# THE CRISIS
## OF THE
## ARISTOCRACY
### 1558–1641

# THE CRISIS
# OF THE
# ARISTOCRACY
## 1558–1641

ABRIDGED EDITION

BY

LAWRENCE STONE

DODGE PROFESSOR OF HISTORY
PRINCETON UNIVERSITY

OXFORD UNIVERSITY PRESS

LONDON   OXFORD   NEW YORK

OXFORD UNIVERSITY PRESS
Oxford    London    Glasgow
New York    Toronto    Melbourne    Wellington
Nairobi    Dar es Salaam    Cape Town
Kuala Lumpur    Singapore    Jakarta    Hong Kong    Tokyo
Delhi    Bombay    Calcutta    Madras    Karachi

TO E. C. S.

'Their inward thought is that their houses shall continue for ever and their dwelling places to all generations; they call their lands after their own names. Nevertheless man being in honour abideth not: he is like the beasts that perish.'

*Psalm XLIX*

# PREFACE TO ABRIDGED EDITION

THIS edition is approximately half the length of the original. In making the excisions needed to carry out this drastic reduction, the following principles have been applied. The scholarly apparatus, including acknowledgements, footnotes, appendices, and discussions of the reliability of the evidence have been omitted. Secondly a great mass of the supporting material, in the form of examples and quotations, has been reduced to a few of the more striking items to buttress each point. And thirdly, there have been dropped a few complete sections which were in some sense diversions from, or by-paths of, the main line of argument. It is evident, therefore, that this is a rather simplified version of the original, and anyone wishing to test the validity of any argument or set of data would be well advised to refer back to it. The statistical calculations of Chapter IV sections I and II are, it appears, particularly controversial, and those who wish to use them should always examine my explanation of how they were arrived at, and also the criticisms that have been made of them. On the other hand it is hoped that the reduction of the obese original to a more slender and elegant shape (at a less elevated price) will improve its physical and intellectual attractions to a wider circle of clients.

*Princeton, October 1965*

# CONTENTS

PREFACE                                              *page* vii

I. INTRODUCTION                                            1

### PART ONE

## THE NATURE OF THE CRISIS

II. THE PEERAGE IN SOCIETY                              15
  I. Concepts of Society                               15
  II. Social Structure                                 21
  III. The Peerage                                     28

III. THE INFLATION OF HONOURS                          37
  I. The Gentry and Knightage                          38
  II. The Baronetage                                   43
  III. The Peerage                                     48

IV. ECONOMIC CHANGE                                    62
  I. Estimates of Income                               62
  II. The Counting of Manors                           68
  III. The Facts of Change                             71
  IV. The Causes of Decay                              76
  V. The Causes of Growth                              88
  VI. Conclusion                                       93

V. POWER                                               96
  I. The Instruments of Violence                       96
  II. The Face of Violence                            107
  III. The Growth of Order                            113
  IV. The Uses of Influence                           125
  V. Conclusion                                       129

### PART TWO

## GETTING AND SPENDING

VI. ESTATE MANAGEMENT                                 135
  I. Leasing Policies                                 143
  II. The Movement of Landed Income                   154

VII. BUSINESS                                         160
  I. Exploitation of Estates                          163
  II. Investment                                      173

VIII. OFFICE AND THE COURT    183

    i. London and the Court    183
    ii. Direct Rewards    191
    iii. Indirect Rewards    199
    iv. The Burden of Office    207
    v. The Impact of the System    212
    vi. The Consequences of the System    217

IX. CREDIT    233

X. CONSPICUOUS EXPENDITURE    249

PART THREE

MINDS AND MANNERS

XI. MARRIAGE AND THE FAMILY    269

XII. EDUCATION AND CULTURE    303

XIII. RELIGION    332

XIV. CONCLUSION: THE CRISIS OF CONFIDENCE    349

APPENDIXES

I. Estimates of Total Manorial Holdings, 1558–1641    355
II. Rewards, 1558–1641    356

INDEX    359

# FIGURES IN THE TEXT

1. Mobility of Land, 1560–1699         *page* 22
2. Grants of Arms, 1560–1639     39
3. Creations of English Knights, 1558–1641     40
4. Creations of English Baronets, 1610–41     45
5. Creations and Promotions of English Peers, 1558–1641     49
6. Numbers and Composition of the Peerage, 1487–1641     50
7. Estimated Gross Rentals, 1559, 1602     65
8. Estimated Gross Rentals, 1641     66
9. Purchase and Sale of Manors, 1560–1639     72
10. Fertility of First Marriages, 1540–1659     78
11. Duration of First Marriages, 1558–1641     270
12. Termination of First Marriages, 1558–1641     283
13. Social Status of Wives, 1540–1659     286
14. Marriage Portions and Prices, 1475–1724     290
15. The Portion/Jointure Ratio, 1485–1734     291
16. Age at First Marriage, 1540–1659     295
17. Education, 1560–1639     311

# THE CRISIS
# OF THE
# ARISTOCRACY
## 1558–1641

# I

## INTRODUCTION

IT has been observed that the map of English social history is full of huge blank spaces, more often than not labelled 'here be the rich'. This book is designed to fill the largest and most important of these areas. It is odd that it should so long have remained unexplored, since for hundreds of years, indeed to within living memory, England was ruled by a tiny group of aristocrats who were the makers of what has traditionally been regarded as the stuff of history—namely national politics and war. This neglect can partly be explained by the character of research into social history in the last fifty years, which for this period has concerned itself mainly with the peasantry—the exploited classes —and with the capitalist solvents of feudalism, the so-called progressive gentry and urban merchants. Nor is the situation very different on the Continent, where intensive work on the medieval *noblesse* has not been matched by comparable studies of the aristocracy in the sixteenth and seventeenth centuries.

The terminal dates for the core of this work and for most of the statistical data are the accession of Queen Elizabeth in November 1558 and the winter of 1641 when civil war had become almost inevitable. In examining attitudes of mind and behaviour patterns, however, the temporal range is extended where necessary back into the early sixteenth and on into the middle or even later seventeenth century. This is only reasonable since such slow-moving factors are relatively impervious to all but the most cataclysmic political events.

If treated with some flexibility, the eighty-odd years between 1558 and 1641 form a very satisfactory unit of time for historical purposes. It includes the period of stability after the Henrician revolution, and the period of disintegration which followed. It sees the most critical phase of fundamental changes in politics, society, thought, and religion. The number of men holding English titles during the period is neither too small to form a meaningful statistical sample, nor too large to become unmanageable by a single historian. Though these 382 noblemen are the principal subject of this book, reference will be freely made as occasion warrants to the thoughts and actions of untitled members of the court *élite* or the greater country landlords. Both the temporal and the class definitions of the title are regarded more as signposts than blinkers.

The main reason for the relative neglect of the aristocracy is that until very recently the materials upon which such a study could be based were simply not available. They lay, unsorted, uncatalogued, unknown, and inaccessible in the great private houses of England. In the last twenty years, however, an archive revolution has taken place. Very many of these private collections are now on deposit in local Record Offices; most of the rest have been listed by the National Register of Archives, and can be examined by properly qualified researchers thanks to the enlightened generosity of their owners. It is only since the Second World War, therefore, that it has become possible to make a serious study of the aristocracy, for the evidence in the national records can only supplement that in the family archives themselves.

A study such as this, which tries to ferret out the most intimate details of the lives and thoughts of a group of men and women long since dead, is only possible, if at all, for periods subsequent to the middle of the sixteenth century. At about this time the growth of literacy among the landed classes led to an explosive increase in the number of private letters that were written, soon to be followed by autobiographical essays, advices to sons, and other revealing personal documents. Secondly, the amount of surviving financial and estate records of noble families increased quite suddenly at this period; thirdly, the expanding role in society of the state machine caused financial records, evidence given in lawsuits, and correspondence with the government to accumulate in the public archives in far larger quantities than ever before. The change in the record material is thus one both of quantity and of quality; there is vastly more of it, and it is far more personal in character.

Though many of the ideas behind this study are derived from the French school of historiography, the approach is made along rather different, admittedly less logically systematic, lines. It is hoped that by so doing it will be possible to avoid over-stressing the strictly economic factors determining social and political change, and to give due weight to the imponderables of ideology and aspiration, prejudice and custom. There are more, and often more potent, motors of individual and group behaviour than those which can be demonstrated in a statistical table.

It is statistics, however, which compose the bony skeleton of this book. As John Smyth of Nibley remarked 300 years ago, 'The old achievements and actions of private men appear but now and then floating in the great gulf of time'. If these fleeting appearances are to be given historical significance it is necessary to be sure that they are typical, a thing which only statistics will reveal. Political history is different, and easier. At any one time there is only one Prime Minister—if that—and at most no more than three foreign or economic policies. But a social group consists of a great mass of men, each an individual human being, and as such a partial variant from the norm. Statistical measurement is the only means of extracting a coherent pattern from the chaos of personal behaviour and of discovering which is a typical specimen and which a sport. Failure to apply such controls has led to much wild and implausible generalizations about social phenomena, based upon a handful of striking or well-documented examples.

There is a second danger from which the social historian can protect himself by paying attention to his statistical controls for the group as a whole. This arises from the fact that surviving private archives are not, as one might at first imagine, a purely random sample. They are a selection, heavily weighted on the side of those families which were rising in the world, and those which were already so rich that total dispersion and dismemberment of their estates were unlikely. They thus favour the up-and-coming at the expense of the failures, and the magnates at the expense of the middling landlords. Studies of well-documented individual families are immensely valuable in themselves, but the temptation must be avoided of generalizing from a selection which is not merely too small to form a sample, but which also contains an inherent bias. Statistics make a dry and unpalatable diet unless washed down with the wine of human personality. They have been used, therefore, merely as controls to check the significance of the tangled jetsam of anecdote and quotation thrown up by three talkative, quarrelsome, idiosyncratic generations of noble men and women.

One of the basic assumptions of this book is that the political and social crisis of the seventeenth century has been largely misconceived in recent years, since it has been interpreted as a product of a changing social structure. In fact relatively little structural change took place in English society between the fourteenth and the nineteenth centuries : what altered was the role of the various social classes within a fairly static framework.

Professor E. H. Carr has recently reminded us that the historian does not exist who is unaffected by his upbringing and background. I cannot pretend to any special immunity from this inescapable limitation of the human mind. All I can do is to offer a personal confession, which may help to rebut the charge of premeditated bias. At first I believed that the difficulties of the sixteenth- and seventeenth-century aristocracy were at bottom financial. Though I am more than ever convinced that the aristocracy passed through a grave financial crisis at the end of the sixteenth century, I no longer support the view that this was the sole, or even necessarily the prime, cause of their troubles. It has become apparent that economic change within a class structure in any case raises grave problems of interpretation and measurement. I am now persuaded that the upheavals of the mid-seventeenth century cannot be explained in terms of any single factor, but only as the product of a great variety of forces, some of which historians have hitherto been content to leave to the sociologist and the anthropologist. This shift from an economic to a sociological interpretation of historical causation is no great personal innovation : it is part of a general reappraisal of historical attitudes since the 1930's.

The second preconception with which I began was that aristocrats were an antipathetic group of superfluous parasites. I still do not relish the spectacle of a tiny handful of families monopolizing huge slices of the available economic resources of an impoverished society, lording it in arrogant ease and luxury over an obsequious, cowed, undernourished, and illiterate mass upon whose labours they depend. But moral indignation is not an aid to clear thinking or a sympathetic understanding of the past. This is the class pattern of most pre-industrial societies the world has known, and it is unreasonable to suppose that it serves no useful function whatever. In any case, what distinguishes the English aristocracy of this period from the *élites* of other times and places is the relative moderation of its appetites for wealth and power, and the relative sense of social responsibility displayed by some of its members.

It is, perhaps, merely evidence of insular complacency to regard the tranquil evolution of English affairs in the last 300 years as a singularly happy dispensation of Providence. But it is difficult to avoid the conclusion that the cause of this tranquillity should be sought more in the reluctance of the over-privileged to fight in the last ditch, than in that of the reformers to push them over the edge. This singular adaptability to changing circumstances by the forces of the Establishment is a feature that above all others has distinguished the history of England from that of her continental neighbours in recent centuries. Despite the weaknesses which seriously reduced their influence over events in 1640–2, the English peerage were already the best educated, most politically conscious, least caste-ridden, least obsequious to monarchy, most open to new talents and new ideas of any aristocracy in Europe, with the possible exception of that of Sweden.

This book sets out to do two things: firstly to describe the total environment of an *élite*, material and economic, ideological and cultural, educational and moral; and secondly to demonstrate, to explain, and to chart the course of a crisis in the affairs of this *élite* that was to have a profound effect upon the evolution of English political institutions. It is therefore at once a static description and a dynamic analysis; it is a study in social, economic, and intellectual history, which is consciously designed to serve as the prolegomenon to, and an explanation of, political history. It does not, however, concern itself with the latter as such, and the role of the House of Lords in the shaping of national affairs is deliberately excluded from its scope.

Since successful politicians and very wealthy gentlemen were normally rewarded by a title, the peers formed at one and the same time the major component of a social *élite*, an *élite* of wealth, and a power *élite*. The kind of life they led, therefore, is of particular importance to a proper understanding of the past. Every society possesses an *élite*, or rather these three *élites*, and the differences between one society and another are in large measure to be sought in the different characteristics of their *élites*: in the relationships between the overlapping groups that compose them, the degree of unity or division among them, the system of recruitment, the ease or difficulty of entry, the religious and ethical framework of their lives.

The secondary object of this book is to describe in as much

detail as can reasonably be tolerated the way of life of this *élite*, a way of life which in its final form lasted with only minor changes well into the twentieth century. The life of a nobleman was one of comfort and leisure, based on a country house, financed mainly from agricultural profits, and supported by a huge train of servants. The code by which these men lived differed radically from that which rose up to challenge and temporarily to overthrow it in the middle of the seventeenth century. The capitalist/Protestant ethic is one of self-improvement, independence, thrift, hard work, chastity and sobriety, competition, equality of opportunity, and the association of poverty with moral weakness; the aristocratic ethic is one of voluntary service to the State, generous hospitality, clear class distinctions, social stability, tolerant indifference to the sins of the flesh, inequality of opportunity based on the accident of inheritance, arrogant self-confidence, a paternalist and patronizing attitude towards economic dependants and inferiors, and an acceptance of the grinding poverty of the lower classes as part of the natural order of things. If in this age of confusion and turmoil many men—even Cromwell himself—seem to straddle the two ideals, this does nothing to minimize the essential contradiction between them.

The central concern of this volume is to analyse a series of changes which help to explain a crucial historical problem. During the first half of the seventeenth century something very odd happened in England. The Commons emerged as a far more important political assembly than the Lords, and peers were unable to exercise that influence over parliamentary elections which they had wielded under Elizabeth, and were to wield again under the Hanoverians. Moreover in 1642 a body of gentlemen and townsmen supported by a handful of dissident peers had the amazing effrontery to challenge the King, the bishops, most of the peerage, and their gentry supporters; it even defeated them. A few years later the House of Lords was abolished altogether, an act of political surgery which twentieth-century radicals are not yet willing or able to accomplish. Thus the middle of the seventeenth century saw the eclipse of the monarchy, of the peerage, and of the Anglican Church. It saw the brief emergence into the open of radical ideas about social, economic, sexual, and political equality. Admittedly all this did not last, and by the end of the seventeenth century the peers, like the Anglican clergy and the

King, were firmly back in the saddle. But it should be noted that the bit and the curb, the stirrup and the whip, were now of a different design.

Why did all this happen? For a long time it was customary to explain these events as a particular crisis arising from particular events, personalities, and policies: the ineptitude of James, the corruption of Buckingham, the obstinacy of Strafford, Laud, and Charles; the rise of puritanism, the growth of a sense of constitutionalism, the development of improved procedural techniques by the House of Commons. Within its terms of reference, each of those explanations is satisfactory enough, and indeed together they still provide the best guide to the issues which divided men one from another when civil war broke out in 1642. But what they leave unexplained is the decay of respect for the Establishment as a whole which opened the way to so comprehensive a challenge.

One suggestion has been a growth in the economic resources, and consequently in the political influence, of a mercantile and industrial class of capitalists whose financial interests were thwarted by the obstinate stranglehold maintained by a decaying feudal aristocracy. This hypothesis, which had a considerable vogue between the wars, has recently taken some hard knocks. The so-called industrial revolution of the period 1540–1640 has been cut down to size, and is now seen as a relatively minor development in terms of money invested or men employed. It is now evident that a large number of the leaders of the merchant oligarchies in the towns, particularly in London, were loyal members of the royal patronage system, beneficiaries of monopoly privilege both in economic affairs and in town government; and it is now known that in any case townsmen at no time comprised more than about 10 per cent. of the membership of the Commons, and that they were not at all prominent in its proceedings.

The picture of the aristocracy painted in this book still further discredits the old stereotype. There was nothing particularly feudal about the peers in 1641: if they fought for the State, they were paid for their services; their seats in the House of Lords bore no relation to feudal tenure; their client gentry were bound to them by personal not feudal ties; the feudal aspect of their relationships with their tenants was confined to the intermittent enforcement of obsolete taxes like fines for wardship; their estate management was as modern as the times and as their paternalist notions of fair

treatment of tenants would allow; their zest for new industrial
and commercial ventures was keener than that of the merchants;
the challenge to their authority came not from capitalists or bourgeoisie, but from solid landowners only one notch further down
the social and economic ladder, the squires and greater gentry. As
for the real new men, the rich merchants, they were too concerned
with scrambling aboard the old status bandwagon to have any
wish to scupper it.

A more promising suggestion was that of a 'rise of the gentry',
conceived primarily in economic terms as the emergence of a
prosperous new class with enlarged estates run on novel commercial lines for the maximization of profits, a class which filled the
benches of the House of Commons, but whose claims to political
power commensurate with their economic resources were consistently blocked by the Crown. This attractive picture was confused
by the discovery that there were very many declining, as well as
very many rising gentry, so that the overall movement seemed for
a time to be in doubt. What has been proved beyond question by
this conflict of evidence is that this was a period of unprecedented
economic mobility among the middle landowning groups, with
families moving up or down in remarkable numbers. That far more
land—and therefore a higher proportion of national wealth—was
in private non-aristocratic hands in 1640 than in 1540 can hardly be
disputed any more. But a more important question is whether the
movement enhanced the wealth of a limited group of great county
families, or whether it increased the number of the lesser gentry,
or both. The latter phenomenon has been proved beyond doubt,
the former is still no more than a probability, though the evidence
seems to be pointing in this direction also. What is not proven,
however, is that the rise in wealth and territorial possessions of the
leading gentry in absolute terms was sufficiently pronounced to
account for their seizure of political initiative.

The alternative hypothesis is that the parliamentary party in the
Civil War was primarily composed of small, backward, declining
gentry whose loyalty to the Crown and the Church had been
undermined by economic hardship. Nearly all the evidence available contradicts this ingenious theory. The impoverished back-
woodsmen of the north and west, far from being parliamentarians,
formed the hard core of the royalist cause, men who fought to the
last for a Court and King from which they had got nothing but

high taxes and contemptuous neglect. The list of leaders and active supporters of the parliamentary cause in 1642, on the other hand, reads like a roll call of the most important of the county families: Barrington, Barnardiston, Baynton, Curzon, Dacres, Dryden, Erle, Hales, Hampden, Hungerford, Knightley, Onslow, Pelham, and Wallop. These were no impoverished or declining gentlemen driven to rebellion by financial plight. It is perfectly true that as the war dragged on more radical elements from lower down the gentry hierarchy came to the fore, first in local then in national government. But this was a consequence of the stresses of war, and does nothing to explain either the initial crisis, which took the form of a generalized breakdown of confidence in government, or the outbreak of war itself.

The socio-political breakdown of 1640–2 had three main causes. The first was a long-term decline in respect for and obedience to the Monarchy, caused partly by the personal ineptitude of kings, partly by growing financial impoverishment, partly by structural defects in the Court system, and partly by the widening gap between the moral standards, aspirations, and way of life of the Court and those of the Country. This movement began in the latter years of Elizabeth, gathered impetus under James, became an avalanche under Buckingham, and could not be arrested by Charles after 1629. The second was the failure of the Established Church to comprehend within itself all but the Roman Catholics. Between them, Elizabeth, Whitgift, and Laud managed to alienate from the Anglican Church an ever-increasing body of influential opinion. The policy of Laud in the 1630's—at least as much in matters of ritual and church organization as in social and economic affairs—was the final instrument which brought the whole edifice to the ground in 1640.

These two factors could not alone have caused the prolonged upheaval of the 1640's if it had not been for a third, the crisis in the affairs of the hereditary *élite*, the aristocracy. For a time this group lost its hold upon the nation, and thus allowed political and social initiative to fall into the hands of the squirearchy. It surrendered its powers of physical coercion to an increasingly powerful state; it permanently alienated much of its capital resources in land; for a period, admittedly not a very long one, its purchasing power declined absolutely; its subsequent decision to jack up rents and fines did much to break down old ties of personal allegiance; it was obliged to share more and more of the commanding heights of administrative and political authority with a confident and well-educated gentry; and, partly because of guilt by association with a corrupt, licentious, and in the end tyrannical Court, partly because so many of its members belonged to a feared and hated religious minority, partly because of the workings of the puritan conscience, it temporarily forfeited much of its influence and prestige. The rise of the gentry is to some extent—though certainly not entirely—an optical illusion, resulting from this temporary weakness of the aristocracy.

This book is primarily concerned with the third of these seismic shifts in English life, although it is designed to throw some incidental light upon the other two. The early Tudors had striven, not without success, to undermine the strength of the nobility, which they had regarded as a menace to quasi-absolute monarchy. In the reign of Elizabeth it was thought that the balance of society was just about right, with the aristocracy filling a useful role as 'brave half paces between a throne and a people', to use Fulke Greville's famous phrase. By the early seventeenth century things had gone too far, and the Early Stuarts began anxiously trying to shore up the tottering edifice. 'Though their dependences and power are gone, yet we cannot be without them', wrote the republican Henry Neville in the middle of the century. This many-sided crisis in the affairs of the aristocracy did not itself *cause* the Civil War, but it created the conditions which made it possible. As James Harington said at the time: 'A monarchy divested of its nobility has no refuge under heaven but an army. Wherefore the dissolution of this government caus'd the war, not the war the dissolution of this government.'

It is instructive to compare this crisis with that of 250 years later, when the dominant role of the landed aristocracy in politics and society finally and irretrievably crumbled. Throughout the nineteenth century a series of forces were working to undermine their position. The growth of party organization and of public meetings reduced the significance of personal relations as a key to political influence; the substitution of merit for nepotism or money as criteria for entry into the Civil Service closed many avenues of profit and employment; the abolition of the Quarter Sessions as a kind of local parliament destroyed another powerful engine of aristocratic authority. Finally the agricultural depression, death-duties, and a progressive income-tax combined to sap the financial foundations of the peerage, just at a time when vast new fortunes were being made in trade and industry. It was not, however, till the turn of the century that they gave in. Their strong sense of public duty, reinforced by evangelical christianity, made them continue to serve in the army and in India, and to dominate the new county councils. Some, like the Cecils, continued to take the lead in national politics. Indeed at the very top their power lingered on years after its base in the country at large had been eroded. Aristocrats of three generations' standing were in a majority in the Cabinet until 1895, and they still formed a third of the 'Caretaker' Cabinet of 1945.

What finished the peerage in the end was the combination of all these forces with a collapse of morale. Education at a major public school and Oxford or Cambridge came to be regarded as a test of status as valid as that of a landed estate and a good pedigree. This upper middle class 'owned no land, but they felt that they were landowners in the sight of God and kept up a semi-aristocratic outlook by going into the professions and the fighting services rather than into trade'. Faced with this challenge, the aristocracy abdicated their responsibilities. From looking after the tenantry and serving the Empire, they took to hunting and Gaiety girls. The King turned away from them, becoming the patron of the moneyed parvenus from the City; they lost the respect of the public and of themselves, and they then deliberately courted disaster by pitting themselves against a popularly elected government. The result was the Parliament Act of 1911, the symbol of the end of the pre-eminent role of the peerage in English administration, English politics, and English society.

The story has a familiar ring to the historian of the aristocracy in the late sixteenth and early seventeenth centuries. Though one was temporary and the other—one assumes permanent in its consequences, the developments of the two periods were similar in many ways. Each saw the permeation of the peerage by new and vulgar wealth, a relative decline in old aristocratic wealth, a decline in aristocratic electoral influence, a decline in the prestige of a title, a decline in aristocratic morals under the leadership of a pleasure-loving king. Both ended in an attack on the powers of the House of Lords, and a change in the social composition of Council or Cabinet.

Words like 'crisis' and 'revolution' should not come tripping too
lightly from the historian's pen. History lumbers jerkily on with
few real breaks with the past. The forces of inertia ensure an
amazing degree of continuity in human affairs, whatever the
strength of the pressures for change that are brought to bear. A
situation like that which faced the aristocracy at this period, however, may reasonably be described as a crisis, for it involved major
readaptation in almost every field of thought and action in order to
fit into a rapidly changing environment.

Granted that change is a continuous process, that every shift has
both earlier antecedents and later developments, it is nevertheless
between 1560 and 1640, and more precisely between 1580 and
1620, that the real watershed between medieval and modern
England must be placed. It was then that the State fully established
its authority, that dozens of armed retainers were replaced by a
coach, two footmen, and a page-boy, that private castles gave way
to private houses, and that aristocratic rebellion finally petered
out; then that the north and west were brought within the
national orbit and abandoned their age-old habits of personal
violence; then that the British Isles, England, Wales, Scotland,
and Ireland were first effectively united; then that political objectives began to be stated in terms of abstract liberty and the public
interest, rather than particular liberties and ancient customs; then
that radical protestantism elevated the individual conscience over
the claims of traditional obedience in the family, in the Church,
in the nation; then that non-conformity and the nonconformist
conscience became established features of the English scene; then
that the House of Commons emerged as the dominant partner of
the two Houses, and actually seized some of the political initiative
from the executive; then that the Lord Treasurer developed as the
leading minister of the Crown, and the Exchequer as the most
important administrative department; then that noblemen and
gentry provided themselves with a bookish education to fit themselves for their new role in society, so that for the first time in
history the intelligentsia became a branch of the propertied classes;
then that the cosmopolitan influence of the Grand Tour first
became a common element in a young man's training for life;
then that London and the Court first began to sing their siren
songs to the rural landlords; then that the ideal of stately, public
living in the country was challenged by that of opulent, private

pleasures in the City; then that foreign trade developed sufficiently
to begin to preoccupy the minds of statesmen, and to make a
London alderman the financial equal of a baron; then that usury
was first openly legislated for, that interest rates fell to modern
levels, that the joint-stock company began to flourish, that colonies
of Englishmen were established across the seas, that England
abandoned its territorial ambitions in Europe and dimly recognized its future as a naval power; then that capitalist ethics, population growth, and monetary inflation undermined old landlord–
tenant relationships and old methods of estate management; then
that England first began to enjoy such modern means of com-
munication as the private coach and the public carrier, the private
newsletter and the public newspaper; then that Shakespeare
and Spenser, Sydney and Donne transformed our literature, that
Inigo Jones introduced Palladian architecture, that Bacon pointed
the way to modern experimental science, and that Selden and
Spelman demonstrated the possibilities of serious historical
research.

It was to this changing, challenging world that the peers had
to adapt themselves between the accession of Queen Elizabeth
and the outbreak of civil war. Their failures helped to open the
way to the political upheavals of the seventeenth century; their
successes laid the foundation of the political stability of the eighteenth century and the partial survival of aristocratic values,
aristocratic styles of life, aristocratic influence in the countryside,
and aristocratic predominance in the cabinet to within the memory
of men still alive today. Using new material, deployed in a new
way, this book tries to tell the story of this adaptation, to identify
and explain its successes and its failures. In doing so it offers a
new explanation of the central event of modern English history
—the breakdown of monarchical and aristocratic government in
1640–1 and its re-establishment on terms in 1660 and 1688.

PART ONE

# THE NATURE OF THE CRISIS

## II

## THE PEERAGE IN SOCIETY

### I. CONCEPTS OF SOCIETY

HIERARCHY and organic unity were the two predominant postulates upon which contemporaries constructed their theories about the nature of society and the functions of government. As the universe was ordered in a great chain of being, so the nation was regulated by obedience to a hierarchy of superiors leading up to the King, so society was composed of various estates of men all settled and contented in their degree, and so the family was ordered by subservience of wife and children to the *pater familias*. Whether in heaven or hell, in the universe or on earth, in the state or in the family, it was a self-evident truth that peace and order could only be preserved by the maintenance of grades and distinctions and by relentless emphasis on the over-riding need for subjection of the individual will to that of superior authority.

> The heavens themselves, the planets and this centre
> Observe degree, priority and place.

Although there are signs of belief in equality of opportunity among the urban bourgeoisie, although the rumblings of radical social egalitarianism can be heard from time to time during peasant risings, and although, as we shall see, there was a growing movement towards individualism, the prevailing temper of the age was the antithesis of the twentieth-century western system of values.

Given these assumptions, it was natural that the supreme virtues should be obedience and the avoidance of change. In 1658 Sir

Henry Slingsby warned his son that '*Subjection* to *superiors* is a precept of high consequence'. Strenuous efforts were made to immunize the minds of youth against the poison of new ideas. 'Hold all innovations and new ways suspicious', advised Sir Edward Coke—and plunged back into the self-appointed task of making radical political notions respectable by dressing them up in garbled medieval precedents. Because of this crushing burden of belief in the need for social stability, all change had to be interpreted as the maintenance of tradition. In religion the reformation was defended as a return to the early church; in politics, parliamentary sovereignty was defended as the enforcement of fourteenth-century customs; in society the rise of new men was disguised by forged genealogies and the grant of titles of honour. One of the most striking features of the age was a pride of ancestry which now reached new heights of fantasy and elaboration. Though it soon became a fad, a craze, a quasi-intellectual hobby for the idle rich, its prime purpose was social integration, the welding of a homogeneous group of seemingly respectable lineage from a crazy patchwork of the most diverse, and sometimes dubious, origins. Genuine genealogy was cultivated by the older gentry to reassure themselves of their innate superiority over the upstarts; bogus genealogy was cultivated by the new gentry in an effort to clothe their social nakedness, and by the old gentry in the internal jockeying for position in the ancestral pecking order. A lengthy pedigree was a useful weapon in the Tudor battle for status.

The English family, both late medieval and modern, has been patrilinear in its structure, and it was upon the origins of the father rather than those of the mother that attention was concentrated. Thus only in a few, usually disputed, cases, did a title descend through the female line on the extinction of all heirs male. This pride in paternal ancestry became ever more openly expressed as the sixteenth century wore on. Those imaginative creative writers, the Tudor heralds, were kept busy contriving vast rolls tracing the ancestry of the nobility back to the Norman conquerors, to the Romans, to the Trojans. Some were not satisfied until they had got back to the kings and worthies of the Old Testament, the Popham family tree beginning with an illustration of Noah seated in a diminutive ark. An outstanding example of devotion to this hobby was Lord Burghley, who passed his leisure in poring over his collection of genealogies of the European nobility in general and of himself in particular. He was a man who delighted to be told that he derived his ancestry from one Owen Whyte who 'came with Harold that was Earl Godwin's son out of Cornwall'—nonsense which only irritated his more realistic son, Robert. This was the period in which heraldry moved into a baroque phase, a lush profusion of improbable quarterings supplanting the simple coats of a less sophisticated and pretentious age. Behind such excesses lay a growing vanity and pride, stimulated by the need to show external proof of status. As early as 1577 Walter Earl of Essex was boasting of his fifty-five quarterings, so England was clearly already well set on the road to the heraldic fantasy world whose finest hour came at the end of the eighteenth century with the 719 quarterings of the Grenvilles depicted on the ceiling of the Gothic Library at Stowe.

It was Thomas Earl of Arundel, who 'thought no other part of history so considerable as what related to his own family', but there is evidence that he was not alone in his opinion. Apart from this passionate genealogical and heraldic research, men began both delving into the history of their families, and writing their autobiographies for the instruction of posterity. The explosion of historical and antiquarian research in the seventeenth century stemmed directly from this self-centred pursuit, and its most valuable work was done in this field. The middle years of the seventeenth century saw a remarkable growth of serious and well-documented family histories based on careful study of private archives. In 1618 John Smyth claimed that with his *Lives of the Berkeleys* he was the first to write 'a genealogical history of any patrimonial family'. The real significance of his work, however, was not its genealogical precision but its emphasis on social and economic history and its reliance on the records in the muniment room at Berkeley Castle. Nor was it long before others followed in his footsteps, inspired, encouraged, and paid for by the noble patrons themselves. This passion for family history was not confined to the peerage, but spread right through the whole upper gentry class. One of the paradoxes of the age was that this excessive adulation of ancient lineage took place at precisely the time when political theorists were laying increasing emphasis upon virtue, education, and the capacity to serve the State as the supreme test of and justification for a leisured class living off the labours of others. But the contemporary obsession with genealogy and the direct association of gentility with a private income prove that birth and wealth still ranked higher than virtue, education, or ability as indicators of status.

From time to time attempts were made to put the authority of the State behind the enforcement of the ideals of hierarchy and social stability. From the very beginning the Anglican Church was harnessed to the task of disseminating official propaganda, homilies on the need for obedience to established authority being regularly read from every pulpit. Since church attendance was compulsory on Sundays, the Government was guaranteed a captive audience for its opinions at least as comprehensive as that provided by the radio and television networks of the twentieth century. Another line of attack upon the same problem was through sumptuary legislation, laying down the most detailed regulations governing the type of clothes and the amount of food which could lawfully be worn and consumed by different classes of persons. The attitude of the Tudors is revealed in the preamble to a Proclamation of 1600 about the carrying of firearms, in which attention was drawn to the 'indecent and disorderly confusion among all sorts and degrees of men (every mean and base person taking to himself that which belongeth to men of the best sort and condition) as is very unseemly and unmeet in a well-governed state'. It was for this reason that in 1636 Charles actually forbade the buying, selling, or wearing of imitation jewellery. There was even Tudor class legislation about sport, archery being prescribed for the lower orders, and bowls and tennis restricted to gentlemen with an income of over £100 a year.

Both government and the public saw a clear distinction between the types of punishment suitable to a gentleman and those reserved to the vulgar. If one seeks to explain why the punishment of Prynne struck contemporaries with such peculiar horror, it was not the barbarity of the sentence but the quality of the person upon whom it was executed. So deep went this feeling of a fundamental distinction of ranks that gentlemen did not hesitate to behave in ways which would today be considered base and even cowardly. When Lord Herbert of Cherbury was shipwrecked at Dover in 1609 he leaped into the only rescue boat, used his drawn sword to prevent anyone but Sir Thomas Lucy from entering, and then deserted the sinking ship and its crew and made for the safety of the shore— an action which he was not ashamed to record in his autobiography.

The inevitable result of such thinking was a deliberate effort to destroy those remnants of democratic government in local affairs that had survived from the Middle Ages. Town Charters were revised and reissued, in every case in order to place electoral power in the hands of a tiny minority. Where this was not done, the control of the town was restricted by mere governmental fiat, as at Sandwich in 1604, when the Privy Council ordered the electorate for the Mayor to be reduced to the twenty-four of the Common Council. Similarly control of the parish was confined to the 'better sort' by the device of the select vestry, while at religious worship the gradations of rank were publicly defined by the erection of private pews, the placing of which was the subject of continual friction and even violence. In the country local government was monopolized by a caucus of leading landed families, and in the national political institution of the House of Commons the same closing of ranks is visible. Not a single merchant was made a J.P. in Essex after 1564, not a single clothier was returned as M.P. in the great cloth county of Wiltshire after 1603, and indeed the proportion of merchants and urban officials in the Commons was a mere 12 per cent. in 1584 and was still the same in 1640. Within the landed classes the hardening of the lines of social cleavage itself reflected and was supported by a shift in the balance of economic advantage from the yeoman leaseholder to the nobility and gentry landlords. The latter began to cream off the agricultural profits in enhanced rents and fines, and as a result it became increasingly difficult for the yeomanry, or even the minor gentry, to improve their economic position.

The last and most serious attempt to buttress the hierarchical concept of society was made by the King and the Privy Council in the ten years of personal rule before the collapse of royal government in 1640. Sale of titles was stopped, as an obvious threat to the system, and efforts were made to reinforce authority at every level: at Court restrictions were placed on entry to the inner closet; at Oxford University the powers of the few were increased by the Laudian Statutes; in London and the towns support was given to the Mayor and Aldermen against the commonalty; attempts were made to regulate industry by the encouragement of guild organization; in society there was a frank revival of snobbery. 'The priviledges of generous blood are more to be cared for than heretofore', it was announced in 1634, a doctrine which looked forward to the revolutionary scheme for a hierarchy of ranks linked to fiscal and other privileges which was being solemnly discussed in 1639. To show that it meant business, the Privy Council did not hesitate to act in ways of dubious legality. Two draymen who ran down the coach of the Earl of Exeter in 1637 were acquitted by a jury. The Privy Council promptly used prerogative powers to have the miscreants publicly flogged and then committed to hard labour in Bridewell. The same year Thomas Bennett was fined £2,000 by the Star Chamber for telling the Earl of Marlborough that he was as good a gentleman as his lordship, for the Bennetts were as good as the Leys. Authoritarian reaction and reinforcement of aristocratic privilege seemed to be marching hand in hand as England edged ever nearer a system of government modelled upon that of Richelieu. The fact that the attempt collapsed so ignominiously in 1640–1 suggests, however, that it was out of touch with social realities.

The key symbols of Tudor and Early Stuart society were the hat and the whip. The former was for ever being doffed and donned to emphasize the complex hierarchy of ranks and authorities. Everyone, every day, many times a day, by removing his hat or by putting it on, gave visible proof of his acceptance of the great principle of subordination universally at work at Court, in the street, in the great household, in the university, and even within the family. The peculiar ferocity with which the Quakers were treated can only be explained if we realize how shattering a psychological blow to the conceptual framework of society was their quiet refusal to remove their headgear. Physical punishment was used, as it had never been used before, as the prime means of enforcing obedience. Whips and stocks were used by the Crown upon its lesser subjects, by the nobleman upon his servants, by the village worthies upon the poor, by the dons upon the undergraduates, by the City Companies upon the apprentices. The possession of these handy instruments was a mark of dignity, a prerequisite of property. Children were flogged into absorbing their book-learning, undergraduates were flogged into compliance with College regulations, servants and apprentices were flogged by their masters, the adult poor were flogged to encourage them not to be poor and homeless, Papists were flogged to persuade them of the superior virtues of Anglicanism, breakers of laws drawn up in their wisdom by the propertied classes were flogged into a recognition of the errors of their ways. Those of gentle birth were flogged like the rest so long as they were children, and between about 1500 and 1660 they were also flogged as adolescents. It was only when a young gentleman went down from the university that he left his adolescence behind him. As a man of birth and breeding he could be assured that from now on he was immune from corporal punishment, an indignity reserved for those of lower social status.

During the early seventeenth century these authoritarian attitudes were having to compete with what can only be described, for lack of a better word, as the concept of individualism. The growth of population faster than food supplies or employment opportunities and the increased use of money and credit led to a more cut-throat competitive society, first in the towns and more slowly in the countryside. The ideal of a society in which every man had his place and stayed in it was breaking down under a combination of material and ideological pressures. Many no longer had a place in which to stay, and those who had were less willing to accept their lot as eternally ordained by God. Humanist education with its cult of heroes was teaching the upper classes that each man was an empire unto himself, whose duty it was to strive for personal glory. Most important of all was the slow working of the puritan conscience, with its stress on man's direct personal relationship with the deity, and its hierarchy of the elect and the damned, the godly and the profane, which might bear little relation to existing social gradations. At the same time a flood of new ideas in astronomy and medicine, history and law, were helping to undermine confidence in the hierarchic principle of social organization as the inevitable and necessary rule of God and Nature. One of the major themes running through this book is the consequent erosion of respect for kings, bishops, noblemen, landlords, and fathers of families. By 1641 rust was eating into the shackles of the Great Chain of Being.

## II. SOCIAL STRUCTURE

Hitherto we have been discussing the official ideology of the age and the measures taken by authority in its support. But all such ideologies are imperfect reflections of the realities of the social system. They tend to glorify the existing upper classes and conceal the benefits they derive from their position. They exaggerate the duties and minimize the privileges of the few. They also present a picture of a fully integrated society in which stratification by title, power, wealth, talent, and culture are all in absolute harmony, and in which social mobility is consequently both undesirable and unthinkable. Reality, however, is always somewhat different.

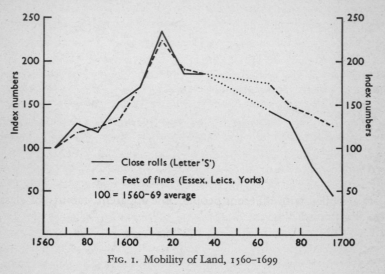

FIG. 1. Mobility of Land, 1560–1699

This ideological pattern and these measures designed to freeze the social structure and emphasize the cleavages between one class and another were introduced or reinforced at a time when in fact families were moving up and down in the social and economic scale at a faster rate than at any time before the nineteenth and twentieth centuries. Indeed it was just this mobility which stimulated such intensive propaganda efforts. The causes of this mobility are discussed elsewhere; here we are merely concerned to register its existence and assess its consequences.

Direct evidence of this mobility is provided by the exceptionally rapid turnover of land as recorded in the Close Rolls, registering the more important land sales, and Feet of Fines (Fig. 1). This mountainous rise and fall must represent a tremendous upheaval in the mobility of land in this country, which is without parallel in either the later Middle Ages or the late seventeenth and eighteenth centuries. The result of this mobility of land was that the gentry was changing in composition with unprecedented rapidity. Exceptionally large numbers of new families were forcing their way to the top, exceptionally large numbers of old families were falling on evil days and sinking into obscurity. There were 641 gentry families in Yorkshire in 1603; by 1642, 180 of these had died out in the male line or left the county, while 218 had first become armigerous, had come into the county, or had set themselves up as cadet branches. This represents a disappearance and replacement of more than one family in four in a space of forty years.

The fact that social mobility, upwards and downwards, was occurring at an unprecedented rate despite all efforts to halt the flux should not lead us to suppose that the whole class structure was breaking down, or even that it was being reshaped to more than a limited extent. Neither the growth in the power of the state, nor the decline in the authority of the King himself, nor the relative rise in wealth and influence of the squirearchy did much to affect the basic system of social stratification. A class is not a finite group of families, but rather a bus or a hotel, always full, but always filled with different people. The apparent stability of class position is an illusion created by the slowness of change and the extraordinary stability of class character, resulting from the chameleon-like adaptability of new families. The social structure itself should be regarded as a continuum with bottlenecks, or alternatively as a stepped pyramid or lozenge. Short of a major revolution and the confiscation and redistribution of land and capital, social mobility may alter the shape of the figure, may broaden or narrow some of the steps; but except over a long period of time it is unlikely either to eliminate the existing steps or to create new ones.

The measure of the resilience of a class structure is its ability to absorb new families of different social origin and convert them to the values and ways of life of the social group into which they are projected. By this test the English social structure of the sixteenth and seventeenth centuries emerges with considerable distinction. Despite the massive tide of wealth flowing into the hands of yeomen, lawyers, City merchants, top-ranking administrators, and successful politicians, they were all successfully absorbed, at different levels, into the ranks of the landed gentry. That a 'middle-class culture' of educated artisans, small shopkeepers, and merchants grew up in Elizabethan England cannot be doubted, but the dominant value system remained that of the landed gentleman. Except for the yeomen, none of the new men had acquired their fortunes from the profits of land, and yet as soon as the opportunity offered all hastened to turn their wealth into a landed estate. Since there was plenty of land on the market there arose no proud dynasties of merchants, no hereditary strain of lawyers (except through younger sons), no unbroken sequence of professional politicians. Only in the royal bureaucracy did there develop a certain sense of professionalism, handed down from generation to generation. As a result the social prestige and the standards of value of the landed classes were never seriously challenged except for a brief period during the Interregnum.

Active personal occupation in a trade or profession was generally thought to be humiliating. The man of business was inferior to the gentleman of leisure who lived off his rents. Retail trade was always degrading, and overseas trade only a respectable occupation for a son and heir if pursued as a hobby rather than as a profession. Indeed Chamberlayne asserted, and apologists like Edmund Bolton and Richard Brathwait admitted it to be the common belief, that by apprenticeship 'a gentleman thereby loses his gentility for ever, till he can otherwise recover it', presumably by making a fortune. In fact, of course, the younger sons of lesser gentry had always been apprenticed to merchants, and after the middle of the seventeenth century the younger sons of great knights and squires and even of a few peers began to be put out to trade. But this development only affected younger sons, who were anyway regarded as expendable, and it can therefore hardly be regarded as more than a very trifling shift of opinion.

The ranking of the professions was only slightly higher than that of tradesmen. Between 1560 and 1640 the Church was not the respected occupation it once had been and was to become again. Even the bishops were not held in much respect, being men 'of a low condicion' as Selden put it. Consequently they were ruthlessly robbed by nobility and gentry under Elizabeth, and it was not until the early seventeenth century that a handful of well-born and well-connected younger sons began to trickle back into the Church, and it was not till 1666 that it could be observed, as a novelty worth recording, that 'many knights' daughters of good fortune now marry the church men'. The position of doctors was

hardly any better, despite the striking financial and social success
of the leading court physicians. John Ferne thought it not a very
honourable profession, and as late as the middle of the seventeenth
century a gentleman was refusing the offer of marriage with the
daughter of a rich doctor since 'the very thought of the clyster-
pipes did nauseate his stomach'. The anal preoccupations of contemporary medicine must have done much to prevent a rise in the
status of the profession. Only the lawyers were not oppressed by
a feeling of social inferiority, even if they were neither loved nor
admired for their arrogance and rapacity.

One reason for the continued social pre-eminence of land
was that it remained the primary source of political influence.
No longer a reservoir of docile manpower, landownership
was now the necessary qualification for a seat in the House of
Commons and a share in local government, as Justice of the
Peace, Sheriff, Deputy Sheriff, Deputy Lieutenant, or Commis-
sioner of musters or subsidies. So long as land retained this vital
role in the structure of power, so long would it reign supreme as
a status symbol; moreover, the political developments of the
seventeenth century, the weakening first of the financial resources
and later of the prestige and influence of the Crown, actually increased the importance of the landed interest. Their social pre-
eminence, and their exploitation of the educational facilities of the
country, meant that it became virtually impossible for a man of
low birth to rise to high office. For nearly 400 years politics was
the monopoly of the gentleman, and it was not until 1906 that
the first man of working-class origin obtained a seat in the
Cabinet.

Along with the supremacy of land went a continued respect for
medieval aristocratic ideals. One of the most characteristic features
of the age was its hyper-sensitive insistence upon the overriding
importance of reputation. Many of the punishments of the day, the
stocks, the pillory, the apology read out in the market-place, were
based upon the theory that public humiliation was a more effective
penalty than a swingeing fine. The extraordinary seventeenth-
century code of the duel, under which men felt impelled to risk
their lives to avenge a casual word, was merely a cancerous growth
from the same cells. A by-product of this cult of reputation was an
insistence upon the aristocratic virtue of generosity. Though contemporaries lamented the decay of hospitality—and it undoubtedly

did fall away during this period—this is less remarkable than the vigorous persistence of the ideal, and in some measure the practice, in direct opposition to Calvinist ideals of frugality and thrift. The prime test of rank was liberality, the pagan virtue of open-handedness. It involved wearing rich clothes, living in a substantial well-furnished house, keeping plenty of servants, and above all maintaining a lavish table to which anyone of the right social standing was welcome. This was the quality most admired by the leading squires and nobles of England, and this that they were most anxious to impress upon posterity.

There is little or no evidence of any weakening in the attachment to this doctrine before the Civil War, despite the fact that it was directly opposed to the Puritan imperative to save rather than to consume. Some early seventeenth-century Puritans like Sir Thomas Heselrige of Noseley, Leicestershire, were content for posterity to know that they were of 'great temperance and sobriety', but the majority of gentry and nobility—even those of a puritan cast of mind—would have scorned so tame an epitaph.

The motive behind this emphasis on liberality was the maintenance of status, which in turn depended more on ways of spending than on mere income. As Sir Thomas Smith remarked in the reign of Elizabeth, 'a Gentleman, (if he will be so accounted) must go like a Gentleman'. This use of expenditure as the acid test of rank means that status bore a closer relation to income than it does in some modern Western communities, like England, where education, accent, and professional occupation are all of crucial importance. It also means that in the effort to maintain status many families overreached themselves, fell heavily into debt, and eventually sold their patrimony and disappeared. At some stage along this dismal road they would be forced to violate another of the conventions of their class and oppress the tenantry in an effort to find the money to maintain expenditure. Thus families like the Treshams were not only financially ruined by their excessive hospitality to their equals, but also socially discredited for their excessive severity towards their tenants.

On the broad view this was a two-class society of those who were gentlemen and those who were not. As a contemporary put it with disarming simplicity, 'All sorts of people created from the beginning are divided into 2: noble and ignoble'. Objectors to this theory, who pointed out that all were descendants of Adam, were brushed off with the argument that 'As Adam had sons of honour, so had he Cain destinated to dishonour'. By the end of the sixteenth century this naïve view did not even begin to fit the facts. From Sir Thomas Smith in 1583 to Sir John Doderidge in 1652, acute observers of the contemporary scene took a less idealized view of the situation.

In these days he is a gentleman who is commonly taken and reputed. And whosoever studieth in the universities, who professeth the liberal sciences and to be short who can live idly and without manual labour and will bear the port, charge and countenance of a gentleman, he shall be called master. . . . And if need be, a King of Heralds shall give him for money arms newly made and invented with the crest and all: the title whereof shall pretend to have been found by the said Herald in the perusing and viewing of old registers.

Despite the blurring of the line by the devaluation of the word 'gent.', despite the relative ease with which it could be crossed, the division between the gentleman and the rest was basic to Elizabethan society. An essential prerequisite for membership of the *élite* was financial independence, the capacity to live idly without the necessity of undertaking manual, mechanic, or even professional tasks. But other equally important qualifications were birth, education, and willingness to adopt the way of life and the system of values which prevailed among the landed classes. Moreover, the source of wealth was just as important as the amount, as many a great London merchant was mortified to discover. When Francis Bacon spoke contemptuously of 'such worms of aldermen' and expressed his surprise at Lionel Cranfield's tact and ability, 'more indeed than I could have looked for from a man of his breeding', he was merely giving voice to conventional wisdom.

This fundamental social division was therefore not based exclusively on wealth—indeed social divisions never are—even though achievement or retention of the higher status was impossible without it. Money was the means of acquiring and retaining status, but it was not the essence of it: the acid test was the mode of life, a concept that involved many factors. Living on a private income was one, but more important was spending liberally, dressing elegantly, and entertaining lavishly. Another was having sufficient education to display a reasonable knowledge of public affairs, and to be able to perform gracefully on the dance floor and on horseback, in the tennis-court and the fencing school.

The upper classes, which comprised the top 2 per cent. or so of the population, divided into three broad groups roughly defined by rank. The first were the plain gentlemen, mostly small landed proprietors but also in part professional men, civil servants, lawyers, higher clergy, and university dons. Above them were the county *élite*—many of the esquires and nearly all the knights and baronets, titular categories which expanded enormously in numbers in the early seventeenth century and which in purely economic terms have an awkward tendency to merge into one another. Finally at the top there were the 60 to 120 members of the titular peerage, itself subdivided into a higher and lower subsection. In this three-tiered division of the gentle classes, the upper gentry are important as forming the link between the other two. They are the men who controlled county politics under the patronage of the local nobleman, who provided the M.P.s and Deputy Lieutenants, and who dominated the bench of Justices. In a large southern county they seem to have comprised about 20 to 25 families, the total being perhaps about 500 in the whole country. These 500 upper-gentry families are in many ways similar in attitudes and way of life to the lower reaches of the peerage, and it was with them, or with the leading elements among them, that social and matrimonial ties were maintained.

Within very broad limits, and admitting many individual exceptions to the rule, the hierarchy of ranks corresponded very roughly to categories of income, though unfortunately for the historian anomalies are too numerous to allow the generalization to be applied to individuals without careful investigation of the particular circumstances. Contemporaries certainly thought that gradations of title meant, on an average, gradations of wealth. This was accepted by Thomas Wilson at the beginning of the seventeenth century and by a much shrewder student of the social structure, Gregory King, at the end.

### III. THE PEERAGE

The titular peerage formed the top layer or layers of this hierarchical, pyramidal structure. In the eyes of the sixteenth century they were a distinct group of the nobility, *nobilitas maior*, as distinct from the *nobilitas minor* of knights, esquires, and armigerous gentry. The criterion of an English peer of the realm was the right to sit in the House of Lords, a right obtained either by letters patent or by receipt of a writ of summons. By the end of the fifteenth century it was the usual, but by no means inevitable, practice to summon all who had previously received a writ, unless they were attainted or under age or otherwise incapacitated. Those who could no longer maintain status because of poverty were quietly dropped from the list. But during the sixteenth century the legal definition hardened on the basis of an inalienable hereditary right. By the reign of Elizabeth ambiguities and uncertainties had been ironed out and there was no longer much serious doubt about who was, and who was not, a peer of the realm. The legal position was now clear.

With the bare title went a number of privileges, legal, financial, and political, which distinguished the aristocracy from the lesser nobility below them. They were favoured before the law in that they could not be arrested except for treason, felony, or breach of the peace. They could not be outlawed, they were free of various writs designed to force men to appear in court, they were not obliged to testify under oath. In consequence they were very slippery customers to catch in the tattered net of the contemporary common-law procedure. They were also free from many of the burdens of local government. They did not sit on juries, could not be pricked as sheriffs, and were not obliged to turn up at county musters.

Hereditary noblemen could in fact, though not in theory, expect that most if not all high offices in the royal household, some embassies, some military commands, and most Lord-Lieutenancies should be reserved for them to the exclusion of mere commoners. Indeed by the reign of Charles I the peerage had achieved almost a complete monopoly of this last office, twenty-nine out of the thirty-three holders being earls or their heirs male, the remainder being made up of two viscounts, one baron, and a bishop. But they could lay no claims to any of the greater offices of state, like those of Lord Treasurer or Lord Chancellor, nor to any fixed proportion of seats on the Privy Council. Holders of high political office were usually given titles to increase the respect accorded to them and to their office, and some important offices were always given to old aristocratic families to secure their support and strengthen their loyalty, but hereditary claims as such were never recognized by either the Tudors or the Early Stuarts.

Finally the peers sat apart, along with the bishops, in one of the two representative assemblies of the kingdom which together, and in conjunction with the King, made up Parliament. Owing to a concentration of modern research upon the lower house, the great power exercised by the Lords in Tudor legislation is in danger of being seriously underestimated. Within this body the importance of lay peers was greatly increased first by the disappearance of the abbots at the Dissolution of the Monasteries, and then by the collapse of the prestige and social standing of the bishops. After 1560 the Upper House was dominated and controlled by the lay peers, the bishops having already taken up their now familiar role of obsequious yes-men for the current ruling clique. Moreover, since peers, unlike commoners, were entitled to vote by proxy, even the aged or infirm who could not stand the journey to London were able to influence decisions by entrusting their proxy to a friend of similar outlook. Looked at as a power *élite*, they consistently filled high political office, they occupied at least half the seats in the Privy Council (if only thanks to concurrent elevation to a title), they formed one of the two legislative bodies in Parliament, they had a near monopoly of the Lord-Lieutenancies, and they were in a position to exercise great influence on county politics and administration by virtue of their territorial holdings and their train of clients. It was the peerage who stole the limelight in the Tudor political system, even if it was the gentry whose interests ultimately prevailed. If the gentry were the ruling, the aristocracy were the governing class.

The significance of these privileges and distinctions should not be over-emphasized. They conferred certain benefits, and served to mark the peerage off from the rest of the community, but they were of limited economic or legal importance. The immunities before the law were helpful rather than decisive, and no one waxed rich merely by being in a position to bilk creditors or evade parliamentary taxes. This is in striking contrast with the situation on the Continent, where a title of nobility conferred favours so enormous as to cut their holders off from the rest of the community upon the fruit of whose labours they existed. English historians in the Whig tradition have in consequence been inclined to picture this country as one with a long history as an open society. This is an over-simplification. Social stratification was very rigid indeed in seventeenth-century England, and mobility from the lower levels into the upper gentlemanly bracket, which had been so common half a century before, was becoming increasingly difficult by 1640. Legal and fiscal inequalities existed, privilege was king. Those who belittle these facts, who pretend that seventeenth-century England was a land of free opportunity, who profess to be unable to distinguish between a gentleman and a baronet, a baronet and an earl, betray their insensitivity to the basic presuppositions of Stuart society.

On the other hand, it is equally misleading to claim that seventeenth-century English society was virtually indistinguishable from that which flourished on the continent of Europe. The permeation of society by merchant wealth, the orientation of foreign policy towards the promotion of economic interests, the influence in the House of Commons of the East Indies or the West Indies interest, the heavy burden of taxation born by the landed nobility, the importance of joint-stock investments and the Bank of England, the relative freedom from personal oppression and economic misery of the peasantry, all point to the fact that there were striking differences between the two societies.

The titular peerage, then, was a status group defined by special privileges of its own, and the major component of a power *élite*. But was it anything more than that? Was it a class in the narrow sense of the word, a body of men with similar economic interests, enjoying similar incomes derived from similar sources? There can be no doubt that landed income was a basic criterion of title. As we have seen, after the middle of the sixteenth century, impoverished peers ceased to be excluded from the House of Lords. One result of the boarding up of this convenient drop-hatch for the indigent was the development of a potential discrepancy between wealth and title. This was why in 1629 the House of Lords petitioned the King to give the Earl of Oxford an estate, so that he could support his dignity. Failing royal aid—and it usually did fail—the only solution was to trade title for money in marriage with an heiress. On the other hand, entry into the higher status groups continued to be directly related to wealth—and landed wealth at that. The result was that, on the average and without prejudice to individual exceptions, legal status remained a reasonably close indicator of financial means.

If we regard the gentry *élite* and the titular peerage as forming a single class, we can see that it is defined in a number of ways. In the first place, its members stood out because of their wealth. As a result of this wealth, they lived in a more opulent style than their neighbours. They mostly married among themselves. They or their sons controlled or filled the county seats in Parliament. They were bound by the same moral pressure to spend freely, to serve the State, and to treat their tenants well. Whatever may be said of the earls, therefore, the baronage at any given time only represents the majority of the greater landowners of the country. Although for some purposes the lives of this non-noble gentry *élite* are freely drawn upon for illustrative material, the statistical skeleton of this book is the titular peerage. This is a defensible procedure since the peerage, embracing as it does about two-thirds of the total families in this economic class—and all those in the really very high income bracket—may fairly be taken as a representative selection.

There is no doubt, however, that the representative value of the peerage changes over the eighty years from 1560 to 1640. A reasonable majority grouping of the greater landowners in 1560, by 1600 it had urgent need to admit new blood to maintain the close relationship of title to landed wealth. This was achieved by James in 1603, but the massive inflation of the peerage under the Duke of Buckingham introduced new elements of uncertainty. A number of the new arrivals lacked the financial backing needed to maintain the position of a baron, while by now some members of the older aristocracy had fallen upon hard times. Moreover, there had been admitted one or two rich merchants. The peerage in 1640 was a landed aristocracy increasingly devoted to money-making, infiltrated partly by a capitalist bourgeoisie obsessed with aristocratic pretensions, and partly by jumped-up lesser gentry who owed their elevation to political favour but some of whom had failed to extract from the Crown the favour of a great landed estate with which to endow their successors. Unattractive though it may be to those with romantic illusions about rank and title, it has been the successful fusion of old blood, new wealth, and political careerism that has given the English peerage its remarkable capacity for survival over the past three centuries.

If the titular peerage was a status group and if together with a further thirty or forty families it formed a single economic class, it remains true nevertheless that there were both marked internal gradations and important differences between the numerous variables in ranking which together formed the social stratification system. Within the peerage dukes, marquises, and earls were in economic resources, political influence, and social prestige set somewhat apart from viscounts and barons. Another obvious division was that of birth, between great families of several generations' standing and those but newly risen to wealth and dignity. At all periods men of inherited position have tended to forget the humble and often sordid origins of their family greatness, and have looked with distaste upon the rise of new men to their own degree of eminence. Bacon remarked complacently that 'new nobility is but the act of power, but antient nobility is the act of time', an observation which is more revealing of his prejudices than of his understanding. Awareness of the difference between the medieval military and the Henrician administrative nobility lingered on among the poor rather than among the aristocracy itself. It found expression in popular revolts like the Pilgrimage of Grace, and cropped up again in the reign of Elizabeth. In 1601 a William Hansley of Market Rasen grumbled publicly that 'there was none of noble blood left in the Privy Council'. 'What are the Cecils', he asked contemptuously, 'are they any better than pen-gent. ?' He, if no one else, saw the difference between a *noblesse d'épée* and a *noblesse de robe*.

More difficult to gauge is the importance of the divisions between rich and poor within the peerage. Both in 1559 and in 1641 the differences in wealth were certainly enormous. In the latter year there was not only a wide gap in the size and value of territorial holdings, but also a gulf between those who could and those who could not exploit mineral resources, drain fens, or develop urban property. There was also a vast, unbridgeable gap between those with plums in the government service, and those without. On the other hand by the seventeenth century a fairly effective rheostat had been devised to prevent a nobleman dropping too far behind or forging too far ahead of the economic group that was suitable to his rank. His title had a market value, and if the going got too rough he could always cash it by marrying the daughter of some low-born but rich and aspiring merchant. From that day to this the glitter of a coronet has always proved an irresistible bait to the City trout. Conversely, stupendous wealth often led to stupendous dissipation, stupendous debts, reckless generosity to younger children, and massive land sales, and it was not till the second half of the seventeenth century that this natural safety valve was blocked off by the legal device of the strict settlement. In the early seventeenth century, therefore, the incomes of most of the peerage tended to bunch around a mean. The enormously rich and the relatively poor were still exceptions and anomalies.

It is helpful for some purposes to look upon the class divisions among those of gentry status and above in a quite different way: to classify them as members either of a 'court' or a 'country' group. According to this method the courtiers are lumped together with the royal officials, some lawyers, the higher clergy, the customs farmers, and the monopoly merchants of the capital to form a single group whose interests were diametrically opposed to those of the rest of the population, the clash between the two being the basic cause of the domestic upheavals in so many countries in Europe in the middle of the seventeenth century. It could further be argued that in England the courtiers proper formed a distinct culture group of their own, particularly in the 1620's and 1630's when religious beliefs, tastes in interior decoration, painting, architecture, sculpture, poetry, and music, attitudes towards sex, drink, and gambling, all differed widely from those prevalent in the country at large. There was also a geographical separation of those who lived in or about the Court and Westminster from those who resided on their country estates, to say nothing of differences in the scale and nature of spending.

This concept is perfectly valid in certain contexts, though it is wrong to treat it as a simple unitary explanation of a very complex political and social situation. It must be accepted that a courtier earl often had more in common with a courtier gentleman than with a country earl. Because of this special interest the ideas and actions of gentlemen who had no particular territorial standing but were powerful figures at Court, men like Sir Walter Ralegh or Sir Thomas Lake, have also been used in this book to illustrate certain aspects of the life of a nobleman. As we shall see, most peers were part-time or full-time courtiers for some of their career, whereas the same cannot be said for any important segment of the gentry, even the *élite*.

It would be foolish to claim that in 1558 and in 1641 all titular peers were men of similar wealth or even of identical interests. Some were the owners of vast territorial possessions stretching over a dozen counties or more, others were confined to a few manors in a single county; some were regularly attendant at Court and frequent holders of high political office; others resided habitually in the country and cultivated their gardens; some, but very few, could trace their ancestry back to the twelfth or thirteenth century, others, but very few, were obscure products of Jacobean capitalism; some were men of the highest cultivation, leading England back into Europe by their judicious patronage of the arts; others were country boors who could talk of nothing but hawks and hounds and the price of mutton; others again were city louts whose vision was limited to alehouses, dice, and drabs. But for all that, they still represented—at any rate up to about 1620—an *élite* with distinct legal and political privileges, a common outlook upon their social duties, and a common motivation arising from a common source of income in the land. As late as 1640 most of them conformed to this pattern, even if there were increasing numbers of exceptions to the rule, the obstinate countryman, the almost landless, the ex-merchant with an eye to maximum profits. Looked at from one point of view, in terms of economic-occupational ranking, they comprised the majority of the class of very large landowners : in the 1630's the Earl of Kingston and Thomas Thynne were both members of it. Looked at from another, in terms of political power, they included the majority of the fairly homogeneous group of influential courtiers : in the 1630's the Earl of Carlisle and Sir Thomas Jermyn were both members of it. But while the earls of Carlisle and Kingston had something in common, the same interest in preserving the privileges of status, the same political club, the same titular rank, the same kinship connexions, Thynne and Jermyn had nothing. Looked at from a third angle, in terms of local power, the peerage included the majority of a fairly homogeneous group whose influence on local affairs was paramount. This was another variable in the stratification system, which did not operate quite like that of influence at Court. In the late sixteenth century Lord Chandos was known as 'King of the Cotswolds' and the Earl of Lincoln lorded it over parts of Lincolnshire, but at Court they were less influential and less respected than a mere favourite like Ralegh, and of negligible consequence in comparison with a powerful official like Sackville or Egerton.

By the mid-sixteenth century there had been established the

doctrine of the fixed hereditary title. As a result the peerage had become a geological formation, the offspring of compacted layers of new men who, generation after generation over a long period of time, had fought their way to the top. Only if a title still brought with it a common ideology, educational privileges, favoured treatment in the struggle for political office, special legal and fiscal privileges, and exceptional opportunities for financial gain could such a collection of individuals maintain its position at the apex of the social pyramid. In the sixteenth and early seventeenth centuries, these criteria were largely, but not wholly, fulfilled. To use a sociologist's terminology, the upper ranges of society in 1558 were not very far off a position of status equilibrium. Although disequilibrium was developing by 1641, the process had not gone so far as to preclude substantial recovery after the Restoration.

The titular peerage should be seen, therefore, as the majority component, and the only common factor, in a whole series of overlapping ranking variables in a hierarchical social structure. Though dear to the simple-minded historian, clear and well-defined classes —either as economic categories or as self-conscious social phenomena—rarely exist in reality. Imperfect though the identification may be, the titular aristocracy is something more than a statistical convenience for the social historian in a hurry. It comprised the most important element in a status group, a power *élite*, a Court, a class of very rich landlords, an association of the well-born.

# III

## THE INFLATION OF HONOURS

'It pitieth me to see all the parts of this kingdom almost in flames of fiery quarells, only for going before, and no man more contentious for it than such as were wont to go behind' (memorandum by a herald in 1604: Bodl. Wood MSS. F 21, f. 22).

T HE most immediately distinctive feature of a society dependent upon monarchy is the existence of titles of honour. Their purpose is to define and to preserve the various gradations of society, both to act as a check upon fluidity and to set the seal of official recognition upon such fluidity as occurs. Since at all periods before the twentieth century social position has depended upon landed wealth, and since that wealth can be rapidly acquired by persons of base extraction, usually by public office, trade, or the law, there has always been a large element of make-believe about the whole business. From earliest times newly enriched families have been hastily provided with genealogies and titles commensurate with their new wealth. The system thus maintains a precarious balance between a rigidly unalterable hierarchy and a situation of absolute mobility. When mobility occurs, it is hastily made respectable by the fiction of gentle birth and the official stamp of rank or title by which Princes contrive 'of vessels of contempt to make vessels of eminency'.

So elaborate a convention will only function satisfactorily if too much strain is not placed upon it. In the first place the hierarchy of titles cannot be left to look after itself: it has to be carefully watched and tended so as to prevent its gradual disappearance. The natural erosion of families by the failure of the male line demands a steady flow of new creations so as to keep up the numbers. As the preamble to the patent of creation of Lord Darcy of Chiche in 1551 observed, 'the pre-excellent estate and dignity of baron, almost wiped out by various chances and by death, cannot be restored to its former splendour unless those who have been most useful to [the King] and the realm as leaders in war and counsellors in peace are advanced to it'. On the other hand there is the contrary danger of elevating too many persons, of too humble social origins, a process which, if accompanied by scandal, exposes the artificiality of the contrivance, and makes it the subject of public contempt and ridicule.

Between 1540 and 1640 there steadily built up an intense acquisitive pressure for outward marks of social distinction. As we have seen, the century witnessed changes in the composition of the English landed classes which were quite unprecedented in their scope. Families rose and fell with extraordinary rapidity, and those that rose, from yeomen to gentlemen, from gentlemen to squires and beyond, urgently demanded some open recognition of their new position. Since a gentleman by his very nature pursued no profession or occupation with an agreed system of advancement, social prestige was the sole outlet into which his competitive instincts could be channelled. The flood of aspirants to the peerage can only be understood if it is set in the context of the tidal wave that was sweeping through all the higher reaches of English society.

## I. THE GENTRY AND KNIGHTAGE

In illiterate societies, changes in the composition of the higher ranks of society are made respectable, and indeed are concealed from public view, by altering the genealogies handed down by oral tradition. The growth of written records, however, makes such a process much more difficult, since more is required than a conveniently feeble memory; fraud, and even forgery, have now to be employed. This thankless task had in 1417 been placed in the hands of the College of Heralds, whose duty it was to smother new wealth beneath a coat of arms and a respectable pedigree. The only real checks on totally unauthorized assumptions of arms were the official Visitations, carried out by the heralds about once a generation between 1530 and 1686. The result of rapid changes in land ownership was an unprecedented torrent of claims for arms in the early Elizabethan period (Fig. 2). In consequence there was a dramatic increase in the number of the gentry. In 1433 there had been only forty-eight families of gentry status recorded in Shropshire, but in 1623 there were 470 who laid claim to it. To do the heralds justice, they did in fact make some efforts to preserve the use of coat armour from utter debasement. For example, they rejected the claims of 47 in Staffordshire in 1583, of 95 in Shropshire in 1623, of 51 in Kent in the 1660's, the public method by which their decisions were announced being calculated to give the greatest possible humiliation to the offending families. But these efforts were too intermittent and haphazard to do much to stop the rot, and in any case were more concerned with preserving the lucrative monopoly of the heralds than with maintaining social

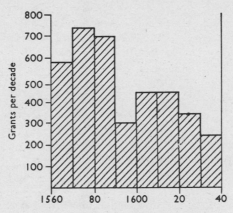

FIG. 2. Grants of Arms, 1560–1639

distinctions. Indeed the ignorance, carelessness, and venality of the heralds soon became notorious. The relaxing of standards by the heralds was dramatized by the revelation in 1616 that Sir William Segar, Garter King of Arms, had been tricked by the York Herald into selling arms (for 22s.) to that overworked man, Gregory Brandon, the common hangman of London—the arms being those of the Kingdom of Aragon with a Canton of Brabant.

The title of knight originally involved military obligations, and even in the sixteenth century it preserved some vestiges of its ancient function in that it was often given under royal commission by military commanders in the field. By now, however, this aspect was falling into the background, and in 1583 Sir Thomas Smith could observe that knights were usually made 'according to the yearly revenue of their lands'.

As in everything else, Elizabeth was remarkably parsimonious in her distribution of honours, and the numbers of English knights failed to increase during her reign, despite the rapid growth of population and the upward thrust of many new families into the squirearchy (Fig. 3). In the last twenty years of the reign, creations were ostensibly fairly large, but the gross figures conceal the fact that the numbers knighted in England actually fell in the next two decades. The bulk of the new knights were made up of adventurers in the Irish wars and volunteers in the various military expeditions

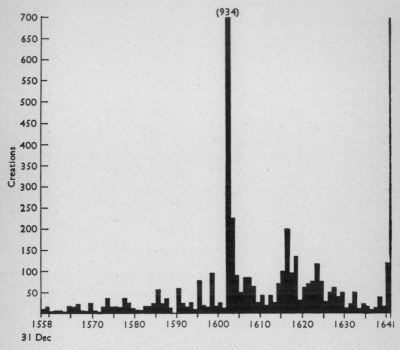

FIG. 3. Creations of English Knights, 1558–1641

of the age, all of whom received their titles from the Lord Deputy or the Lord General. Essex was particularly generous with these favours and thereby incurred the Queen's indignation. Worst of all was Essex's behaviour in his brief and inglorious Irish expedition of 1599 when he created as many as eighty-one knights, without even the justification of a military victory and against the express orders of the Queen. It was this act more than any other that rankled in the Queen's breast and prevented Essex's restoration to favour. The consequences of his action, coupled with the extreme parsimony of the Queen, was to create the curious situation whereby numbers of young gentlemen were swaggering about London as knights, while their fathers in their country manor-houses were obliged to content themselves with the humbler title of esquire. Worse still, a number of bankrupt and low-born adventurers in the Essex entourage had also acquired the dignity. The knightage had certainly not fallen into contempt, but its very uneven distribution was causing considerable ill-feeling among the wealthy gentry. The number of knights had probably fallen very slightly during the reign to about 550, over 25 per cent. of whom were creations of the Earl of Essex.

With the accession of King James on 24 March 1603, royal parsimony was suddenly replaced by the most reckless prodigality : in the first four months of the reign he dubbed no fewer than 906 knights. By December 1604 England could boast of 1,161 new knights, which means that the order had suddenly been increased almost threefold. It could not be denied that Elizabeth had been unwisely sparing in her distribution of honours, and that a large number of substantial families deserved some public recognition of their position, style of living, and service in local administration. But the careless distribution of knighthoods by King James— forty-six at a go before breakfast at Belvoir on his way south— could only bring the order into contempt. In James's favour it must be admitted that he could have had no personal knowledge of those he knighted, and that he was under considerable pressure. He was only too anxious to please his new subjects, who pressed themselves and their claims upon him at every step. If James had been profuse in knighthoods on his journey south, it was his proclamation ordering all worth £40 a year to present themselves that opened the flood-gates. Philip Gawdy, who witnessed the occasion, said that among the throng was 'a scum of such as it would make a man sick to think of them', including shepherds and yeomen's sons and sons of London pedlars. Nevertheless the title was still eagerly sought for, although James had now for-gotten his former indignation at the sale of knighthoods and was distributing the right of nomination among his courtiers. From them these rights passed, like stocks and shares, into general currency among London financial speculators, so that in 1606 Lionel Cranfield bought the making of six knights from his friend Arthur Ingram for £373. 1s. 8d.

Although laments at the passing of older and better traditions were entirely ineffectual, and the sale of knighthoods continued to flourish, the practice was undoubtedly causing increasing irritation. The older county families were indignant at having to adopt such shabby methods to obtain what they regarded as their natural deserts, and resentful as the way opened to newer but less scrupulous families to obtain precedence over them. Though they perforce bought their wares in the market, they became more and more hostile to its continued existence.

After the decision to create baronets in 1611, the flood of knighthoods fell off to half its former rate. By 1615, however, the failure of the Addled Parliament and the consequent desperate search for new sources of revenue led James to relax his restrictions on new creations. From an average of 31 a year for 1610–14 they rose to 120 a year for 1615–19, reaching a peak of 199 during the expensive Scottish journey of 1617. John Chamberlain observed that there was 'scant left an esquire to hold up the race', and that the dignity had sunk yet lower with the knighting of men such as the Earl of Montgomery's barber, the husband of the Queen's laundress, and an ex-innkeeper from Romford. Next year, things went from bad to worse with the admission of an ex-convict, Ralph Burchinshaw, 'but whether that honor will repair his ears that he hath lost is a question'. So great did the pressure of numbers become that the King himself began to treat the ceremony as a joke and to make fun of it, if two stories recorded by Archie the Fool are to be believed. One relates how James, when faced with a Scottish gentleman with a long and unpronounceable name, simply dubbed the man with his sword, and said 'Prithee rise up and call thyself Sir what thou wilt'. Surprisingly enough, the accession of Charles caused a marked reduction in knighthoods, to a level of 45 a year from 1626 to 1630, falling subsequently, after the major policy decision to cease selling titles, to a mere 22 a year from 1631 to 1640 and rising again under renewed political and financial stress to over 100 a year in 1641–2.

Knighthood was the first dignity which the Crown openly allowed to be sold, not by the King himself but by deserving courtiers and servants. The causes of this development are clear enough. Fierce pressure from below from a squirearchy too long starved of titles, a financial stringency that precluded the distribution of direct cash gifts to servants and followers, a laudable desire to please both courtiers and clients, the fact that offices, monopolies, and favours were already being granted to courtiers for resale, all led the easy-going James to succumb to temptation and make knighthood a saleable commodity. Fluctuating according to the conflicting needs to reward followers, to keep up the price, and to preserve the dignity from falling into complete contempt, sales continued until Charles's decision after the death of Buckingham to put a stop to all such practices. Financial necessity, however, then obliged him to turn to the socially less deleterious but politically more disastrous expedient of fining large numbers of the gentry for their failure to take up knighthood at his coronation. James having debased the dignity till it was hardly worth having, Charles then added injury to insult by mulcting very large numbers of the gentry of £173,537 between 1630 and 1635 for having spurned it.

By this inflation, by the venal methods of acquisition, and by the lack of care exercised in sifting the origins and standing of would-be purchasers, the respect for the Crown as the fount of honour was weakened, and the hierarchical structure of society was undermined. Knighthood fell into contempt, and men began seeking some further title of distinction.

## II. THE BARONETAGE

One of the weaknesses in the hierarchy of dignitaries as it existed before 1611 was the wide gap that yawned between the mere knight and the peer of the realm. First advocated by Bacon in 1606, it was not till 1609 that the idea of a new order came to the fore, as the result of a report drawn up by Sir Robert Cotton on possible sources of revenue, which included the sale of titles and gave historical precedents for such sales. And so early in 1611 the Government decided to put on the market a new hereditary dignity of baronet. Salisbury is said to have opposed the scheme since he feared it would anger rather than placate the gentry, but his star was now on the wane and it was Northampton, aided by his protégé Cotton, who persuaded James and the Council to adopt it.

At this early stage every effort was made to preserve the new dignity from drifting into the inflationary condition of the knightage. The baronets were given precedence immediately below the barons, and were guaranteed that the numbers would never be allowed to rise above 200. Moreover, James personally promised not to fill up such vacancies as might occur by the failure of the male line. Choice of candidates was restricted to those who could prove that their family had been armigerous for at least three generations, and that they owned land in possession or reversion worth £1,000 a year. And finally, still further to distinguish him from a mere knight, each baronet had to swear an oath that he had not given a gratuity to a courtier to obtain nomination. In return for the conferring of the title, the aspirant was asked to pay the cost of maintaining thirty soldiers for three years in Ireland, for the plantation of Ulster. This was the theoretical position, but in fact all that was demanded was a direct payment into the Exchequer of £1,095 and there was no guarantee what the money was to be used for. Nevertheless in these early years the money was honestly employed, if not all in Ulster, at least in Ireland.

As soon as the announcement was made there began an intense scramble for precedence by the leading county families, during which Northampton and Salisbury in particular were eagerly lobbied by rival claimants. In view of the enormous attention paid to questions of prestige, the first baronetcy in the county was a prize worth fighting for. One of the most serious political consequences of these new creations in the eyes of later commentators was that they set the countryside by the ears by exacerbating jealousies and hatreds between local families who otherwise would have been content to share vague claims of precedence. And this feature was certainly very marked indeed in the struggle of 1611 about the arrangement of the first ninety-odd baronets. Already, however, the first hint of corruption had begun to creep in. The seventy-second baronet was Sir Paul Bayning, a mere rich London merchant, who obtained this favour by paying £1,500 down instead of the usual £1,095 in three instalments. 'A worthy baronet', an official defensively (or sarcastically) noted against his name on an Exchequer list of receipts.

It was not until 1618, however, that the urgent necessity of finding some commodity other than cash with which to reward deserving suitors obliged King James, no doubt under Villiers's persuasion, to begin treating baronetcies in the same way that he had long been treating knighthoods (Fig. 4, p. 45). The original scheme of a direct cash payment of £1,095 to the Exchequer was abandoned, and 'the making of a baronet' was granted to courtiers to be resold on the market to the highest bidder. From the start the King took little care either to check the suitability of the candidates or even to restrict his bounty to those of suitable social status to be entrusted with such powers. For example in 1622, when the City of Lincoln was trying to raise money to drain and deepen the Fossdyke, James 'further to manifest his affection . . . did grant to the said city the making of three baronets'. In this

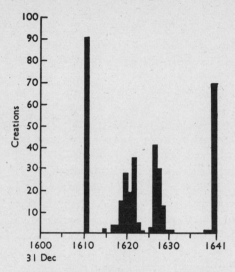

FIG. 4. Creations of English Baronets, 1610–41

case the distribution of an honour still sought by the leading gentry of the county was entrusted to the care of a caucus of provincial aldermen.

The way such grants were handled is vividly described by the King's Master Shipwright, Phineas Pett:

The 20th day of November [1619], attending at Theobalds to deliver his Majesty a petition, his Majesty in his princely care of me, by the means of the honourable Lord High Admiral, had before my coming bestowed on me for supply of my present relief the making of a knight baronet, which I afterwards passed under the broad seal of England for one Francis Radclyffe of Northumberland, a great recusant, for which I was to have £700. But by reason that Sir Arnold Herbert (that brought him to me) played not fair play with me, I lost some £50 of my bargain.

One result of the new policy was the alarming fall in the sale price of baronetcies, from £700 in 1619 to a mere £220 in 1622. By offering over 100 in five years Buckingham and the King were flooding the market. As the price fell, so the quality of the purchasers declined, and the unworthy character of some of them soon became public knowledge. In 1623 the scandal became flagrant when the Earl Marshal's court attempted to degrade a Shropshire baronet, Sir Thomas Harris, 'for baseness and other bad qualities'. But though encouraged by James, who declared his adherence to the original promise that none could be created who had not been armigerous for three generations, little could in fact be done. Harris, who was a successful Shrewsbury draper of yeoman stock, fought back vigorously and the Earl Marshal discovered that he could not touch his patent under the great seal, and could merely have him 'declared and pronounced no gentleman'. With the open recognition of a baronet who was no gentleman, another serious blow had been dealt to public respect for the hierarchical structure of English society.

Between 1618 and 1622 James was drawing heavily upon a strictly limited fund, as he had bound himself by the terms of the patents not to create more than 200 baronets, and there were already 198 by the end of 1622. Though weak, James was an honest man, and when he granted a baronetcy to Sir Thomas Playters in 1623, he announced that it was the last he intended to make. King Charles, less easy-going but fundamentally weaker and more dishonest than his father, began with the best of intentions. Despite lobbying from various quarters, he at first stuck to King James's resolution to abide by the solemn promises of the patents and to make no more baronets. But in December 1626 the needs of the French war and the ascendancy of Buckingham tempted him to break his principles and his promises and to give the Villiers clan—the Duke, his wife, and his mother—a free hand in the distribution of some eighty-five new baronetcies, all in excess of the stipulated 200. Though other influential courtiers managed to get some of the pickings—a client of the Earls of Holland and Warwick secured a corner in Essex baronetcies—the main sales were handled by the Duke. Sir John Oglander recorded how a hawker of baronetcies came peddling his wares around the country houses of the Isle of Wight, and, royalist though he was, he added the ominous comment: 'But a time may come, which may be either by Parliament or by his Majesty, that . . . their honour may be buried in the dust, as the Duke's was very shortly after the making of those upstart baronets.'

This flood of new baronets pushed the price down to £200 or less, and the usual quarrels broke out between buyer and seller over payment. In one case Charles had to intervene personally on behalf of the seller, threatening the buyer with a summons to appear before him; in another the seller fought a successful test case in Chancery to enforce the contract.

In the summer of 1629 Charles, now freed from the influence of Buckingham, turned his face resolutely against any further sale of titles of any kind. Absolute monarchy would manage its finances without stooping to such undignfied and socially harmful practices. Only one baronet a year was made in 1630–1 and 1639–40 and none at all between 1632 and 1638. In May 1641, however, this policy was reversed, and a new flood of creations began which in under two years added a further 128 families to the 290-odd already elevated. The purpose of this change was probably partly to buy support against the opposition in Parliament. If so it proved a dismal failure, for of those created up to the end of 1641 rather more became active Parliamentarians than active Royalists. Even as a device to raise money and to reward courtiers it had limited success, since sellers exceeded buyers. As early as July 1641 the price was down to £400 and there can be little doubt that it subsequently fell still lower. Many potential purchasers, like George Evelyn of Wotton, must have refused the offer because of the prevailing political uncertainty and for fear that the new titles might be challenged and overthrown by Parliament.

Writing during the enforced leisure of the Interregnum, the royalist Sir Edward Walker remarked that the creation of the order of baronets 'hath been a greater cause of debasing nobility and undervaluing gentry, and hath generally given more offence and scandal to all degrees than any dignity that ever was devised'. The history of the order does much to support this claim. The original device of 1611, including as it did a direct cash payment to the Crown, was in itself a blow to the prestige of monarchy, despite the social and financial safeguards. The subsequent disputes over precedence and the opposition of the knights aroused bitter feelings, which were greatly exacerbated when baronetcies were sold by courtiers to mean persons from 1618 to 1622 and 1626 to 1629. King Charles's breach of the solemn engagement not to make more than 200 English baronets seriously diminished faith in the royal word, as well as arousing indignation among the existing holders of the title. Such revival of confidence as occurred between 1629 and 1641 was then shattered once more by the fresh spate of sales. The result was to heighten the competitive friction among the leading gentry, to alienate many of them from the Crown, to undermine respect for aristocratic institutions and titles, and to drive the ambitious to seek yet further honours in the peerage itself.

### III. THE PEERAGE

Under the early Tudors the size of the peerage had undergone only one major fluctuation. The deliberate refusal of Henry VII to elevate new men, coupled with natural wastage assisted by attainder, had resulted in a contraction of the male peerage from about 57 to 44. But this policy was soon reversed under Henry VIII and by 1529 the numbers were back again in the middle fifties, a figure which remained virtually unchanged until the end of the century. But this apparent stability conceals a very substantial turnover, with new creations just keeping pace with attainders and natural extinctions. Between 1509 and 1553 some forty-seven titles had been created, restored, or resumed, the great majority representing the elevation of successful soldiers and administrators after 1529. But things were very different under Elizabeth. If she was frugal in her distribution of knighthoods, she was even more conservative in the creation of new peerages (Fig. 5, p. 49). This attitude stemmed not so much, as with her grandfather, from a deliberate intention to reduce the powers and numbers of the peerage as from a snobbish and increasingly unrealistic wish to maintain the peerage as a caste for men of ancient lineage. From personal observation Francis Naunton concluded that 'a concurrence of old blood with fidelity [was] a mixture which ever sorted with the queen's nature'. This comes out very clearly from the eighteen peerages which she did create, revive, recognize, or admit, of which six were merely restorations of former titles, two were inherited in the female line, three were granted to younger sons of peers, two to heirs or coheirs of ancient houses, and three to royal cousins. Only Lord Burghley and Lord Compton (who came of knightly stock) belonged to new families without either ancestral claims or blood relationship to the Queen. This parsimony was, of course, no more than normal Tudor practice, broken only during the revolutionary decades of the 1530's and 1540's, but it had now to be maintained under very different conditions. In a period of rapid changes in land ownership so conservative an attitude could only lead to an ever-widening breach between title

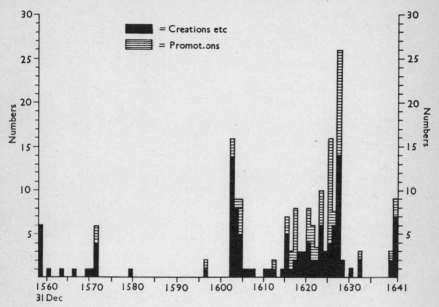

FIG. 5. Creations and Promotions of English Peers, 1558–1641

and status on the one hand and power and wealth on the other. Moreover, owing to inexorable erosion by the failure of male heirs, to say nothing of extinction by attainder, it also caused a slight numerical decline in the size of the peerage (Fig. 6, p. 50). Here as in other fields the Queen's meanness became more marked in the last years of her life, and between 1573 and 1603, apart from admitting Lord Willoughby d'Eresby to the title inherited on his mother's side, and belatedly promoting to an earldom Lord Howard of Effingham, the hero of the Armada, she only created one new peer, himself the son of an attainted duke, the heir general of an extinct barony, and a royal cousin.

James came south in 1603 with a reputation for generosity over the granting of titles, and as soon as he arrived he was faced with a demand for new creations that had been dammed up for nearly twenty years. Eminent courtiers and officials like Sir Robert Cecil and Sir Thomas Egerton, leading county families like the Petres, Spencers, and Danvers, all had claims which could hardly be denied. The large number of creations and promotions of the first three years of the new reign was no more than was called for in

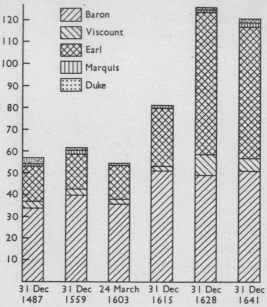

FIG. 6. Numbers and Composition of the Peerage, 1487–1641

view of the growth of population and the rise of new families, and the choice of candidates was on the whole judicious. The process by which the choice was made, however, appears to have been more open to criticism.

From the beginning there were rumours that the traditional practice of accepting petty gratuities was tending to degenerate into corruption. The first clear evidence of the open sale of a title by James comes in 1605, when Arabella Stuart was given a patent for a peerage with a blank for the name to be filled in at her pleasure. A week later Sir William Cavendish got his patent passed on Arabella's nomination and there is clear evidence that he was finally brought to pay for it. In his accounts the payment is left vague but unmistakable: 'presently after my Lord's creation, paid at Sir William Bowyer's house which he paid over, the sum of two thousand pounds.' All in all, what with this purchase price, the gratuities to others, the fees for the creation, and the clothes and food bought for the occasion, his title cost the new peer nearly £2,900.

In spite of some dubious transactions, the peerage in 1615 still retained its full dignity and respect. Hardly anyone had been admitted to its ranks who was unworthy of the honour by birth and wealth. The system of granting honours, though open to abuse, had not yet degenerated into plain corruption. The King himself had sold no titles for cash and, with the exception of Arabella Stuart (and possibly one other), no private person had ever been given the right of nomination. The increase of numbers by about 40 per cent. over 1603 (and 1558) was certainly substantial, but not unreasonable in view of the number of respectable gentry families newly risen to outstanding wealth and position.

In 1615, however, there occurred a radical change of policy, to a system of direct cash sale of titles by the Crown, and the granting of nominations as rewards for courtiers. It is no coincidence that this change of policy coincided with the rise to favour of George Villiers, future Duke of Buckingham. The Villiers ascendancy meant the dispossession from office of the Carr dependants, and ultimately of the Howard faction. Not all could be removed, like Suffolk, by the frontal assault of a charge of corruption, and the others had to be compensated for their disappointment. With the failure of the Great Contract in 1610 and the abrupt dissolution of the Addled Parliament in 1614, the Crown had lost hope of parliamentary supplies and was trying to manage without them. The pressure to use the sale of titles as rewards for the hungry Villiers family, as compensation for the outgoing politicians, and as means to raise ready cash was therefore almost irresistible. Advised by Bacon, and no doubt encouraged by Villiers, James at last took the plunge and consented to a direct sale of peerages as the only means of raising ready cash. 'Baronies were wont to be given by entaile, but now they go by bargain and sale', observed the wits in the aisles of Saint Paul's.

In the thirteen years from 31 December 1615 to 31 December 1628 the numbers of the English peerage rose from 81 to 126, and at the same time the number of earls increased still faster, from 27 to 65. These phenomenal increases, of 56 per cent. in the

peerage as a whole, and 141 per cent. among the earls, constitute
one of the most radical transformations of the English titular
aristocracy that has ever occurred. Nor was this all, for at the same
time the Irish peerage was being enlarged to an even greater
degree. There were 25 Irish peers in 1603, but between then and
1641 the Stuarts created 80 more. Of these some 50 were Englishmen, at least 30 of whom had no connexion with Ireland whatever.
All but five creations took place between 1616 and 1630 and they
seem almost without exception to have been the result of gift or
purchase from the Villiers family, whose rapacious stranglehold
on the colony was almost complete.

Naturally enough, the records of the sordid intrigues and bargains that lay behind this inflation are neither as full nor as reliable
as one could wish. Many of the participants were ashamed of their
own conduct. For example, in 1624 John Holles was very anxious
to conceal the fact that he was about to pay for his earldom, and
asked for promotion to the Council of War as 'some excuse unto
the world . . . why his Majesty should receive him unto this
honour'. But for all this secrecy there were plenty of well-informed
commentators—including John Holles himself—to report how
things were arranged, and sufficient negotiations were conducted
in writing to have left ample traces in private correspondence.

The creations of these thirteen years fall into a variety of categories. There were those like Bacon, Conway, Coventry, or Dudley
Carleton, who achieved their dignities as the natural reward for
political services and obsequiousness to Buckingham, and almost
certainly paid little or nothing for them. There was an analogous
group like Mohun, Weston, and Goring who were promoted to
buttress Buckingham's political position in the House of Lords in
1628 ('Mohun in a Lordlike way will best be your servant', Sir
James Bagg had observed to the Duke some months before). And
then there were those who from ambition or necessity had made
marriage alliances into some ramification of the wide Villiers clan,
and thereby obtained office or title as a marriage portion. As
Fuller observed : 'Most of his neices were matched with little more
portion than their uncle's smiles, the forerunner of some good
office or honour to follow on their husbands.'

The last and most important group of new peers are those who,
in one way or another, paid roundly for their honours. The rarest
category comprises those who handed their money straight into

the Exchequer. The official receipt-books only record five such
payments. This dearth of official evidence is caused by the fact
that in most cases the money went to a courtier, usually Buckingham, and that in others it was directly assigned for a specific purpose. In 1616 the large sums required to launch Lord Hay on an
expensive embassy to Paris and Madrid were raised by selling
two baronies to Sir John Holles and Sir John Roper for £10,000
each. The two peers were created and paid their money on 9 July,
and three days later Lord Hay set out, 'for that he could not move
till this weight set his wheels going'. When he returned he was
given the making of two barons as additional compensation for
his outlay, and was made a viscount in return for money with
which to buy hangings to furnish houses along the route of the
royal journey to Scotland. And in 1624, when enormous sums were
needed to pay for the Duke of Buckingham's embassy to Paris, a
new round of sales of titles was begun in order to raise £30,000.

While the commonest of these urgent needs were for the cost of
embassies or progresses, the sale of titles was also used for the
widest purposes. A case that shows the intimate connexion between the sale of titles and the other forms of royal grants and
favours is that of Sir Thomas Monson, a Lincolnshire landowner
and successful Jacobean courtier. In the early 1620's Sir Thomas
became involved in a very complicated transaction with the Earl
of Middlesex connected with debts to the Crown incurred by
officials in the Ordnance Office. The Earl bought out Monson's
interest in the estates of one of the officials in return, amongst
other things, for 'the making of 6 Baronets'. But James's refusal
to exceed the stipulated total of 200 baronets made it impossible
for the bargain to be fulfilled, and instead Monson was given the
right to enfranchise the copyholders on the royal manor of Wake-
field. Before the grant could be implemented, however, James
died and Charles refused to confirm it. Monson kept pressing for
an alternative reward, and in 1628 he persuaded a committee of
privy councillors to recommend that he be granted the making of
a baron, to be taken in his own person.

There can be no doubt that the commonest method of obtaining a peerage, particularly after 1624, was payment to the Duke
of Buckingham, his relatives, or his followers among whom he
frequently distributed the proceeds. Usually, however, the money
went direct to the Duke himself. In 1624 Sir Francis Leake paid

him £8,000 for his barony and Lord Houghton £5,000 for his earldom. The cool effrontery with which Buckingham told the King of Leake's offer and of how he was preparing the patent provides remarkable evidence of the relationship between James and his favourite: 'Here is a gentleman called Sir Francis Leake who hath likewise a philosophers stone; 'tis worth but eight thousand; he will give it me if you will make him a baron. I will, if you command not the contrary, have his patent ready for you to sign when I come down; he is of good religion, well born, and hath a good estate. I pray you burn this letter.' Ireland during these years was virtually a colony of exploitation maintained by the Villiers family. Between 1618 and 1622 the Duke secured £24,750 from the sale of nine peerages, eleven baronetcies, four knighthoods, the Lord Chancellorship, and a seat on the Privy Council in that unhappy island. This corrupt tyranny continued until his murder and in 1627–8 we find Lord Barrymore paying him £1,000 for a barony and the Earl of Cork £2,000 for two baronies for his younger sons. One way or another—and the ways were many and devious—most creations between 1615 and 1628 led back to George Villiers, Duke of Buckingham, and the Commons were well justified in 1626 when they made 'the trade and commerce of honor' one of the chief grounds for their impeachment of the Duke. As they said, even if he did not altogether begin the traffic, 'he was the first that defiled this virgin of honour so publicly'.

The motives and the mechanics of the wholesale distribution of titles between 1615 and 1629 are now clear enough. An indolent king in desperate straits for money with which to finance his day-to-day pleasures and to reward his courtiers, a prevailing tradition of gratuities and bribes for services rendered, a long-standing custom of the sale by individuals of minor offices in the administration and the law, the accession to power of a new and unscrupulous favourite bringing with him a crowd of relatives and dependants all clamouring for the spoils, the financial success of the sale of baronetcies, all combined in 1615 to exert irresistible pressure. Occasionally the King sold titles directly, more often he either sold them and turned over the money at once for some specific purpose like an embassy or a progress, or gave the benefit of a nomination to a deserving courtier, creditor, or disappointed place-seeker. In all cases where the King granted the nomination to others, it should be emphasized that in theory all he was giving away was the profits. The grantee had to find a suitable candidate, but the King retained the ultimate right to accept or reject the offer. Nevertheless the choice lay with the grantee, and so far as we know this right of veto was in fact rarely exercised. Most commonly the distribution of these favours was carried out not by the King but by Buckingham, to the profit of himself, his relatives, or his dependants. The reckless inflation of both the English and Irish peerages coincides with the rule of the Duke and it formed an important element in making him one of the best-hated men in English history.

Naturally enough the price of peerages, like those of knighthoods and baronetcies, tended to fluctuate according to the laws of supply and demand. In the first five or six years, from 1615 to 1621, a barony was held at about £10,000, at which price at least five were sold and probably more. But by 1622 Chamberlain reported that the price was dropping, and it is clear that in the middle 1620's the price fell by about 50 per cent. Evidence for viscountcies is less reliable and abundant, but it seems that they were sold for £10,000 in 1620, about £8,000 in 1625, and had dropped to £4,000 or £5,000 by 1627. Until about 1620 the normal price of converting a barony into an earldom was the same as for a barony itself, namely £10,000, but a few years later it was down to £4,000. Irish titles, which were freely sold throughout this period, underwent the same decline in value.

This widespread system of 'temporal simony', as the Earl of Clare described it, was put to an end by Felton's knife. Free from Buckingham's corrupting influence, within a few months Charles realized the damage being done to his conceptions of monarchy and society, and firmly put a stop to all such practices in future. Nor can there be any doubt that this was a deliberate decision of Charles himself. It was not till 1641 that Charles renewed the practice of selling honours. He began, as has been seen, with baronetcies, and in the summer of 1641 he created a number of new peers, one of whom—Lord Capel was reputed to have bought his title. The last of such sales occurred as late as October 1648 when the captive Charles at Carisbrooke promised to make Lord Brudenell an earl in return for a mere £1,000. By now it was all the monarch had to offer, and even this promise could not be honoured till the Restoration.

The immediate consequences of this process of inflation of titles of honour and their distribution by open sale are obvious enough. But what of the wider social and political effects? During the long years of the Interregnum a number of royalists looked back over the history of the previous half-century to try to discover how it was that the institution of monarchy had fallen into such disrepute. Without exception they all agreed in laying great emphasis upon the sale of honours. Gervase Holles thought that 'that way of merchandise . . . was one cause (and not the least) of [the] misfortunes . . . of our last-martyred King'. Sir Edward Walker thought the same: 'It may be doubted whether the dispensing of honours with so liberal (I will not say unconsiderate) a hand, were not one of the beginnings of general discontents, especially amongst persons of great extraction.' The Marquis of Newcastle saw a direct chain of causation. First 'so many beggarly people [were] made great Lords and Ladies in title that were not able to keep up the dignity of it' that respect for the peerage declined; and then, once 'Noblemen were pulled down, which is the foundation of monarchy—monarchy soon after fell'.

There is a good deal of evidence that respect for the titular peerage was declining in the early seventeenth century. An important cause of this development was the partial divorce of titular rank from both wealth and status, caused by the fact that titles could be bought for money; that mere merchants or merchants' sons like Hicks, Craven, or Bayning could acquire them; that a few of the new peers, particularly Villiers' relatives and hangers-on, lacked the financial resources to maintain the position their titles demanded; and that they had become so numerous that familiarity bred contempt. Assuming a population in 1630 of about 5 million, there were about twenty-five peers per million people, which, apart from the first decade of the nineteenth century, is the highest ratio ever reached. The peers under Charles I were a more upstart group than at any time in the previous 200 years—far more so than at the present day, when the pattern more closely resembles that of 1558.

Condemnation of this development was widespread in the early seventeenth century. Emphasis on moral revulsion is not a misplaced application of a twentieth-century standard of values but recognition of the attitude of mind of a generation still deeply affected by renaissance ideas of nobility as the hallmark of both personal merit and ancient lineage. It saw the inflation of honours as the cause of the introduction of the dread notion of 'parity'. No hierarchy, no King, warned Shakespeare; 'No Bishop, no King', argued James; 'No Nobility, no King', concluded Newcastle. There was truth in what they said. It is not without significance that this first epoch of direct sale of titles culminated in the temporary abolition of the House of Lords and the monarchy, just as another epidemic of sales from 1891 to 1921 witnessed the removal of most of the political powers of the Lords and the final erosion of the residual authority of the Crown.

Handled discreetly, the sale of titles could have been adjusted to changing circumstances without causing too much offence, without shattering the established order, and with some profit to the Crown. As it was, supply often tended to outrun demand since many families scorned to traffic in so squalid a market. Moreover, it is a nice point whether the embattled gentry were more infuriated by the sale of honours before 1629 or by the alternative devices of distraint of knighthood and forest fines of the 1630's. By this last-minute change of heart the Crown failed to restore much confidence in its integrity and merely aroused further indignation over the illegality of its measures. It got the worst of both worlds.

Another drawback, which was pointed out by Sir John Bramston, was that the creation of so large a number of hereditary titles gravely reduced the political influence of the Crown. So long as the commonest honour of knighthood was not hereditary, generation after generation of leading county families were obliged to seek Crown favour and undertake public service, if only to maintain their social position within the knightly class. But once they had acquired a hereditary baronetcy or peerage, they and their descendants could more easily afford the luxury of political opposition.

It was left to Bacon to draw attention to a more fundamental problem, which was the strain this inflation was placing on both the national economy and royal finances. Men with titles felt themselves obliged to maintain a way of life commensurate with their degree. The result of a titular inflation was therefore to increase conspicuous consumption and this used up more and more capital in unproductive ways. For the maintenance of this style of living the nobility had to rely in large measure on lavish royal

rewards and favours, which in turn endangered the stability of
royal finances and created friction among the taxpayers, who were
not among the beneficiaries of the system. The consequence was
the growing cleavage in thought, behaviour, pattern of life, and
economic interests between 'Court' and 'Country'. There is much
truth in this analysis of Early Stuart politics and finances, and it is
curious that it is only mentioned in passing by Bacon, and was not
developed by others.

The consequence to which all commentators drew attention
was the incitement to faction. For a time the House of Lords itself
was rent by divisions between groups of different origin. The
older peerage despised the new, and their contempt found violent
expression in 1621 when Arundel publicly taunted Spencer with
his ancestry. There were also jealousies between new peers of
long-standing gentry stock and those of base blood, which again
were ventilated openly when Lord Digby called Lionel Cranfield,
Earl of Middlesex, 'an insolent merchant'. Large numbers of the
peers, particularly those of ancient title, were offended by the
elevation of George Villiers first to a marquisate and then to a
dukedom, and in the 1620's there developed what had not been
seen since the days of Wolsey or Protector Somerset, a large group
of peers actively ranged against royal policies and the royal
favourites. By no means all this opposition group came from the
older peerage, and some of its members owed both title and fortune to recent royal patronage. John Selden thought little of such
ingratitude, and remarked acidly: 'The Lords that fall from the
King after they have got estates by base flattery at court and now
pretend conscience, do as a vintner; that when he first sets up,
you may bring your wench to his house and do your things there;
but when he grows rich, he turns conscientious and will sell no
wine upon the Sabbath day.'

It was argued by both Walker and Newcastle that an important
factor in creating this opposition group in the Lords was the lack
of sufficient public offices to satisfy the ambitions of so numerous
a nobility. Every peer thought himself entitled by virtue of his
dignity to a share in at any rate the more decorative offices of state
or court, and when rebuffed he tended to join the country party
out of pique. Newcastle went still further and ascribed the opposition in the Commons to encouragement from the Lords. 'The
House of Commons had not been factious but for them, for as

soon as ever one is made a Lord, he thinks himself then capable of the greatest place in England, though most unfit, partiality hath such force; and if he be denied, then he grows factious and makes parties and joins with the House of Commons to disturb your Majesty's government.' We need not agree with the Marquis in his over-cynical analysis of political motivation, but it remains true that the growth of a powerful opposition in the House of Lords deprived the King of his last bulwark against an indignant Commons, and that this growth was encouraged by the sale of titles.

The inflation of honours not only provoked divisions within the peerage, but also inspired fierce jealousies between order and order, rank and rank. The peers fought bitterly for the defence of their and their children's privileges, first against the baronets and later against the English gentry who had acquired Irish and Scottish titles; the baronets quarrelled with officials, magistrates, and lawyers over issues of precedence; the knights were profoundly resentful of the baronets, with their hereditary privileges and superior rank; the squirearchy were furious at having to give way to a mob of knights often of low birth and mean estate. The numerical increase in all ranks, the creation of a new order, and the glaring injustices of the distribution of titles tended to set the whole governing class at loggerheads. In France, where titles carried with them substantial fiscal advantages, a not dissimilar situation actually increased the King's power by splitting his enemies into jealously warring groups incapable of collective action. By building up a hierarchy of vested interests, the monarchy effectively divided class from class and so was able to triumph over all. Although the idea was toyed with from time to time, the English Crown never brought itself to link titles to solid material advantages, and as a result the inflation of honours merely resulted in widespread disaffection. Hostility to the author of such a system was stronger than hatred of inferior or jealousy of superior ranks and orders.

As set out by the royalist commentators of the 1650's, the folly of the inflation of honours by the Early Stuarts seems obvious enough. There were, however, a number of facts and arguments which they ignored. In the first place, the sale of titles was a significant source of revenue to the Crown between 1603 and 1629. Of course only a tiny fraction of the money ever came to the hands

of the King himself, since the early attempts at direct crown sales
soon degenerated into grants to courtiers of the rights of nomination. But had titles not been available James and Charles would
have been obliged to reward their courtiers and officials in other
ways, possibly by direct grants of money, annuities, or lands.
Knighthoods, baronetcies, and peerages are merely three items in
a rich and varied range of wares by the sale of which the Crown
endeavoured to finance an extravagant and parasitic court in the
teeth of opposition from Parliament and the country. Admittedly
such lavish generosity was unnecessary for the maintenance of the
court structure; some happy mean between the parsimony of
Elizabeth and the extravagance of James would have been better
in every way. But given the characters and outlook of James and
Buckingham, a flow of grants and favours on a huge scale was
inevitable, and the profits to courtiers of the sale of honours must
be regarded as part of the financial resources of the Crown, though
not one that figures in the official accounts.

If so, we must discover how important a part it was. No precise
figure can be given, but it should be possible to arrive at the order
of magnitude. I estimate that the *minimum* total profits to Crown
and courtiers for the sale of all honours between 1603 and 1629
was about £620,000. This gain certainly did not compensate for the
unpopularity and loss of prestige resulting from this traffic, but
it is only fair to set it on the other side of the scales. The inflation
of honours was not the sole cause either of the decline in the
prestige of the peerage or of the growth of faction in the countryside. The peerage suffered from other disadvantages, amongst
them close identification with the moral turpitude popularly
ascribed to the Court, and the fact that in 1640 some 20 per cent.
were Papists, while the country gentry had been prone to faction
long before the struggle for ranks and titles began.

The further objection to the arguments of the royalist commentators is that they were too much obsessed with the mechanics of
supply to notice the phenomenon of demand. They were correct
to draw attention to the undermining of respect for rank and title
by the speed of the inflation, by the system of open sale, and by the
unsuitable nature of some of the purchasers. But they were wrong
to attribute the growth of a sense of 'parity' merely to these abuses.
Though clumsy in operation, the inflation was in principle no
more than recognition of an established socio-economic fact, that

the class pyramid in its upper ranges had become much broader at the base and rather lower at the top than it had been at the accession of Elizabeth. The huge expansion in the numbers of men calling themselves gentleman, esquire, knight, baronet, baron, viscount, and earl is not merely the result of the greed and folly of heralds, courtiers, and kings. Even if the heralds had been sea-green incorruptibles, Buckingham and the courtiers men of austere and blameless lives, and King James a man of iron will and an overflowing treasury, a substantial increase in titles must still have taken place. The insatiable demand for status and honour between 1558 and 1641 is proof of the truth of what has been called 'Tawney's Law': that the greater the wealth and more even its distribution in a given society, the emptier become titles of personal distinction, but the more they multiply and are striven for.

# IV

## ECONOMIC CHANGE

> . . . your fair titles
> Are but the shadows of your ancestry;
> And you walk in 'em, when your land is gone,
> Like the pale ghosts of dead nobility.
> RICHARD BROME, *The Damoiselle*, I. i

ACED with the problem of demonstrating changes in the economic position of different classes in society, the historian is tempted to content himself with giving a series of examples to illustrate a general hypothesis. The hypothesis is propounded to explain a political situation, and the capacious rag-bag of social history is then rummaged for supporting evidence. But this approach is rendered virtually useless by the irritating variability of human nature. No matter how triumphantly a given class is rising to the top, no matter how inexorably another is being depressed, there will always be numerous individuals who perversely insist on running directly contrary to the general trend, or who contrive to remain stationary in a period of dynamic change. Any theory of social movement can therefore always be supported by an imposing array of individual case-histories. Thus for the century before the Civil War there have been discovered affluent peers and decaying peers, successful courtiers and ruined courtiers, rising gentry and decaying gentry. The inadequacy of the method has been effectively demonstrated by this bewildering conflict of evidence. Since he cannot discover by any other means what examples are typical and what are exceptional, the historian is forced back, whether he likes it or not, upon statistical analysis and quantitative measurement.

### I. ESTIMATES OF INCOME

Full understanding of the economic position of the peerage and of changes that occurred in that position demands accurate data about the gross and net incomes of each individual at various points of time. Armed with such information it would be possible

to work out the total income of the group, the mean income, and
the distribution pattern, and to compare these three at forty-year
intervals. But the quests for the Golden Fleece and the Holy Grail
were less fraught with all but insuperable difficulties. The path is
obscured by the paucity of records, the difficulty of interpreting
such records as do survive, the ambiguities about the meaning of
the word 'income', and the uncertainties about the precise significance of the different meanings.

Although there has been preserved a far higher proportion of
the original archives of the peerage than of any other social group,
it is still only a very small part of the whole, and its distribution is
uneven. Roughly speaking, the greater the family the higher the
chances of survival of its archives; the papers of wealthy earls
have come down to us in far greater profusion than those of minor
barons. This is because the larger the estate the smaller the likelihood of total disintegration and dispersal. There is a fair chance
that at least the hard core of a huge sixteenth-century estate has
passed on intact down to the present day, often through daughters
or close relatives, and that in consequence the family archives have
been preserved in some country house or other. With smaller
families, however, time and chance have taken a heavier toll, and
substantial records usually survive only for the very few families
whose line of descent runs unbroken from that day to this.

Even when family records exist, they rarely tell the historian
precisely what he wants to know. A serious problem is what is
meant by 'income', a word upon which historians have placed a
wide variety of interpretations, each of which is perfectly valid for
certain purposes but must not be confused or compared with any
other. The smallest useful category is the 'disposable income', put
forward recently as a useful guide to the breaking-point in the
finances of a great magnate. This is the residue of the gross personal income, after the deduction of jointures, interest payments,
irredeemable annuities, rents for leases, the cost of estate management and repairs, and the upkeep of a reasonable establishment.
This is not a concept used by contemporaries, who when calculating net income tended to confine their deductions to rents for
leases and fee-farm rents, and sometimes to annuities as well.
Another 'income' consists of the gross personal receipts. These
gross receipts might be artificially swollen by taking on a lease
whose profits were offset by the rent, or by recovering lands in

jointure in return for the grant of an annuity, and therefore have only limited value unless the fixed charges are set off against them. All these types of personal income raise two further questions, of which the first is whether or not to include the profits of office. If what is required is the total income of the individual, they must obviously be taken into account; but if it is the long-term assets of the family which are being calculated, they must be ignored. The second question is whether or not to take account of the burden of debt. It was perfectly possible for a man to enjoy a large gross revenue, half or more of which was eaten up in interest payments. Sooner or later these debts would have to be cleared off, probably by the sale of land, and to ignore them can therefore give a very misleading impression of capital resources. If what is wanted is the net cash at the disposal of the individual for current needs, the receipts from land must always be offset by the interest charges on loans.

So far all definitions of 'income' that have been offered have been concerned with property in possession. For some purposes, however, it is necessary to add in reversionary interests. This is because the personal income of the model nobleman was not a constant, but fluctuated in a series of huge steps as various sections of the estate were temporarily withdrawn from his control. When he came into his own on his father's death, the young lord might find that he only enjoyed a part of the total family estates, some of the rent being set aside for a jointure for his mother, some for life interests for his younger brothers, and some allocated to trustees to raise marriage portions for his sisters or pay his father's debts. On his mother's death and the payment of his sisters' portions he would at last begin to enjoy the full income of the estate, with the minor exception of that devoted to the support of his brothers. But when his eldest son grew up he had to give him an allowance, and when the boy married he was obliged to settle on him and his wife an important slice of the total income. Moreover as his daughters grew up he probably found it prudent to make part of the estate over to trustees, to use the income for raising capital for the marriage portions.

Given this bewildering multiplicity of choice, the historian must select the type of 'income' which is most suitable to his current purpose, and must take great care not to attempt misleading comparisons between wholly different categories. The 'income' for which most evidence is available is the gross rental of land in possession plus that of assured reversions in possession of wife, son, or mother. This formed the basis of tax assessments, and can most frequently be found from records in private archives. Despite its limitations, therefore, this is the type of 'income' which must first be used as a basis for calculations.

One of the principal objects of this book is to demonstrate and measure change, and financial change is only meaningful if account is taken of changes in the level of prices. The most recent and authoritative index is that compiled by Professor Phelps Brown in order to measure changes in the price of goods—mostly food—consumed by the labouring classes. It is therefore necessary either to employ the Phelps Brown index as it stands, or to scale it down by some arbitrary amount to make allowance for labour costs in

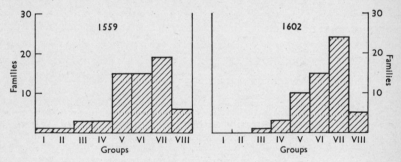

FIG. 7. Estimated Gross Rentals, 1559, 1602

aristocratic expenditure, and then to scale it up again by another arbitrary amount to make allowance for other expenses. On balance it seemed better to leave the index unaltered, despite its imperfections. Throughout this book, whenever reference is made to adjustment to allow for rising prices, it is to be understood that the index used is that of Professor Phelps Brown.

In Figs. 7 and 8 the peerage has been divided at three selected dates into eight categories, grouped in descending order of rental income. The placing of individual families in these categories is a hazardous operation, and there can be little doubt that a few have been placed one above or below their true position. Nevertheless it is probable that the table gives a reasonable picture of the distribution of landed wealth throughout the peerage, and a very rough approximation of the total gross rental.

It is surprising to find that of the eight families in the top four groups in 1559 only the Herberts were of recent origin; all the others had acquired their wealth and lands before the accession of Henry VIII. On the other hand, ten of the fifteen in the next group were members of the new administrative and military *élite* raised up in part or in whole by Henry VIII, and endowed largely from the spoils of the monasteries: Browne, Manners, and Mordaunt;

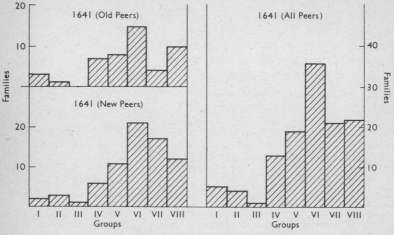

FIG. 8. Estimated Gross Rentals, 1641

Paget, Paulet, and Rich; Russell, Seymour, Wriothesley, and Windsor; these were some of the greatest names in Tudor England, the families that supplied much of the political weight and the administrative talent to maintain the Elizabethan system.

By 1602 there is no one at all in the top two groups. Only two survive of the eight families who in 1559 filled the first four groups, but they have been joined by two newcomers, the Cecils and the Sackvilles. The number in the next group is also down by a third, none of the survivors being new families. The number in the bottom category has scarcely altered, and the chief difference in the distribution pattern is a reduction in the number of really large estates, a contention that is supported by manorial counts. A comparison of the mean gross rentals in 1559 and 1602 shows a rise from £1,680 to £2,430; after adjustment by the price index, this indicates a fall of about 20 per cent. in real terms between the two dates.

There are striking differences between the distribution patterns of 1602 and 1641 (Figs. 7 and 8). Of the surviving old peerage families, the number in the top brackets has risen remarkably while the number in the bottom group has also increased; the gap between rich and poor was evidently widening again. Of the 73 newcomers to the peerage in 1641, 12 were in the 4 top groups, and indeed 6 of them were among the 10 richest landowners in England. On the other hand, no fewer than 29 of the 73 were in the two bottom rental categories, though it must be remembered that some of them were drawing very large incomes indeed from official sources.

Hitherto all calculations have been confined to gross rentals of land in possession, together, so far as they can be discovered, with those of assured reversions in possession of close relatives. To obtain true gross income, these figures must be adjusted to take into account landed profits which did not come in the form of rent, profits of industry and commerce, and profits of office and crown favour. In order to obtain a picture of the income at the disposal of the family for its own purposes, this total must then be further corrected by subtracting the burden of interest on loans. To do this means embarking upon a sea of speculation with not much more navigational aid than an erratic compass and a child's atlas. There are few pointers to the average value of casualties, and the full profits of office, including those of corruption, monopolies, and the sale of offices, can only roughly be guessed at in the fitful light of contemporary estimates, which may or may not have been well founded. The conjectural nature of any such calculations is thus sufficiently evident, and some will regard their compilation as a thoroughly unscholarly exercise in guesswork. But if the historian confines himself exclusively to what he can prove in a court of law, he soon becomes an antiquary, a chronicler, or an acidulated critic of his rasher colleagues. However hazardous and uncertain the task of quantification may be, it must be attempted if we are to obtain a picture of the overall economic situation of the peerage.

In 1559 the price revolution had been under way for several decades and fines for beneficial leases were of considerable importance on those estates of which there are adequate records. Together with profits of courts, sales of wood, and receipts in cash and kind from estates under direct management, total casualties may perhaps be put at rather more than 20 per cent. of the rentals.

The total receipts from land were thus about £135,000 and the mean receipts per peer £2,140. Dependent on various assumptions, the mean net income of a peer, as adjusted by the price index, was £2,200 a year in 1559 and £1,630 in 1602, a drop of 26 per cent. By 1641 the mean income had risen again to £5,040, or the equivalent of £2,290 in money of 1559, which is roughly the same as the mean income of the sixty-three peers eighty-two years before. In terms of net income adjusted to agricultural prices, therefore, the wheel appears to have come full circle. It should be noted, moreover, that the figures suggest that about three-quarters of the peers of 1641 enjoyed incomes amply large enough, given prudent management, to support their titles. In the late eighteenth century Lord Shelburne told Boswell that 'a man of high rank, who looks into his own affairs, may have all that he ought to have, all that can be of any use or appear with any advantage, for five thousand pounds a year'. If this is true, and if the rise in prices between 1640 and 1780 is taken into account, most noblemen must have been quite comfortably off on the eve of the Civil War.

## II. THE COUNTING OF MANORS

Any conclusions that may be drawn from these rough calculations may fail to carry conviction unless they can be supported by numerical evidence not supplemented by guesswork of any kind. The only possibility seems to be the counting of manors, a method first used by Professor Tawney over twenty years ago. But the counting of manors itself raises formidable problems, and the serious and well-founded objections raised against Tawney's original calculations can only be met by the application of more sophisticated statistical techniques to more rigidly controlled data.

The first question to ask is whether or not the manor is a meaningful unit of measurement. The counting of manors, it has been claimed, is about as useful, and has much the same psychological effect, as the counting of sheep, one reason being that a manor is not a unit of wealth but merely a definition of rights over a semi-obsolescent tenurial system. This is technically quite correct. But up to the Civil War most manors included not only the by now financially almost valueless rights of overlordship over freeholders, but also substantial ancient demesne lands, mills, rights over the waste, and the power to exact entry fines from

copyholders, often at the lord's discretion. In most villages, therefore, the lord of the manor or manors was the owner of the most
valuable property in the parish.

Non-manorial agricultural property cannot seriously have
affected the landed fortunes of most of the nobility, at any rate
before the 1620's. Lesser men might enjoy relatively substantial
incomes drawn from a wide scattering of small properties, but
the sheer scale upon which the nobility operated forced them to
deal mostly in large units. Sensible noblemen increased the value of
their manors by snapping up peripheral holdings when they came
on the market, but in comparison with the cost of manorial purchases these non-manorial acquisitions are usually relatively small,
and the process does not invalidate the hypothesis that a major
change in the number of manors held must reflect a real shift in
landownership.

The most serious objection raised against counting manors is
that the range of values they embrace is so vast and so random as
to reduce all calculations to futile arithmetical exercises. The crux
of the argument is therefore concentrated upon the problem of
the dispersion of values. That the manor was a variable economic
unit no one in his senses would deny, and attempts to classify
individual peers or gentry by the numbers of manors they held
are bound to fail for this reason. To give but one example, the
Ishams owned only two manors, but enjoyed a gross landed
income of no less than £1,600 a year in 1637, at a time when other
families needed a dozen manors or more to arrive at such a figure.
The question at issue, however, is whether the dispersion of
manorial values is so wide and so different at different periods as
to render useless manorial counts involving hundreds or thousands
of items a question that can only be answered by the application
of statistical techniques.

Samples of manorial values have been taken for 1535 and for
the years around 1602; the former is derived from the *Valor
Ecclesiasticus*, an official inquiry into the value of all ecclesiastical
estates. It supplies gross annual values, including those of ancillary
holdings such as mills, etc., classified under the same heading.
The second sample is taken from the Close Rolls over a period of
thirteen and a half years from 39 Elizabeth to 6 James I, which
give the prices at which manors were actually sold. The comparisons we wish to make are between the position in 1559 and that

in 1641, but unfortunately there is at present available no third set of figures yielding data for mean values and the dispersion of values for 1641. On the other hand it is inherently improbable that the dispersion of manor values relative to the mean changed over the years, and the application of statistical techniques to the two sample distributors of 1535 and 1602 confirms that this is so. It cannot be *proved* that the dispersion of manor values did not change between about 1602 and 1641. But since it remained so stable in the previous sixty-seven years, there is a strong prima-facie case for supposing that it did not alter very much in the next thirty-nine.

The most important question is whether the dispersion of manor values as revealed in the two samples is so wide that it prevents useful conclusions from being drawn about changes in real values from changes in manorial numbers. At first sight the range of values disclosed in the two samples appears to confirm the gloomiest forebodings of the critics. In the *Valor Ecclesiasticus* sample the annual values run from under £2 to over £165, and in the Close Rolls sample the sale values run from under £100 to over £10,000. But an inspection of the frequency distributions shows that in both samples there was a marked concentration of manors towards the lower end of the range of values. In calculating the sampling error in the counting of manors, there are two independent variables, the size of the dispersion and the number of manors in the sample. The larger the dispersion and the smaller the number of manors in the sample, the larger the sampling error will be. Since one manor may be up to 100 times more valuable than another, the use of manorial counts as indicators of real wealth is only possible, if at all, *provided that the comparisons relate to large numbers of representative manors*—representative in the sense that they are statistically random samples. It is clear that sampling errors will be considerable when the dispersion of values is as great as it has been found from our two samples, and that it is only by dealing in large numbers that they can be reduced to manageable proportions.

How did the amount of the property of the peerage of 1558 compare with the amount of the greatly enlarged peerage of 1641? How much mobility was there in aristocratic landownership, and was there any significant variation in the rate of mobility? Allowing for price changes, did the amount and the real value of the property of peerage families extant in 1558 increase or decrease in the next eighty-three years, and at what speed? Some of these questions may be answered by constructing statistical tables of manorial holdings, working out the sampling errors inherent in each, and then seeing whether any useful conclusions can be drawn from the results.

To make the sample as large as possible we have selected not the 57 peers Elizabeth found on her accession in November 1558, but the 62 peers extant on 31 December 1559, together with the earls of Kent, who resumed an old title in 1572 and whose estate had not appreciably altered since 1558. Appendix I provides an approximate picture of the situation for all peers all over the country, showing that in 1558 these 63 families held 10 per cent. more manors than did the 121 peerage families in 1641. Between 1558 and 1641 the average manorial holding per peer had therefore dropped by about half. The fall is due partly to the very small landed possessions of a number of Early Stuart peers, and partly to the erosion of the holdings of the older peerage: in 1641, 9 out of 48 surviving pre-1602 peerage families and as many as 29 out of 73 surviving Early Stuart peerage families held fewer than 10 manors. Partly it was also due to the decline of the really great territorial magnates. The older grandees had suffered particularly heavy losses and few newcomers had emerged to take their place. There were 39 peers holding more than 40 manors in 1558, of whom only 14 survived at this level in 1641, while only 9 of the later creations were manorial owners on a similar scale. In terms of landownership, though not of course of gross landed income, much less total income from all sources, the top level of the English social pyramid had been substantially reduced between the accession of Elizabeth and the outbreak of the Civil War.

### III. THE FACTS OF CHANGE

Every kind of manorial count shows that the holdings of the surviving peers of 1558 had fallen by about a quarter by 1602 and by a further fifth by 1641. Since the mean value of manors relative to the price index is believed to have declined slightly in the first period, and risen considerably in the second, only the first provides convincing evidence of declining real income. Both, however, are proof of a shrinking in the landownership of the older peers and therefore in their capital resources—exploited or un-exploited—and their political authority. Nor was the balance redressed by the new families who had risen into the peerage, for in 1641 the number of really large manorial holders, old and new, was down by over a third, and the average holdings per peer were down by a half as compared with 1558.

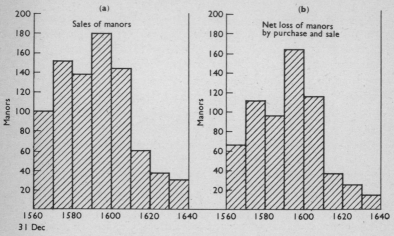

FIG. 9. Purchase and Sale of Manors, 1560–1639

A further point which emerges from the tables is that, in those families which survived, the gains from marriage with heiresses were very much greater than the losses to heirs general and younger sons. The decline among the surviving families, therefore, is entirely to be ascribed to the disparity between crown grants and purchases on the one hand, and sales on the other (escheats were of negligible consequence for families which survived in the male line). There was a very high rate of turnover of property throughout these eighty years, the losses almost amounting to the total holdings of 1558. There is reason to believe, however, that these losses were not spread uniformly over the whole period. Fig. 9 shows all purchases and sales all over the country, the dates of which are precisely known, made by the forty-two families extant from 1558 to 1641. The figures strongly suggest that after the first decade of the seventeenth century there was a very sharp fall in sales, as families at last managed to balance their budgets. By far the worst period of sales was from about 1585 to 1606, during which time the net losses were so alarming that one may reasonably talk about a financial crisis of the aristocracy, which was arrested soon after the death of Queen Elizabeth.

Until similar studies have been carried out for other periods, it is difficult to be absolutely certain whether or not this picture of widespread decay in ownership of landed capital among surviving families is a phenomenon particularly confined to the late sixteenth and early seventeenth centuries, or whether it is common to all times. There are, however, some significant pointers. In her unpublished study of the peerage from 1485 to 1547 Miss Helen Miller has noted that rapid rise and fall was the exception to the rule. The contrast between the two periods is so dramatic, particularly in the figures for losses, that one may reasonably conclude that it represents a real change in the trend of aristocratic fortunes.

### Comparative Gains and Losses

| Dates | Years | No. of families | Gained 10+ manors | Static | Lost 10+ manors |
|---|---|---|---|---|---|
| 1485–1547 | 62 | 90 | 27% | 69% | 4% |
| 1558–1641 | 83 | 74 | 10% | 35% | 55% |

The same contrast emerges if one compares the 1558–1641 period with the late seventeenth and eighteenth centuries that succeeded it. Professor Habakkuk has argued that the latter period was a time of growth rather than decay in aristocratic landholding and of increasing stability in landownership. It thus looks very much as if both rapid mobility and marked decay were temporary phenomena peculiar to the late sixteenth and early seventeenth centuries.

The more speculative calculations of 'income' tell much the same story. They support the view that a shrinkage of manorial holdings by about a quarter during the reign of Elizabeth meant an equivalent, or almost equivalent, shrinkage in landed income after adjustment for changes in the price index. At the same time the burden of interest rose and the profits of court and office stagnated if they did not decline. Receipts from land rose throughout the reign, especially towards the end, and may almost have caught up with the cost of living. But they could not compensate for these other factors, much less for the decline in the amount of land held. As a result the financial position of the peerage was substantially weaker in real terms than it had been forty years before, the greater magnates being particularly severely hit. Nor was this all. The amount of land throughout the century at the disposal of the private landlord had been substantially increased by massive sales of crown land, for which private buyers paid over £800,000 during the reign of Elizabeth. Since the number of manors dispersed among the tenantry by sale by landlords was still very small, the property held by the middle and lesser landlord groups, subsumed under the portmanteau heading of gentry, must necessarily have increased. Relative to those of the gentry, the financial resources of the peerage must therefore have shrunk even faster than any of these figures would suggest.

The next forty years present superficially a much more encouraging picture. Though the burden of interest on debt continued to rise, and though the average amount of land held probably fell a little, receipts from land were rising very rapidly in almost all areas, and those who could obtain a niche at the Court were enjoying rewards undreamed of under the parsimonious Elizabeth. Moreover, some fortunately situated magnates were now drawing large revenues from urban rents in the booming west end of London and from their hitherto largely worthless estates in Ireland, while the benefits of draining the fens in East Anglia and Lincolnshire were just beginning to show themselves. In consequence the net income of the peerage in 1641 was on an average at least as great in real terms as it had been in 1558—and very much greater than it had been in 1602.

The recovery of the peerage in terms of purchasing power does not mean that their financial position relative to other classes in society was back to what it had been in 1558. At a subsistence or near-subsistence level, income has an intrinsic value of its own, for even marginal changes may mean the difference between life and death. At the level of society with which we are concerned, income is mostly devoted to ostentatious consumption in the battle for status. In consequence wealth is relative, and only has meaning in relation to the wants that it satisfies and to the competitive posture of other members of the society. Now there is every reason to suppose that between 1558 and 1641 there had been a striking growth of population, trade, and industrial and agricultural production, and the gross national income must have greatly increased. Since the real mean income of the peers failed to show comparable buoyancy, it follows that their share of the whole must have declined. Since their share of the total of land in private ownership had also declined, their position both among the landowning classes and in society as a whole was much inferior to what it had been.

That it was the relative not the absolute position which mattered was reflected in the gloomy calculation of a peer in 1628 that the House of Commons could buy up the Lords thrice over, despite the recent doubling in the numbers of lay peers. Moreover wants had altered and increased over the years so that identical real incomes no longer provided identical satisfaction. Upper-class needs were now more exclusively a matter of money rather than services, and the development of a taste for luxuries had raised the levels of expenditure all round. It was Plato who observed that poverty consists not so much in small property as in large desires, a truism which should be sufficiently self-evident in the age of the affluent society. A nobleman of 1641 who enjoyed the same or even greater purchasing power than his grandfather in 1558 was far from being as content with his lot; nor did his wealth stand out with the same pre-eminence in an increasingly opulent society of squires and merchants.

In any case, to assume that the financial recovery of the aristocracy meant the end of the crisis in their affairs is to fall into a vulgar error. The crisis was not purely economic, it was moral and social as well, and the methods adopted to solve the one merely exacerbated the other. The shrinkage of the territorial possessions of the aristocracy seriously constricted their zone of influence, 'As oft as thou sellest a foot of land, thou disposeth of a furlong of thy credit', Sir John Strode warned his son. 'Northern thoughts . . . measures honour by the acre', ruefully reflected the 3rd Earl of Cumberland as he sold off his ancestral estates. The jacking-up of rents and fines on what was left undermined the old relationship of dependence and loyalty between landlord and tenants, and so continued the erosion of prestige. Some peers became active promoters of fen drainage, and in doing so aroused the fury of whole counties and classes. Wealthy the aristocracy certainly were again in 1641. But growing financial reliance upon Court favour meant association with an institution that was coming to be regarded as an invention of the Devil, and though some noblemen laid hands on the gold beneath, all were defiled by the pitch. Moreover, the search for office and favour drew them up to London and so further weakened the links with the countryside. In short, their financial recovery was achieved by trading respect and loyalty for cash, and the proceeds were spent—fully spent— on pleasure rather than power.

The crisis of the aristocracy thus passed through two phases, the second being the direct outcome of the first. Under Elizabeth their capital holdings in land and their incomes deteriorated, both relatively and absolutely, as a result of which respect for their titles and their authority was diminished. The cure for this financial crisis was sought in vigorous reorganization and exploitation of the estates which were left, the result of which was to contribute to this second and graver crisis, the crisis of confidence which came to a head in the reign of Charles I.

## IV. THE CAUSES OF DECAY

The late sixteenth and early seventeenth centuries are character- ized by an exceptional speed of turnover of land, as shown in the graph on p. 22. Now it takes two to make a sale, and the assump- tion that a want has only to be expressed to be satisfied by the free workings of the market is far from true in an unsophisticated economy. The cause of this activity in the land market cannot have been a sudden wave of buyers unaccompanied by a sudden wave of sellers. Throughout this great upheaval in the market, land went on selling at a fairly steady 16 to 20 years' purchase, giving a return of $6\frac{1}{4}$ to 5 per cent. at a time when interest rates were 10 per cent. or more. This premium was paid largely because there was no alternative form of long-term investment other than land, and because with it one bought social prestige. It also suggests that there were more potential buyers than sellers, and that the market was controlled more by the supply than the demand.

Part of the supply of land for the market came from the Crown, which at irregular intervals was raising the wind by selling off parts of its landed capital. Between 1536 and 1554 the Crown raised at least £1,260,000 from sales of ex-monastic property, and gave away an unknown but very substantial amount as well. Thereafter there were five more periods of royal land-sales during which about the same amount was received as in the first great wave of selling. But these crown sales are not in themselves an adequate explanation of the intense activity of the land market. In the first place, the sales are not on a large enough scale. The total number of manors sold between 1560 and 1629 merely by the forty-two peerage families, which lasted from 1558 to 1641 must have just about equalled those sold by the Crown itself (Fig. 9). Secondly, the chronology is all wrong, the very large crown sales under Charles I coinciding with a sharp fall in land transactions. Thirdly, sales by the Crown cannot account for the exceptional turnover of landed families to which all contemporaries drew attention, and for which Professor Tawney and others have found statistical evidence. Internal transfer of land within the propertied classes must have been the prime stimulus to the land market. What needs to be explained is not so much why a lot of small men were finding it hard to make both ends meet, but why so many important established families were obliged to sell their patrimony. To set the problem in perspective we must first look at certain features of human biology which are common to all times and all places.

One of the most powerful forces working for fluidity within a society were, and are, the limitations nature has placed upon the human capacity to reproduce. In this period as in others a surprising number of families died out altogether because of failure to provide a male heir. This came about despite the fact that one of the principal objects of marriage was to ensure continuity of title and of family estates. So urgent was this need that even the most disastrous of marriages tended to hold together until it had been achieved. Capacity to reproduce is affected by diet and disease, by inherited propensities, and by age and duration of marriage. It has been calculated that in 1925 7 to 8 per cent. of all married women in England were completely non-fecund, and other studies have suggested that 12 per cent. of all marriages are likely to be infertile. In the sixteenth and seventeenth centuries a male heir was even less easily come by than is the case today, for, despite an earlier marriage age, other factors raised the recorded figure of childlessness to a much higher level. These were firstly ill-balanced diet, tight corseting, lack of fresh air and exercise, liability to infection, all of which seriously impaired female health and encouraged miscarriages and still-births; secondly, the high adult mortality rate, which meant that only about a half of all marriages were completed (i.e. lasted throughout the whole fertile period of women); thirdly, the fact that, if M. Goubert is right, female fertility in the seventeenth century ended very early, at about 41. As a result the recorded evidence shows that 19 per cent. of all first marriages among the nobility between 1540 and 1660 were childless and no less than 29 per cent. produced no male children (Fig. 10). These figures are undoubtedly exaggerated by failure to record some children who died in infancy, but since only two noble children out of three survived their fifteenth year at this period they are an optimistic estimate of the proportion of first marriages which produced an adult male of marriageable age to carry on the line.

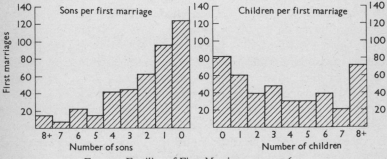

FIG. 10. Fertility of First Marriages, 1540–1659

This emphasis on the degree of childlessness should not obscure the fact that there were a large number of very prolific marriages. If one-third of first marriages produced one child or none at all, one-third also produced more than six. In a fertile couple conceptions were probably far more frequent in the upper classes than in the lower owing to the almost universal practice of putting babies out to wet-nurses. Lactation, which among the poor might last for years, is said to be quite an effective contraceptive agent. As a result the recorded average of children per fertile aristocratic first marriages was as high as five. On the other hand the lethal attentions of doctors and poor nourishment from wet-nurses of dubious reliability were two hazards to which the children of the aristocracy were particularly prone, and it is possible that infant mortality among them was also exceptionally high in consequence.

The danger of the extinction of the family in the male line was aggravated by the low reproduction rate of younger sons. Living for the most part on very modest annuities, they tended to be badly placed to obtain a second wife if the first died young. Moreover, a fair number did not marry at all, and sought a living in the army or at sea, professions with a very high wastage from disease. Large families were thus mainly confined to that minority of eldest sons whose marriages were highly fertile.

So eccentric a fertility pattern wrought havoc upon family stability and continuity. Of the 63 noble families of December 1559, 21 had failed in the male line by December 1641, and 26 by December 1659. There is nothing unusual in an extinction rate of 40 per cent. per century, indeed it is probably rather low in comparison with earlier periods. This inexorable attrition destroyed any prospect of maintaining the peerage as a self-perpetuating closed caste. If the Crown did not bestir itself to plug the gaps, in 250 years or so there would be no one left to sport a title.

A further biological cause of economic instability was the failure, not of the total male line, but of the direct descent from father to son or grandson. If there were daughters of the marriage, a proportion—and possibly a high proportion—of the estate would pass to them as heirs general and thus become detached from the title, which would pass to an uncle, nephew, or cousin. There were 32 partial failures among the 63 families in our sample, 16 of which involved heirs general. Only a third of the 63 families lasted for 83 years without either total or partial failure of succession.

Heirs general did not only diminish the estate of existing peers; they also swelled the fortunes of those who were lucky enough to secure them in marriage. Since so many peers married within the aristocracy and since they so diligently pursued heiresses, a good deal of the dismembered property fell into the hands of existing noble families. In cases where the heiress married into the gentry, the result more often than not was to hoist the husband up into a higher-income group and to add to his social status. Consequently within a very few years he is found to have acquired a title. Although there were certainly exceptions, the great bulk of peerage property which descended via heiresses passed into the hands of noblemen or men who, largely as a result of their wives' inheritance, were shortly to be ennobled. The degree to which existing peers and their sons monopolized the attentions of aristocratic heiresses is thus critical to the survival of the group and to the exclusion of newer men.

Between 1559 and 1641 the 63 families of 1559 left 58 heiresses, either as a result of collateral descent or of total failure of the male line. Four of these 58 married after the attainder of their father, and so were not heiresses at all, and 6 died before reaching marriageable age. Of the remaining 48, 23 married existing peers or their heirs male, and only 12—and they mostly women who brought very little with them—married men who failed, either in their own person or that of their son and heir, to obtain a title. Thanks to their active pursuit of heiresses, noble and otherwise, on balance the existing peerage acquired far more by their wives than they lost by their daughters.

There are, however, certain other losses which can be attributed indirectly to the lack of a son or grandson to whom to pass on the estate. Some of the most profligate peers of the day, men who most seriously reduced their family inheritance, were childless or without male children, and often on very bad terms with the relatives who were to succeed them. Other economic strains imposed by the structure of the family were the result of long-lived widows and a superfluity of children. By common law, widows were entitled to a third of the estate, and the substitution of the jointure for the dower only moderately reduced the proportion usually allocated for this purpose. Peers were in the habit of taking another wife as soon as one had died, and the natural toughness and longevity of women once they had survived the child-bearing cycle meant that jointures were a regularly recurrent burden rather than an occasional cross to be borne for a few years at infrequent intervals. If we take the forty-two peerage families which endured from 1559 to 1641, there occurred in these years 141 deaths of holders of the title or adult married heirs male. In 102 cases, or 72 per cent., widows survived to enjoy their jointures. A family could on an average expect to be paying widows up to a third of its income for over half the time. Naturally enough, noblemen afflicted with long-lived women found it difficult to maintain customary standards of living and yet keep out of debt. Though all were recklessly extravagant, it is none the less noticeable that six of the seven aristocratic conspirators in the Essex rebellion of 1601 had suffered in varying degrees for years past from the burden of widows. This was not the main cause of their difficulties, but it was a contributory factor.

Equally harmful financially was an excess of children to be

provided for. Despite the urgent need to secure the succession, an
overfull quiver was by no means a cause of unmixed satisfaction.
All too often the wife gave birth every two years or so with monotonous regularity, until the cycle was ended by death. In 1536 the
Earl of Wiltshire complained of poverty partly because his wife
'brought me forth every year a child', and both Lord North and
the Earl of Northumberland advised against 'a multitude of unprofitable children'. The rise in the size of portions made girls
peculiarly expensive and unwanted, though boys were still welcome so as to protect the direct male succession against the ravages
of accident and disease. After three boys had been born, however,
which was a situation which developed in at least one family in
every five, there was a strong incentive to call a halt.

It is therefore curious that there are few signs at this period of
any practical steps being taken to prevent conception. Substantial
though the financial incentive was becoming, however, the large
number of really huge families suggests that only a minority of
the English nobility before the middle of the seventeenth century
were willing or able to take practical steps to limit the burden of
children. Whether this policy of *laissez-faire* was due to technical
ignorance, to the inadequate urgency of the incentive, or to moral
or theological objections to interference in the biological process,
we are not at present in a position to say.

So far we have discussed biological factors which at all periods
are working to open up the land market. We must now turn to
factors specific to the period in question, in order to explain its
exceptional features. An over-fertile wife and an excess of paternal
affection could result in particularly serious damage to the long-
term fortunes of a family. Marriage portions given with daughters
were rising much faster than the price index (Fig. 14, p. 290), and
finding the capital could either plunge a family into debt for years
or else lead to the temporary detachment or outright sale of a
portion of the estate. What made this rise so harmful to family
finances was the practice firstly of paying the portion not to the
bridegroom but to his father, and secondly of using it for current
expenditure and not capital investment. Normally the marriage of
a son, especially an eldest son, was a means of raising ready money,
often on advantageous terms, and this was a frequent and well-
recognized means of clearing off debts. When in 1596 Sir Hugh
Cholmley found himself much in debt and unable to clear it off

by sale of lands owing to an entail, he dragged his eldest son away from his studies at Cambridge and married him off to a girl with a portion of £2,000. This financial incentive was an important reason why peers tended so swiftly and frequently to take themselves a second wife after the death/of the first. It was the absolute freedom with which the father of the groom, or if his father were dead the groom himself, might dispose of the marriage portion which made the inflated offers of squires and merchants so very tempting.

In the sixteenth and early seventeenth centuries, therefore, the marriage portion did little to advance the long-term fortunes of the family. Moreover on the bride's side the money was often found, especially in the sixteenth century, by breaking into family capital and selling lands, and peers who had difficulty in breaking entails hastened to push through Acts of Parliament to allow them to sell land to raise portions for daughters. Borrowing was also a frequent recourse, but a dangerous one when interest rates were at 10 per cent. and mortgages liable to forfeiture for non-payment. It was not until the early seventeenth century that it became common to convey parts of the family estates to trustees for a period of years to raise the money out of income. At its worst the system increased the ability of and temptation to the holder of the estate to raise money for current needs by selling himself or his eldest son for ready cash, and to sell land or run up debt on very unfavourable terms in order to provide the ever-increasing portions needed to marry off his daughters. The cost of the operation fell most heavily on the next generation, who would have to pay off the debts and live off an estate permanently truncated by land sales or temporarily reduced by jointures and trusts to raise portions.

The peculiar conventions governing the financial arrangement of marriage were made more dangerous by the confusion and weakness of the current land law. An Elizabethan father experienced very great difficulty in ensuring that his eldest son would not dissipate the entailed property in riotous living or undue generosity to daughters and younger sons. All he could do was either to make a simple entail, or to give himself and his son a life tenancy in the estate at the time of his son's marriage, with reversion to the heirs male. But the entail could usually be overthrown at any time after the father's death by the simple legal fiction of suffering a recovery, and even when it could not, it could sometimes be got round by making the purchaser a lease for 10,000 years, a device which was used by the Earl of Derby in 1597. As for the life tenancy, it was only watertight after the birth of a son to the marriage and before he reached his majority. The efficacy of the life tenancy was not proof against the manœuvres of the spendthrift waster or of the heir determined to defraud his younger brothers. On the other hand it certainly made it more difficult for estates to be dispersed, and an examination of Royalist Composition Papers shows conclusively that by 1642 the great bulk of aristocratic property was now held on life tenancy.

Elizabethan fathers tended to settle only a proportion of their lands on their eldest son and to reserve the remainder for the payment of debts and provision for younger sons. The importance of younger sons in breaking up family estates should not be exaggerated. If we ignore the special case of Sir Robert Cecil, in the twelve and a half counties covered by the *Victoria County History* the number of manors which passed permanently away from the 74 Elizabethan peerage families to younger children between 1558 and 1642 was less than 50. Since they started in 1558 with about 690 manors, and in all some 1,100 passed through their hands during this period, it is clear that grants to younger children were a significant but not a very important factor in the break-up of the family estates. The reason for this is that the outright grant of land to younger sons was being superseded by the grant for a period of years, or more commonly for the two lives of the son and his bride. By this arrangement the property maintained the son during his life and provided a jointure for the widow, but then reverted to the senior member of the family, leaving the children of the marriage to fend for themselves. In the early seventeenth century increasing familiarity with professional occupations for younger sons made fathers prefer to give them annuities and rent-charges rather than property, even for two lives.

At the same time more and more noblemen adopted an alternative to land sales as a means of paying debts or raising cash for marriage portions: in their wills they conveyed part of their property to trustees for a period of years, to use the income for these specific purposes. Next, they began setting up these limited trusts during their own lifetime, a form of enforced saving which suddenly became very popular indeed when the outbreak of war in

1642 forced fathers to make hasty provision for their children in case of their own death in battle or the seizure of their estates.

Finally, in the middle of the seventeenth century there was developed a legal device by which an unbreakable life interest was created at marriage in virtually the whole of the estate by settling the reversion on trustees for contingent remainders. This 'strict settlement', which gradually became standard practice in the late seventeenth century, made detailed provision for widows' jointures, younger sons' annuities and daughters' portions, so that the hands of the current holder of the estate were now very closely tied.

The result of all these various developments, culminating in the late-seventeenth-century strict settlement, was to increase the amount of property settled on the son and heir, and very severely to restrict the powers of alienation of the estate that was so settled. The sixteenth and early seventeenth centuries thus form a temporary phase during which it was exceptionally easy and exceptionally tempting to sell property or grant it away from the heir male. It would be difficult to overestimate the significance of these changes from the inflexible to the permissive to the inflexible in the legal arrangements for preserving property. They must be one of the most important of all causes for the extraordinary activity of the land market at this period. We must not, however, fall into the error of supposing that the working of the law is an autonomous force acting entirely on its own. In the early sixteenth century the propertied classes desired flexibility in the disposal of land: the lawyers provided it. By the late sixteenth and seventeenth centuries they realized the dangers and wanted rigidity: after half a century of obstruction, the lawyers finally supplied the demand. The law, as always, was a product as much of the social environment as of ossified tradition.

The root cause of these changes in the disposal of land was a shift in attitudes of mind towards property, towards the independence of children, and towards a man's responsibility for the long-term interests of the family. It is wrong to regard Sir Orlando Bridgeman, the inventor of the strict settlement, as a *deus ex machina* who suddenly transformed the fortunes of the landed classes. He merely provided a device which fitted in with what had for some time been current thinking. What had changed since the early sixteenth century was less the technicalities of the laws of conveyancing than the aspirations and sense of family responsibility of the landed classes. Men now wanted to preserve and increase their family patrimony, they were more devoted to the winner-take-all doctrine of primogeniture, they were content to surrender a good deal of freedom in the management of their estates, and they were willing to reduce, indeed almost to eliminate, the financial control they had previously exercised over the marriages of their children. The landed classes willed the end: the conveyancers and the judges at last provided the means.

The fourth interlocking factor in the situation beside changing terms of marriage, changing techniques of conveyancing, and changing family aspirations was changing facilities for credit. For a long time interest on loans was in theory altogether forbidden, which meant in practice a rate of 12 per cent. or more; from 1572 there was imposed a legal maximum and practical minimum of 10 per cent. which fell to 8 per cent. in 1624 and 6 per cent. in 1651: interest rates were halved in eighty years. Between 1570 and 1620 far greater use was made of borrowing by the landed classes than ever before, but despite the growth of fluid capital in the City the amount of money available was always less than the demand. It was not till the scriveners tapped a new range of small investors that supply exceeded demand and the interest rate fell to a more reasonable level. At the same period there was considerable theoretical, and some actual, danger to borrowers on mortgage that failure to pay on the stipulated day, which was rarely more than a year ahead, would involve the total loss of the security. By the early seventeenth century, however, the Court of Chancery was offering protection to creditors and the mortgage was no longer the fearful thing that once it had been. The period between 1580 and 1620 is therefore one at which the landowner was in a most disadvantageous position. He was borrowing on an unprecedented scale, but he was paying very high interest rates, and his security was liable to forfeiture for non-payment on the day. After about 1620, however, rates fell and the security was protected.

It was these ideological, legal, and financial changes which turned marriage from a destructive to a constructive agent. Firstly, the strict settlement made it impossible to raise marriage portions by the sale of land, which greatly encouraged the setting up of trust deeds well in advance; secondly, long-term borrowing became safer and even reasonably economical; and thirdly, fathers agreed that portions should be used not for their own private purposes but to purchase more land to be settled on the heirs. Portions were no longer either raised by sale of land or squandered by the bridegroom's father on current consumption. From being a cause of family decay in the late sixteenth and early seventeenth century, by the late seventeenth century the financial arrangements of marriage had become a cause of family growth; in its perfected form the system enabled the aristocracy to hoist themselves up by their own bootstraps.

At this period conspicuous consumption was a cause of family decay second only to biological failure. This can happen to any-one at any time, but it was extraordinarily common among the nobility and greater gentry in the late sixteenth and early seven-teenth centuries. Tastes which found favour with a Medici prince were sedulously copied by a less richly endowed English earl. The majority of the Elizabethan and Early Stuart peers and greater gentry were second- or third-generation *nouveaux riches*, who were reaping the fruits of the fierce scramble for power and wealth of 1529–53. These are generations from which heedless dissipation may normally be expected, and the absence of legal obstacles to the sale of capital made irresponsibility all too easy. In the ab-normally fluid situation of the late sixteenth and early seventeenth centuries, with large numbers of relatively new families pouring into the gentry, the knightage, the baronetage, and the peerage, the struggles of the status-seekers were particularly violent. The enormous inflation by King James in the numbers of all ranks in itself greatly increased the incentive to spend more freely, 'men of honour being not seldom compelled to proportion their layings out to their dignities, not their port to their ability'. A self-perpetuating cycle was thus set up. Over-consumption led to sale of land, which generated social mobility and psychological in-security among the purchasers; in its turn insecurity caused a struggle for status, exacerbated by the inflation of honours, which found expression in competitive consumption.

When analysed, the conspicuous consumption of these years took four main forms. The first was the maintenance of pomp and circumstance in royal service, whether as President of the Council of the North, which undid Henry Earl of Huntingdon, or as ambassador extraordinary, which plunged Edward Earl of Hertford into debt; the second was the cost of attendance at Court in the hope of office, which in the long run was likely to empty the purse of the average baron, unless the Crown came to the rescue. This was the cause of the ruin of the Sandys, the Windsors, and the Norths. The third and largest group, which overlaps and is inextricably mixed up with the second, were those attracted to the pleasures and vanities of London, who entered into a round of dissipation which in time inevitably undermined both health and fortune. Proportionately far more peers than gentry possessed or rented a London house, and the consequences of this gravitational pull reached catastrophic dimensions between 1575 and 1625. Before, the pull was still relatively weak; after, the Government drove men from London, and in any case it was becoming more difficult to sell land so as to provide the ready money.

The fourth and last group were those who stuck to the old country ways under the new conditions: men who continued to keep open house to all comers, to dispense lavish charity, to keep hordes of domestic servants and retainers; to live, in short, as a great medieval prince. Like the Stanleys, these were often men who were also most conservative in their estate management, which added to their difficulties. Such open-handed country ways were on the whole an Elizabethan phenomenon, and by the early seventeenth century most noblemen had adopted a more modest manner of rural living. To make matters worse, during the reign of Elizabeth many of the nobility were trying to live up to two or even three ideals at once. They were keeping up the rural pomp of the feudal nobleman while at the same time cultivating the urban tastes of the renaissance courtier and giving expensive and unrequited service to the Prince.

After about 1620, however, the tide began to turn. This change cannot be explained on financial grounds. If Caroline noblemen were more economical, it was certainly not because they were worse off than their fathers. The true explanation lies in changing standards of values, changing codes of behaviour, changing fashions of competition, which affected both 'Court' and 'Country' alike. From living publicly in the hall and state-rooms, they withdrew into dining-rooms, bedchambers, and closets. They gave up the vast impersonal family monument in favour of the small life-like bust, since they now wanted to assert their personality rather than the sheer grandeur of their line. They were deeply affected by the rising tide of puritan propaganda against waste, extravagance, gambling, and drinking. At bottom, the cause of the change was the rise of individualism, privacy, puritanism, and the cult of the virtuoso.

Between the beginning of the sixteenth century and 1640 prices, particularly of foodstuffs, rose approximately sixfold. The worst was over by 1560, but during the next eighty years prices just about doubled. This secular movement, which was caused primarily by a very sharp growth of population, put an unusual premium on energy and adaptability and turned conservatism from a force making for stability into a quick way to economic disaster. Landed families which stuck to the old ways, left rents as they were, and continued to grant long leases soon found themselves trapped between lagging incomes and rising prices. The significance of this lag should not be exaggerated. There is no evidence that the gap was ever very wide, and it did not last for more than forty years or so. The Elizabethan nobility ran into difficulties more because of mounting expenditure than because of declining landed incomes in terms of purchasing power. On the other hand the rapid rise in incomes after 1590 was of major consequence in enabling them to recover their prosperity.

## V. THE CAUSES OF GROWTH

If one turns from the causes of decay to the causes of growth, it is clear that many of these factors could be made to work to precisely opposite effect. If extravagant expenditure was the cause of the undoing of many, thrift and judicious investment were a key to stability and growth. 'Great is the rake and bottomless the mine of timely and discreet frugality', observed Waterhouse, who was never at a loss for the moral aphorism. The ethics of saving, however, were ambiguous, for there was a strong traditional obligation to live well and spend freely. The miserly were universally despised. 'Niggardliness [is] . . the worst evil can befall noble persons', the Marquis of Argyle warned his son. One of the most common pieces of advice was to keep recurrent expenditure down to two-thirds or even a half of gross income, so as to save something for emergencies. Bacon—of all people—actually advised keeping down to one-third of income. These were counsels

of perfection, but there can be no doubt of the truth of the pro-
position that it was necessary to save to be able to meet extraordinary expenditure on such things as marriage portions, calls for
government service, the irresistible temptation of building, or the
unavoidable necessity of litigation.

If failure to adjust to the price revolution caused hardship to
some, those who raised rents and fines and reduced the duration
of leases found that they could comfortably weather the storm.
Others, who were in a position to exploit the growing demand for
food, housing, and goods, steadily increased their fortunes.
Enclosures increased yields, fattening cattle and sheep for the
insatiable London market brought substantial returns, wool-
growing was profitable before 1620, mining and metal-working
could sometimes be turned to good account, urban development
in London was a gold-mine, fen-drainage could convert largely
useless acres into highly profitable land. Many hundreds of small
gentlemen did well out of farming and increased their inheritances,
and thousands rose from the yeomanry into the gentry. It is significant, however, of the limits placed on thrift by the demand for
consumption to match status and the slowness with which agricultural profits can be reaped, that only two peerage families, the
Spencers and the Pierrepoints, seem to owe their fortune and thus
their elevation primarily to economy and astute estate management. A crucial factor in the retention or increase of an existing
fortune, these were very rarely prime causes for the acquisition
of a really great one.

At this very high level, trade is equally of relatively minor
significance. The total volume of overseas trade in the late sixteenth century does not show any very striking growth, and the
amount of merchant capital being ploughed back into land was
probably not so very much greater than it had been in the late
Middle Ages. Between the accession of James and 1621, however,
trade boomed and a growing number of merchant fortunes sought
an outlet in land and title. But only three merchants, Hicks, Bayning, and Cranfield, and one merchant's son, Craven, managed to
secure one of the ninety-four titles conferred from 1602 to 1641,
and Cranfield owed his elevation more to his political than his
commercial activities. Only 9 of the 417 baronets created between
1611 and 1649 were themselves merchants, though 21 were the
sons of merchants and 34 married merchants' daughters. Of the

25 upper-gentry families of Somerset before the Civil War, only
one owed its rise to trade.

The same is largely true of the lawyers, those rapacious beneficiaries of the litigiousness of the age. Some legal profits went
via marriage to support existing families; more, almost all of it
acquired from fleecing the nobility and gentry, was spent on purchasing land from the victims. But most lawyers needed to enter
politics if they hoped personally to rise as high as the peerage, and
the Lord Chancellorship or Lord Keepership was almost the only
semi-legal office which regularly led to a title. Others rose by
political office after training in the law, and others amassed sufficient wealth in the law to justify the granting of a title a generation
or more later.

In the 65 years from 1560 to 1625, 55 lawyers reached the top of
the profession as Lord Chancellor, Master of the Rolls, or Judge
of one of the two Common Law courts. By 1666, 13 of these 55
families had entered the ranks of the peerage, and 17 had joined
the baronetage. This process was nothing new, for, as Fuller observed—with some exaggeration—'The study of the common-law
hath advanced most antient extant families in our land'. Nevertheless there can be little doubt that both the numbers and the wealth
of the profession increased dramatically at this period, and that its
impact upon the lower levels of the landed classes must have been
much greater than it had ever been in the past.

When all is said and done, however, the really important causes
of rise into the peerage were not thrift, the administration of land,
trade, or the law. They were precisely the same two factors as had
been decisive in the Middle Ages, firstly royal favour—usually,
but by no means always, a sign of intellectual capacity—and
secondly marriage. Attendance at the Court of a penurious or
unfriendly prince could, and often did, lead to disaster. On the
other hand, royal service was a factor, and often the most important factor, in the rise of most aristocratic families. The majority
of the 1559 peerage were of Tudor origin, created by virtue of
royal favour. Some were enriched by service to Henry VII and
Henry VIII in the early French Wars, others were substantially,
and in some cases almost entirely, the product of the great share-
out among officials, soldiers, and courtiers of the property seized
from the Church between 1536 and 1553. Two-thirds of the new
Jacobean peerage had made or increased their fortunes by office-

holding under the Crown, and the ancestors of others, like Arundell of Wardour or Denny or Petre, had been office-holders half a century before under Henry VIII, but had had to wait for their promotion.

If office and favour was lacking, there was always marriage. Family after family rose up in the world by the simple device of piling estate upon estate by the judicious choice of brides. It was generally appreciated that two or three gentry rolled into one, or an aristocratic coheiress and a gentleman combined, were the financial equivalent of a baron. In the circumstances of the day, such entrepreneurial activity usually resulted in the granting of a title. This acquisitive process is not always an autonomous factor, however, for it must be remembered that quite often it was royal influence which directed an heiress into the arms—or should one say the clutches?—of one aspirant rather than another. Many of the older peers owed their position very largely to their prudence in choosing and their skill in capturing rich brides. The Touchets were a small Derbyshire family who married the heiress of the Audley estate and title. The Bourchiers were younger sons who married the Fitzwarin heiress in one generation and the Dinham in another. The Stanleys rose by successive marriages with heiresses. Many of the Jacobean peerage were similarly the product of amalgamation by marriage. The Fanes climbed to be earls of Westmorland on the backs of the Mildmays (who had absorbed half the Sharington estate) and the Nevills; the Finches to be earls of Winchelsea on the backs of the Moyles and the Heneages.

The classic case is that of the rise of the Cavendishes. The foundations of the family fortunes were laid by the redoubtable Bess of Hardwick. As Horace Walpole put it, in his vulgar way,

> Four times the nuptial bed she warm'd
> And every time so well perform'd
> That when death spoil'd each husband's billing
> He left the widow every shilling

Ruthless, aggressive, and ambitious, she spent her life working to further the interests of her children by her second husband, William Cavendish. The estates of the first, Robert Barlow, and of the third, William St. Loe, were all devoted to this purpose. On becoming the wife of the great Earl of Shrewsbury she married two sons and a daughter to the children of this fourth and last captive, and so hitched the Cavendish family on to the coat-tails of the Talbots. During the Earl's lifetime she devoted her energies to transferring money from the Talbot estate to the mounting assets of herself and her children. After his death she used her ample jointure for the same acquisitive purpose. Her second son William married first a coheiress of Henry Kighley, who brought in a comfortable Yorkshire estate, and then a Warwickshire heiress; her third son Charles married first a Kitson coheiress and then an Ogle coheiress and his son in turn married the Basset of Blore heiress. No wonder that by 1640 both Cavendish lines had acquired earldoms, and that both were among the twenty richest families in England. The psychological cost, however, was not small. The ferocity of the quarrels of Bess of Hardwick with George Earl of Shrewsbury threatened the peace of the north and necessitated the shocked intervention of the Queen herself. The marriage of Henry Cavendish to Grace Talbot was not a success, quite apart from its sterility (he publicly spoke of her as harlot and openly took a mistress); that of Mary Cavendish to Earl Gilbert did not go too well, while William Lord Cavendish's determination to use his son's marriage to improve his political prospects shattered the boy's happiness and blighted his life.

Though royal favour and marriage were the most important factors in causing the rise of a family into the peerage, the two often went together, while over a period of time other factors were bound to come into play. It was unusual to rise to the peerage by marriage alone, though that was certainly true of the Berties, to quote but one example. Even in the case of the Cavendishes marriage was not the only factor, for the extraordinary administrative capacity of Bess of Hardwick and the 1st Earl of Devonshire counted for much in increasing the value of their estates. Moreover the property acquired by marriage might derive ultimately from a wide variety of courses. The Cavendishes absorbed the ancient peerage estate of the Ogles, the ancient gentry estates of the Bassets of Blore and the Barlows of Barlow, the courtier estate of the St. Loes, and the merchant estate of the Kitsons. From this point of view their origins are hopelessly mixed. These multiple origins and the degree to which they vary in their significance as one moves up the social hierarchy make nonsense of attempts to attribute economic growth among the landed classes as a whole to any single cause, whether it be efficient land management, as Professor Tawney has suggested, or Court and office, as Professor Trevor-Roper would have it. The former may be true for the yeomanry and lesser gentry, but is manifestly inadequate to explain the build-up of the massive fortunes required to maintain the dignity of a baron. The latter may be true for many of the aristocracy, but is manifestly inadequate to explain the rise of the gentry. The very uneven distribution of royal favour among courtiers, the limited profits to be derived from the majority of lesser offices below those virtually monopolized by the peerage, the restricted number of offices available, and the relatively small proportion even now of the total gentry class which haunted the Court and was in a position to derive benefit from it, all suggest that the lower one descends the social scale, the weaker becomes the influence of office and the Court as a factor in social mobility.

Important to a majority of the aristocracy and to many of the leading squires, Court and office can have been of little consequence to more than a tiny minority of middling and lesser gentry. Even in the case of the peerage the significance of royal favour or office must be qualified by an appreciation of the time factor. In any reign a number of families acquire great wealth from royal service. Some are promptly attainted, some dissipate their capital in the next generation or two, some die out; others hang on to their gains, improve and increase them by shrewd management or marriage, beget heirs male, and thus establish a great noble family. More was needed than the initial fortune, whatever its source. Endurance was also an important prerequisite, and this of necessity involved a wide variety of factors.

## VI. CONCLUSION

Both the speed of social change in the late sixteenth century and the generally downward trend of aristocratic finances were governed by a complex of deep-seated forces, economic, political, legal, social, and intellectual. For a relatively brief period maximum scope was offered for the free play of the two great agents of destruction, sterility and stupidity: sterility, which results in partial or complete failure of inheritance, and stupidity, which allows excessive expenditure, improvident marriage, and incompetent estate management, and which blocks the way to appointment to the more responsible—and more lucrative—offices of state. The instability of landed fortunes at this period was not the product of some strange freak of genetics which caused an abnormal proportion of stupid and dissolute children, or no children at all. To the inevitable changes wrought by the eccentricities of human reproductive capacity were added in the late sixteenth century exceptional temptations and compulsions to overspend on conspicuous consumption, royal service, or marriage portions, exceptional need for adaptability in estate management, novel opportunities and exceptional dangers in large-scale borrowing. Compensations were lacking during the reign of Elizabeth, owing to exceptional stinginess in the distribution of royal favours and snobbish objections to marriage with heiresses of lower social status. To make matters worse, legal obstacles to breaking entails and selling land were exceptionally weak, and moral objections to the dismemberment of the family patrimony exceptionally feeble. A landed aristocracy has rarely had it so bad.

On the other side, a few massive fortunes were being piled up in the law, in trade, and in certain government offices, the owners of which were all seeking security and status through the purchase of a landed estate; under James some great properties were being carved out of the royal patrimony for the benefit of favourites; and all the time there was the upward thrust of those landed families who could profit from booming farm prices and who were content to save and reinvest their gains instead of consuming them in gracious living.

After reaching a climax in 1610–20 the rate of economic change in the landed classes declined sharply. For one thing the shock of the 1620–1 economic crisis and the temporary fall in land values may have frightened off some buyers, and the subsequent prolonged slump in wool prices must have adversely affected a large number of small-scale sheepowners. For another the prospects of the great landlord rapidly improved. Even the most incompetent could not fail to profit from the massive rise in average rents in the early seventeenth century, and thereafter the levelling off of prices reduced the importance of inefficient estate management. New sources of income opened for some with the draining of the fens, the growth of urban housing around London, and the demand for iron and steel; a select few grew rich on royal bounty; a more intensive pursuit of heiresses had a snowball effect upon the greater landed fortunes; swingeing taxes on land after 1642 affected the lesser landowner more severely than the greater; the life interest and later the strict settlement made dispersal of land by sale more difficult, cheaper interest rates and the equity of redemption on mortgages made it less necessary; the growing obsession with property influenced the thinking of all but the most irresponsible of wastrels, the system of social stratification hardened. By the late seventeenth century England was ripe for the Venetian oligarchy of the Hanoverian era, presiding over a landed society which was far more stable in its composition than it had been a century earlier.

# V

## POWER

Nothing plagueth England but the many breaches and ever unsure, never faithful, friendship of the nobles.

L. HUMPHREY, The Nobles, 1563

THOUGHTFUL and observant contemporaries were unanimous in picking out the two most striking social phenomena of their time. The first was the extraordinary skittishness of land as it passed from hand to hand, the second the far-reaching changes in both the nature and the degree of power exercised by the nobility. Power takes many forms: it may be composed in varying degrees of physical force, economic pre-eminence, and social or personal prestige; it may express itself in coercion, authority, or manipulation. That preponderant power was exercised by the nobility over English society in the Middle Ages is generally accepted, and few would deny the crucial role of the Whig oligarchs in eighteenth-century local and national politics. But by then the nature of that power had fundamentally changed, for it had ceased to rely on coercion as an instrument. It no longer possessed, or claimed to possess, that power of the sword which Hobbes supposed to be the essential sanction of authority. If the course and causes of this change could be traced, and if it could be proved that there was a short-lived phase of uncertainty and weakness as the old dog learned new tricks, it might be possible to throw fresh light on the changing function of the aristocracy. This in turn might reveal something important about the political crisis of mid-seventeenth-century England.

## I. THE INSTRUMENTS OF VIOLENCE

Before the sixteenth century physical force had been widely dispersed among the nobility and gentry and had been readily used by them in pursuance of personal ends. The medieval system of values placed obedience to the public authority and devotion to the common good below individual loyalty—whether feudal,

between the lord and his man, or contractual, between the lord
and his retainer, or personal, between unequals as the lord and his
private following, or between equals as brothers-in-arms. Under
such circumstances disruption of public order by private violence
was inevitable. Always present throughout the Middle Ages, this
endemic disorder had taken political colouring in the fifteenth
century and had weakened the authority of the Crown and hindered the working of the law. The greatest triumph of the Tudors
was the ultimately successful assertion of a royal monopoly of
violence both public and private, an achievement which profoundly altered not only the nature of politics, but also the quality
of daily life. There occurred a change in English habits that can
only be compared with the further step taken in the nineteenth
century, when the growth of a police force finally consolidated
the monopoly and made it effective in the greatest cities and the
smallest villages. In the early twentieth century even the lower
classes lost the habits of violence which their betters had been
obliged and persuaded to give up nearly three centuries before.

The first task of the Tudors was to rid the country of the over-
mighty subject whose military potential came not far short of that
of the monarchy itself. This meant destruction of individuals by
attainder or confiscation; refusal to create new great families by
gifts of lands and swelling titles; encouragement of a counterpoise
in the more numerous families of lesser rank and pretensions;
diversion of noble time, energy, and money to royal service at the
Court; and development of the monarchy as the one overriding
focus of allegiance and loyalty. The result was a shift in the structure of power from the Lords to the Crown and the Commons.
English history is full of examples of bodies or classes of men who
have tried to exercise a power so arbitrary and excessive that they
have stimulated opposition and have then moderately (but never
completely) declined. The difference between a Duke of Buckingham in the early sixteenth century, with his castles, his armouries,
and his hundreds of armed retainers, and a Duke of Newcastle
in the mid-eighteenth century, with his Palladian houses, his handful of pocket boroughs, and his spreading political connexion,
is a measure of the change in English society.

The Tudors tackled their problem from four angles. They tried
first to control and then to reduce the size of the force of retainers
magnates were in the habit of attaching to themselves; they tried

first to control and then to prevent the building of castles and their stocking with excessive quantities of modern weapons; they sought to change men's attitudes of mind, to persuade the nobility themselves that resort to violence was not merely illegal and impolitic but also dishonourable and morally wrong; and to persuade the dependants and tenants of the nobility that loyalty to their lord should not extend to support of private quarrels by force of arms, much less to the taking up of arms against the sovereign. Far from being accomplished within a few years by mere legislative fiat of Henry VII, this was a task which could only be achieved by a hundred years of patient endeavour on a broad front using a wide diversity of weapons. It called for a social transformation of extreme complexity, involving issues of power, technology, landholding, economic structure, education, status symbols, and concepts of honour and loyalty. The story is not one of royal intentions, which are plain enough in the statute book, but of royal achievement, which can only be dug out of the obscure records of local and family history.

The first target for attack was the system of maintenance. Stimulated by royal demands for military service in the Hundred Years War, in the fourteenth century nobles had surrounded themselves with increasing numbers of armed servants. In addition they had consolidated their political and military power, both in war and in peace, by mobilizing their tenants and by exchanging oaths and making formal indentures for service and loyalty with local knights and gentry. Both the core of armed servants and the outer layer of retained gentry wore the lord's livery and badge as a sign of their allegiance. This system had been developed to assist the King in his wars abroad, and under favourable circumstances it could help to build up a stable political structure at home. But in the intervals of peace and in the reigns of weak monarchs like Henry VI it was easily perverted to private and disruptive ends. The servants became hired bullies ready to serve their master's turn against his enemies, whether the poor and defenceless, a rival magnate, or at a pinch even the King himself; and the lesser landowners were sucked into a vortex of allegiance and dependence which alone could offer the psychological support and physical protection the King could no longer supply.

The evils of the system were manifest in the overaweing of juries, the defiance of courts of justice, the perversion of all organs of local government, and ultimately in armed rebellion against the sovereign. The livery of an earl or duke inspired greater respect than the holding of a public office, and was the more sought after for this reason. The ultimate royal goal may have been to get rid of the whole practice of maintenance, but for a very long time this was entirely impractical. The first object of the Tudors was therefore not to destroy the system but to check its evils, and to turn it to their own advantage. Only when they had erected an alternative power structure dependent on office distributed by themselves could they afford to knock away this dangerous but useful prop. They had to lean on something while they were finding their feet.

And so Henry VII passed a series of Acts asserting without any possibility of doubt that the prime loyalty of every subject was to the Crown, and only secondly to his 'good lord'. He forbade royal officials and royal tenants to be retained by any other person, he enforced the obligation of all royal officials and annuitants to serve the King in war; finally in 1504 he made a serious attempt to put teeth into Edward IV's statute of 1468, restricting the use of livery to household servants. *Pour encourager les autres*, he threatened to fine Lord Bergavenny a nominal £70,000 for retaining 471 men in Kent.

The force of this repressive measure, which in any case was restricted to the life of Henry VII, was soon undermined by the Tudors' need for the services of their nobles and leading gentry to provide them with an army. Whether to launch an expedition abroad, to ward off foreign invasion, or to crush internal rebellion, it was to its loyal magnates that the Crown was obliged to turn in an emergency. Lacking a standing army of its own, lacking paid local officials of its own, it had to rely on the armed retinues of noblemen and gentry for help in war, and on the power structure of good lordship, indenture, and livery for local political control in peace. Though in theory the King could raise a conscript army chosen from a national levy of all able-bodied men between 16 and 60, in practice the administrative difficulties of mustering, selecting, training, and arming this force were for long almost insuperable. Moreover, the militia was primarily intended for local defence, and could not be used abroad. In the few foreign campaigns undertaken by Henry VII the armies were therefore raised in the usual way by the nobility and leading gentry from their servants and tenants. In 1513–14, Lord Bergavenny, who seven years before had got into trouble for retaining, turned up with 984 tenants, servants, and friends at his heels. The importance in this system of the titular aristocracy was shown in 1523, when it produced no less than a third of the total army. Internal troubles like the Pilgrimage of Grace or Wyatt's rebellion were suppressed by the same means, and the early stages of the great French Wars of the 1540's were fought by the usual indentured retinues, raised thanks to the continued enforcement of the obligation of tenants to serve their lords in war.

Some efforts were already being made to find alternative, and politically safer, means of raising troops. Henry must have been acutely aware of the dangers of the existing system, and in 1544 he achieved a major victory by sending militia conscripts out of the country to serve as reinforcements for the indentured army at Boulogne—a totally illegal exercise of the prerogative which apparently passed off without question, and set a useful precedent for the future. Once the principle had been accepted that conscripts could be sent overseas, the militia organization became potentially a really useful instrument. Its exploitation was hindered by the use of foreign mercenaries in the late 1540's and early 1550's, but Mary's reign saw the development of the office of Lord Lieutenant to supervise the musters, and also the passing of an Act which prepared the basis for the conscript armies of the future.

After 1558 Elizabeth proceeded, somewhat spasmodically, to develop the system. In 1573 she ordered that out of the general body of the militia there should be chosen picked men, to be equipped at public expense and more regularly and professionally trained in the use of weapons. These 'trained bands' were still controlled by the magnates, but now in their capacity as lords lieutenant and not in their own right. The peer and his retinue were being replaced at home by the deputy lieutenants and the trained bands, and abroad by Ancient Pistol and his forced levies. Since service in the former provided exemption from conscription, they were soon filled with men anxious to avoid the draft, while the latter were selected by Mr. Justice Shallow for their uselessness to the local community, and were actually shipped abroad only because they were too supine to run away or too poor to bribe their captains. Militarily, therefore, the change was little short of disastrous, despite the obvious political advantages.

And so in moments of extreme crisis Elizabeth still turned to her magnates for assistance. They were the better able to help since they had continued to use their control of local administration to exempt their own tenants from the county muster system, so much so that on one occasion the Cheshire Sheriff and Justices had to confess themselves unable to furnish the numbers required in the certificate of musters, since so many were servants and tenants of the Earl of Derby. The old tradition of private loyalty in time of war was thus preserved among the tenantry of the nobility and greater gentry, while the rest of the population was being organized on a territorial basis. Dr. Goring has shown how under the Early Tudors England was operating a dual military system, the one quasi-feudal and the other national. Though the relative importance of the two was shifting fast, the same duality persisted right through the reign of Elizabeth. At the time of the Armada the national levies were assembled, but a corps of shock troops of 1,500 foot and 1,600 horse was supplied by the tenants and servants of the nobility and leading gentry. The letter written to the Queen by the Earl of Pembroke from his Pembrokeshire fastness on 28 July 1588 was as reassuring in its expressions of loyalty as it was alarming in its medieval implications. 'I will, whensoever it shall like you to command, attend your service with 300 horse and 500 foot at the least of my followers, armed at my own cost and with my own store.' It is a measure of Elizabeth's caution that, even in this great crisis of the reign, this offer of a sizeable private army was not accepted.

Well into the second half of the reign of Elizabeth the greater nobles were still able to attract both younger sons of gentry as household servants, and their elder brothers as liveried retainers: as late as the 1590's Gilbert Earl of Shrewsbury could turn up on a special occasion like St. George's feast attended by men as substantial as Sir George Booth and Sir Vincent Corbet, both of them worth well over a thousand pounds a year and yet still willing to wear his lordship's livery. On the other hand the dependence of the gentry on the nobility was on the decline. Fulke Greville noted that Elizabeth 'did not suffer the nobility to be servants one to another, neither did her gentry wear their liveries as in the ages before'. One explanation was a change in educational habits. The gentry now sent their sons to schools to acquire book learning, rather than into the household of a nobleman to acquire a patron. As Lord North observed in the middle of the seventeenth century: 'It is certain that families of noblemen are clean other then they were anciently; for within memory of some yet alive, it was usual for persons of the inferior gentry to put their sons into such service for breeding.' Now they began to be educated either at home with a private tutor or at Eton or Westminster instead.

Below this top level of client squires, the nobleman still collected around him a host of men on the lower fringes of the gentry who had no inhibitions about seeking livery. These suitors were impelled by a desire to avoid taxes and county musters, to overawe their enemies, or to increase their standing in the locality. The livery of a great lord had a cash value in an increasingly mercenary age. In 1593 Charles Chester offered the Earl of Essex's steward Gelli Meyrick £100 'if you will procure me my lord's cloth'. During the reign of Elizabeth this local clientage was increasingly threatened by the encroaching pretensions of the rival court factions. As the conflict at Court became more acute, and as the number of jobs and offices in the patronage of the Court expanded, so local loyalties were replaced by the more rewarding allegiance to the great favourite. This centripetal effect is first noticed during the Burghley–Leicester conflict in the early years of Elizabeth, when it was alleged that in every shire there were many J.P.s who openly wore the livery of my Lord of Leicester. This development, which prepared the way for the political connexion of the eighteenth century, was all the more decisive because the politicians insisted that dependence upon them should be absolute; they were as resentful of competing loyalties as the most jealous of mistresses. The ancient ties of loyalty to the local magnate withered away in a fetid atmosphere of total commitment to one or other of the Court factions.

After the client gentry, the second element in a fifteenth-century nobleman's following was the retinue of personal servants who attended him wherever he went. This practice of enlisting a substantial private bodyguard persisted well into Elizabeth's reign, despite the much advertised efforts of the Early Tudors to suppress it. As late as the 1570's the Earl of Oxford was accompanied not only by his gentlemen followers, but also by 100 tall yeomen in livery with the Blue Boar recognizance on the left shoulder. Nor had knights and squires abandoned their retinues. Until his

death in 1579 Sir Richard Cholmley lived in state at Roxby surrounded by dozens of retainers and servants, who when not otherwise employed used to sneak into the kitchen and spear the meat
out of the cooking-pot on the points of their daggers. There can
be little doubt, however, that the function of these bravoes in the
late sixteenth century was as much one of display as of military
force. Moreover by the early seventeenth century they were superfluous in either capacity. Neither Salisbury nor Buckingham felt
the need for a large bodyguard to protect him or to give him
status, for the ingredients of prestige had now shifted to more
showy but less warlike items. 'Tall fellows' were no longer in
such high demand.

Evidence of these changes is provided by the reduction both of
liveried retainers and of household servants. In the mid-fifteenth
century 299 men had worn the livery of George Duke of Clarence;
in the early sixteenth the Earl of Northumberland kept 171 in his
household alone and the great Cardinal Wolsey in his prime had a
checkroll of no fewer than 422 domestic servants. By the mid-
seventeenth century most large households were down to between
30 and 50, which was about the number needed for convenient
running of the establishment. Contemporaries thought that the
decline partly set in between 1590 and 1620. William Harrison
could still complain that 'No nation cherisheth such store of them
[idle serving men] as we do here in England', but by the second
decade of the seventeenth century Fynes Moryson was talking
of the 'great trains and large housekeepings of lords and gentlemen' as things of the past. Thus, whereas in 1587 the Earl of Derby
kept a staff of 118 at Knowsley, in 1702 his successor managed to
run the place very comfortably with only 38.

As important as the decline in numbers was the change in the
character and social origin of the servants. In a great medieval or
Tudor household there were many younger sons of gentry, who
went into aristocratic service as the most convenient way of continuing to lead a life of ease and leisure. They had formed the core
of the bodyguard and the close personal attendants of the lord,
and it was at just this level that the reduction of staff was most
marked. In 1553 the Duke of Northumberland had 40 gentlemen
and 30 yeomen ushers in his household, the Marquis of Northampton 34 gentlemen and 13 yeomen. After the Restoration
important grandees like the dukes of Richmond and Albemarle

were content to be accompanied by six footmen and two or three pages. There were two reasons for this change, both stemming from the same desire for personal liberty and privacy: firstly, the magnate no longer required a crowd of gentlemen to attend him wherever he went, preferring to move around accompanied by a footman or two; and secondly, the gentry themselves now regarded personal service as socially humiliating. Contemporaries, who were well aware of the fundamental significance of these changes, had witnessed the collapse of a style of living and a scale of values which had flourished from the days of Beowulf to those of Sir Philip Sydney.

After the client gentry and the servants the third element in a nobleman's sphere of influence was his tenantry. As late as the middle of the century and after, land was prized as much for the 'manred', or influence over men, as for the financial gain or the social cachet it brought with it. The payment Tudor magnates expected were marks of deference, electoral obedience, military service in time of war, and occasional support with armed force in a private quarrel. John Smyth of Nibley recorded that whenever Henry Lord Berkeley visited Berkeley Castle he was met and escorted by '300, 400 and 500 horse of his kindred, friends and tenants ere he came to Berkeley town, . . . which confluence of train how it daily doth and more is likely to degenerate, let his posterity observe and declare to their generations'. Nor did the Elizabethan tenantry confine themselves to ceremonial marks of respect, for they continued to be ready to turn out in force to fight their master's battles. In 1598, Gilbert Earl of Shrewsbury sent 120 men to arrest an enemy and Edmund Lord Sheffield countered with a defence force of 60. In an earlier episode in 1593 the Earl is said to have mustered some 400–500 men to work all night long on the destruction of another enemy's fish-weir on the Trent at Shelford. Already, however, such loyalty was becoming rare, and in 1600 Henry Earl of Lincoln was trying to bribe men at 1s. a day to help him in his feud with Sir Edward Dymock. It is hardly surprising that after 1620 we hear no more of these massive turnouts, either to welcome and escort the magnate on his progress through the country or to rally in arms to support him in his private quarrels.

What helped to keep the system in being till the end of the sixteenth century was those periodic calls by the Crown upon the lords for help in an emergency. As a result many peers continued to try to enforce upon their tenants an obligation of military service in addition to paying the rent. Roger Earl of Rutland levied an aid in 1599 to help pay for his Irish Expedition, and Sir Francis Darcy actually dragged his tenants through the Court of Chancery to make them contribute to his military expenses, while tenure by military service—tenant right—flourished on the Borders into the early seventeenth century. With the accession of James in 1603, and the end of these military demands by the Crown upon the peers and gentry, this form of pressure on the tenants ceased and the tenant–landlord relationship became more exclusively one of rent. Of course the service element persisted right into the nineteenth century—peers mustered their tenants in volunteer military groups both in the Civil War in the seventeenth century and at the time of the Napoleonic invasion scare —but it was no longer an important, far less a decisive, element in the relationship. The military results were summed up by Sir Walter Ralegh with his usual exaggeration: 'there were many earls could bring into the field a thousand barbed horses, many a baron five or six hundred barbed horses, whereas now very few of them can furnish twenty to serve the King.'

Second only to the problem of manpower was that of fortification and equipment. Although by the end of the fifteenth century the Crown had established itself as the only power in the land with a train of siege artillery, its greatest subjects still thought it worth while to spend money on fortification. The last private castle to be built from scratch in England was Thornbury in Gloucestershire, erected by that dangerous potentate the Duke of Buckingham in the years before his execution in 1521. Although it was never finished, it was of impressive size and strength, and provides ample justification for Henry's high-handed action. Happily for England, the effectiveness of Thornbury was never put to the test of civil war, but throughout the century there is occasional evidence of serious military defence works by the peerage. The last and most striking case is that of Kenilworth, a medieval castle which was modernized and heavily fortified by the Earl of Leicester in the 1570's. Surrounded by extensive flooded ground, it was one of the strongest places in England and was fully equipped by Leicester to stand an extensive siege.

Thereafter evidence for fortification dies away, and by the reign

of King James most noble castles were becoming almost as
ruinous as those of the Crown itself. Many, particularly in the
north, were deserted by their owners in favour of more hospitable
seats in the friendlier countryside of the south, and were stripped
of their roofs for the sake of the lead. Those who stayed behind in
the north or west gave light and elegance precedence over
defence. They destroyed the military value of their castles by the
insertion of huge mullioned windows, as did Sir John Perrot at
Carew Castle in Pembrokeshire, and the Earl of Worcester at
Raglan Castle in Monmouthshire. Cuthbert Lord Ogle may have
continued to sulk in real fortified medieval castles at Ogle and
Bothal, but by 1612 Sir Charles Cavendish was actually building
himself a sham one at Bolsover—sure evidence that the thing was
functionally as dead as the dodo. In the south, court peers were
now building ostentatious, outward-looking palaces like Holdenby, Burghley House, or Longleat rather than frowning for-
tresses turned in upon their courtyards. Moats and drawbridges,
portcullises and arrow-slits became things of the past. Though the
Civil War was to prove that many a great house could by im-
provisation be turned into a defensive position, men were no
longer building with this end in view.

Neither men nor castles are of much value without arms, and it
was in their accumulation of weapons that Tudor noblemen most
clearly revealed their military potential. Here again the attitude of
the Crown was ambiguous. By 1547 it had built up an enormous
armoury of modern arms. But this needed to be supplemented by
smaller scattered depots for immediate defence of local areas.
Until the county muster and trained-band system had been set on
foot in the middle of the century, and until the local authorities
had been bullied into financing and equipping their own arms
depots, which did not happen until quite late in Elizabeth's reign,
there was no alternative to allowing—and indeed obliging—
noblemen to purchase and store in their own armouries sufficient
weapons to fit out a small army in time of emergency. The rise
and fall of the aristocratic armoury is thus a product of changing
methods of national defence, as well as of the shifting ambitions
and fears of noblemen themselves.

Such evidence as we have suggests that stockpiling of weapons
was of modest proportions before 1550, reached a peak between
1550 and 1600, and thereafter declined. The most formidable

assembly of weapons on record was that stored in the heavily fortified castle of Kenilworth in the 1570's and early 1580's by the Earl of Leicester. There were over 100 guns, 1,500 shot for them, ample supplies of powder (which had been made on the spot by a powder-maker hired for the purpose), over 450 small-arms, and other weapons for nearly 200 horse and 500 foot. The purpose of these extraordinary preparations is not certain. It may have been insurance in case of civil war at the Queen's death; it may have been a blackmail weapon with which to browbeat Elizabeth if he began losing favour at Court; it may have been for protection against attack by his enemies, who were legion. At all events he turned Kenilworth into a fortress that could compare in strength with the royal castles of the Tower and Berwick. Not for over half a century had a subject possessed such formidable military resources. If only he could have ensured the loyalty of his men, Leicester was in a position to defy all comers, even perhaps his sovereign. He was the last of his kind in English history.

Ambiguous though some of the evidence is, there can be little doubt that the general trend in the early seventeenth century was towards a reduction of these great private arsenals. In 1577 Harrison had reported that 'as for the armories of some of the nobility . . . they are so well furnished, within some one baron's custody I have seen three score corselets at once, besides calivers, hand-guns, bows and sheaves of arrows, pikes, bills, pole-axes, flasks, touchboxes, targets, etc. the very sight whereof appalled my courage'. A generation later Ralegh observed that at one time 'the noblemen had in their armories to furnish some of them a thousand, some two thousand, some three thousand men, whereas now there are not many that can arm fifty'. If he exaggerated the degree of the change, he was right to regard this as one of the most important transformations to have occurred during his lifetime.

## II. THE FACE OF VIOLENCE

Given that the keeping of retainers, the stocking of arms, even the fortification of castles continued into the late sixteenth century, it is hardly surprising that the true story of the Tudor struggle to monopolize violence is far more long-drawn, far more complicated, and far less triumphant than is generally supposed. The issues men fought over were prestige and property, in that order. What might ostensibly appear as a quarrel over a piece of land or an office, in fact was at bottom a struggle for position and authority within the county society. The gentry squabbled over church-seating, striving for the best pew in the parish; the squirearchy fought for election as knights of the shire and for appointments on local commissions; the nobility strove to maintain or acquire pre-eminence in the distribution of county patronage; the Court aristocracy fought for the ear and attention of the monarch. In a society that was even more obsessed with status than with money, intangibles of this sort aroused passions which often could only be appeased in blood.

Englishmen of the educated classes today enjoy the reputation for unusual reserve and exceptional self-control under the most provoking circumstances. In the sixteenth and seventeenth centuries tempers were short and weapons to hand. The behaviour of the propertied classes, like that of the poor, was characterized by the ferocity, childishness, and lack of self-control of the Homeric age, and unless we can grasp these basic psychological premisses we cannot hope to understand the true dimensions of the Tudor problem. The educational and social systems of the age inculcated ideals of honour and generosity. Impulsiveness was not reproved, readiness to repay an injury real or imagined was a sign of spirit, loyalty to a friend in a quarrel was a moral duty, regardless of the merits of the case. This absence of restraint was all the more serious since men in the sixteenth century were so exceedingly irritable. Their nerves seem to have been perpetually on edge, possibly because they were nearly always ill. The poor were victims of chronic malnutrition, the rich of chronic dyspepsia from over-indulgence in an ill-balanced diet: neither condition is conducive to calm and good humour. Moreover, a gentleman carried a weapon at all times, and did not hesitate to use it. It was none other than Philip Sydney who warned his father's secretary that if he read his letters to his father again 'I will thrust my dagger into you. And trust to it, for I speak it in earnest'. The Sydneys were not a particularly violent family, but it was Philip's nephew who stabbed his schoolmaster with a knife when he threatened to whip him.

The language used by men of breeding and high social standing is often so intemperate as to be almost deranged, and this petulant childishness of language was matched by childishness of deed. When Henry Earl of Lincoln was quarrelling with a neighbour at Chelsea, he bought a load of London night-soil and stacked it on a wharf where the fumes would give the greatest annoyance. Meeting the Sheriff of Dorset on the highway, Henry Howard, future 2nd Viscount Bindon, repeatedly galloped past him at full tilt in order to splash him with mud, and then knocked his hat into the puddles. Speech and pranks such as these did not of themselves endanger the security of the State or undermine respect for the law. But they are symptomatic of a readiness to resort to direct action that in an age of armed retainers could easily lead to rioting and even minor warfare between rival gangs.

The situation was exacerbated by the total lack of rules within which such violence as occurred could be confined. When personal conflict between principals took place, no holds were barred. Even teeth were not excluded, and when Thomas Hutchinson was attacked by Sir Germaine Poole, 'getting him down he bit off a good part of his nose and carried it away in his pocket'. When armed retainers were employed, there were equally no conventions about fair play. Surprise ambushes, attacks from the rear, onslaughts by overwhelming numbers were all legitimate tactics in the sixteenth century, and brought no disrepute upon the organizer. In 1578 Edward Windham was attacked in Fleet Street in broad daylight by twenty-five retainers of the 2nd Lord Rich, urged on by their master with bloodthirsty cries of 'Draw villains, draw', 'Cut off his legs', and 'Kill him', an assault that Windham met by firing a pistol at his Lordship and then fleeing into the French ambassador's house. Stories of this kind, which could be indefinitely repeated, prove beyond possibility of doubt that up to the end of the sixteenth century men saw nothing dishonourable in attacking by surprise with superior forces, and nothing in hitting a man when he was down. By the second decade of the seventeenth century, however, such behaviour was becoming discreditable and is much less frequently met with.

Given the absence of honourable conventions in the prosecution of a quarrel, it is hardly surprising that some of the retainers of noblemen were indistinguishable from hired bullies, men who were ready to beat up or even occasionally to kill at a word from their master. Men who today would be temperamentally attracted to a parachute regiment or the secret police found satisfaction in the sixteenth century in the armed retinue of a great nobleman.

The retention of bodyguards and the ability to bring out the tenantry in case of need meant that insecurity continued to prevail in many areas of the countryside. The basic distinction between the Highland and the Lowland Zones remains valid for the sixteenth century, for the former still preferred traditional methods of settling disputes to obedience to the law. As late as 1607 the President of the Council of Wales reported that violence was still endemic, intimidation of juries common, and blood-money and the blood feud often preferred to the cumbersome machinery of the law. Nor were things much better in the north. Even in the relatively peaceful area of Wentworth Woodhouse, south of Sheffield, in the early seventeenth century Sir William Wentworth was still advising his son to make sure that 'the doors at night be surely shut up by some trusty ancient servant, and your men so lodged as they may defend your house'. Up here too the blood feud and blood-money remained an important element in the pattern of human relationships, operating quite outside an only partly effective legal machinery. In the Hoghton murder case of 1589 only three jurors dared appear for the trial, and two and a half years later the Earl of Derby recommended dropping proceedings and leaving the issue to be patched up with blood-money. So long as the landed classes subscribed to an ethical code which demanded satisfaction for injury outside the courts of law, the 'peace in the feud' was a more effective instrument for the regulation of violence than the authority of the central government. Many of Shakespeare's plays deal with this issue of personally inflicted revenge, and it was clearly a concept still familiar even to London society at the turn of the century.

It is hardly surprising that disputes among peers and greater gentry tended to tear county administration apart and reduce it temporarily to impotence. In the reign of Elizabeth feuds like those between the Stanhopes and the Markhams in Nottinghamshire, the Fiennes and the Dymocks in Lincolnshire, the Danvers and the Longs in Wiltshire, the Muschampes and the Collingwoods in Northumberland, the Mansells and the Heydons in Norfolk, all threatened the peace of the county. They were dangerous since they drew in with them by family alliances not only most of the other squires of the county, but also the magnates. If those

responsible for local government were themselves the breakers of
the peace, there was little hope of justice being done.

Sometimes great lords tyrannized over a county administration
and protected criminals. In Gloucestershire in the 1570's, Giles
Lord Chandos used armed retainers with guns at the ready to
frighten off the under-sheriff, protected servants of his who robbed
men on the highway near Sudeley Castle, so that the inhabitants
dared not arrest the thieves nor the victims prosecute their
assailants, rigged juries, and put in a high constable of the shire
who used his office to levy blackmail on the peasantry. When
summoned to the Council of Wales he did not deign to come,
retorting loftily that 'I had thought that a nobleman might have
found more favour in your Court, than thus hardly to be dealt with
(as I am) like a common subject'. Nor were things much better in
Gloucestershire thirty years later. A yeoman who refused to lend
money to the 3rd Lord Stafford's son found his cattle driven off
into Thornbury Castle. When he went to protest he was seized,
beaten up, robbed, and thrown into a dungeon, where he lan-
guished while the cattle were killed or sold—proceedings justified
by the Staffords on the grounds that the inhabitants of the village
were only villeins anyway.

In the face of such behaviour by men like Stafford or Chandos,
there was little that the local J.P.s could do, even if they wished to.
Many of them were attached by family ties or good lordship to an
influential peer and were careful to preserve the interests of their
patron. Whether as J.P.s, jurors, or witnesses, men naturally
tempered their desire for justice with a prudent eye to their personal safety, and were unwilling to run great risks. Attempts by
the local administration to deal with feuds between nobles and
squires usually ended in failure. Adequate to cope with problems
like poor relief, the repression of sturdy beggars, or the fixing of
prices, issues upon which the landed classes were reasonably
agreed, perfectly competent to deal with most lower-class disorders, it was quite unfitted to enforce peace upon quarrelling
magnates, much less to punish the guilty. For one thing, it was
the habit until the turn of the century to appear at quarter sessions
and assizes with a following of armed retainers who could on
occasion be used to threaten the court.

If the countryside remained liable to civil disorder up to the
turn of the century, the same was true of the towns. Professor

MacCaffrey has noted that violence in the streets of Exeter was only effectively curbed by about 1600. In London itself the fields about the City and even the main arterial roads were continual scenes of upper-class violence. Bloody brawls and even pitched battles occurred in Fleet Street and the Strand, and little protection could be offered by the authorities until hours or days after the affair was over. Owing to the growing attraction to London of the nobility and squirearchy, rural quarrels tended to get transferred from the quarter sessions, the horse-races, and the hunting matches of the country to the streets of London. It was in London that Lord Eure was attacked by a gang of his Yorkshire enemies, the Woodringtons.

Even the Court itself was not entirely immune from violence, although mutilation could be inflicted upon those who broke the peace within its verges. Physical assault at Court came under the jurisdiction of the Marshal's Court, and was always regarded as an exceptionally grave offence, since it might easily endanger the personal safety of the monarch. But the Court could not hope to remain entirely insulated from the brawling and beatings-up that were taking place near by.

Since Elizabeth found it prudent not to take vigorous action against the nobility except when open rebellion seemed imminent or had actually occurred, she was forced to turn a blind eye to much sporadic violence among her courtiers and their followers, a policy of not so masterly inactivity which is best illustrated by the story of the Oxford–Knyvett feud.

In 1580 Anne Vavasour gave birth to an illegitimate son, the father being the Earl of Oxford. In consequence, the Earl quarrelled violently with Anne's patron, Thomas Knyvett, a Gentleman of the Privy Chamber. Both were prominent and influential courtiers, Knyvett having daily access to the Queen, and Oxford being the son-in-law of the all-powerful Burghley, and himself a former favourite of Elizabeth for whom she still had some affection. Early in 1582 it was rumoured that Oxford was planning Knyvett's assassination. In March there was a duel, in which both were wounded and one of Oxford's men killed. In June several of Knyvett's men met and wounded two of Oxford's in Lambeth Marsh. A few days later there was an unsuccessful attempt to murder Knyvett one evening as he was disembarking at Blackfriars stairs—a favourite place for attack as the victim struggled helplessly up the slimy steps. Next month there was a fresh battle between the two factions, in which Knyvett personally killed one of Oxford's men. Knyvett promptly got the Queen to urge Lord Chancellor Bromley to have the case, to which he was to plead *se defendendo*, tried in a privy session during the vacation, where the affair could be hushed up. When the Lord Chancellor refused, he was sharply told by Hatton, 'My good lord, it is very necessary you take care to please the queen in this case'. Bromley's reluctance to tamper with the processes of the law was eventually overcome, and a coroner's verdict of *se defendendo* was duly returned. Next February a servant of Oxford was killed, presumably by a Knyvett supporter, and buried in St. Botolph's, Bishopsgate. In March Oxford's men murdered Long Tom, an ex-follower of Oxford who had switched his allegiance to Knyvett.

Thanks to the studied neutrality of the Queen, two great courtiers were allowed to commit murder after murder with complete impunity. Both in the brutality of their tactics and in their immunity from the law, the nearest parallels to the Earl of Oxford and Sir Thomas Knyvett in the London of Queen Elizabeth are Al Capone and Dion O'Banion, Bugs Moran and Johnny Torrio in the Chicago of the 1920's. It is against this sinister background of rival court factions with their hired killers and 'cutters', of sporadic murder and violence in the streets of London, and of occasional pitched battles in the countryside, that the wisdom of Elizabeth's tactics must be judged.

### III. THE GROWTH OF ORDER

The picture hitherto has been one of irresponsible violence of word and deed, controlled hardly at all by the forces of order. Taken by itself this is very misleading, for throughout the sixteenth century great, and ultimately successful, efforts were being made to contain violence and bring it within tolerable limits. Above all there was the steady pressure of the central government striving to impose its own rules and to stiffen the local authorities into enforcing the law with less obvious respect of persons. The instruments employed were the Privy Council, the Court of Star Chamber, and the two Councils of Wales and the North, the last two having been specifically set up to deal with the problem of feudal disorder in the Highland Zone.

At the centre the Privy Council worked in private, receiving complaints, instituting inquiries, issuing warnings, enforcing arbitration, summoning the recalcitrant to London for weeks of boring and expensive attendance upon its good pleasure, and on some occasions committing the obstreperous to prison for a spell. The Star Chamber was the Council working in public as a court of law, where proceedings against rioters could either be instituted by the Attorney-General or more commonly by the aggrieved party, and where the influential could be punished for their misdeeds by fines, imprisonment, and public humiliation. In fact, however, it was never used to tame the magnates. There is no evidence that noblemen were prosecuted in Star Chamber under Henry VII, and under Elizabeth the court was more useful to magnates wishing to punish poachers on their deer-parks than it was to gentry or lesser men seeking protection against the tyranny of their superiors. The Star Chamber was an invaluable instrument for diverting the gentry from armed conflict; it was the Privy Council itself, acting without due process of law, that controlled the nobility.

Casual violence over personal issues, even when it involved substantial numbers, was something no Tudor monarch or Privy Council was prepared to take too seriously. Rural riot and intimidation were dealt with by encouragement of tedious litigation in the courts or by forced arbitration over the subject under dispute by the Council, rather than by the swift punishment of the use of force itself. Brawls in London were regarded with rather less tolerance than those in the countryside and were often prevented from developing into full-scale gang-warfare by clapping one or both contestants into the Fleet for a few days to allow passions to cool. Here too, however, neither the Queen nor the Council showed much determination in punishing the breach of the peace itself, and the greater and more influential the nobleman the more warily they trod. Even when blood had actually been shed, they still acted with extreme caution. On the whole the Council preferred to allow even crimes of violence to be the subject of private litigation in the courts of law, and when a jury could not be rigged to bring in a favourable verdict, a pardon for the aggressor could usually be obtained—at a price—from the sovereign.

As soon as personal feuding looked like turning into treason,

however, the Council acted promptly enough. The quarrel over
the Dacre inheritance was allowed to rumble on unchecked, but
when the north erupted into open rebellion, it was suppressed
with ruthless savagery. The peace of Nottinghamshire had been
broken for years by the open clash of armed bands of Talbots and
Stanhopes without goading the Privy Council into more than
verbal rebukes, and without any serious punishment of any but
minor participants in Star Chamber. But once Gilbert Earl of
Shrewsbury's religious loyalty was called in question, he was very
soon laid by the heels.

The extreme caution, even timidity, displayed by Elizabeth and
Burghley in the face of aristocratic violence is striking evidence of
the insecurity of their position. They relied on the slow shift of
habits and customs during a prolonged period of peace, and on
the steady growth of independence among the squirearchy, rather
than on ruthless intervention from the centre to enforce the law.
By degrees, over a period of time, they hoped to tip the balance
in favour of good order and to reduce the irresponsible authority
of the magnates. As Lord Buckhurst explained to Gilbert Earl of
Shrewsbury in 1592:

Your Lordship must remember that in the policy of this Common
Wealth, we are not over-ready to add increase of power and countenance to such great personages as you are. And when in the country
you dwell in you will needs enter in a war with the inferiors therein,
we think it both justice, equity, and wisdom to take care that the weaker
part be not put down by the mightier.

The victim of assault was encouraged to complain to the Council
or launch a suit in Star Chamber, and if he rarely obtained redress
and punishment of the main offender, he at least was protected
from further attack and had the satisfaction of seeing his enemy
officially rebuked. Although there is no evidence that severe
penalties were ever inflicted upon a great nobleman after 1556,
the punishment of inferior agents was a telling blow to the prestige
of their patrons. The lengthy process of sixteenth-century lawsuits allowed tempers to cool, acted as a lightning-conductor for
local violence, and transferred the field of battle from the countryside to Westminster. Slowly the Tudors taught the lesson that
there was a higher authority whose will could in the last resort
override that of even the greatest magnates in the realm. The

curious thing is that this flabby policy was a success. In 1626 Lord Keeper Williams complacently remarked that 'in ancient time the records of the Court of Star Chamber are filled with battles and riots so outrageous, whereas now we hear not one in our age'. This was an overstatement, but it is true that by the third decade of the seventeenth century cases of violence were declining, as men increasingly turned to the more sophisticated weapons of fraud, forgery, and perjury.

As well as wielding the stick, the Crown could also dangle the carrot. By its extensive disposal of patronage, it had great powers of leverage over the nobility, which it did not hesitate to use. It was not only that families whose loyalty was suspect could be frozen out of public office. Equally significant was the fact that men with a reputation for violence often found it hard to obtain favour at court. An exception to this rule is the appointment of Ralph Lord Eure as Lord President of the Council of Wales— unless it was thought that only a man accustomed to murder and violence was capable of handling the Welsh.

But this pressure by the central government would by itself have been incapable of mastering violence if there had not also occurred changes in occupational habits and in the mental and moral climate of opinion. During the long period of peace from 1562 to 1588 the nobility lost the habit of military service, and even during the war years of the 1590's only a minority took an active part in military campaigns. Another twenty years of peace after 1604 meant that they were now almost entirely absorbed in private and civilian pursuits, and no longer looked to war as a natural outlet for their energies. The movement of the aristocracy out of the countryside into London and about the Court greatly accelerated this shift by providing alternative fields of competition, intrigue, and pleasure. By 1640 the bellicose instincts of the class had been sublimated in the pursuit of wealth and the cultivation of the arts. It was to take a bishop—Bishop Wren of Ely—to complain that this development was sapping the moral fibre of the nation.

The change in occupational habits was accompanied by a change in concepts of duty, by which the ancient obligation to serve the Prince in war gave way to one of service in government and at Court. At the same time education was changing in content, with greater emphasis on book-learning and less on the medieval code of honour. The striking increase in the number of nobility and gentry who acquired a smattering of training in the law at the Inns of Court inevitably increased respect for this venerable weapon for bringing down an adversary. The spread of the puritan ethic throughout the landed classes led to the superimposition of a training in deferred gratification—deferred, that is, until the next world —upon the tradition of immediate satisfaction of impulse. The development of vital religious, ideological, and constitutional issues reduced the purely personal element in local and national politics and therefore the incentive to resort to private violence to achieve victory. Finally, the tenantry became increasingly reluctant to give active support to their lord in his private quarrels, as the old-style nobleman keeping open house to all comers in his country seat changed into a largely absentee rentier concerned more with raising rents than preserving loyalties.

A consequence of the decline of violence was an astonishing growth in litigation. Societies being weaned from habits of private revenge always turn to the law with intemperate enthusiasm, but by any standards the growth of litigation between 1550 and 1625 was something rather exceptional. In the common-law courts the number of plea rolls *per annum*—admittedly a very crude and suspect criterion—suggests a sixfold increase for the Common Pleas and a doubling for the King's Bench. Cases brought before the Courts of Requests and Star Chamber appear to have multiplied at least tenfold over the same period, while by 1621 Chancery was issuing about 20,000 subpoenas a year.

The decline of violence was only one cause of this legal explosion, though the fact that no less than 15 per cent. of Star Chamber suits in the reign of Elizabeth came out of Wales is not without significance. All the pride, obstinacy, and passion that hitherto had found expression in direct physical action was now transferred to the dusty processes of the law. From the point of view of the state the manifold inadequacies of the legal system had their advantages. So long as there was a remote prospect of ultimate victory, men would turn hopefully to the law as a weapon against their enemies. Once launched, the suit would with its complexity and prolixity consume their time, their energies, and their substance for years and years on end. The very deficiencies in the machinery of the law, its great cost, its appalling slowness, its obsession with irrelevant technical details, made it an admirable instrument for the sublimation of the bellicose instincts of a leisured class. Sixteenth-century litigation combined the qualities of tedium, hardship, brutality, and injustice that tested character and endurance, with the element of pure chance that appealed to the gambler, the fear of defeat and ruin, and the hope of victory and the humiliation of the enemy. It had everything that war can offer save the delights of shedding blood. It gave shape and purpose to many otherwise empty lives.

Litigation, therefore, remained the most popular of indoor sports, despite unanimous agreement upon the folly of such behaviour and the rapacity of lawyers. No nobleman of the day was without his string of suits against tenants or rivals, mostly about property. William Earl of Salisbury, who was not an unduly litigious person, had 29 in train in 1621, 20 in 1634, 13 in 1637. As the Earl of Huntingdon told his son, 'suits in law are grown so common that he that hath not some is out of fashion'. Riotous attacks on an enemy's person or property were going out, litigation was coming in. The two phenomena are not unconnected.

At the very time when increasing pressure was being brought to bear on private violence by the central government and when important modifications were taking place in men's way of life and ideas about their social responsibilities, there also occurred a technological change which made personal assault a very much more dangerous business. In spite of the substantial numbers involved and the fact that all combatants were armed, there was relatively little actual killing in the sixteenth century. If many of these great feuds turn out on close inspection to resemble the battles of Tweedledum and Tweedledee, the main reason was that the standard weapons used were the heavy sword with a single cutting edge and the buckler or shield. These weapons allowed the maximum muscular effort and the most spectacular show of violence with the minimum threat to life and limb. Fighting with them was not much more dangerous than all-in wrestling.

After about 1560 the broadsword began to give way to the needle-sharp rapier, with which it was only too easy to kill a man by running him through the body. The introduction of this new weapon thus had consequences exactly the reverse of that of the contraceptive: the one increases, the other decreases, the risks attendant upon two instinctive and pleasurable acts, fighting and making love. The rapier was as dangerous a weapon as a sports

car in the hands of a high-spirited young man with little sense of
self-control and no rules of conduct to regulate his behaviour.

Such a situation was clearly intolerable, and no sooner had the
rapier come into fashion than its use was severely restricted by a
set of rules and conventions of theological rigidity. A powerful
cause of the decline of casual and unregulated violence involving
the clash of groups of retainers, servants, and tenants, was the
development in the minds of the landed classes of a new ethical
code—the code of the duel. From our point of view, the two
important features of the duel are that it normally involved the
principals alone and not their friends and servants—for in England the group duel never caught on in the way it did in France—
and secondly that it was strictly controlled by rules which assured
fair play. The murderous assault by superior numbers, the surprise
ambush, and the blow from behind were no longer tolerated in
polite society. A duel was an isolated episode whose consequences,
even if fatal, offered little moral justification for subsequent ven-
geance by indignant friends and relatives.

Violence in word or deed was thus regulated, codified, restricted,
sterilized. The traditional ambition of the propertied classes to
demonstrate their personal courage and to avenge any disparage-
ment of their virtue or their honour was given an outlet which at
last affected no one but themselves. As Bodin and others argued
for France, the first consequence of the triumph of the code of
honour of the duel was to diminish faction quarrels and to lessen
the danger of aristocratic civil war.

It must be admitted that contemporaries took a less optimistic
view of the social consequences of the duelling code. This was
because a rigid stereotyping of the conventions led to an absurd
elaboration of punctilio, so that a gentleman of quality found himself under obligation to challenge an opponent for the most trivial
of verbal slips. A touch of bad temper, a loose word spoken to an
acquaintance or even to a friend demanded instant redress, and
might well result in bloodshed or death in the fields the next
morning. In particular, the giving of the lie was elevated into an
injury so deep that it could be expiated only in mortal combat.
Young men being naturally headstrong and hot-tempered, such
a code took a heavy toll of lives, and it was the appalling wastage
of gentle blood which so horrified contemporaries. De La Noue
claimed that in France more noblemen died annually from duelling

than soldiers were killed in several battles in the civil wars. When
carried to these lengths, the duel became a major moral and social
scourge, although one that did not directly threaten the stability
of the monarchy or the security of the state.

Intellectual opinion in England ranging from Sir Walter Ralegh
to Sir Francis Bacon was equally critical of the duelling code,
puritan moralists were unanimous in their condemnation of this
system of licensed manslaughter, and King James made strenuous
efforts to curb its development in England. It was the events of
1613, however, which really alarmed the King and galvanized the
Government into serious action. In that year there were six challenges or duels among the Court aristocracy and it looked as if the
English nobility, like fighting cocks in a ring, were about to
indulge in wholesale mutual slaughter. The situation horrified a
man as genuinely pacific as James, and he decided that something
more positive was needed than mere personal intervention to
patch up quarrels among his friends. And so in 1613 he joined in
the fray with a lengthy proclamation against 'the bloody exercise
of the duello'. As usual, however, James's bark was worse than
his bite and, despite Bacon's proud boast 'I hope I shall not know
a coronet from a hatband', he was in fact as careful to avoid
offending the rich and influential as was his master. It was two
lowly gentlemen who were picked on as victims for exemplary
punishment in Star Chamber, while the peers and courtiers who
had set the example continued to be allowed to go free. England
remained a country 'wherein a poor man was hanged for stealing
food for his necessities and a luxurious courtier . . . could be par-
doned after killing the second or third man'.

Feeble though this policy was, it nevertheless produced results,
if only because it was buttressed by the moral force of puritan
thinking. The earnest endeavours of the Privy Council and the
King to prevent aristocratic duels and to arbitrate over quarrels
now offered an avenue of escape from the tyranny of the code of
honour. Challenges continued to be sent and accepted, but were
now accompanied by sufficient publicity to allow the Government
time to intervene and stop proceedings. As a result, the worst
evils of the duel were effectively contained in England, and never
reached the proportions they achieved in France. The number of
duels reported by contemporaries reached a peak in the second
decade of the century and thereafter declined—at any rate until

the Civil War. In the early seventeenth century the duel thus succeeded in diverting the nobility from faction warfare with armed gangs without leading to a dislocation of social intercourse by incessant fighting over trivial slights, real or imagined.

The success of the Tudors in weaning the landed classes from their ancient habits of violence and subjecting them to the discipline of the law involved a social revolution of far-reaching consequences. From their point of view, the acid test of their policies was their success in bringing the whole country under central administrative control and in defeating aristocratic rebellion. Until the late sixteenth century, however, they could not hope to achieve this, and they had to be content to rule the country on the old system of reliance on loyal local magnates. Elizabeth was distrustful of the independent northern magnates, the more so since their loyalty to the Anglican settlement was highly suspect. In 1565 Mary Queen of Scots was openly expressing her hope of winning over all the great magnates north of the Trent—the earls of Derby, Shrewsbury, Northumberland, Westmorland, and Cumberland— since she believed that they were all 'of the old religion'. Faced with this potential threat to her throne, Elizabeth had no alternative other than to undermine their position. She deprived the Earl of Northumberland of the Wardenship of the Middle March, deliberately built up a rival gentry clientele under his enemy Sir John Forster, and put a southerner of proved loyalty, Lord Hunsdon, in charge of Berwick and the East Marches. Many of the northern gentry began to acquire the habit of looking south to London for favour and advancement, and to see positive advantages in defying the Percys.

Exasperated by such studied neglect, the Earl and his friends exploded into rebellion in 1569, the last episode in 500 years of protest by the Highland Zone against the interference of London. It was compacted of rivalries among the nobility of the north, the 'old goodwill of the people, deep-grafted in their hearts, to their nobles and gentlemen', fidelity to the Catholic religion, the misery of a decaying pastoral area harried and made desolate by border raiding, and temporary unemployment in the clothing industry of the West Riding due to a stoppage of trade with the Low Countries. Even this combination of motives, however, could not prevent the speedy disintegration of the Rebellion at the first sign of opposition, while down in Norfolk hardly a tenant stirred to help their lord, the Duke of Norfolk. It is nevertheless a measure of Elizabeth's sense of insecurity that she ordered the summary execution by hanging of over 700 of the rank and file of the rebels, instructions which were happily frustrated by the commanders on the spot. Compared with the savage reactions of Elizabeth and Burghley, James II and Judge Jeffreys acted with compassion and restraint in their handling of the Monmouth Rebellion. The North was taught a lesson which it did not forget. Never again would the cry 'A Percy, A Percy', 'A Dacre, A Dacre' evoke a Pavlovian response of unthinking loyalty among the gentry and peasantry of the North.

To ensure that the victory was final, energetic measures were taken to weaken the influence of the local aristocracy. The earls of Northumberland were henceforth confined to Sussex, and as a result the Percy clientage withered on the vine. Such ties of loyalty as might have persisted among their tenants were finally snapped by the ruthless raising of rents and fines carried out by the 9th Earl from his prison in the Tower in the early seventeenth century. The Nevilles, earls of Westmorland, who had already been excluded from central and local offices, were now exiled and lost all their estates, never to be restored. The Cliffords, earls of Cumberland, were tamed by bringing the 3rd Earl south to be brought up as a ward of the puritan Francis Earl of Bedford. He was thus converted to protestantism, and his aggressive instincts were channelled into harmless jousts in the tiltyard and privateering adventures at sea. By 1600 the Earl was no more to his tenants than an absentee landlord whose rare appearances in their midst meant nothing but a fresh rise in rents and fines. The last Lord Lumley moved south of his own accord, the better to savour the fantastic splendours of Nonesuch Palace, and to pursue the humane pursuits of book collecting and connoisseurship. The Dacre estates, which had been swallowed up by the Howards, were sequestered by Elizabeth after the attainder of Francis Dacre in 1569 and the Duke of Norfolk in 1572. This successfully disposed of all but two of the old leading families, and Elizabeth took care that no new families were given large land grants in the north, and that none of the greater squires was elevated to the peerage.

Personal extravagance and biological accident dealt effectively with the last two northern magnates, the Stanleys, earls of Derby, and the Talbots, earls of Shrewsbury, of whom the former was uncrowned king of Lancashire, and the latter dominated a wide swathe of territory from Yorkshire across Derbyshire, Nottinghamshire, and Staffordshire, down into Shropshire and Herefordshire. Both families failed in the direct male line, leaving heavy debts and three heiresses behind them; the Stanley estates were either sold or partitioned soon after 1594 and the Talbot estates soon after 1618. It is noticeable that in both cases the Crown did all it could to facilitate dismemberment. This only left the lesser peers, the Scropes, the Darcys, the Whartons, the Eures, and the Ogles, who were comfortably and harmlessly occupied in the administrative routines of the Council of the North. By the accession of James, the North was in the safe hands of carpet-baggers, bureaucrats, lawyers, and loyal local landowners of medium rank.

The story is the same for Wales and the Welsh borders, from which the most serious threats to royal authority had sprung throughout the Middle Ages. The power of the last great border magnate had been broken by the execution of Edward Duke of Buckingham in 1521, an act of decisive importance in English history since Buckingham was a man of towering strength, the like of which was never to be seen again. The elimination of Buckingham was no more than an essential preliminary to the task of taming Wales and the Marches. A few years later the gross tyranny and corruption of the 2nd Earl of Worcester and his Herbert henchmen in South Wales and the borders forced the government to undertake a major administrative reform. The marcher franchises were destroyed and the Council of Wales set up in the 1530's as an instrument dominated by English marcher gentry to bring the Welsh up to English standards of civilization and good order. After these revolutionary steps there was little trouble from the Welsh border magnates. There can be little doubt, however, that for a time in the 1590's the 2nd Earl of Essex lorded it over a large area of Wales and the Marches. The Essex Revolt of 1601 was essentially a metropolitan affair, an episode in a faction fight between two groups of courtiers for control of the Queen's purse and person. But had the revolt in London achieved even momentary success, it might have lit the fuse for a violent explosion in South Wales and Denbighshire, as the Vaughans and the Salusburys of Rug took bloody revenge upon their rivals in local government. As it was, however, the London end of the conspiracy collapsed in a matter of hours and this possibility was never put to the test.

The Essex Revolt and the Main Plot two years later were the last occasions on which a disgruntled nobleman took up arms for no higher purpose than to secure what he judged to be his due. As a method of conducting party politics, armed rebellion was by now a thing of the past. Twenty-five years later Buckingham aroused hatreds far deeper and more widespread than those inspired by Cecil in 1600–3, but the mere idea of armed revolt against the favourite was now unthinkable. Impeachment had become the orthodox weapon of revenge, and Buckingham's assassination owed nothing to aristocratic conspiracy. If some dissatisfied noblemen worked off personal spleen against the Crown in the crisis of 1640–2 by supporting Pym and the Commons, they were given their opportunity by, and took refuge behind, deep-seated political and religious grievances.

These last, hopeless, gestures of aristocratic rebellion were at bottom no more than dramatic episodes in the struggle by the Crown to establish its unimpeded control over local administration. Understanding of Tudor problems and Tudor policies is impossible unless it is realized that the traditional view of their reliance upon the lesser landowning classes is partly misconceived. Up to about 1570 the Tudors were obliged to govern as had medieval kings before them, mainly with the co-operation of the aristocracy. Only in the later years of Elizabeth did there occur a decisive shift to dependence on the squirearchy and gentry. By 1600 the great territorial empires of the mid-sixteenth century were things of the past: increasing royal interference, discriminatory use of royal patronage, and the growing ambition of the squirearchy had combined to undermine their foundations. Sheriffs, J.P.s, and commissioners were all appointed in London, and slowly came to look as much to the Crown as to the local magnates for their advancement. The authority of the magnate over the local gentry was now coming to depend less upon his territorial power than upon his influence in London. The gentry were still content to look after an earl's interests in the countryside, but only if in return he could get them offices and favours at Court and if he could put effective pressure on the judges.

## IV. THE USES OF INFLUENCE

In the fifteenth and early sixteenth centuries the great nobles dominated politics and local government by their command over their tenants, by their nucleus of armed followers, and by their influence over the retained gentry, who were drawn into their orbit by the need for protection and patronage in dangerous times. In the eighteenth century these great nobles were still very influential in politics and local government thanks to the patronage that went with a substantial holding of land, to the power of the purse to buy electoral votes, and to mobilization of the resources of public office effectively monopolized by the Whig oligarchy. The eighteenth-century 'connexion' was more personal, more reliant on crown support, more dependent on the subtle arts of management and the simple techniques of corruption, more liable to sudden—if temporary—collapse in gusts of public indignation over real issues like Wilkes or the American War. It was none the less one of the most important features of English political life before the nineteenth century. The manner in which the nobles were induced and obliged to abandon the threat and actuality of violence as a means of control has now been described, and it remains briefly to examine how successful they were in creating a new network of influence upon the ruins of the old mixed system of force, authority, and persuasion.

At the same time as they were being weaned from violence, the influence of noblemen over county elections was being automatically reduced by the shrinking of their territorial holdings. To the extent that land was passing out of their hands into those of lesser landowning groups, their influence over county elections was proportionately reduced. Fewer manors meant fewer freeholders whose opinions could be influenced, and therefore fewer votes when it came to the push. Sir Robert Sydney, future Earl of Leicester, was strongly advised to hold on to his property 'for by it you shall be ever able to have many freeholders at your command, which in a man's own country is specially to be regarded'. It was the inexorable shift to economic rents in the early seventeenth century which was probably the most fatal blow of all, for it undermined the loyalty of tenants on the property which was retained. Landlord–tenant relationships never became wholly dominated by the ethos of the market-place, and ties of sentiment

lasted well into the eighteenth and nineteenth centuries. After the
initial bitterness of swallowing the pill of economic rents had
worn off, there were still heart-strings as well as purse-strings
upon which a great nobleman could pull in time of need. But there
can be no doubt that the influence of a nobleman over his tenants
was declining, especially in the first years of the new economic
relationship; his influence over his freeholders was weakening as
they became alive to political issues and increasingly haunted by
problems of religion; his influence in the country was weakening
as his territorial possessions contracted and as he spent more time
in London; and his leadership of the greater gentry was crumbling
as they acquired more education, more administrative experience,
and more grievances.

The only compensating factor was the creation of the office of
Lord Lieutenant, which gave the local nobleman control of the
militia, and enabled him to manipulate musters and war-taxation
to help his friends and penalize his enemies. But appointment to
this office depended as much on court favour as on local influence,
few if any peers could reckon on it as of right, and in any case
executive authority rested with the gentry in their capacity as
deputy lieutenants. Thanks to extensive territorial possessions, a
spreading connexion of influential relatives, and the acquisition of
a host of local offices at the disposal of the Crown (including the
Lord Lieutenancy), it was possible for the 3rd Earl of Huntingdon
in the late sixteenth century to run the borough and the county
virtually as a private bailiwick. As long as he lived his will was
unchallenged by any save the Crown itself, but as soon as he was
dead, the power of the Hastings began to crumble. He was an
Elizabethan, not an Early Stuart phenomenon, and even he relied
on royal support to maintain his position.

If aristocratic control of county elections was weakening between 1540 and 1640, the same period saw two developments
which were to lay the foundations of the eighteenth-century
patronage system. In the first place the distribution of monastic
estates meant the acquisition by the nobility of a very large
number of advowsons and lay rectories. Of course the bulk of the
lay patrons were gentry, and the most important single patrons
were the Crown, the bishops, and Oxford and Cambridge colleges.
Nevertheless, in 1640 the aristocracy could appoint the parson in
between 5 and 10 per cent. of all parishes, and when after the

Restoration the Church enhanced its social standing and its political influence, this was to be a most useful source of patronage.

Secondly, the sixteenth century saw a flood of seats in the House of Commons put at the disposal of the nobility by a complaisant Crown. Between 1547 and 1584 the House was enlarged by the creation of no fewer than 119 new borough seats. Some, such as the Cornish seats, were presumably intended to strengthen royal control over parliament, but the great majority were merely an easy and ostensibly harmless way of gratifying an influential suitor seeking an extension of his private patronage. If the Tudors ever stopped to consider the political consequences of their action, they presumably calculated that a courtier could be relied on to nominate supporters of official policies, and that mere tradesmen would not dare to challenge the royal will. But there was no guarantee that the son and heir of the courtier would take the same view, nor that the electorate would continue meekly to accept these high-handed directives.

The full extent of the political patronage exercised by the peerage is still not clear, but the work of Sir John Neale has revealed enough to show how pervasive it was in Elizabethan England. The degree of control exercised by the magnates over the boroughs varied from the absolute and arrogant mastery of Pembroke over the village worthies of Wilton to the delicate exercise of tact and influence that was needed to handle substantial corporations like those of Lincoln or Salisbury. The number of Commons seats more or less at the disposal of the peerage in their private capacities in the mid-Elizabethan period is not precisely known, but it may have been as much as a fifth of the total. In addition, court peers who were Wardens of the Cinque Ports, Captains of the Isle of Wight, and Chancellors of the Duchies of Lancaster or Cornwall exercised wide influence by virtue of their office—five seats for the Cinque Ports, three or more for the Isle of Wight, and thirteen for Lancaster.

Finally there was the patronage both offered to and sought by the great court favourites like Leicester, the Cecils, and Essex. As the struggle for power at Court intensified in the 1590's, both Cecil and Essex began spreading their net wider and wider, sucking into the battle all with hopes and ambitions at Court, overriding many local loyalties and smashing many petty tyrannies in the process. Individuals found themselves forced to choose between two mutually suspicious and intolerant patrons. This polarization continued throughout the first decade of the reign of James, and probably reached its peak in the 1614 Parliament.

Such little evidence as is available suggests that thereafter the influence of the Court magnates steadily weakened. The rise of vital political issues, constitutional, economic, and religious, aroused the urban electorate and emboldened them to throw off their chains. By the middle 1620's it was becoming hard for a courtier to get a nomination, and hard for a magnate, whether in or out of Court, to maintain his old pre-eminence in local elections. Authority tended to pass either to the urban oligarchies themselves, or more commonly to local gentry, and particularly to those with a reputation for radical opinions. The final débâcle came in 1640 when the high tide of political passion broke the dykes of clientage and temporarily engulfed the ancient traditions of aristocratic control and influence. The Earl of Holland was as powerless at Reading as was Lord Finch at Cambridge; Salisbury was ignored at St. Albans, Suffolk was rebuffed at Dorchester, Paget failed at Great Marlow. The Court was ruined and discredited, and by too close association with it the aristocracy was politically discredited too. Though their numbers had doubled in the previous decades, it is doubtful whether on this occasion they effectively influenced more than 10 per cent. of elections. A year later salt was ostentatiously rubbed into the wounds when the Commons ordered boroughs to ignore the contents of all letters from peers, and to report them to the House for investigation.

At this, the lowest point in aristocratic influence over elections, there were visible the first hints of the secret weapon which was to prove so effective in quelling these disturbing signs of electoral independence. In the 1640 election for the first time candidates resorted to really lavish entertainment as an inducement to the electorate. Candidates for shire elections spent in hundreds of pounds, candidates for boroughs in tens, and if such sums were still within the means of the gentry, there were already signs that the longer purses of the nobility would eventually prevail. This could not happen, however, till costs rose from hundreds to thousands of pounds, as they did in the late seventeenth century when votes were sold for cash. In 1640 inducements were limited to food and drink. At Abingdon Sir George Stonehouse of Radley 'prevailed by his beef, bacon and bag pudding, and by permitting as many of them as would, to be drunk at his charge'. So long as these relatively unsophisticated conditions persisted, the greater gentry of the locality were more than a match for either the county magnate or the politician from the Court.

## V. CONCLUSION

Many forces converged to remove at last the centuries-old danger of aristocratic violence, but the most important single factor was the shrinkage both in numbers and in scale of the over-mighty subjects of the Crown. This decline in its turn had many causes, partly economic, partly legal, partly psychological, which have already been set out at length, but there can be little doubt that the action of the Crown was of vital significance. By occasional executions and irreversible attainders and by refraining from building up new landed families to replace those which died out, the Tudors succeeded in reducing the numbers of great territorial landlords. By 1620, of the handful of families who dominated late-fifteenth-century society and politics, only the Howards survived, and they were tame enough. After 1572 there was not a duke in the country until the revival of the title for Richmond and Buckingham by James I. Those great families which survived found that their habits of spending were causing a contraction of their territorial possessions, which in time had far-reaching effects on their authority. The decline in the number of families holding some 70 manors or more from 18 out of 62 in 1559 to 6 out of 121 in 1641 is not very significant in terms of real income; in terms of influence, however, it would be difficult to deny its importance.

Secondly, there was a change in men's ideas of loyalty. The influence of the nobles over client gentry and tenantry was being weakened by their increasing absenteeism due to attendance at Court, and by the shift to economic rents which severely reduced the service element in landlord–tenant relationships. Tudor monarchy and the Price Revolution were both working to the same end. The key to early- and mid-sixteenth-century society is to be found in the word 'manred', meaning control over persons for military service, a word which, significantly enough, had disappeared from the English language by the middle of the seventeenth century. Its place in the scale of aristocratic values was taken by rent, even rack-rent. Semi-feudal potentates from the highland zone, an earl of Northumberland or Westmorland, were as anachronistic in the England of Elizabeth I as was El Glaoui of Marrakesh in the Magreb of the mid-twentieth century. The all-pervading influence of the central government was seeping steadily into the remoter areas, subsuming local loyalties under allegiance to itself, wearing down the recalcitrant by administrative and legal pressure, and cowing the rebellious by the sheer scale of its resources. The growth of religious enthusiasm was leading men to wonder if God was not a better master than an earl. In the midst of a fierce quarrel with the Earl of Huntingdon in 1628, Sir Henry Shirley gave voice to this feeling by asserting that 'he cared not for any lord in England, except the Lord of Hosts'. In time such an attitude undermined the position of the King himself, and by 1664 a tutor in a noble household was teaching that a gentle-man's 'highest ambition is to be a favourite in the Court of Heaven'. To begin with, however, puritanism was a powerful solvent of subordinate loyalties and thus temporarily strengthened the hand of the Crown.

Thirdly, the nobility themselves were losing the military capacity to challenge their sovereign, and the technical capacity for leader-ship in war. As armies grew in size with the domination of the field by the infantry pikemen and as the technical services like pioneers and ordnance increased in importance, war ceased to be an exciting *chevauchée* led by high-spirited young men out for a lark. Now that small-arms had been invented, strength, courage, and skill on horseback were no longer any protection against sudden and ignominious death. War was no fun any more, and the tiltyard at Westminster Palace had to serve as a substitute for the fields of Crécy and Agincourt. A military commander had now to be an expert in logistics, in transport and victualling, in engineering and administration. The nobility were ill-adapted to such a change, which in any case deprived war of most of its aristocratic glamour. From this point of view, as from so many others, the period from 1560 to 1640 is one of transition. Between 1552 and 1642 England enjoyed several prolonged periods of peace, and the opportunities for military service were consequently sharply reduced. About three-quarters of the peerage—which means virtually every able-bodied adult peer—had seen service in

the wars of the 1540's, but by 1576 only one peer in four had had
any military experience. In the early seventeenth century only
about one peer in five had seen action, and the proportion both
fit and experienced in 1642 was even smaller. One of the reasons
why King Charles lost the Civil War is that the English aristocracy
no longer knew how to fight. If the Earl of Newcastle had had the
professional expertise of Sir Ralph Hopton it might have been
a very different story.

Fourthly, the nobility were losing their nerve. As their utility
in war declined, they tried to protect their position by a romantic
and artificial revival of the chivalric ideal, expressed in literature
by Malory's Arthurian legends, by Lord Berners's translation of
Froissart, and by Stephen Hawes's *The Pastime of Pleasure*. These
calls for a spiritual regeneration in military prowess to justify
social and economic privilege were doomed to failure in the face
of technical changes in war and the revolution in concepts of
duty. Reformers like Roger Ascham bitterly attacked Malory for
exalting adultery in bed and murder in the battlefield. The advent
of the county muster and the trained band destroyed the concept
of a military *élite*, and the nobility and gentry turned instead to
royal administration in the shires. As their military power ebbed
they began to doubt their capacity and duty to act as self-appointed
watchdogs over royal policies.

They were slowly discouraged from keeping either armed bodyguards or numerous liveried retainers, their castles fell into ruins,
their military equipment rusted in their armouries. Like the rest of
the population, they were deeply affected by the heavy barrage of
propaganda from pulpit and printing-press on the subject of the
necessity of loyalty to the sovereign. Elizabeth was extolled as
God's Lieutenant on earth, and rebellion castigated as a grievous
sin, as contrary to the natural law of subjection to superior
authority, as a grave threat to human happiness and prosperity,
and as doomed to failure anyway, since contrary to God's will.
On the periphery of these arguments there lurked a crude
nationalism:

> If that you stick together as you ought,
> This little isle may set the world at nought,

urged one of the propaganda pieces put out on the occasion of
the 1569 rebellion. The divine right of kings, passive obedience,

national feeling, were all devices used by the Elizabethans to secure loyalty to the throne. By the end of the century rebellion was becoming not merely very chancy, but also very disreputable, and it is not surprising to find that in 1601 Southampton had to be fortified by readings from Aristotle's *Politics* to nerve him for revolt.

These doctrines were particularly effective when allied with the widespread Calvinist theories of predestination and of the direct intervention of the Almighty in human affairs. The object of rebellion was to free the King from evil advisers. If it succeeded, it proved the justice of the cause; if it failed, this was clear evidence that the enterprise was contrary to the will of God. And so, although there were several aristocratic rebellions against the sovereign throughout the sixteenth century, not a single one of the defeated conspirators maintained the justice of his cause on the scaffold. Without exception they acknowledged themselves justly condemned to death for an offence against God and the King, and professed themselves the King's good and loyal servants. These public expressions of devotion to the Moloch of the State—confessions curiously reminiscent of those pronounced in Stalinist treason trials—were not the result of torture, for a nobleman's rank effectively protected him from racks and pincers. It is certainly possible that promises and threats about the disposal of the property and the treatment of the heirs may have played their part, but it is difficult to avoid the conclusion that the main explanation of these abject confessions was a profound belief in the inviolable sanctity of the state, to the preservation of which it was the moral and religious duty of the defeated rebel to devote his last moments on earth. There was thus a failure of confidence as well as a failure of power.

Fifthly, and lastly, the nobility found themselves increasingly bound to the Crown by ties of fear and hope. The numerous acts of attainder of the fifteenth and sixteenth centuries were intended as much for threats of retribution in case of further disobedience as for punishments for past rebellion. Most families regained part or all of their land, now held on sufferance from the Crown. Obligations and recognizances for huge sums were freely used by Henry VII as blackmail weapons for good behaviour. The late Tudors allowed arrears of debt to pile up until the debtor became hopelessly entangled and dependent on the good pleasure of the sovereign for respite or remission. Moreover, as the Court machine swelled in importance, so did the amount of gifts, offices, and honours at its disposal, and those who wished to have a share in these benefits were well advised to display their loyalty and obedience to the Crown.

The crucial victories of the Crown over the nobility were won between about 1570 and 1620. It was then that the great territorial empires were at last broken up, then that the massive bands of armed retainers were cut down to size, then that the nobility abandoned their age-old habits of casual violence, which now became the mark of dangerous eccentricity. The new sense of responsibility was affecting both old and new by the early years of the seventeenth century, and recorded acts of violence by the nobility declined sharply after 1600. If the doubling of the numbers of the peerage is taken into account, under Charles I such acts per peer per decade averaged only one-fifth of what they had been in the latter days of Elizabeth. The combined tally of violence and duels suggests that the chances of a peer's being involved in some form of physical assault during an adult life-span of twenty years fell from about two in three to two in ten. Private warfare and the blood feud were rapidly declining, and if baronial revolts continued to splutter into brief and increasingly ineffective life, by 1603 their day was done. Upper-class violence was far from dead in 1640, but it had at last been brought within manageable proportions, and was now largely canalized within the rigid formalities of the personal, private duel. As Sir Walter Ralegh put it, with only minor exaggeration: 'The Justices of Peace in England have opposed the injustices of war in England; the King's writ runs over all; and the Great Seal of England with that of the next constables will serve the turn to affront the greatest lords in England that shall move against the King.' A decisive step forward had been taken in bringing order and civility to English society.

As a result, the outbreak of civil war in 1642 differed markedly from all previous uprisings. Before, earls had stocked their castles, summoned their retainers and tenants, and sallied forth at the head of their private armies, confident in their technical ability and material resources to conduct a campaign. In 1642 the war began with attempts to capture the county magazines and to assume control of the trained bands, issues which were usually decided less by the whim of a great magnate than by the interests and affections of the majority of the leading county families. Although noblemen still filled the highest posts in the armies, there was a desperate search for professional soldiers to stiffen the headquarters staff, for the nobility in general no longer possessed the requisite experience. Although both sides had recourse to the issue of commissions to prominent supporters to raise their own troops— Newcastle's Whitecoats, for example—the extensive use of the trained bands of the counties and the emergence of the New Model Army in 1644 showed the bankruptcy of the old military system. Henceforward the only hope of challenging the authority of the State was to lie in seizing some of its military stores and suborning part of its armed forces. Private enterprise was no longer adequate for the purpose.

PART TWO

# GETTING AND SPENDING

---

## VI

## ESTATE MANAGEMENT

You have the lease of two manors come out next Christmas;
you may lay your tenants on the greater rack for it.
J. MARSTON, The Malcontent, III. i

WHEN all is said and done, the foundation of aristocratic
wealth, power, and honour rested on the land. There
have been many periods of English history in which
little more was needed to look after this inheritance than the
maintenance of an efficient routine of checks and audits for the
prevention of fraud. Any fool with minimal application to business
could do the job reasonably well. 'It requires no great sense, no
parts, little or no sagacity or penetration, nothing but a very
moderate degree of steadiness and clearness of head', remarked
Lord Shelburne in the late eighteenth century. Such, however,
was not the case between 1560 and 1640, for the times demanded
ceaseless rethinking and initiative. Landlords now had to run,
simply in order to stand still. Prices, and especially food prices,
were rising fairly continuously, the Phelps Brown index of con-
sumables rather more than doubling over this eighty-year span.
Income from land had to be adjusted to keep pace, and this meant
the introduction of radical changes in every aspect of estate
management. Secondly, this was a period of rapid growth of
population and of economic output. More and more land was
being brought under cultivation, towns, and particularly London,
were growing fast, mining and industrial activity were expanding.
If landlords were to take advantage of these new opportunities,

they had to be alive to the possibilities and ready to risk money on their exploitation. The handling of these more speculative enterprises is of a different order from straightforward administration of agricultural property, and discussion of them is postponed to the next chapter. A third factor upsetting traditional patterns was the increasing tendency of peers to hang about in London instead of residing on their estates. Many of them were becoming semi-absentee landlords, and the shift of interest from manpower to income is in part a reflection of this change, coupled with the disappearance in the new nation-state of the need and the desire for personal dependence. Finally, many peers found themselves in serious financial difficulties and thus had a powerful incentive to overhaul their estate administration in order to increase their income. Change was not merely desirable; it was obligatory.

Anyone who has read the hundreds of catalogues compiled by the National Register of Archives, who has examined some of the great body of material now collected in the County Record Offices, who has worked through the accumulated deposits of time of old-established families in their original settings in the muniment rooms of country houses, cannot help being struck by the change that occurred between the early sixteenth and early seventeenth century. For the former period the records are few, scattered, imperfect, and largely confined to muniments of title; for the latter they exist in almost embarrassing profusion, and are of many different kinds, even including that greatest rarity, private correspondence.

Why men suddenly began to preserve these records is not at all clear. Many of the documents, particularly accounts of expenditure, can have had little or no practical value once they had served their immediate purpose of discharging the accountant of his responsibility. This accumulation is the product of a literate, record-conscious society, increasingly obsessed with its own past, and turning more and more to old parchment for illumination.

The documentary basis of estate management was not only increasing alarmingly in both the quantity compiled and the quantity preserved, it was also changing in its technical character. It was written on paper rather than parchment, in books rather than in rolls, in English rather than in Latin, in arabic rather than in roman numerals. Despite these changes in form, the contents and purpose of accounts remained unaltered from the Middle Ages.

The spread of double-entry book-keeping had not the slightest effect upon the landed classes, all of whose accounts continued to be arranged on the thirteenth-century charge-and-discharge system, designed not to strike a true balance of income and expenditure, but to calculate what was nominally due by the accountant. The object was the prevention of fraud, not the calculation of profit and loss. The declared account is thus meaningful only in terms of its immediate purpose of calculating the obligation of the accountant to his lord at the year's end. To ascertain the actual cash received or the true balance on the year's working often demands more information than the account can be made to disclose.

Further difficulty is caused by the fact that a single account never, or hardly ever, embraced the full range of a lord's receipts and expenditure. Each accountant—indeed each manorial bailiff— was a world unto himself, getting and spending within his own sphere, and knowing and caring little for the responsibilities of his colleagues or for the over-all picture of his lord's finances.

Given a multiplicity of independent accounts, a charge-and-discharge system, a wildly fluctuating income from fines, imperfectly recorded payments in kind, and totally haphazard accounting of such 'foreyn' receipts as New Year's gifts, bribes, or the profits of office, it is hardly surprising that many great noblemen had the greatest difficulty in discovering just what their financial position really was, and even more so in assessing the comparative profitability of alternative courses of action. The only warning indicator was a mounting load of debt, but its causes could not be discovered without very detailed investigation, and sometimes not even then. Of the great magnates only the 2nd Earl of Salisbury could really be said to have had a proper grip on the situation. For the vast majority of the great estates, Lord Berkeley's servant John Smyth of Nibley must be allowed the last word: 'The irregularities and disorders of our days may not appear in accounts to posterity; we will spend all and more at the year's end, and not be able to say how or wherein.'

The administrative organization which produced these records varied considerably from family to family and from generation to generation. The smaller the estates the more flexible and primitive the methods employed and what concerns us here is how the really great properties were run. Certain general principles governed all arrangements. Because of poor communications, if the estate consisted of compact groups of properties widely separated one from another, particular receivers would necessarily have to be appointed for each geographical area. The second factor was the degree to which the lord habitually resided and spent his money in London. If he did so to any considerable extent, a London agent was necessary to collect the cash from the receiver-general and/or the particular receivers of the rural estates, and to supervise the expenditure in the capital. The London agents of families like the Manners or the Cliffords in the early seventeenth century effectively replaced the receiver-general as the most important of the financial officials. This was a very similar development to that in the Early Tudor royal administration by which the Chamber squeezed out the Exchequer. It could only be avoided if the lord normally lived in the country, or if the main estates were sufficiently close to London to allow the receiver-general to fulfil both functions.

The service itself made an attractive opening for an able young man with a career to make in the world, for the prospects of promotion were quite good. Within the aristocratic household the hierarchy of officers allowed for advancement over the years, and there was always the chance of moving sideways into another great household or onwards into royal administration.

The landed property administered by the officials working on the estate side of management was expected to provide four things: an obsequious and obedient source of manpower; supplies of food and fuel for consumption in the household; a regular annual income to meet normal running expenditure; and occasional large sums to pay for emergencies such as service on an embassy or the marriage of a daughter. The main problem was to strike the right balance between these four conflicting needs, a search complicated by the traditional insistence on the reduction of overheads and the elimination of capital investment in the estates.

The profits of a great estate were derived from a wide variety of sources. There were free rents, paid in respect of their duty to the manorial lord by the freeholders. These had never been large sums, they were fixed in amount, and were now of negligible consequence owing to the declining value of money. There were rents of assize paid by copyholders according to the custom of the manor. These also were small fixed sums, which by the early seventeenth century had shrunk in value, but copyholders were also obliged to pay a fine on each change of ownership by surrender or succession. If the fine too was fixed by custom it was not worth much, but if it was 'arbitrable' it could be stepped up to keep pace with the rising monetary value of the land. These fines were levied in the manorial court, which was also responsible for collecting the heriots or best beasts from the estates of dead copyholders and for other minor penalties. All these sums were overshadowed by the rents paid by tenants farming demesne rectories or mills held on lease. At each new letting the lessees also paid fines, which often amounted to very large sums indeed. Finally there were the profits of the demesnes kept in hand. These might consist of industrial or mining profits, profits from the sale of woods, or profits of sheep and cattle ranching or arable husbandry, part of which would be taken in the form of provisions for the household.

Apart from a shrinking home farm, the only demesnes which a nobleman consistently kept in hand were his woods—though if the opportunity offered itself, he was usually ready enough to lease them out to an enterprising iron-manufacturer. Otherwise he hung on to his trees, treating them less as a crop to be culled annually on reaching their sixteen-year maturity, than as a piggy-bank in which he could store up capital over long periods. Come a rainy day, he could chop down the trees and lay hands on his capital. The Elizabethans in particular drew heavily upon this reserve in times of trouble. Well might Pepys define woods as 'an excrescence of the earth created by God for the payment of debts'.

Setting aside woodlands, which constitute a special case, the first question a nobleman and his officials had to decide was whether or not to go in for large-scale demesne farming. This had been standard practice in the boom period of the thirteenth and early fourteenth centuries, but had tended to fall out of favour as prices and consumer demands levelled off. Now that demographic growth and inflation were again in full swing with agricultural prices well in the lead, one would have expected a major switch back to demesne husbandry. This was indeed the policy adopted with strikingly successful results by many European aristocrats, particularly in the East, but the English nobility were very reluctant to follow their example.

The reason for this failure to move with the times was a

pathological fear of being cheated by dishonest officials, a theme
which recurs again and again with monotonous regularity in all
memoirs and 'advices' of the period, and which dictated the archaic
form of account-keeping. From a distance of 300 years it is very
difficult to judge how far these arguments were sound. Certainly at
other periods and in other places, landlords have managed to run
large demesnes without being ruined by the malpractices of their
servants, and without straining themselves with excessive attention to business. On the other hand, there may be some validity
in these fears. Since similar conditions tend to produce similar
psychological reactions, it is probable that the labouring classes
in Elizabethan England were as feckless, lazy, and incompetent
as those of pre-industrial societies with a surplus underemployed
labour force today. In any case, given the methods of accounting
for demesnes and for leaseholds and given the system of beneficial
leases, the relative merits of the two systems could not easily have
been worked out. If English noblemen at this period did not
develop great farms like the Prussian junkers, the explanation lies
in current prejudice and custom rather than in a rational calculation of optimum economic advantage.

It must be admitted, however, that some of the most enterprising and active of the Elizabethans went in for demesne farming on
a moderate but substantial scale. The difference between the Elizabethan rentier and entrepreneur does not fit the Marxist stereotype of the contrast between the old and feudal and the new and
capitalist; it is rather a product of a different use of time and
energy. Those who were wholly occupied in politics and at Court
were content to lease out their estates; those who lived in the
country were more ready to undertake the hazards and labour of
direct management, although owing to the difficulties of control
nearly all were frightened off the labour-intensive activity of arable
farming. Great demesne farmers were primarily concerned with
sheep and cattle ranching on extensive enclosed pastures, either
carved out of the old demesne, or in former deer-parks, or in
freehold closes.

It has been argued that throughout the whole of the first half
of the sixteenth century there was a premium on sheep-rearing,
thanks to the soaring price of wool. After the collapse of the
export boom in 1551, however, this margin tended to disappear,
and greater emphasis was placed on the production of meat to

feed the rising population, particularly in the great city of London. Discussion of sheep-farming in the sixteenth century has for too long been conducted on the erroneous assumption that sheep are perambulating empty woolly bags. In fact by the late sixteenth century all flocks of which we have record were being managed as much with an eye to mutton as to wool.

The demands of a great household for meat were very heavy, at least 50 beeves and 400 to 500 muttons a year, so that the smaller of the demesne ranches can reasonably be regarded as no more than home farms. In the sixteenth century, however, there were a considerable number which were unquestionably being operated for profit. The greatest sheepmaster of the Elizabethan age was not some thrusting member of the rising capitalist gentry, but the senior nobleman of England, Thomas Howard, Duke of Norfolk, who in 1571 owned as many as 16,800 animals in East Anglia alone. Since this is an autumn count, it must represent the basic stock carried over from year to year, after the surplus lambs had been sold off. It is instructive to compare this with the flock of the Spencers of Althorp, the only family to rise into the peerage primarily by the profits of sheep-farming. At no time was their permanent flock larger than about 13,200, with an addition of 4,300 to 5,000 lambs each spring.

If there were a number of fairly large-scale demesne farmers in the reign of Elizabeth, they were rare by the 1620's, and almost extinct by the outbreak of the Civil War. One reason for this decline was the levelling off of prices after the slump of 1620–1, which led to a contraction of profit margins; another was the secular trend which was redressing the balance between meat and wool prices on the one hand and those of corn on the other. Unless noblemen were prepared to go in for arable cultivation—which they were not—the incentive to keep their pastures in hand rather than lease them out was substantially reduced. The third and fourth decades of the seventeenth century saw a general shift to leasing by the great pasture farmers of the Midlands: the Spencers and the Cranfields among the peerage, the Fitzwilliams, the Temples, and Heneages among the squirearchy. By 1640 all the prominent land-owners of whom we have record had reduced their demesne husbandry, many of them to the narrow limits of a home farm to supply some of the needs of the household.

Even the home farm itself was normally on a far smaller scale than the size of the aristocratic household would seem to warrant. Few noblemen doubted that it was wasteful to purchase basic supplies on the open market, but many sought less cumbersome ways than arable farming for obtaining their needs in wheat, barley, rye, malt, and pease. The rectory in the village where the great house lay was usually owned by the lord, who was therefore entitled to the great tithes. If he took them in kind instead of leasing them out he found himself supplied with large, and indeed sometimes superfluous, quantities of corn. The second alternative was to take part of the rent from the more substantial tenant farmers near the great house in the form of a fixed quantity of foodstuffs, a device which both supplied the household and offered some protection against inflation. Thus in 1611 the Earl of Rutland got all his oats and most of his wheat and pease in rent corn, his malt partly from rent corn and partly from tithe corn, and only his rye and barley from the home farm at Woolsthorpe near Belvoir Castle. His beef and mutton came from cattle and sheep fattened in his parks, his lambs from his own flock and from tithes, his rabbits from his own warren.

From these three sources, demesnes, tithes, and provision rents, most peers of whom we have record were receiving foodstuffs to the value of between 5 and 10 per cent. of their gross cash income from land, to which must be added something for free carriage. As wood fuel became scarcer, more and more noblemen began going over to coal for at least part of their heating requirements. Now coal is heavy and dirty and often has to be transported long distances. Rather than use their own carts or hire them for the occasion, many peers in the late Elizabethan and early Stuart period preferred to put this disagreeable obligation upon some of their tenants as a condition of their leases.

Even the deer-parks tended to go the same way as the rest of the demesne as the quest for profit grew more intense in the early seventeenth century. After all, the most fanatical of Nimrods could hardly exhaust the possibilities of all the eighteen deer-parks owned by the 1st Earl of Pembroke in the early years of Elizabeth. And so park after park, even that around the great house, was let as pasture for cattle and sheep, or on occasion cleared of trees and ploughed up. 'Men of late', wrote Norden in 1607, 'have disparked much of this kind of ground and converted it to better uses.' The records of the aristocracy bear him out.

Never agricultural entrepreneurs on a very large scale, noblemen contracted their activities in the early seventeenth century so that by 1640 the great majority were little more than rentiers, and often absentee rentiers at that. Given the prevailing economic conditions this change may well have produced the optimum financial return, but it certainly had important social consequences. It focused attention upon the ever-sensitive problem of rent and made this the flash-point of conflict in rural society; it detached the nobility and squirearchy from direct contact with the soil; and it plunged an already leisured class into even greater idleness.

## I. LEASING POLICIES

It is platitudinous to observe that men's deeds are as often as not considerably at variance with their words, and that this discrepancy causes scant concern to all but the most squeamish. On the other hand dismissal of stated social aspirations simply because they are more honoured in the breach than the observance is as foolish as acceptance at their face value. Neither absolute cynicism nor absolute *naïveté* are much use in assessing the relative weight of idealism and self-interest in influencing the behaviour of so erratic and unpredictable an animal as man. It is therefore not entirely superfluous to examine the moral obligations which were supposed to govern landlord–tenant relations. This was not one of those periods in which it has been regarded as right and reasonable for a man to do as he likes with his own, regardless of the assumed laws of God and the alleged interests of society. A landlord was expected to cherish old tenants and to moderate his demands upon all, whether old or new. Ralegh's famous and much-admired advice to his son counselled a landlord to 'use thy poor neighbours and tenants well, pine them not and their children to add superfluity and needless expences to thy self'. The prevalent doctrine of social responsibility was buttressed by the teachings of the clergy. 'Divines will also have it', reported Dudley Lord North, perhaps a little doubtfully, 'that Gods blessing doth not accompany such persons as are too hard on their tenants.' These restraints pressed particularly upon the aristocracy, who were expected to set an example in moral rectitude.

This body of doctrine was part of the wider concept of the superior virtues of the Country over the Court, the notion that in

some recent golden age landlords—and particularly aristocratic
landlords—had lived quietly in the countryside, dispensing charity
and good cheer and acting as kindly protectors of a loyal and
contented peasantry. The serpent in this Garden of Eden was the
Court, which lured landlords away from their tenants and involved
them in wasteful extravagance, thus making it psychologically
possible and financially necessary for them to squeeze the uttermost farthing out of their estates. There is no need to point out
that this theory involves an over-sanguine interpretation of late
medieval rural society—the Peasants' Revolt and Jack Cade's
rebellion are sufficient indicators of a different reality—but there
was some truth in the idea that the Early Tudor nobleman had
been paternalistic in his attitude towards his tenants, in return for
obedience, loyalty, and service.

Consider, for example, the assumptions that lie behind the
popular eulogy of that old-fashioned Elizabethan nobleman,
Henry 3rd Earl of Huntingdon

> His tenants that daily repaired to his house
> Was fed with his bacon, his beef, & his souse.
> Their rents were not raised, their fines were but small,
> And many poore tenants paid nothing at all.
> No groves he enclosed, nor felled no wood,
> No pastures he paled to do himself good.
> To commons and country he lived a good friend,
> And gave to the needy what God did him send.

No doubt the failure of the Elizabethan nobility to adjust the
receipts from land to the changing value of money was due in
large part to innate conservatism, laziness, inertia, and a failure to
grasp the long-term significance of inflation. But some of it must
surely be put down to the workings of this moral code which
made men feel that they had an obligation not to rock the boat.
How otherwise, indeed, are we to explain why the long series of
anti-depopulation Acts passed through a parliament of landlords
with such little difficulty, if such practices, though profitable, were
not also thought to be wicked? It is not surprising to find that
Henry Lord Berkeley died in an atmosphere of virtue and debt,
with a reputation as 'the best landlord that England had'. Evidence of noblemen and squires managing their estates on these
easy-going paternalist lines runs through to the eighteenth century

and beyond, and is a factor in slackening social tensions which economic historians ignore at their peril.

The question of landlord–tenant relations has been exhaustively discussed by Professor Tawney and others, but there is still room for a re-examination of the problem from the point of view of the landlord rather than that of the tenant. The most numerous group of tenants, though not necessarily the most important financially, consisted of those who held their estates by copy of court roll.

In the early seventeenth century the surveyor John Norden thought that most copyholders must originally have enjoyed fixed fines, but that as prices doubled and trebled in the early sixteenth century they were forced by landlords to agree to arbitrable fines, meaning that the fine was subject to negotiation at each change of tenant. The issue of entry fines was one of the two main causes of landlord–tenant friction in the sixteenth century, as landlords strove to obtain their fair share of the rising agricultural profits and tenants tried to take full advantage of their rights. The Court of Chancery became the arbiter in these disputes, and was always ready to support the tenants if they could prove their legal position. If they won their case, it meant that they were established in a position not very different from that of a freeholder, and that the lord was deprived of all but a tiny and diminishing fraction of the true value of his property. Even if they lost, however, things were still inconvenient for the lord, since he had to take his profit almost entirely in the form of entry fines.

Let us look at the Hampshire estates of the Earl of Southampton as surveyed in 1624. Only on one manor, Dogmersfield, were the fines of a fixed amount, an attempt by the Earl's officers to overthrow the tradition having been defeated in the Courts seven years before. Copyholders on all the other manors were subject to arbitrable fines, and as a result the survey revealed the following situation:

|  | Present rent | Potential value to the lord |
|---|---|---|
| Freeholders | £14 | £14 |
| Copyholders | £272 | £2,372 |
| Leaseholders | £1,582 | £2,815 |
| Total | £1,868 | £5,201 |

The Earl could hardly hope to obtain eight-ninths of the value of the copyhold estate from irregular fines, if only because the tenants would lack the foresight to accumulate capital over the years for such huge payments. It was therefore in the interest of the lord to turn copyholds into leaseholds, and so to bring the annual rent more nearly into line with true values and reduce the size of these occasional fines.

By brandishing the stick of arbitrable fines, the lord could often force copyholders to surrender their copies and take leases at higher rents and lower fines. By 1624 the Earl of Southampton had already converted five copyholds at Beaulieu, and all over the country the same process was at work. The rights and wrongs of the process of converting copyhold into leasehold are far from clear. Copyholders of inheritance with fixed fines were the fortunate beneficiaries of a legal accident, which thanks to price inflation transferred all but a fraction of the profits of their estate from the lord to themselves. It was natural for landlords to attack this new distribution of profits, natural for copyholders to take maximum advantage of their good fortune. Copyholders with arbitrable fines found themselves faced with demands for larger and larger capital sums to be raised at irregular intervals, and unless they held a copy of inheritance they were liable to be turned out unless they could pay. On the other hand the lord was certainly not getting his full due from the trivial rents and the erratic fines, and it was very much in his interests to shift to a leasehold system at higher rents.

Since demesne husbandry and copyholding were both shrinking, the major emphasis on any great estate was increasingly placed on the administration of leaseholds, a subject of some complexity. Every time a lord made a lease, he had to decide three things: what the estate was worth, how long a lease he was prepared to grant, and in what proportion he was going to divide the profit between the entry fine and the rent.

So long as prices were virtually static there was little demand for efficient surveys, since new lettings were mere slavish copies of the old. But in the sixteenth century two factors emerged to upset this stable pattern. The upheaval in landownership meant that there sprang up a host of new landlords anxious to discover just what it was they had acquired, and the rise in prices made it imperative to survey and value the property before each new letting in order to know what to charge. Consequently the surveyor changed from being primarily an antiquarian lawyer skilled in seeking out and describing complicated medieval tenures, and became in addition a geographical and geometrical technician as conversant with the plane table and trigonometry as with Coke upon Littleton. The new world of mathematics and instrument-making was called in to redress the balance for the old landlord.

The late sixteenth and early seventeenth centuries saw the making of a very large number of more or less accurate surveys, now measured by the latest techniques, and often accompanied by a 'plot' or detailed ground plan of the estate. The plot was a cherished document which would be of practical value for decades to come. In 1607 John Norden explained that 'a plot rightly drawn by true information describeth so the lively image of a manor and every branch and member of the same as the Lord sitting in his chair may see what he hath, where and how it lyeth, and in whose occupation every particular is, upon the sudden view'. The construction of accurate estate maps was made possible by the application of new mathematical expertise to data provided by new instruments. The pocket compass gave the cardinal points, the four-perch line, soon to be replaced by the iron link-chain, gave accurate linear measurements. By considerable labour it was possible by these means to make reasonably approximate assessments of area. In the early seventeenth century this improved but still clumsy method was superseded by triangulation, introduced as a result of geometrical theory, made practicable by the invention of the plane table and the theodolite, and made easy by the publication of John Napier's logarithm tables.

This intellectual and technological revolution—for it was no less—meant that by the beginning of the seventeenth century it was at last possible for the lord of many manors to keep a close check upon his agents and his agents upon the tenants. It was of even greater benefit to the noble owner of many properties than to the small gentleman who could ride over his estates in an afternoon. With the aid of accurate measurements of acreage and up-to-date valuations, it was possible to plan a leasing policy. Late-sixteenth century leases usually ran either for 21 years or 3 lives (the latter for technical reasons usually stated as 99 years or 3 consecutive lives, whichever was the shorter). In most of the north and in the south-west as far east as parts of Berkshire, leases were for lives, usually 3. All over the south and the Midlands, in Hertfordshire, Buckinghamshire, Bedfordshire, Essex,

Huntingdonshire and Northamptonshire, the 21-year lease seems to have been almost universal. The causes of these customs are unknown, but their origins go back to the late Middle Ages and therefore do not concern us here. What is important for our purposes is the extreme frequency of the lease for lives in the southwest, in contrast with the more flexible lease for years which prevailed over much of the Lowland Zone. It was a difference which by the mid-seventeenth century was to have important consequences upon the trend of landlord incomes in that area.

If the duration of the lease was governed to a considerabe extent by custom, so also was its character. Over the greater part of England in the late sixteenth century tenants held their farms under beneficial leases, and it is therefore vital to grasp the significance of this system. Under it a tenant paid a large cash fine, usually over a period of two years, and a low annual rental. In return he received a long lease, usually 21 years or 3 lives, which gave him fair security of tenure. In almost all cases the tenant was made responsible for upkeep, repairs, and hedging and ditching, though he might be allowed the use of timber from the hedgerows. There was usually a heavy penalty clause preventing him from ploughing up established pasture, and the more efficient landlords like the 2nd Earl of Salisbury demanded a guarantee that all the manure produced on the farm should be ploughed back into it, and that the fertility of the arable be preserved by allowing one year fallow in three.

There is some reason to suppose that fines did not begin to play an important part in most landlords' income until the early sixteenth century. The duration of leases seems to have increased at this period and fines were imposed to compensate landlords for the rise in the level of prices. There was clearly a strong sense of obligation not to tamper with ancient rents, just as there was on copyhold estates, and this obliged landlords to take their share of the growing profits of agriculture in the form of entry fines. As prices rose to ever greater heights, so did the importance of the fine relative to the rent. From the point of view of the landlord the principal advantage of the system was that it might enable him to raise large capital sums at short notice, by demanding large entry fines for re-leasing his lands, if necessary in reversion, if necessary for a long time to come, if necessary at a reduced annual rent. A landlord could thus raise immediate cash, the cost of the

operation being paid for in the form of loss of potential income in
the years to come.

Because the system was in effect a form of mortgage on the
future, part of the costs of the cash raised by a lord in fines was
passed on to his successors as a loss of rent. Each landlord was
thus strongly tempted to take his profit and let the heirs go hang,
as his father had done before him. If he shifted to rack-renting he
would almost certainly receive less in his own lifetime than he
would have done if he had stuck to large fines and small rents,
even though in the long run the financial advantage was enormous.
Like flogging in public schools, the beneficial lease was an institution in the perpetuation of which its former victims always
ended by acquiring a vested interest.

The tenant was even more strongly in favour of the beneficial
lease than the landlord. In so far as he was able to make the complicated calculations necessary, he would have realized that in the
long run he paid less in rents, fines, and hypothetical interest on
the fines, than he would have done if he had paid an annual rack-
rent. If he had managed to save up the money for the fine, the
system was absurdly advantageous to him. Although at this period
leases for years were still commonly allowed to run out before
renewal, leases for lives were very frequently granted in reversion,
thus giving the tenant very nearly absolute security of tenure,
which is always a most sensitive issue in landlord–tenant relations.

On any rational view, however, the defects of the system for both
sides outweighed the advantages. The tenant found his capital tied
up in what was the equivalent of a loan on mortgage to his landlord, and the land was thus starved of the capital needed for improvement and stocking. If the estate was held on lease for a life
or lives it was pure chance when it would expire, an uncertainty
which acted as a disincentive to long-term saving. This was a particularly serious matter since it was not yet possible to take out a
life-insurance policy. Even when the duration of the lease was a
fixed term of years there was no means of knowing what the lord
would demand for a fine, and therefore how much would have to
be saved.

On the other hand it is not difficult to understand why the
average tenant clung so tenaciously to the beneficial lease. Not
only did he pay less in aggregate, but the uncertainty of timing
and duration of the fines fitted in with his vision of life on earth.

When man is at the mercy of disease and the weather, in health today, crippled or dead tomorrow, gorged today and starved tomorrow, with money to burn today from the sale of a bumper crop, plunged into debt tomorrow because of harvest failure, the human condition is one of perpetual flux. The beneficial lease was just one more card in a large pack of jokers, and leaseholders and the customary tenants positively preferred a few years of misery and hardship while the fine was being paid, followed by a long period at a low rent, to the regular payment of a reasonable annual sum.

In 1608 the Earl of Shrewsbury tried to get his Staffordshire tenants to offer larger rents now in return for a reduction of fines in future, but the majority refused outright. The surveyor pointed out to them that they held their land on lease with fines running up to £80 'the which fines perhaps would undo or greatly hinder many of them, and especially of the poorer sort', but they replied that they 'had rather smart one year than every year'. The possibility that the sole beneficiary of the system would be the village usurer was one tenants preferred to ignore.

The disadvantages of the beneficial lease to the landlord were far more glaring. Irregular fluctuations of income made budgeting very difficult, and as normal credit machinery improved, it became less necessary to reserve the power to raise capital from the tenants. Loans from city financiers replaced fines for new leases. Moreover during the sixteenth century the ratio between fines and rents had been progressively getting out of hand. As prices rose, landlords who stuck to the convention of charging ancient rents found themselves having to take a larger and larger proportion of their income in irregular fines. In the west, where the tradition of maintaining old rent was hardest to break, on the eve of the Civil War landlords like the earls of Bath and Berkshire and lords Petre and St. John were getting a third or more of their income in the form of fines.

Even if the duration of the leases was not excessive and if reversions were avoided, the method of calculating fines was almost always defective. In the first place the assumptions made about the value of a life interest were seriously inaccurate. In the absence of actuarial statistics about expectation of life it was generally assumed that 1 life was the equivalent of 7 years, 2 lives of 14 years, and 3 lives of 21 years. This may perhaps have been true in the high mortality period of the fifteenth century, but it was certainly an underestimate by the late sixteenth century.

It was not till the second decade of the seventeenth century that landlords were provided with data by which they could tell at a glance what fine they ought to charge. By 1617 Lord Paget owned a book of 'Arithmetical questions touching annuities and leases', and in 1622 Thomas Clay published his *Briefe and Neccessary Tables for the Valuation of Leases, Annuities etc*. Before this they must have relied heavily on guesswork. The fine was worked out in terms of so many years' purchase of the difference between the annual rent and the annual value as revealed in a recent survey. Since the fine was in the nature of an advance, allowance had to be made for interest at the current rate, so that the higher the rate the smaller the fine. To take an example, if a property valued at £30 per annum is let at an annual rent of £10, the fine is a multiple of the residual value of £30—£10 = £20. For a new lease of 21 years, the fine at 10 per cent. interest works out at 8·2 years' value, or £164, and at 8 per cent. at 10 years' value, or £200. The reduction in the rate of interest from 10 per cent. to 8 per cent. in 1624 thus benefited the propertied classes in two ways; in fact it enabled them to borrow more cheaply and in theory it justified the imposition of larger fines for beneficial leases.

Even when these tables had been published, few landlords applied them strictly. It is not until the eve of the Civil War and later that there is evidence of landlords' charging the full rate to old tenants, the Earl of Bridgwater in the late 1630's, the Earl of Salisbury in the 1650's (and probably earlier), and the Duke of Somerset in the 1660's.

The interest content of a beneficial lease was very large. Let us assume that the rent charged on a lease was half its true value, which seems to have been an acceptable figure around the turn of the century, and that leases for 21 years were commonly being sold at about 7 years' purchase of the difference between the rent and the true value. Over 21 years the landlord therefore received in actual cash:

$$\tfrac{1}{2}+(\tfrac{7}{21}\times\tfrac{1}{2}) = \tfrac{2}{3} \text{ of the annual value of his property.}$$

In the long run the family was therefore sacrificing one-third of the annual value of the property in order to allow the current lord to borrow from his tenants on mortgage at a high rate of interest.

It would be a very long time before landlords became aware of the full implications of the system. The curtailment or abandonment of the beneficial lease depended firstly on the production of more sophisticated mathematical data which showed up the folly of the system, and secondly on the growth of credit facilities to provide an alternative source of ready cash in time of need. In the early seventeenth century both these desiderata were met, and it is therefore not surprising to find two processes in motion: a reduction in the duration of leases, and a rise in rents and a concurrent decline in the size of fines, leading in some cases to annual tenancies at rack-rents. On the basis of fragmentary evidence, it looks as if the shift to rack-rents on short leases was only really getting under way in the 1630's, although noble landlords had been increasing the rental element in their receipts for some decades before this.

Another way of increasing a landlord's income from the tenantry was to enforce the payment of every obsolete and obsolescent feudal due for which a legal case could be extracted from medieval records. This revival of fiscal feudalism in landlord–tenant relations on aristocratic estates is a product of that legal antiquarianism of the 1630's which lay behind Laud's attempts to restore the finances of the Church by delving into pre-Reformation rights to urban tithes, Charles's demands for distraint of knighthood, forest fines, and scutage, and Parliament's insistence on rights and privileges extracted from medieval rolls. The hunting down of ancient dues became a favourite occupation of some of the more scholarly minded aristocratic agents. On behalf of Lord Berkeley, John Smyth of Nibley took perverted pride in enforcing rights of wardship by actions of 'Ravishment del gard', levying an 'aid pur faire fitz chevaler, according to the statutes of 3 Ed I and 25 Ed III', and in claiming a composition in lieu of villein works not performed for over a hundred years. The profits were so trivial that they can hardly have been worth the labour involved in seeking them out and the irritation caused to the victims, but the process provides an interesting example of the way private landowners in the 1630's were turning to medieval precedents in order to increase their incomes.

The commonest ways of increasing landed income in the seventeenth century were undoubtedly to convert as much land as possible to leasehold; to employ the new techniques of surveying to have it accurately measured and plotted; to use the new mathematical tables to work out fines; to shorten the duration of leases; to go over increasingly to rack-rents; and to enforce the payment of obsolescent feudal dues. These were all ways of getting a larger share of the existing profits of agriculture from the tenantry. But it was also possible to go in for various forms of improvement which would not only alter the division of profits between tenant and landlord but would increase the gross agricultural output from which these profits were derived. Apart from fen-drainage, which is more in the nature of a large-scale entrepreneurial undertaking and is dealt with in the next chapter, the most obvious and most common form of direct improvement was inclosure, by which all surveyors were agreed that it was possible to increase the value of both arable and pasture land by 50 per cent. or more. Why this is so is not clear, but it is presumably a combination of better drainage by the ditches, more wind-breaks by the hedges, better stock control, reduction of time spent in travel from strip to strip, elimination of wasteful grass balks (in so far as they existed), and greater sense of personal responsibility where land was cultivated in severalty.

Few aristocratic landlords were guilty of the ruthless depopulating inclosures that so horrified contemporary moralists. Many put pressure on tenants to agree to a voluntary or semi-voluntary redistribution of holdings, so that they could consolidate and then enclose their demesne in the open fields and their share of the wastes and common. It was not too difficult for the lord, the rector, and the larger farmers to agree on a course of action which would be mutually profitable, though excessive rapacity over waste and common could do serious harm to the economy of the poorer cottagers. Once consolidated and inclosed, the demesne could be let off in blocks of 100 acres or so to substantial farmers from whom major increases of rent could be expected. Most great landlords of whom adequate records survive were carrying out such inclosures in the early seventeenth century.

So far as can be seen, this was almost the only kind of agricultural improvement for which noblemen were prepared to pay. Not that inclosures demanded all that much money anyway. When the huge 2,200-acre ranch at Brigstock was cut up into small closes by the 2nd Earl of Salisbury in 1635–9 it only cost him £380. To take one detailed example, 130 acres were surrounded with 30,000 quicksets for hedges together with 3 gates and 6 posts for a total expenditure of £16. 13s. When it was a matter of major reconstruction or of additions to a farmhouse, men like the 4th Earl of Pembroke and the 2nd Earl of Salisbury were usually prepared to make a compensatory reduction of the fine for a new lease. Apart from this, all other improvements were left to the tenants, the theory being that their leases were of sufficiently long duration to encourage them to carry them out on their own behalf.

## II. THE MOVEMENT OF LANDED INCOME

The most important—and the most difficult—questions have been left to the last. Did noblemen succeed in increasing their landed incomes to keep pace with the price revolution? Were they more or less successful than the gentry? Was there a period of slackness followed by a period of efficiency? Were puritan and parliamentary sympathizers more efficient and more ruthless than their Anglican and Royalist fellow-peers? It is very doubtful whether it will ever be possible to give categorical answers to these questions. The problem of changes in income is bedevilled by that arch-enemy of the economic historian, the beneficial lease. How is he to deal with a situation in which income is taken partly in fines and partly in rent, when the proportion of the one to the other varies from decade to decade and from lord to lord, when fines come in at wildly irregular intervals and are sometimes not recorded in the normal estate accounts? Rises in income may take place at very different times from one estate to another. Spectacular leaps occur when very long leases at old rents at last run out, and these may distort the general picture.

For evidence we are obliged to rely upon some very flimsy material: comparison of valuations and extents which may have been calculated on different bases; comparisons of rentals which may represent a widely varying proportion of the full annual receipts; comparisons of gross income in single years, which may not be representative of the average. Each has serious weaknesses, but if they all point in the same direction they may in aggregate make possible certain tentative deductions.

The evidence indicates that on most estates rents at least doubled between about 1590 and 1640. Since agricultural prices only rose by about a third this must have been an exceedingly prosperous period for the English landlord. It is surprising to find that there is very little evidence for more than a momentary pause in the upward rise in rents during and after the agricultural and commercial crisis of 1620–1. It looks very much as if the shrieks and groans of landlords which echoed in and out of Parliament at that time were out of all proportion to the pain that was being suffered. By and large, between 1590 and 1640 the greater English landlords were riding the crest of a wave which was powerful enough to carry along with it all but the most grotesquely incompetent or old-fashioned. The only qualification of this generalization is that in the south-western areas the strength of custom was sufficiently powerful to ensure the persistence of the three-life lease at old rent and large fines, which may well have prevented landlords with all or most of their property in that area from obtaining their full share of the feast.

Why the 1590's should have marked the turning-point on so many estates is not hard to fathom. The most important factor must have been the demographic explosion beginning about twenty years before, the cause of which is still obscure. There must have been a great mass of young men reaching manhood in the 1590's and pressing hard upon the available agricultural land. Landowners must have found themselves besieged by prospective tenants outbidding each other in their desperate search for a holding. Secondly, this was just the time when very many of the aristocracy found themselves in serious financial difficulties, and were therefore particularly anxious to increase their incomes. To this economic incentive on both sides may be added a number of less tangible factors. This decade saw the last of the age-old habit of regarding land not only as a source of money, but also as a means of obtaining military aid and outward signs of loyalty and esteem. The rapid rise in agricultural prices during this decade must have opened landlords' eyes to the necessity and justice of tampering with ancient customs in order to cope with the effects of inflation. The passage of time had at last dulled the fears aroused by the widespread peasants' revolt of 1549, and the moral effect of the militant preaching of the 'Commonwealthsmen' of that period on the subject of rack-renting, inclosing, and fine-raising landlords: it is no coincidence that the first formal relaxation of anti-inclosure legislation occurred, admittedly temporarily, at just this moment. In the 1590's many forces thus converged to break down the psychological blocks which for forty years had deterred many aristocratic landlords from tackling the problem of raising their share of agricultural profits.

It must be asked whether contemporaries were right to attribute particular ruthlessness in the handling of estate administration to those who were themselves in severe financial straits through over-consumption in London or at the Court; and whether Max Weber and his followers are correct in associating puritanism with the less agreeable manifestations of the capitalist ethic. Examination of the situation and opinions of those who defied the standard moral code demanding generous treatment of tenants tends to support both these assumptions. The individual peer who started to squeeze his tenants hard was usually forced to act by a crushing burden of debt. This debt *might* be the result of maintaining on inadequate resources the medieval traditions of generous hospitality in the country. Such was the experience of Sir Thomas Tresham and the 3rd Lord Vaux. It was much more likely, however, to be excesses at the Court which drove men to extremes: if George Earl of Cumberland restricted himself to squeezing the richer lessees, Henry Earl of Lincoln and Edward Lord Morley both got a bad reputation for their treatment of their tenantry; all three were attempting to recoup losses caused by a life of extravagance in London. No such excuse can be made for the 9th Earl of Northumberland, whose natural misanthropy was exacerbated by long imprisonment in the Tower, where he whiled away the time by extorting the last drop of profit from those northern tenants whom he knew he would never be allowed to see again.

It is noticeable that early Elizabethan Puritans like the 3rd Earl of Huntingdon and the 2nd Earl of Bedford were conservative landlords who did little to improve their estates or to squeeze their tenants. But in conformity with a hardening of attitudes towards the poor which some have detected among puritan thinkers and divines, we find that later on an abnormally high proportion of those with a record of severity were men of puritan sympathies. But casually collected impressions cannot provide very effective ammunition to use in the battle over the relationship of religion and the capitalist ethic and more specifically Puritanism and 'progressive' estate management, so called. To be convincing much more extensive data would have to be collected on a much more systematic basis.

In any case the thesis must not be pushed too far. A Puritan like the 1st Lord Montagu of Boughton was exceptionally hostile to the ethics of the acquisitive society: 'God hath made you a landlord of many tenants', he told his son; 'count that a greater blessing than if he had made you a master of ten thousand of sheep. . . . Travail not too much to be rich. . . . He that is greedy of gain troubleth his own soul.' It was in his insistence on frugality that he fully conformed to conventional puritan ideology. As Weber pointed out, two other elements in this ideology made a more potent contribution to nascent capitalism than any freeing of man's lust for profit from the trammels of moral restraint. The first was the stress on the moral virtue of hard work and the immorality of idleness. Living as we do in a modern industrial society in which almost everyone works for his living, it is very difficult to understand the significance of this doctrine. In the sixteenth century the rich and well-born were idle almost by definition, a huge labour force was absorbed in slothful and parasitic personal service, and the poor were as feckless and unreliable as they are in any society where under-employment is the norm, education non-existent, and security unknown. When the 1st Lord Spencer planted a wood on his estate at Althorp, he celebrated the occasion by setting up a stone inscribed 'Up and be doing and God will prosper'. He was expressing a sentiment of whose novelty and importance he was perhaps not altogether aware. The second doctrine was that of the virtue of thrift, of deliberate under-consumption for the sake of sobriety and the avoidance of debt. This ran deliberately counter to the prevailing aristocratic ethic of generosity and hospitality, and was a factor in capital accumulation which it is impossible to evaluate, but which cannot have been small. The adoption of this new scale of values helps to explain why the seventeenth century saw a great increase of capitalist activity without any very revolutionary change in sixteenth-century ideas about such things as the just price, usury, or landlord–tenant relations.

It has been suggested by Professor Tawney that the decline in the prosperity of the aristocracy relative to that of the squirearchy was in large measure due to differences in efficiency in estate management. The essential difference is between 'Court' and

'Country'. Men who live on the spot and devote themselves to the humdrum tasks of administration will obtain a higher economic return from their estates than those who are content to leave things to their officials, and devote themselves instead to the affairs of the Court or national politics, to the busy round of London society, to the pursuit of pretty girls or fallow deer. This is true regardless of the intelligence and knowledge—or lack of them—of the landlord, for 'the eye of the most ignorant owner operates upon his agents like witchcraft', as Lord Shelburne observed in the eighteenth century. The most conspicuously successful great landowners of the period—the 1st Lord Spencer, the 1st Lord Brudenell, the 9th Earl of Northumberland, and the 1st Earl of Devonshire—have left sufficient evidence in the form of letters, memoranda, marginalia, and suggestions on accounts, to prove that they all personally directed their own affairs.

Efficient management meant the operation of demesne estates, the conversion of copyholds, inclosure by agreement, taking in the waste, raising rents on new lettings, shortening terms of leases, switching from beneficial leases to rack-rents, changing lease-holders to tenants at will, all of which required not merely routine honesty and competence, but the power and will for radical decision-making. When things got desperate, even such easy-going spenders as the 3rd Earl of Cumberland and the 1st Earl of Bridgwater had to roll up their sleeves and negotiate in person with the tenants for bargains for new leases. Although one highly efficient landlord, the 2nd Earl of Salisbury, relied largely on the zeal of exceptionally capable servants, it is generally true that in this period of rapid change in the agricultural scene the personal attention of the landlord was of crucial importance.

Under these circumstances, it is easy to see that the smaller landlord living on his own estate and the larger landlord with nothing to do but to manage his properties were far more likely to prosper than the landlord, great or small, who was absorbed in public affairs or courtly pleasures and intrigues. This being so, one would expect to find that the country landlord usually ran his estate more efficiently than the courtier, and the evidence of the peerage, together with that accumulated by Miss Finch for Northamptonshire and Professor Simpson for East Anglia, would tend to confirm this view for the late sixteenth century. Since a far higher proportion of the peerage than of the squirearchy were at court, the peerage were on balance at a disadvantage. This was an important but rarely a crucial factor in governing the prosperity and decay of families, which was more commonly determined by other causes. Different expenditure patterns were more influential than different management policies, even in the late Elizabethan period when the premium on innovation was highest.

It was only for a relatively short period that the balance of advantage favoured the medium-size, personally directed estate against the vast rambling accumulation of properties owned by an indolent or preoccupied absentee. New surveying and mapping techniques and the growth of more systematic accounting methods gave great lords the same intimate sense of control of their estates as did the more direct knowledge of his every field possessed by the smaller gentleman; the general shift away from demesne farming lessened the need for personal attention. When the process was complete, when prices had levelled off and the landlord had become a rentier pure and simple, it could safely be said that 'a gentleman's account is a trifle to a merchant's—one hour or two in a week will do it'.

When that day came, the advantages of personal supervision on the spot which had been so significant in the late sixteenth century would substantially diminish, and the disadvantages of size and dispersal disappear altogether. As fewer nobles in proportion to total numbers obtained jobs at the Court and in national politics, as more squires found their pleasures in the City rather than the country, absentee landlordism in any case became more evenly diffused throughout the upper range of society and less markedly a characteristic of the aristocracy. The disadvantages in estate management under which the aristocracy laboured in the late sixteenth century were therefore only temporary and were caused by features peculiar to the age. When times changed in the seventeenth century and when they set their minds to the problem of more efficient management, the many who still owned thousands of acres of under-exploited land were able to make a striking recovery. The evidence of their success is writ large in the family archives of the early seventeenth century; some of the fruits of this success were harvested in the latter half of the century in the revival of aristocratic influence in national and local politics.

# VII

## BUSINESS

IF we are to get the business undertakings of the nobility in their true perspective we must look at them through the eyes of contemporaries. By singling out a single, and in terms of rewards a secondary, branch of the many-sided economic activities of the nobility, we give it an apparent significance which it certainly did not possess to those who took part in it. 'Où est le profit, là est l'honneur' was a fifteenth-century slogan, and aristocratic codes of behaviour have generally proved feeble defences against the temptations of really big money. But it is a mistake to be too cynical, and there is no doubt that Elizabethan and Early Stuart peers would have been astonished and disgusted to find themselves described as men of business. Their upbringing had taught them to despise 'base mechanick arts', to look down upon shopkeepers and merchants, and to regard as degrading direct participation in all but the commanding heights of economic enterprise. Their energies were primarily directed towards the ends of spending rather than to the means of getting, and it was with the various ways of conspicuous consumption that they preferred to busy themselves. When the money ran short, as it often did, the most obvious steps were—in this order—to marry an heiress, to seek some lucrative office or patent from the Crown, to exploit the untapped resources of their estates, or to invest in some speculative enterprise. Contemporaries regarded the last two alternatives as fundamentally similar in character and classed mining or urban development as branches of estate management— as indeed they are. It is because we wish to bring out the role of the aristocracy as entrepreneurs and risk-takers in a capitalist economy that we isolate these aspects of management from the more traditional ones of raising rents and fines and producing corn, cattle, and timber.

There was no legal obstacle to participation in most forms of large-scale business, although there were limits beyond which it was thought improper to go. It seems doubtful whether the 8th Lord Audley was expressing a real difficulty when he told Thomas

Cromwell in 1532 that 'because I am a baron I may not do as all
other merchants do', and asked for a 'licence to practise the feat of
merchandise as frankly and freely as other merchants hath'. There
is really no other evidence whatever to suggest that it was thought
improper to engage in foreign commerce or shipping. Nor was
there anything shabby in marketing the produce of one's estate,
and no one thought the less of the 1st Lord Spencer for going up
to London every year to sell his own wool and mutton. But buying
and selling on the internal market was petty huckstering, and
beneath the dignity of a gentleman. It was perfectly in order for
Sir Percival Willoughby to own ships and transport his coal down
the Trent to Lincolnshire, but disreputable to buy corn there to
provide a return freight for resale in Nottingham. To persuade
him to agree it was urged that 'your worship need not be seen
in the premises, but only your servants'. Similarly in industry
there was criticism when in the early 1560's James Lord Mountjoy
set up house on the site of his alum-mine and works at Canford in
Dorset and spent his time doing the daily chores of a factory
manager. As he admitted, 'some say that I vary from my vocation
far to become a miner'. But if a peer restricted himself to a director's role rather than a manager's, demesne farming, the opening-
up of mineral resources, the starting of metallurgical industries,
the development of urban property, participation in privateering,
trading, and colonizing companies, were all entirely respectable
activities.

Apart from their intelligence and initiative, such as it was, the
aristocracy contributed to business enterprise at two levels: in
terms of undeveloped capital assets which could be exploited or
used as security to raise capital; and in terms of influence at Court
for the obtaining of licences and monopolies. Upon their broad
acres there grew huge tracts of virgin woodlands and beneath
them lay untapped reserves of minerals. The woodlands were
often of poor quality and sited too far from centres of population
to be able to provide cheap fuel for domestic purposes. The only
hope of turning them to profitable use was to start up some
industry on the site which was a greedy consumer of charcoal.
Until it was discovered how to use coal for smelting, iron-works
perfectly fulfilled this requirement, and it is not surprising to find
the nobility taking the lead in iron-manufacture. At this period
landowners acted on the assumption that they were free to work

all the minerals on their own estates except precious metals and copper, and except in those areas where mining rights were regulated by ancient customs. It was on the demesnes and in the parks and woods of the nobility and greater gentry that mining could be carried out with least social disturbance, without interference in the agricultural life of the village and without the almost insuperable complications of land ownership in fields partitioned on the strip system.

Great landed estates were essential to economic enterprise in other ways than the supply of untapped raw materials; they could also be used to provide security for the borrowing of capital. Except in a few isolated instances, it is impossible to discover how much of the money for capital investment was raised by the peers themselves. Undoubtedly some of them financed out of current income industrial and mining ventures which required only limited capital. When more was needed, leases could be granted for low rents and large fines; woods could be cut down; rent-charges could be sold. But this was often not enough, and the financial contribution of the peerage was less the hard cash they had at their disposal than the harnessing for productive purposes of their enormous powers of borrowing. The money was mostly put up by the great London aldermen and merchant financiers on the security of aristocratic mortgages, statutes, and bonds. But even if a good deal of the capital came ultimately from the City, this does not lessen the significance of the role of the aristocracy. It was they, not the merchants, who were the risk-takers in new business ventures, and it was only by the pledge of aristocratic landed security that mercantile capital could be drawn into them.

The second important contribution of the nobility to entrepreneurial activity was their influence at the Court and in local society. The period before the Civil War was one of extensive economic controls. First imposed as a deliberate system of regulation of economic life for socially desirable ends, these degenerated fairly rapidly into a ramshackle bunch of monopoly patents, either sold for ready cash or more often given away as rewards to importunate courtiers. As a result the industrialist with a new technique, the prospector for rare minerals, the fen-drainer, the explorer, the colonizer, even the London speculative builder, all needed a friend at Court to obtain the necessary patent or licence. The natural intermediaries for these concessions were the peers, since their social position gave them ready access to the monarch and the Court, and their family ties linked them to many of the leading political figures. Moreover certain undertakings, particularly fen drainage, could only be launched with the active co-operation of the local authorities, and here the nobility were indispensable, thanks to their influence over all levels of county administration.

One result of this situation is that the peerage is nominally associated with almost all the major economic projects of the day. In fact, however, there is a wide variation in the degree of personal involvement. At one end of the scale is the 6th Lord Mountjoy's patent for alum, in the search for which he squandered half his life and much of the family fortune. At the other is the 1st Earl of Carlisle's grant of the Caribbean Islands in 1627, his lordship's interest in the settlement of the West Indies being largely confined to extracting a rake-off from the real undertakers. Consequently it is necessary to approach the problem of aristocratic participation in projects requiring a government patent with some care: mention in a patent may mean anything from full entrepreneurial initiative and investment to the receipt of a percentage in return for a little wire-pulling in high places.

## I. EXPLOITATION OF ESTATES

Since inclosure, conversion from arable to pasture, and the raising of rents all caused social unrest and might even lead to rioting, there was a strong incentive for landlords to turn instead to the extraction and refinement of mineral ores. The only snag was that the rights of landowners over these ores were far from clear. A test case of 1568 between the Queen and the 7th Earl of Northumberland established beyond question the already recognized fact that the Crown had no rights over non-metallic minerals, but it merely confused the situation over metals. The ancient principle that the Crown owned all mines of precious metals was reaffirmed, but with only three dissentients the judges also asserted that the Crown could claim possession of all ores that contained the slightest trace of gold or silver. It was on the basis of this judgement that the Queen staked her claim to the country's copper-mines, which were therefore excluded from the field of aristocratic enterprise. As Northumberland's counsel pointed out, the judgement theoretically meant that 'the Crown would have all the mines of base metal in the realm', for the greatest metallurgist of the day, Agricola, had recently observed that 'in nature generally there is some amount of gold in silver and in copper, and some silver in gold, copper, lead, and iron'.

Fearful of the massed opposition of landowners, neither Elizabeth nor James in fact made any attempt to use this legal judgement to extend the authority of the Mines Royal Company over any other metal than copper. This limited monopoly was rigidly enforced, however, and in 1602 the Company was preparing to start digging in the Earl of Derby's park at Knowsley, an intrusion upon his property which his lordship can hardly have regarded with favour. Characteristically enough, it was left to Charles I in 1638 to commit the folly of trying to extend royal claims to lead, offering the owner of a mine, Lord Herbert of Cherbury, 10 per cent. of the production as a gesture of royal good-will. The Later Stuarts were more cautious, and any remaining ambiguity was cleared up by an Act of Parliament passed in 1688–9, the *annus mirabilis* of the rights of property.

In 1540 the riches that lay buried beneath the English countryside had hardly begun to be exploited, and the next half-century saw a remarkable growth of mining activity. In this the nobility and greater gentry took the lead, sometimes on a very large scale, despite the frequent warnings issued by the prudent or the disappointed. 'Whosoever is a mineral man must of force be a hazard adventurer . . . as if he were a gamester playing at dice or such unlawful games', observed Bevis Bulmer, who spoke with personal feeling. In 1667 Stephen Primatt included in his pamphlet for investors the warning that 'mines of what nature or kind soever in England are for the most part very great casualties, and the profit of them very uncertain'.

The truth of these gloomy prognostications can easily be demonstrated from the history of the coal industry, in which many of the greater gentry of the north and midlands, the Lowthers of Westmorland, the Willoughbys, the Strelleys and Beaumonts of Nottinghamshire, plunged heavily and often disastrously. Of Huntingdon Beaumont and Sir John Ashburnham it was said that they 'wholly buried their estate in the said coal-mines'. One reason for these frequent disasters was that as mines became deeper draining costs rose rapidly, particularly in view of the failure of pumping technology to keep abreast of the growing depth of seams. 'Instead of draining the water, their pockets are drained.' The second factor that made large-scale investment in coal-mines so imprudent was the great difficulty in marketing from 'land-sale' areas. Transport costs were extremely expensive—three miles by land could add 60 per cent. to the pit-head price—and alternative fuels were available. The wastes and commons of the countryside were still covered with brushwood, while for the really poor there was always cow-dung, furze, or bean-haulms. As a result some areas such as Nottinghamshire seem to have witnessed a real crisis of over-production in the Early Stuart period, a crisis that brought hardship and even ruin on some of the leading gentry families in the county.

The peers were largely unaffected by these disasters since hardly any of them were large-scale coal operators. One of the few exceptions was John Lord Lumley: he leased out some small pits at Lumley and worked the bigger ones himself. These coals were said to be the best in the county and were assured a ready sale. Water transport down the River Wear gave access to the sea and the London market as well as to the Lord's salt pans at Hartlepool. And so in 1662 we find Lumley's heir leasing five pits but keeping six or more in the park in his own hands. His income included £600 a year from these directly operated pits, £300 a year in rents of the other mines, and £140 a year for way-leaves from other mine-owners. Most peers were content to sink one or two tiny shafts at shallow depths in order to supply the purely local needs of themselves and the tenantry, an operation which involved relatively small capital investment and which gave an equally modest return. A typical example of this kind of 'land-sale' mine is that worked by George Earl of Shrewsbury in his park at Sheffield. In the early 1580's it was producing about 1,200 tons of coal a year and yielding a net profit to the Earl of about £65.

In the sixteenth and seventeenth centuries the two principal centres of lead production were the Mendips and Derbyshire. In the Mendips extraction of the ore was left to the miners but smelting was originally in the hands of the four 'Lords Royal', the owners of the four chief manors in the district. Though the picture is obscure, it would seem that the interest of the land-owner in the development of the Mendip lead was generally restricted to the exaction of his 10 per cent. profit, and that the industry was largely financed by small peasants and Bristol merchants.

Things were rather different in Derbyshire. Although a good deal of the mining was in the hands of the miners themselves, the smelting works on which the industry depended were operated and financed by the local nobility and greater gentry. They bought the ore from the miners, processed it in their own mills, introduced new technological inventions, transported the finished product to the port of Hull, and negotiated for its sale to London merchants.

In 1564 the assay-master of the Mint, William Humfrey, and a German engineer from Saxony, Christopher Schütz, obtained a patent for refining and smelting lead. George Earl of Shrewsbury provided them with the necessary capital and helped them set up their works on his estate at Beauchief Abbey, just south of Sheffield, where they introduced an improved blast furnace and a new type of sieve for the ore, both of which marked a great technological advance. In the 1570's and 1580's the Earl of Shrewsbury may well have been the largest single lead smelter in the country, particularly after his marriage with Bess of Hardwick had put him in temporary possession of the estates of her former husbands, including Barlow near Chesterfield. By the turn of the century, when the works had passed under the control of Sir William Cavendish, future 1st Earl of Devonshire, the annual running expenses were between £1,300 and £3,000 and the annual production between 240 and 350 fodders. With evidence of these and several other large works it is clear that in the Derbyshire area the processing of lead ore was principally in the hands of the great landowners, who alone had the capital to set up the works, the ready cash to pay for the high overhead costs, and the woods to supply the necessary fuel.

Ironstone is to be found in many parts of England, particularly in the Weald, the west midlands, and in Yorkshire. English iron production increased rapidly during the Elizabethan period, owing partly to increased demand, and partly to the introduction of the water-powered blast furnace and hammer. In this expansion the nobility and the leading gentry played the decisive part, the bulk of English production at any given time being in the hands of the great country families.

The chief incentive to the great landowner to set up an ironworks was the prospect of turning his woods into a source of revenue. But lust for quick profits brought Nemesis in its train, since the consumption of fuel by these early blast furnaces was very high indeed, about 16 to 20 cords, or 2,100 to 2,500 cubic feet of wood, per ton of bar iron. As the rocketing price of wood amply proves, a fuel crisis undoubtedly developed in the early seventeenth century, the explanation of which lies in the combination of very high transport costs and improvident cutting policies. It was not until the third decade of the seventeenth century that landowners began to crop their woods in a far-sighted and rational manner. Before this they had usually been content to take high short-term profits from the ironworks at the cost of destroying the adjacent woods.

Although over half the production of iron was in the hands of the upper gentry, the peers were both the pioneers of technological innovation and among the largest individual producers of whom we have record. In the Sussex Weald one of the first and probably the largest works, including an ordnance factory, was set up by the 3rd Duke of Norfolk in the early 1540's, and was greatly expanded by Lord Seymour of Sudeley in the late 1540's, when annual production was well over 200 tons. In 1549 the value of the stock was over £2,000 and more than fifty workmen were employed, as well as large numbers of wood-cutters. These works were designed to consume the Duke's woods in Worth Forest and on the demesne of Sheffield.

The second main iron-working region was the north, particularly Yorkshire. Here, so far as we know, the lead was again taken by the peerage. Among the few Elizabethan works of which we have record are the two furnaces and a forge of the Talbots, earls of Shrewsbury, in the Sheffield area, which were set up by 1566 and were producing between 60 and 160 tons of bar iron a year in 1591 3; the furnace and forge of the Manners, earls of Rutland, at Rievaulx, which were producing 160 tons of bar iron in 1602; and those of the Cavendishes in Derbyshire, which were producing between 100 and 180 tons a year between 1598 and 1601.

In the early seventeenth century the west midlands, the Forest of Dean, and South Wales overtook the Weald and developed into the most important centre of the industry in the country. In Shropshire Robert Dudley, Earl of Leicester, was leasing out very large works at Cleobury Mortimer in the 1570's and 1580's, and the 2nd Earl of Essex owned furnaces and forges at three different sites in the 1590's. George Earl of Shrewsbury built a furnace at Shifnal in 1564, and another at Whitchurch near Goodrich before 1575, which with their attendant forges were producing about 170 tons of bar iron a year in 1591–3.

The surviving accounts suggest that the nobility's influence on the industry passed through two phases. In the first, which lasted well into the Elizabethan period, they took the lead in starting up works, in introducing the new blast-furnace technique, and in finding the capital. At this period works were usually kept in hand, the day-to-day running being entrusted to a manager and the profits paid directly to the lord. But after the initial excitement of launching the new enterprise had evaporated, the great nobles tended to get bored with the responsibility of operating the works directly with a manager, became reluctant to risk the fluctuating hazards of the market, and preferred to lease out their works to a contractor. A further incentive to leasing was provided by the fact—or probability—that by the early seventeenth century the heroic age of the industry was at an end and that both production and profits were increasing only slowly, if at all. Under these circumstances there was no longer any obvious advantage in direct management. Consequently in the Weald, where the expansionist phase ceased thirty years earlier than elsewhere, we find that nearly all the nobility had leased out their works by 1574.

If to most of the nobility the profits of ironworks were of minor financial significance, there were a few in whose calculations they played a very important part indeed. These cases only occurred when and where it was possible to escape from inelastic local markets and to find new and expanding outlets. For example, large-scale production took place in the west midlands in order to supply the nailers of Staffordshire and Birmingham, and in southwest Yorkshire to feed the cutlery industry at Sheffield. Elsewhere, for example in Ireland or at Rievaulx, increased production depended on opening up a water-route for transport of iron to the great London market. Under the spur of such opportunities a number of peers were tempted into expanding the scale of their enterprises, though in most of these cases this involved cutting down their woods faster than they could be replaced by natural growth. The result was temporary or permanent local deforestation, a rise in fuel transport costs, and the necessity of buying wood from others at the enhanced market price, with serious consequences on both output and the profit margin. The classic example of this is the case of the 1st Lord Paget, who took to large-scale development of the iron industry on his Staffordshire estate after his loss of office in 1558. By the late 1560's he and his son had erected two furnaces and three forges and ten years later they were producing up to 330 tons of bar iron a year. But the 2nd Lord was buying wood by 1581, further reckless exploitation by Sir Fulke Greville finally exhausted local fuel supplies, and the industry in the area then collapsed and moved to Birmingham.

Although the possession by the nobility of large tracts of woodlands put them in a very favourable position when the expansion of the English iron industry began, they must be given the credit for taking full advantage of the opportunity. Peers and leading gentry were responsible for and took the profits from the bulk of the national output, and for many years the peers themselves were the technical pacemakers and largest individual producers in the industry. Sixteen of the Elizabethan peers—that is 22 per cent.—and seven of the Early Stuart creations built, operated, or leased ironworks during this period, and for a few of them over short periods the profits provided a very important part of their revenues.

The need to find a market for their output induced some of the leading iron-manufacturing families to experiment with novel technological processes. In 1565 Sir Henry Sydney, in partnership with his receiver-general and a London merchant, took the initiative in bringing over fifty-five Flemish technicians to set up forges for making steel in the Abbey at Robertsbridge in Sussex, and and at Boxhurst in Kent, the ore being sent by sea from the Glamorgan estates. Though the enterprise was ruined within eight years by competition from Baltic imports, it is significant as the second English experiment in steel manufacture. In an undated letter, probably of the early 1570's, one of his agents advised George Earl of Shrewsbury to erect a steelworks to satisfy the very high demand for the expanding cutlery trade of Sheffield. Shrewsbury took the advice and built the third known English plant, which by the 1590's was producing between 30 and 45 tons a year, showing a cash profit of between £200 and £400 a year.

In the early seventeenth century a number of inventors

developed the cementation process of steel-making in a reverberatory furnace and in 1626 a fourteen-year patent was granted to one
Thomas Letsome, who claimed to have perfected the technique
thanks to the use of the money and ironworks of Richard Lord
Dacre of the South. It was the 5th Lord Dudley who pioneered
the first experiments with a reverberatory furnace using coal for
smelting, and one of the earliest recorded English slitting mills,
certainly the earliest in the midlands, was that attached to the
4th Lord Paget's forge at Bromley in 1622. In 1623 the 3rd Earl
of Southampton spent £1,000 in setting up alongside his twenty-
year-old Titchfield ironworks the first plate mill for tin-plate in
England, going into partnership with a London girdler in order
to stock it. No doubt the idea of introducing this new technique
into England came from the girdler, but the Earl was responsible
for putting up the capital and launching the venture, for which he
was to receive 50 per cent. of the profits. Thus nearly every
technological innovation in the smelting and further processing
of iron and steel was financed and operated in the first instance,
not by City merchants or *nouveau riche* gentry, but by established
aristocratic families.

It is significant that most of the evidence for mining and industrial enterprise comes from the late sixteenth century. After
about 1600 interest in these fields undoubtedly slackened, owing
largely, no doubt, to the frequently disappointing results. In any
case there had now emerged two new and much more successful
ways of improving revenue : fen drainage and urban development
in London.

In the fifteen years before the Civil Wars partially and temporarily successful attempts were made to drain over half a million
acres in Yorkshire, Lincolnshire, and East Anglia. This gigantic
operation, in which well over £400,000 were invested, was first
begun in the Hatfield Level. It was financed principally by Dutch
merchants, strongly supported by the huge fluid resources of that
successful merchant the 1st Viscount Bayning, whose executors
lent Vermuyden some £25,000 secured on a mortgage of the land
to be drained.

The greatest undertaking of all, however, was the draining of
the 307,000 acres of the Great Level. After a good deal of negotiation and competition, the contract for the operation was awarded
to a syndicate headed and organized by the 4th Earl of Bedford.

The family had a tradition of fen drainage, for in 1590 his father Sir William Russell, future Lord Thornhaugh, had brought over three Dutch experts to survey and estimate costs for draining his property at Thorney. In the enterprise of the 1630's Bedford was no mere titled figurehead but the active leader of the syndicate and the holder of three of the twenty shares. Since the total cost was said to have been £100,000, this means that the Earl's investment was £15,000. Other shareholders included the Earl of Bolingbroke, Lord Gorges, and Lord Maltravers, prominent officials like Sir Robert Heath, and substantial landowners like Sir Miles Sandys and Sir Thomas Teringham. The Earl of Bedford was awarded 12,000 acres for his share and by 1640 the Thorney estate was peopled with French and Dutch immigrants whom he had settled there, and for whom he had built a church. In 1641 the receipts from Thorney were about £1,000 and in the two years 1660–2 they had risen to about £5,000 a year. Though part of this may be due to abnormal fines, in these two years the former fens were producing one-third of the Earl's gross landed income.

The particular prominence of the nobility in fen-drainage schemes of the 1630's is due to the convergence of all their assets. As very large landowners in the flooded area, they stood to gain most from draining, particularly if directed by themselves (for example, it was alleged that Lindsey had taken care to make his own land fit for arable while that of the others in the drained area was still only fit for rough pasture); their great local influence was essential in order to give a lead to the gentry and to bring force to bear on the riotous fen-dwellers, while their social position made them the most suitable agents for negotiating for a concession from the Crown. And lastly they could use their estates as security to raise money for investment in these distinctly risky undertakings. The Earl of Bedford's heavy debts at his death in 1641 prove that he was financing part of his operations on credit, and the 2nd Earl of Portland certainly mortgaged his two Whittlesey manors for £10,000 to the great court physician Sir Theodore Mayerne in order to raise money to drain his 4,000 acres of marsh in Whittlesey Fen in the Great Level. Like so many other peers, Portland took the risk, but got his capital from London.

These politically hazardous and expensive projects of fen drainage were far less attractive than the glorious certainties of property development in London. At the Dissolution of the

Monasteries much of the area between the City and Westminster
had fallen into the hands of the Crown, but with supreme lack of
foresight it was all given away or sold in the next thirty years,
mostly to the nobility and greater gentry. By 1600 the rapid growth
on the one hand of Westminster as an administrative centre, the
seat of the Court and of the law courts, and on the other of the
City of London as a centre of conspicuous consumption, made
the whole of the intervening area ripe for development and stimulated demand for high-class residential housing conveniently
situated near the Inns of Court and the shops on the one hand,
and the Palace and Westminster Hall on the other.

Since the strip between the Strand and the Thames was for the
most part occupied by aristocratic palaces, development mainly
took place in the area bounded to the north by Holborn and to the
south by the Strand, and stretching between Saint Martin's Lane
and Chancery Lane. The greater part of this enclave was now
owned by the nobility, and it was to their energy and initiative
that its rapid and sensible development was due.

Though there were some notable exceptions, noblemen generally preferred to avoid investing their own capital in this development. The usual policy was to survey the property, divide it into
lots, and let it out on thirty-one-year building leases. At the end
of the thirty-one years the fully developed property reverted to
the landlord, who then re-let on short leases with fines and at
high rents. By this means the landlord controlled and directed
the development of his property, but the capital was supplied
either by the individual tenant or by a speculative builder who
took the lease of a block and built to sublet. The cost to the landlord was the postponement for a generation of the full economic
return. Thus in 1608–10 the 1st Earl of Salisbury bought for less
than £500 some 9 acres of land running up the west side of St.
Martin's Lane as far as the future Newport Street. The strip was at
once divided up and let on thirty-one-year leases at a rent of 1s.
a foot frontage, with obligation on the tenant to build. At this
stage the tenants were left free to build as they liked, the only
restrictions being against setting up any trade or occupation or
using the buildings as inns or alehouses. When these building
leases ran out in 1642, rents jumped to £750 a year and heavy
fines were imposed for new leases of houses on what was now
the fashionable side of a very fashionable street.

There were a few striking exceptions to this pattern of entre-preneurial initiative without capital expenditure, of which a project of the 4th Earl of Bedford was one of the most adven-turous. As early as 1612 the 3rd Earl had begun developing his Long Acre property, so that by 1618 his London rental was already over £500 a year. But it was not until 1631 that the 4th Earl embarked on the major venture of the Covent Garden piazza. Under pressure from Charles I he agreed to plan the whole as an imposing architectural unit forming three sides of a square. The buildings and the church were designed by Inigo Jones and Isaac de Caux, and formed one of the principal sights of London. Accounts survive for one block of residential houses and for the church. On this basis one may estimate with reasonable certainty that the whole undertaking cost the Earl rather over £28,000. As a result of this activity the 5th Earl's London rental rose to over £1,300 a year by 1652, to which must be added substantial receipts from fines, which in two exceptional years 1660–2 amounted to no less than £5,700. By the Restoration the Earl must have been drawing well over £2,000 a year from his Covent Garden and Long Acre property.

Smaller development projects were almost certainly financed by large contractors or small builders on building leases, and no doubt in many cases little or no initiative came from the land-owner, who merely allowed others to develop his estates. It is clear, however, that the largest and most architecturally ambitious projects were the result of entrepreneurial initiative and often personal investment by the noblemen themselves. The role of the aristocrat in the development of London in the early seventeenth century was at least as important as it was after the Restoration and in the eighteenth century.

## II. INVESTMENT

So far we have discussed entrepreneurial exploitation of aristo-cratic estates. Many peers were not content with the vigorous cultivation of their own garden and looked elsewhere for an outlet for their surplus energies. Aristocratic investment at sea was no new development, for several of the late medieval nobility had been shipowners. These noblemen had no use for the safe bet, the steady return. Their ships were not employed on the regular trade routes of Europe, but were sent out over the uncharted oceans in pursuit of more spectacular, and sometimes chimerical, objectives. Before 1585 they were interested in deep-sea fishing, exploration, and the development of new trade routes. George Earl of Shrewsbury owned the *Bark Talbot* at least as early as 1574, and her only directly commercial voyages of which we have record are two trips to Newfoundland, presumably in search of cod. Robert Dudley, Earl of Leicester, owned the 400-ton *Galleon Leicester*, which was Fenton's flagship in the abortive East Indies voyage of 1582, sailed on the West Indies expedition under Drake in 1585, and fought against the Armada in 1588. On the earl's death in the same year she was officially valued at £1,500.

With the outbreak of open war with Spain in 1585 aristocratic interest concentrated upon the more exciting, but sometimes equally unprofitable, pursuit of oceanic privateering. Most of these privateering ventures were financed and directed by rich London merchants like Sir John Watts and some lesser west-country merchants, but the nobility also took a prominent part in them. The merchants were content with minor depredations on Spanish shipping from Brazil and the West Indies, ensuring a modest but regular profit; the noblemen preferred large-scale operations which were semi-military in character and carried a high degree of risk. Their undertakings were, for once, over-capitalized.

Foremost among aristocratic privateers was the 3rd Earl of Cumberland, who organized no fewer than eleven voyages between 1586 and 1598, in six of which he went to sea in person. His motives were mixed. According to his wife he lived the extravagant but unrewarding life of an Elizabethan courtier 'till we had wasted our land and substance, [when] in hope of better fortune of the sea than we had of the land, he ventur'd many thousands, which we saw come empty home'. Her emphasis is on the hope of gain, which was undoubtedly a powerful influence. But the repeated exposure of his person to the dangers and miseries of life in an Elizabethan warship suggests that there were other incentives as well. As Thomas Fuller delicately put it, 'his fleet may be said to be bound for no other harbour but the port of honour, though touching at the port of profit in passage thereunto'. There can be little doubt that Cumberland was partly inspired by the same lust for adventure that made him the best

jousted at court tournaments and a somewhat indiscriminate pur-
suer of women. Behind his desire to strike a blow against Spain
lay ambition to bring glory to his name, a desire more easily
achieved than that of financial gain. In the end he alleged that he
had spent £100,000 on his voyages, to pay for which he was
obliged to speed up the sale of his estate. He had, he said, 'thrown
his land into the sea'. Cumberland was by far the most prominent
noble shipowner of the late 1580's and 1590's, but he was not the
only one. The activities of the others were on a less heroic scale,
and a few actually made a profit on their ventures. There is plenty
of evidence that among the landowning classes the most active
participation in privateering came not from the 'mere' gentry, as
has recently been suggested, but from the peers and courtiers.
Those who tried, with varying success, to profit from war and
privateering during the 1590's were not the 'party of the excluded'
but the 'party of office'.

One of the most spectacular developments of the early Elizabethan period was the state-supported introduction into England
of new industrial and mining techniques from abroad. In both
the main pioneering companies, The Mines Royal and Mineral
and Battery, the Court peerage played a prominent role, and it was
thanks to the encouragement and initiative of Sir William Cecil,
later Lord Burghley, and the Earls of Leicester and Pembroke
that they were launched at all. Neither these nor other more fanci-
ful projects were profitable and the more prosaic development
of ironworks and coal-mines was probably of greater importance
to the national economy. On the other hand they created an
atmosphere of industrial experiment and innovation, encouraged
the prospecting for minerals, introduced foreign technicians, and
provided England with a brass and copper industry.

Precisely the same handful of court peers and privy councillors
played an important part in Elizabethan maritime enterprise.
Their attention had probably been drawn to this field by the
lucrative trading privileges with which the early Tudors had
occasionally rewarded influential courtiers. The degree of aristocratic backing varied widely according to the type of undertaking.
Purely commercial ventures, even novel experiments like the
Muscovy Company or John Hawkins's slaving expeditions to the
Caribbean, were financed and directed by merchants, though not
without some stiffening from the Court. A rather different mixture

of Court and City lay behind the Barbary Company, which was
formed in 1585. This appears to have been an organization imposed on the merchants trading to Barbary, partly to allow the
Earl of Leicester to enforce a monopoly of the export of metals to
and the import of saltpetre from Morocco, and partly to make
the merchants pay for a resident ambassador, whose expenses
would otherwise have fallen on the Queen. Leicester's venture
turned out badly, and he must have lost the whole of his £3,000
investment. But there is evidence that he had been dabbling in the
Moroccan trade in co-operation with a group of merchants at least
since 1581, and the Barbary merchants were obliged to pay him
£1,000 for his unwanted services in foisting a company on them,
so that his net losses may not have been as large as they appear.
From the merchants' point of view, the episode was a salutary
warning of what to expect from co-operation with a none-too-
scrupulous court favourite.

In contrast to these mixed aristocratic and mercantile enterprises, some attempts to reach the East were almost wholly
dependent on the Court. Drake's circumnavigation was largely
financed by the Queen, Leicester, and Hatton, though Burghley
and the rest of the more responsible ministers would have nothing
to do with it. For the planned follow-up commanded by Fenton
in 1581 about 70 per cent. of the £7,000 that was raised came from
the Court group, including five earls and three barons.

An examination of Elizabethan attempts at colonization shows
the same pattern. The first voyage to Guiana in 1584 was financed
and led by Robert Dudley, the illegitimate son and putative heir
of the Earl of Leicester, while Ralegh's voyage the next year was
heavily backed by the Cecils. It was only the less politically hazardous attempts to settle the North American continent which could
attract a wider range of interests. The more serious colonizing
projects of Gilbert in the 1580's were boycotted by the London
merchants, and had to be financed partly by the Court group led
by the Earls of Leicester, Warwick, and Sussex and Lords North
and Burghley, partly by a syndicate of small merchants of Southampton and Exeter, and partly by catholic gentry hoping to found
a religious asylum overseas. It is interesting to note that without
the aid of the great London merchants even this wide support was
inadequate to float the venture, which remained seriously under-
capitalized.

It is clear that Elizabethan maritime ventures sprang from the initiative and financial backing of two very restricted social groups: the great merchants of London (and to a small extent the west country) and the peers and leading courtiers. The relative importance of the two groups varied widely in different ventures, but almost invariably a good deal of the initiative, and nominally of the money, came from the second. A systematic study of the evidence would suggest that the riskier the venture the more important was the role of the Court and peerage. Thus George Best explained that Frobisher 'perceiving that hardly was he harkened unto of the merchants, which never regard virtue without sure, certain, and present gains, he repaired to the court', where he was taken up by the Earl of Warwick.

In the Early Stuart period the pattern was rather different. By now the wealth of the London merchants was dwarfing that of all but the richest peers and officials, their self-confidence and willingness to take risks were increasing, and the joint-stock company provided machinery to harness this latent power. The tentative and largely unsuccessful experiments of Elizabethan peers and courtiers were taken up again and put on a sound business footing by such huge concerns as the East India and the Virginia Companies. Although in the Virginia Company the country gentry appear for the first time as a significant group in maritime investment, there can be no doubt that the aristocracy was still the most active section among the landed classes. Well over a third of the total peerage invested in the company at any one time, and one, the 12th Lord De La Warr, took a keen personal interest in this colonial venture and in fact died on a voyage to Virginia.

Those joint-stock enterprises of the early seventeenth century which had a more exclusively aristocratic composition fall into two groups, supported respectively by the Court and by the opposition. An example of the first is the Council of the New England Company, which was formed of forty 'persons of honour and gentlemen of blood', headed by great court figures like Buckingham, Lennox, Hamilton, Arundel, and Holderness. Efforts to attract merchant investors failed, and as a result the venture was under-capitalized and was wound up in 1635, having achieved very little other than the partition of the land allotted to it.

In contrast with these court projects are the companies directed and supported by the puritan opposition. The Massachusetts Bay

Company was sponsored in 1629 by the 4th Earl of Lincoln to assist the emigration of the Godly. The initiative and a fifth of the first capital of the Providence Island Company came from puritan peers, and the remainder from the gentry. It admittedly included a courtier, the Earl of Holland, but he came from a puritan family and was drawn in to provide useful contacts in the right places. The real initiative, and as time went on more and more of the capital, came from the Earls of Warwick and Lincoln, Viscount Mandeville, and Lords Brooke, Grey of Groby, and Saye and Sele. Spurred on by the stimulus of religious enthusiasm, these peers were more zealous in administration and more prompt with their subscriptions than the courtiers, although the results were hardly commensurate with the effort. Similarly it was his Catholic faith, not hopes of profit, that drove Lord Baltimore to attempt a settlement first in Newfoundland and then in Maryland.

What conclusions can be drawn from this examination of noble participation in business? On the personal plane the activity of some individuals was astonishing in its range. In the Elizabethan period the most active entrepreneur in the country was not some busy merchant or thrusting member of the new gentry, but a peer of ancient stock, George Talbot, 9th Earl of Shrewsbury. It was almost certainly of him that Bacon was thinking when he wrote: 'I knew a nobleman of England that had the greatest audits of any man in my time, a great grazier, a great sheep-master, a great timber-man, a great collier, a great corn-master, a great lead-man, and so of iron, and a number of the like points of husbandry; so as the earth seemed a sea to him in respect of the perpetual importation.'

In addition to all this Shrewsbury was an active investor in trading and exploring ventures, with a share in the Muscovy Company voyage in 1574, in Fenton's attempt to reach the East Indies in 1582, and Carleill's colonizing project of 1583. The nearest rival to Shrewsbury in the range of his operations was Robert Dudley, Earl of Leicester, and yet the Earl of Warwick and Lord Burghley were not far behind him.

In the Early Stuart period there is equally impressive evidence of a wide range of activity. To give but one example: the 3rd Earl of Southampton started a new ironworks, financed a tin-plate mill, developed his London property in Holborn and Bloomsbury, sponsored the first voyage that led to the foundation of the Virginia Company, of which he was a leading member, belonged to the East India and New England Companies, and backed Hudson's exploration of the North-West Passage; his son was the prime mover in a scheme to colonize Mauritius. It would, I believe, be impossible to draw up a list of City merchants or country gentry with such a wide range of interests.

The effect on aristocratic finances of this extraordinary activity was very varied. Many lost heavily, especially during the Elizabethan period. The big gains were derived from the exploitation of the resources of private estates, although those who were foolish enough to indulge in large-scale coal-mining experiments were liable to suffer losses. Ironworks were always profitable, sometimes and for short periods playing a really important part in the finances of certain peers, though the returns tended to diminish as local fuel resources became scarce. On the whole, however, industry was not the road to great riches. Only one man, the tinmaster Lord Robartes, achieved his wealth and thus his title mainly as a result of industry, and even he was perhaps as much dependent on the shrewd investment of his tin profits in money-lending.

The really startling and permanent increases in revenue were achieved by the handful of peers who took advantage of the phenomenal growth of London and profited by the draining of the fens. By the 1640's nine earls were drawing over £1,000 a year from their London property, and by the 1660's about half the Earl of Bedford's landed income was coming from London and the fens. Beneficiaries on anything approaching this scale form a minority, though a significant one; if they gained at all, peers more commonly gained hundreds of pounds rather than thousands as a result of their efforts.

The profits to the aristocracy of joint-stock investments were rarely of any real importance. Though many were ready enough with their money, the amount involved tended to be small in comparison with the total resources of the individual and the potential profit was consequently limited. Moreover, the cautious tended to avoid such investment altogether, preferring to follow the advice offered by his brother to the 1st Lord Montagu when the latter was contemplating buying East India Company stock: 'Your money in sheep rather than ships I think is the better adventure.' A man as calculating and successful as Sir Edward Coke openly boasted as evidence to his sagacity 'that he had never cast his penny into the water'.

The extent to which the peerage was involved in these business activities is a question which can only be answered in statistical terms. If we treat the Blounts as a single unit, there were 158 peerage families extant between 1 January 1560 and 31 December 1639. Of these, 25 per cent. are known to have profited by mining or industrial operations on their estates, 9 per cent. to have taken part in fen-drainage, 15 per cent. to have owned and promoted building in London. On the investment side, 14 per cent. were shipowners, and 63 per cent. put money into trading, colonial, or industrial concerns. Three out of every four families were engaged in one or other of these activities. The figures are of varying significance. Obviously only those who happened to own or acquire property in the appropriate areas could take part in iron- or lead- or coal-mining, in fen-drainage or in urban building round London. So many non-economic factors affected joint-stock investment, and so much of it was casual, indeed trivial, in character that it would be ridiculous to regard this figure as a measure of genuine business enterprise.

It is important not to mistake the significance of this aristocratic contribution to economic growth. The only industry in which the role of the peerage was quantitatively very impressive was iron-manufacture. To Dr. Shubert's list of some 132 blast-furnaces erected before 1642, there may be added another four to make a total of 136, 38 per cent. of which were built by, owned by, or operated under lease from members of the titular aristocracy. The peerage were responsible for only a very small proportion of the total output of coal, and their share in the lead-smelting industry was significant rather than important. Though very important in privateering, their share of English shipping was quantitatively negligible compared with that of the merchants. Although there is too wide a diversity in joint-stock investment to allow any summary generalization, there is no doubt that even in the Elizabethan period the sum total of aristocratic capital subscribed must always have been inferior to that of the merchant community.

The role of the aristocracy in acting as a stimulus to economic growth is not to be found in these quantitative calculations. It only emerges from an examination of the quality of their activities, their nature, and their timing. It was they, rather than the merchants, who were the risk-takers, the frontiersmen, the pioneers in technological and geographical advance, the reason being that their motives were not exclusively financial. The desire for gain was of course never absent, but it would be wrong to suppose that it was in all cases the only, or even the primary, incentive. When the strongly Protestant James Lord Mountjoy said that he tried to develop native supplies of alum in order to retrieve his fortunes and to harm the Pope, there is no reason to assume that the second explanation was pure hypocrisy. When Burghley and Leicester invested and lost considerable sums in the Mines Royal and Mineral and Battery Companies, there is no reason to doubt that they were in part inspired by a patriotic wish to encourage English industrial self-sufficiency, as well as by hopes of large profits. The support given by Leicester, Hatton, and Walsingham to Drake's predatory exploits was at least as much due to the desire to strike a blow against Spain as to hopes of rich booty. Again many of the joint-stock ventures of the Early Stuart period were either gestures of loyalty by courtiers to enterprises fostered by the Crown, or were controlled and backed for their own purposes by the leaders of the Country party. Warwick and Southampton dreamed of reviving the Elizabethan anti-Spanish policy; Lincoln and Saye and Sele were anxious to find a refuge abroad for Puritans threatened by the Laudian Church; Baltimore was seeking a similar haven for Catholics.

The desire to acquire a larger income with which to maintain an ever more lavish style of living was obviously behind the development by the nobility of the resources of their own estates such as the opening up of mines and industries, urban building, and fen-drainage. Even here, however, the issue is not a simple one. Most peers personally promoted and directed the first stages of an enterprise, and then once it was established retired into the passive role of rentier. This practice was largely dictated by the difficulty of finding anyone to bear the initial risks; but may it not also be evidence that noblemen were attracted by the excitement of a new undertaking, only to get bored as soon as the novelty wore off?

Even the more straightforward joint-stock investments cannot automatically be treated as products of hard-headed capitalist calculation. They are better regarded as a natural extension of the taste for gambling which was just now absorbing more and more of the time and resources of the aristocracy. There is no

psychological difference between placing £100 on a throw of the
dice and investing it in a risky voyage of exploration, between
buying a share in the Virginia Company and backing a horse. The
financing of entrepreneurial activity in the early modern period
may be more closely related to the gambling instinct than historians of capitalism are normally willing to admit. This could
explain the prominent role of the aristocracy in support of the
more forward-looking projects of the age, so many of which were
almost inevitably doomed to financial failure.

The economic importance of noblemen at this period arises from
the fact that they continued to pursue gain by speculative rather
than by capitalist means. Still traditionalist in their outlook, they
were continuing to gamble in a new environment of joint-stock
organization and industrial expansion. Consequently it was they,
and not social groups more deeply affected by the spirit of capitalism, who provided the economy with just that element of risk
money without which it could not have moved ahead. In many
cases the contribution of the nobleman was not so much in money
as in credit, his function being to provide the security on the
mortgage of his estates by which capital was raised from City
merchants for investment in novel ventures. The nobleman took
the risk and paid the interest, and the merchant put up the money,
a pattern which is as true of the Earl of Cumberland and privateering as it is of the Earl of Bedford and his fen-drainage and urban
development. It was this combination of aristocratic enterprise
and willingness to take a chance with surplus merchant capital
seeking a safe investment which made so many important
economic developments possible. By itself, neither could have
achieved the same results.

Owing to the inevitable fragmentation of knowledge, it is
difficult for the historian to compare situations he discovers in his
own selected period with those of other ages. There is some reason
to believe, however, that in the century between 1540 and 1640
the business enterprise of English noblemen had its greatest
impact on economic growth. Later on, although their activity
remained constant or even increased, their relative importance
declined as that of merchants, industrialists, and gentry increased.
This phenomenon of aristocratic leadership in the early modern
period fits in well with what is already known about the class in
northern Europe as a whole.

# VIII

## OFFICE AND THE COURT

The prince's court the only mart of preferment and honour.
A gulf of gain.
GABRIEL HARVEY (*Marginalia*, ed. G. C. Moore-Smith
Stratford on Avon, 1913, p. 142)
Seldom do courtiers prosper.
SIR JOHN WYNN, 12 June 1618 (NLW, Wynn MSS. 2855)

THE most striking feature of the great nation states of the sixteenth and seventeenth centuries was the enormous expansion of the Court and the central administration. This
development was characterized by the acquisition by the Crown
of greatly expanded financial and military resources, the extension
of royal control over outlying areas, the development of a self-
supporting bureaucracy with a vested interest in the perpetuation
and extension of royal authority, a concentration of business and
pleasure on the capital city, and the efflorescence of a brilliant and
expensive court life. Everywhere the nobility was sucked into this
vortex, to become generals in the royal army, functionaries in the
royal administration, or attendants upon the monarch in the performance of the elaborate rituals of the Court. For a variety of
reasons they were drawn to the centre and became increasingly
dependent on the Crown for their support. Once-formidable local
potentates were transformed into fawning courtiers and tame
state pensionaries. With important local differences, this model is
true of France or Brandenburg, Spain or England, Milan or the
Netherlands. But these local differences are of fundamental importance in explaining the very varied evolution of the European
governmental systems in the seventeenth century, and England's
experience of this centripetal tendency was as unique as was the
final political outcome.

### I. LONDON AND THE COURT

The magnetism of the English Court can only be fully appreciated if it is first set in the context of the parallel and interconnected

attractions of London itself, as a centre for both business and pleasure. For although the Court swelled in size and importance under its own impetus, its growth was further stimulated by the migration to London of ever-increasing numbers of nobility and gentry. Once lured into the metropolis, whether for a season or for semi-permanent residence, they mostly tended sooner or later to gravitate to the Court. To understand the extraordinary fascination of London in the sixteenth century, one must realize that it was not merely the only city but also the only substantial town in England. Some 320,000 people were packed into the metropolis in the 1630's, at a time when no other urban centre could muster more than about 25,000 souls, and when the total population of England and Wales did not exceed five million. It was not merely a difference in degree, it was a difference in kind: London was unique in a way which it is not today.

The prime importance of London was as a place of business, and in particular of legal business. No man of substance was without his quota of lawsuits with tenants, relatives, or neighbours, suits which were liable to draw him up to London term after term, to haunt dusty offices in the Temple or Lincoln's Inn, and to wander under the echoing roof of Westminster Hall, listening to the endless disputations of the barristers in the four corners of the chamber. As a result an ever-increasing flood of litigious nobility and gentry poured into London as each law term began, a flood which ebbed with the end of term, but whose wash was strongly felt at Court, whither many resorted to fill in the tedium of the interminable delays in the rusty workings of the Common Law. Lord Berkeley was merely an exceptionally conscientious model of his kind, as for many a year he was to be seen 'with a milk white head in his irksome old age of 70 years, in winter terms and frosty seasons, with a buckram bag stuffed with law cases, in early mornings and late evenings walking with his eldest son between the four Inns of Court and Westminster Hall, following his law suits in his own old person'.

Much other business besides that of the law could draw a nobleman to London. It was the only place where large loans could be raised at short notice; it was the centre of skilled conveyancing if marriage settlements were to be drawn up; it was the great market where cattle- and sheep-masters like the 1st Lord Spencer would go to sell their meat and wool; it was the headquarters of the trading and colonizing companies, whose directors were now beginning to include a fair sprinkling of nobility and gentry; and it was the seat of Parliament, that huge social gathering whose sessions, though rare and brief, drew up to London from time to time a substantial majority of the peerage and some 500 or so of the gentry.

Equally important was the growth of the London 'season', demanding the attendance of all with claims to elegance and fashion. The evidence suggests that this developed with astonishing speed between about 1590 and 1620. Sir John Oglander records that in the reign of Elizabeth the gentry of the Isle of Wight 'when they went to London (thinking it a East India voyage) they always made their wills'. By the 1620's, however, the ordinary at Newport, which once had been the meeting place of '12 knights and as many gentlemen', was now deserted, and club dinners were being held in the City for the gentry of each county. By the middle of the century Thomas Fuller could call London 'the inn-general of the gentry and nobility of this nation'.

Perhaps the most important reason for this surge into London was the contrast between the boredom and loneliness of country life and the excitements and gaiety of the metropolis. With increasing numbers of the nobility and gentry passing their most impressionable years at the Inns of Court, the knowledge of urban delights became more widely spread. In London were to be found 'rich wives, spruce mistresses, pleasant houses, good diet, rare wines, neat servants, fashionable furniture, pleasures and profits the best of all sort'. 'You have all the money and women at London', grumbled a Lincolnshire attorney in 1672. Here was the great clearing house for every sort of commodity for elegant living. Up and down the main roads there rumbled the carts of the carriers, bringing metropolitan goods and fashions down into the country. Thus in a single consignment Sir Robert Sydney sent his wife at Penshurst, a coach, a picture, my Lady's pedigree, and a piece of parmesan cheese.

With these goods went the news-letters, retailing the scandalous gossip of the capital and exciting both pious horror and secret longings to savour these forbidden fruits. Week after week a handful of gifted and industrious 'intelligencers', the first journalists the country had ever seen, sent their letters out to absent noblemen, diplomats abroad, and inquisitive country gentry. Spiced

with lurid court scandal, and barbed with satirical comment on
the antics of the royal favourites and the growing corruption in
the administration, these letters were incidentally a powerful source
of mischief.

London was becoming not merely the hub of business and of
information, but also a centre of organized pleasure and tourism.
On show were the lions at the Tower, the baiting of Harry Hunks
the bear at Paris Garden, the wonders of Holden's Camel and
Banks's horse Morocco. There were the two playhouses for noblemen and gentlemen, Blackfriars and the Globe, leaving the Fortune and the Red Bull to the citizens and apprentices. And of
course there were the numerous prostitutes and the streets of
brothels. For the more seriously inclined, there were the royal
tombs at Westminster, as great an attraction in the seventeenth
as in the twentieth century. The first guide-book to the tombs was
published by Camden in 1600, foreign visitors always included
them in their itinerary, and peers and gentry up from the country
flocked in to see them. When Sir Bassingbourne Gawdy's son had
'seen the lions and the tombs at Westminster', he evidently
thought he had done the town. And then there were the special
occasions—coronations, funerals, royal marriages—dazzling spec-
tacles that attracted huge crowds from the country. At the time
of the royal entry into London in 1603 Anne Newdigate down at
Arbury in Warwickshire received a tempting summons: 'Either
come up now and see this bravery or close your eyes whilst you
live . . . and let Jack's coal-pits pay for all.' 'Let 's to London,
there 's variety' was a suggestion often heard in a Jacobean manor-
house.

One of the most powerful forces making for the growth of
London as a fashionable resort was the spread of the private
coach. It was not till the 1590's that such vehicles became common
even among the aristocracy. Before this time many a wife must
have quailed at the physical strain of the long journey on horseback. Now all but the really ill could jolt and bump their way to
town without more than minor discomfort, and the temptation
to come up was in consequence enormously increased. 'Women
love themselves best, and London next', remarked the Earl of
Warwick in 1632, and King James also blamed the female sex for
the expansion of London which he so much deplored. In fact, the
men needed little encouragement. They too deserted the family

seat because of 'abhorrence of solitude'. In country house after country house there could be heard the yawns and sighs of boredom and loneliness. Sir John Harington described himself to his smart friends as 'a private country knight that lives among clouted shoes in his frieze jacket and galoshes'. George Manners prayed for 'better times and fortunes than always to live a poor base Justice, recreating myself in sending rogues to the gallows', and Sir Charles Percy complained to his London friends from Dumbleton in Gloucestershire that 'if I stay here long you will find me so dull that I shall be taken for Justice Silence or Justice Shallow'. As for the Highland Zone, it was considered as remote as Siberia and Lord Burghley urged Bess of Hardwick not to 'live so solitary . . . there in Chatsworth amongst hills and rocks of stones'.

Occasionally a more pastoral note is struck, an idealization of country life as expressed in such poems as Jonson's *To Penshurst* and *Sir Robert Wroth*. This view combined the ancient theories of Horace and Martial with one aspect of the current doctrine of the English gentleman, whose duties both social and administrative called for his presence on his estate : as the dispenser of hospitality, justice, and charity, he was obliged to reside in his country seat, and his migration to London for long periods of the year led to an impoverishment of the district, materially, socially, and spiritually, as well as creating a vacuum of authority for the maintenance of public order.

To support this vague romanticizing of country life, there was widespread complaint about the terrible expense of life in the City. It was a Wiltshire gentleman up from the country who in a letter to his wife summed up a century of rustic indignation about 'that expensive town and hell-hound tradesmen that makes no [more] conscience to cheat an honest country gentleman than [a] whore to cantering, which sticks plaguily in the gizzard of me'. The other great objection to the City was that it was a morally corrupting place, a conviction strengthened by the pamphlets and plays describing the London underworld and the vices and knaveries of the town. Despite God's awful warnings in the great plague and the great fire, Sir Richard Wynn in 1666 was still struck by 'the pride, pomp, luxury, and treason of this damned place'. If the City had an evil reputation, that of the Court was still worse. Incalculable harm was done to the prestige of monarchy by the gold-rush atmosphere of gambling, sex, and drink created by the lavish generosity and the genial tolerance of King James. Sir John Harington's artful description of the drunken orgy at Theobalds in 1606 on the occasion of the visit of the King of Denmark, when courtiers both male and female were staggering and spewing in the royal presence, did little to increase public respect for King James and his friends. It was not mere puritan prejudice that led Lucy Hutchinson to look on the Court as 'a nursery of lust and intemperance', for men like Roger Manners, Sir John Harington, and Lord Herbert of Cherbury, who had lived there long, all bore witness to the truth of this belief.

For all that, until they were forcibly expelled in the 1630's, an increasing number of nobility and gentry spent an ever greater part of their lives in London, and when they were there most of them tended to hang about the Court. The clearest evidence of this shift towards London is provided by the number who owned or rented London houses. By 1560 some thirty, or about half the peerage, had a town house, and almost all the earls were lodged in remarkable splendour. This had been achieved during the previous thirty years by the forcible expulsion of the bishops from their great medieval mansions. Under orders from the Crown, bishop after bishop had surrendered the patrimony of his see, so that by 1560 the row of palaces between the Strand and the Thames linking Westminster with the City were occupied by noblemen.

Once this church booty had been distributed, centrally placed sites suitable for huge London mansions became very hard to find, and in consequence the proportion of peers who actually owned their own houses did not greatly alter between 1560 and 1640. Instead, there took place two important developments. The first was the subdividing and subletting of the Thames-side palaces, which were now too large for the needs of even the grandest of private magnates. These houses had all been acquired and occupied by leading political figures, whose officials, clients, and suitors had filled the spacious halls and rambling suites of chambers. Their descendants were rarely politicians of the first rank, and now had no need for such lavish accommodation. They were therefore only too ready to cut off sections of their palaces and let them, sometimes furnished and sometimes unfurnished, to peers who needed a London *pied-à-terre*.

More important than this subletting of the older palaces was the astonishing early seventeenth-century growth of urban building

on leasehold in the west end to the north of the Strand. This
provided a mass of high-class dwelling-houses fit for noblemen,
court officials, and important members of the squirearchy. Covent
Garden, Queen Street, Drury Lane, and St. Martin's Lane were
built with this clientèle exclusively in mind, and part cause and
part effect was a great increase of peers occupying leasehold property. By the 1620's and 1630's there is evidence of fifty-nine peers
living in rented houses or lodgings as against forty-one with
houses of their own. The rents of these houses, especially if they
were fully furnished, were comparable with London prices of the
mid-twentieth century.

By the 1630's at least three-quarters of the peerage, and probably more, had acquired for themselves by ownership or lease a
fairly permanent residence in or about London. The number of
gentry who had similarly taken on London houses must have run
into several hundreds, to say nothing of those who went into
furnished lodgings for the Christmas season. All the more shattering was the determined effort by the Crown in the early 1630's
to reverse this trend and drive peers and gentry back into the
country.

From the earliest feudal times the fortunes of the nobility have
depended as much upon the favours and ferocities of monarchs
as upon their own hereditary resources. The political history of
medieval England is largely taken up with a prolonged struggle
of the Crown with its barons, a struggle characterized by rebellions, executions, attainders, confiscations, and the lavish redistribution of the lands of the fallen among the royal followers.
There was hardly a succession to the throne before that of King
Charles in 1625 which did not bring with it a sudden turn of
fortune's wheel, the fall of some great magnate, the seizure of his
lands, and the elevation of a new favourite or group of favourites
upon the ruins of the old. In the early seventeenth century John
Smyth of Nibley attributed the extraordinary stability of the fortunes of the Berkeleys over a period of 550 years to the fact that
they managed 'neither to have been often clouded with the frowns
of their princes, nor to have sat too near to their immoderate
favours; but to have the warmth of the Court in a moderate
distance, not in too near nor scorching an aspect or reflex'. Despite
these warnings, the peers in the sixteenth century swarmed to
Court in ever-increasing numbers, for court attendance and

service to the State was now an ideal, a social convention, a pleasure, and a necessity.

By the middle of the sixteenth century the concept of service had begun to change in character, as the secularization of the State and the expansion of the bureaucracy created more and more openings in the higher ranges of government. Social conservatives —and there were few at this time who were not conservative— were anxious that the nobility should occupy these posts so as to prevent government falling into the hands of men of low birth and inferior status.

The publication of an English translation of Castiglione's *Il Cortegiano* in 1561 served to crystallize this attitude by giving the widest publicity to a new social ideal, that of the educated and refined Renaissance man. This ideal did not pass unchallenged in sixteenth-century England, for running parallel to it was a modified, anglicized version in which prime stress was laid on service to the Prince in either the court or the country, and in which piety and virtue played a larger part. If many of the gentry were fascinated by the Court, the aristocracy were won over to it almost to a man, and it was only personal experience of the Court of King James and growing piety of a puritan temper which damped enthusiasm in the early seventeenth century. Even now the call of duty and the pricking of ambition remained, though in many cases the sense of vocation had gone.

By virtue of their rank the peerage had automatic right of access to the Privy Chamber and the Ante-Chamber, the two rooms where much of the life of the monarch was spent. It was expected of a peer that he should show his devotion to his Prince by putting in at any rate an occasional appearance, if only at some of the important feasts and celebrations. Even an opponent of the Court like the 5th Earl of Huntingdon advised attendance for several weeks in each year, though it is significant of the changing attitude that his son should have amended the duration to a few days.

These theoretical notions of obligation were not the only incentives that drove the sixteenth-century nobility to come to Court and to seek royal service. There was that 'perpetual and restless desire of power after power that ceaseth only in death' which Hobbes, who spent his life in an aristocratic household, came to regard as one of the principal motives of human behaviour. Not all peers were satisfied with the exercise of authority over servants, tenants, and local officials, and many sought a wider field in which to employ their talents and to savour the sweets of power. Their predicament had been exacerbated by the decline in demand for their military services and by the more intellectual content of their education. Many had laboriously fitted themselves for public service, only to find the doors of office closed upon them, and their efforts at self-improvement merely left them disenchanted with the oafish pleasures of the countryside. Finally there was the urge to avoid the torments of boredom and melancholia. As Dr. Johnson once observed, 'all the importunities and complexities of business are softness and luxury compared with the incessant cravings of vacancy and the unsatisfactory expedients of idleness'.

Attendance at Court was more than a duty and a pleasure : it was also a necessity. So wide a range of gifts and favours flowed from the Prince that it was essential for every nobleman to have some influence at Court if he was to prosper. 'As fishes are gotten with baites, so are offices caught with seeking', remarked Burghley in 1568. It was not merely those who aspired to posts in the central government who had to lobby in the Court, but also those content with a rural life, to whom it was essential to obtain the rangership of a forest, a stewardship, the lease of a manor, the insertion or omission of a name on a commission'. As the Crown's control of these powers of nomination slipped more and more into the hands of courtiers, who in turn exercised this authority to help their friends or to line their pockets, or both, so the need to establish personal contacts at Court became more and more necessary, not merely to the aristocracy but also to the greater gentry. Another of Burghley's maxims was that a man without a friend at Court was 'like a hop without a pole'. By the 1580's the key to advancement lay at the Court, which with the decline of the over-mighty subject developed into the unique market-place for the distribution of an enormous range of offices, favours, and titles.

## II. DIRECT REWARDS

An astonishing proportion of contemporary correspondence is devoted to the fortunes of the chase after the elusive and many-coloured fruits which tumbled so arbitrarily and irregularly from the cornucopia of the Court. It is only by a close analysis of the bewildering variety of rewards, and of the shifting chronological pattern as different items rose and fell in importance, that we can hope to understand the fascination the Court exercised upon contemporaries.

In the seventeenth century the greater offices of state and household were each worth several thousand pounds a year, although the official fees were only a few hundred. The difference was made up by using cash balances for private money-lending, by the sale of inferior offices, by New Year gifts from lesser officials, by private fees, and by more disreputable sources such as bribes for the corrupt exercise of authority. For example, the office of Lord Treasurer carried with it a fee of £366, but was worth some £4,000 in 1608–12, and £7,000 to £8,000 in the middle years of the seventeenth century. The Mastership of the Court of Wards carried a fee of £133 and was worth about £3,000 in 1608–12. Nevertheless the overheads were heavy. There was the cost of purchase of the office in the first place, which often amounted to two or more years' income, and there was the general expense of life at Court and the maintenance of a suitable establishment. Even these great office-holders relied for support on a flow of extraneous gifts and favours from the Crown.

The most obvious of these gifts was of land, either in lease for lives or terms of years; or entailed on heirs male or heirs general, with or without the reservation of a fee-farm rent; or by way of exchange with the land of the suitor. This last is a very important category, especially during the reign of Henry VIII, and one whose significance has been underestimated. In the 1540's the King was anxious to give every influential man of property a vested interest in the secularization of monastic estates. Some he drew in by outright gift, others by sale, others again by the surrender of some of their ancient patrimony in exchange for lands which a few years previously had belonged to the Church. Under Elizabeth the practice of exchanging lands continued, but now as a mark of favour by the Crown rather than with any ulterior political motive. These exchanges were sought by peers either to simplify estate management, or to take advantage of the very low valuations placed on crown property.

More common under Elizabeth were grants of leases of crown lands, very many of which went to minor officers of the household and others to the great court favourites. One contemporary

thought that 'her Majesty hath granted more leases in reversion
to her servants and captains and such like in her time than hath
been granted since the Conquest'. A striking example of this
policy is the grant in 1587 of a reversionary lease of 21 years after
1615 to Sir William Gardiner of some rich pastures at Bermondsey
at a rent of £68 a year. By 1612 the property was reckoned to be
worth £932 a year over the rent, and the day the lease ran out in
1636 the rent rocketed from £68 to £1,071.

A much cheaper method of gratifying the courtiers was to
blackmail the bishops and deans and chapters into giving beneficial leases on very favourable terms. This cost the Crown nothing
—except of course the prestige and self-respect of the episcopacy,
which in turn reflected on the monarchy—and so Elizabeth turned
to it with avidity. Sir John Harington observed that the Elizabethan courtier was more accustomed to 'pray on the church than
in the church', and Thomas Wilson concluded that the clergy's
'wings are well clipped of late by courtiers and noblemen, and
some quite cut away, both feather, flesh, and bone'. Such amputa-
tion tended to be painful, and the anguished shrieks of the dissected
clergymen echoed shrill but unattended throughout Elizabethan
England. As Bishop Cox of Ely pointed out, the procedure
smacked all too clearly of the double-cross. Was this to be the
bishops' reward for their support during the 1530's and 1540's
for the liquidation of monastic property which 'had rescued abundance of the English from beggary and enriched others with
wealth and others advanced to honours'? But what could the
good bishop expect, when as Archbishop Sandys himself admitted, 'the ministers of the Word, the messengers of Christ . . .
are esteemed *tamquam excrementa mundi*'? It was no good. No
longer was the episcopacy closely linked by blood and social
position to the nobility; no longer did a Scrope or a Percy hold
the see of Carlisle, a Courtenay the see of Exeter, a Bourchier
Canterbury itself. Men of lowly origin, they were now defenceless
against the rapacity of their betters. And so when the summons
for surrender came, the majority of the bishops, for all their squeals
of dismay, nevertheless gave in without undue obstinacy. They
sighed as lovers of episcopal property, they obeyed as sons of the
Supreme Governor.

These leases extorted from the Church by the Crown on behalf
of courtiers were all the more valuable since, once granted, it was

very difficult indeed for a renewal to be refused to the family
descendants. As a result leases tended to remain in the same
aristocratic family at the same old rent from generation to generation, being periodically renewed on payment of a fine, which was
usually grossly inadequate. The estates of many peers consequently
included a fair amount of leasehold property, some of it held of
the Crown but mostly derived from bishops, deans and chapters,
and Oxford and Cambridge colleges, who were equally open to
royal pressure. These leases were sometimes an important feature
of aristocratic income; but it was a source that was cut off sharp
as soon as there ascended to the throne a monarch aware of the
political theory which made bishops one of the prime supports of
monarchy. Rather than rob his bishops, King James preferred to
dirty his hands elsewhere, or to carve slices off the royal patrimony
instead.

The other and more important type of land grant was in perpetuity, either as a free gift or burdened with a fee-farm rent to the
Crown. It was the policy of the Tudors to keep intact the hard
core of estates the Crown had owned under Henry VII, and to
confine themselves to the redistribution of such lands of others as
had come their way. The vast monastic estates left ample room
for generosity after 1537, and under Henry VIII and Edward VI
a new administrative aristocracy sprang up out of the ruins of the
monasteries.

Elizabeth was reluctant to continue too far the process of
dispersal, and preferred where possible to look to other sources,
of which the principal was again the unfortunate bishops. She did
not hesitate to keep bishoprics vacant for long periods in order
to help a friend. The bishopric of Ely was unfilled for thirteen
years, first to subsidize the Portuguese pretender Don Antonio,
and then to support the Earl of Oxford, who had run through his
own patrimony in riotous living. Another device was to maintain
the bishops in a state of perpetual circulation, thus enabling the
Crown to enjoy almost unlimited first-fruits. One such plan in
1575 suggested eighteen transfers and two perpetual vacancies,
which would bring in £21,690 'without any just cause of much
offence to the bishops', and the idea was revived every time there
was a courtier to be gratified or a military campaign to be paid for.

These were all measures to obtain temporary rather than permanent control of episcopal revenues, and it was an innocuous

sounding Act of Parliament of the first year of the reign which
enabled Elizabeth to lay hands on enough land to gratify her
courtiers. The Act empowered the Crown to carry out a forcible
exchange of property with the bishops at every vacancy, ostensibly on equal terms. In practice the Queen got rid of a great mass
of widely scattered impropriations and tenths, most of which had
a fixed monetary value which could not be increased. In return she
took over large and compact estates whose rents could be raised
to keep pace with the price revolution and which had plenty of
growth potential by improvement. Under the terms of the Act
she immediately seized land worth over £3,000 a year from various
sees, which in three sample counties meant that now no less than
14 per cent. of crown lands had once belonged to the bishops.
When Ely was at last filled in 1599, some twenty or more manors
went to swell the landed revenues of the Crown. 'Dr. Eaton hath
eaten the bishopric of Ely; the clergy wish him choked with it'
reported Harington. By the end of the reign it was said that
Exeter had been reduced from twenty-two manors to two. Well
might the Bishop of Winchester protest, with a passion which
wrought havoc with his spelling, 'I never was a whorder of
money'; well might the Bishop of Llandaff suggest that 'his true
title should be "Aff"', for the Land was gone'.

Generally, these exchanged lands were kept in royal hands,
and their real significance is that they enabled Elizabeth to distribute other land, especially in order to build up a new following
of courtiers and nobles in the first few years of the reign, without
making serious inroads into her total rental income. The estates
that were actually distributed by Elizabeth tended mostly to be
former property of others which had come to the Crown by
escheat or attainder. There was a steady trickle of felons' lands,
which could be shared out among the faithful. Other land which
came to the Crown by escheat on the failure of heirs male was
usually regranted within a few years, Warwick Castle passing to
Fulke Greville within ten years of the death of the Countess of
Warwick. Almost as important was the land of traitors. Throughout the Middle Ages and the sixteenth century it was customary
for the Crown to reward its supporters with some of the estates
of the defeated. There were, however, certain conventional limits
within which this game had to be played. It was thought improper for the Crown to ruin a family irremediably by giving all

its land away to others. So long as a substantial proportion was kept in crown hands there was always the prospect, indeed the probability, that a revival of royal favour would bring about the recovery of the estate. This concept of 'the justice of inheritance' provided an insurance cover against the hazards of unsuccessful rebellion.

The most remarkable example is provided by the history of the estates of the dukes of Norfolk. The victim of the last great treason trial of the reign as Henry VIII degenerated into bloody and suspicious paranoia, the 3rd Duke survived the block thanks to the sudden death of the King, but did not recover his estates until 1553. In 1572 the 4th Duke was in turn attainted for treason and executed and his estates divided between the Queen, his eldest son the Earl of Arundel, and his son by a second marriage, the future Earl of Suffolk. In 1589 the Earl of Arundel was attainted and his estates further divided between the Queen and his son and heir. In 1603 the Howards were high in the favour of King James, who restored the bulk of the estates to the family, part going to the hereditary claimant, the Earl of Arundel, but most to his uncles the Earls of Suffolk and Northampton jointly. These last two divided their joint grant in 1609, and the Earl of Arundel later inherited Northampton's share and bought that of Suffolk, so finally reassembling the bulk of the inheritance of the 4th Duke.

It must be remembered that the 'justice of inheritance' only applied to the greatest magnates—mere knightly families could be totally dispossessed without qualms—and that in any case it was only thought desirable to preserve a certain part of the estate. The rest was at the disposal of the Crown to reward its followers, and their distribution was a moral and political obligation which it was dangerous to evade. Those who hurried north to crush the Rebellion of the Northern Earls in 1569, those who encircled Essex House on the afternoon of 8 February 1601, did not do so entirely from altruistic devotion to their beloved Queen: there were pickings to be had and they were determined to stake their claims. As Lord Burghley pointed out after the former uprising: 'It is necessary that the lands of the rebels be dispersed by sale and gift to the good subjects, that thereby they may in respect of the lands become more earnest servants to the Queen's Majesty against the rebels.' It was the same policy as that of Henry VIII in building up a vested interest in monastic property. After 1603 this source dried up, for the growing political maturity of the age would no longer tolerate the executions and confiscations of property of fallen favourites and politicians.

Failing land, there was money, the one thing that Elizabeth could not bring herself to give away, but which James in his early years distributed with splendid prodigality, particularly to his Scottish friends. So far as can be discovered, a gift of £7,000 out of the sale of some seized cochineal in 1598 was the only grant of this nature the old Queen ever allowed herself to make—though she was once cajoled into lending £1,000 to Lord Stafford, to enforce repayment of which she soon extended his lands. Other loans made by Elizabeth were purely for political or military purposes, and repayment was always ruthlessly exacted.

Things were very different after 1603. In the first seven years of the reign some £88,000 was given away to Scotsmen, over £15,000 of it in the first few months. In the *annus mirabilis* of 1611 no less than £43,600 was given away to peers—mostly Scottish—and £20,000 the year after. It was not until the accession of Charles I that the flow of cash gifts really began to diminish, though the new king celebrated his accession with a present of £10,000 to the Earl of Kellie. Cash grants were now in recompense for expenditure incurred, for example on an embassy, or in return for the surrender of some other grant or office. For the most part, therefore, they are inextricably interlocked with the whole range of miscellaneous grants, and cannot be studied in isolation.

If land was scarce, and immediate capital sums were hard to come by, the Crown could resort to the payment of annuities, either for lives or for term of years. This again was a grant rarely made by Elizabeth, and then of modest size and largely confined to personal female friends, like the Countesses of Kildare and Kent and Ladies Hunsdon and Burgh. As a result of this austere policy Elizabeth managed to keep the cost of the administration, both in fees and pensions, down to under £30,000 a year, despite the mounting tide of inflation. Carried to such lengths, the policy was both unreasonable and dangerous since it provided the temptation—indeed the stark necessity—for corruption among public officials if they were to maintain their standard of living. A revision of stipends or a substantial rise in the number and amount of pensions to supplement them was clearly needed in order to maintain

the efficiency of the administrative machine. It is therefore important to decide how far the dramatic rise in pensions, which had
soared to about £140,000 a year by 1626—that is to say about a
quarter of the total cash revenue of the Crown—was due to the
legitimate demands of government service, and how far to the
growth of a parasitic court aristocracy preying upon the revenues
of the Crown.

Some pensions to the nobility were in compensation for loss of
office, an expenditure made necessary by the practice of granting
offices for life, and by James's desire for frequent changes in his
officers. Thus the accession of James made superfluous the garri-
son of Berwick—and its captain—and so Lord Hunsdon had to
be compensated with an annuity of £424. There remain those pensions—the majority—which were gifts in their own right as
rewards for courtiers, most of them with no specific service as
their justification and merely given away to support the living
standards of the courtiers. To the favoured few the benefits were
prodigious, particularly during the open-handed era of the Duke
of Buckingham. At one time or another the Duke of Richmond
and his mother received pensions of £4,100 a year; the old Earl
of Nottingham enjoyed others totalling £3,700 a year, of which
£2,017 were continued to his widow and children; the Earls of
Salisbury, Montgomery, and Northampton and Viscount Conway had £3,000 a year each, and the Earl of Cambridge £2,500.
These were the principal beneficiaries, to whom annuities represented a substantial portion of their total income, but there were
many others on a more modest scale. In the Early Stuart period
one in every three peerage families was at one time or another a
pensioner of the Crown. In 1630 pensions, excluding those to the
royal family, were costing the Crown about £125,000 a year, of
which £39,000, or almost one-third, was going to a mere twenty-
two noble families, and the remaining two-thirds was spread over
many hundreds of courtiers and court and administrative officials.
If pensions were to some extent a necessary expenditure for the
maintenance of Court and Civil Service, they were also to no small
degree an extravagant system of outdoor relief to a minority of
highly favoured noblemen.

If the Crown felt itself unable to hand out these cash sums, it
could fall back on the less obviously painful expedient of allowing
courtiers and officials to run up very large debts, some of which

were themselves incidental by-products of royal generosity. A very great deal of the land dispersed by the Crown after 1540 was burdened with perpetual fee-farm rents, which in the case of large grantees often ran into three figures. By the end of the century almost every peer in England owed such rents to the Crown, and it was not difficult to fall into arrears. The most remarkable case was that of the Earl of Huntingdon, Elizabeth's trusted Lord President of the North, on whose death in 1595 it was discovered that he owed some £8,000 in fee-farm rents, some of them dating back forty years.

Parliamentary subsidies were also allowed to fall far into arrears. When a real effort was made to tighten things up in about 1610, it was found that almost every peer in England was behind in his payments, many indeed scandalously so. The earls of Derby and their wives owed £1,338 unpaid taxes stretching back to 1589, the Earl of Shrewsbury £1,853 from 1585 onward, the Earl of Huntingdon £422 from 1581. The earls of Oxford had not yet paid a subsidy due over half a century before.

The really spectacular debts, however, arose in various ways from the holding of office, one of them being the retention of revenue balances due to the Crown. Sir Christopher Hatton died owing the Queen £42,139 from his office as Receiver of First Fruits and Tenths; the 2nd Earl of Essex owed over £11,000, mostly for his father's Irish expedition of 1573 and for his Sweet Wine Farm. These staggering arrears meant that an official could live vastly beyond his means in his lifetime, leaving the Crown to extract the money as best it could from the heirs. This it usually did, not by peremptory demands for an immediate lump sum, but by placing an extent on the estate and exacting a fixed rent over a period of years. In 1608 there were extents on the lands of peers for debts dating back to before 1588. This easy going attitude towards heavy crown debtors was of considerable financial importance at a time when the interest rate on borrowed money was as high as 10 per cent.

### III. INDIRECT REWARDS

Each of the three types of direct grant, of land, cash, and annuities, involved a strain on royal finances, and was liable to vigorous opposition from the current Lord Treasurer. After about 1580, therefore, courtiers were obliged to look for less painful ways of maintaining the flow of rewards, not because they were equally acceptable but for lack of anything better. As one applicant rightly pointed out, 'monopolies are scandalous, reversions of office uncertain, concealments litigious, forfeitures rarely recovered'. An examination of these obscure possibilities involves plunging into a labyrinth whose paths were once familiar enough to a Leicester or a Buckingham, but which today can only be reconstructed by patient archaeological digging. Every alternative to the direct grant was basically a licence to individuals to use royal authority to levy money on their own account from the consumer or the taxpayer. Though these grants took an extraordinary variety of forms, they fell into three main categories : the delegation to courtiers of the Crown's rights of taxation; the delegation to courtiers of the Crown's power over the regulation of economic activities, whether in manufacture, trade, distribution, or conditions of employment; and the delegation to courtiers of the Crown's authority as the fount of honour and the patron of office. The first two categories are in origin interlocked since the Crown's authority to regulate exports and imports and to vary customs rates derived from its duty to look after the economic health of the nation.

The idea that the Sovereign is responsible for regulating economic activities goes back far into the Middle Ages, but it was only in the sixteenth century that it resulted in a ubiquitous system of state control authorized by parliament and embracing almost every aspect of the nation's affairs. Each Tudor parliament gave birth to a new litter of economic bills until the local J.P.s were weighed down by the burden of these 'stacks of statutes'. There are several reasons why at first the landed classes welcomed this development. They disliked social change and wanted restrictions on the growth of such subversive novelties as the money-market and industrial and commercial capitalism. They were haunted by the need for economic self-sufficiency in case of war, and therefore accepted such varied measures as restrictions on the export of essential commodities and the import of luxuries; state subsidies for, and state control of, armaments manufacture and shipping; regulation of the main export trade in cloth; and monopoly protection for new industrial projects in order to provide a favourable trade balance. They were fearful of agrarian and urban unrest and so put up with legislation to limit inclosures, to stabilize cloth manufacture, and to regulate wages.

As time wore on, however, the objectives of social justice and national advantage tended to become displaced in the eyes of the Crown by its urgent need for fiscal profit, and towards the end of Elizabeth's reign this elaborate system of controls began to change its nature. The difficulty of enforcing these regulations led the Crown to fall back on professional informers working for profit, and on leasing powers of regulation to individuals in the hope of harnessing private greed to the service of the State. As a development out of this leasing system, Elizabeth began to give these contracts to courtiers on relatively easy terms.

The earliest large-scale experiments in subcontracting royal administration occurred in the Customs service, where various branches of the ancient subsidy and most of the new impositions were leased out to private individuals. On the face of it the system was advantageous to the Crown, which obtained a fixed rent in excess of the average over the previous seven years and was relieved of all responsibility for collection. Provided that trade in the commodities concerned was expanding, and provided that improved administration could diminish smuggling, the subcontractor was assured of his profit. More and better-paid customs officers could always cut down on smuggling, and trade boomed in luxury imports under Elizabeth and in almost all commodities under James until the slump of 1621. Such were the potential profits that there was ample room for the courtier to insert himself, and to take his cut as intermediary between the contractor and the Crown.

The pioneer in this field was the Earl of Leicester, who in the late 1560's and early 1570's took over leases of duties on the import of silks and velvets, oils, currants, and sweet wines, thus acquiring a virtually complete stranglehold on Mediterranean trade. From the Sweet Wine Farm alone Leicester drew a clear rent of £2,500 by subcontracting to the man who actually handled the business, Mr. Customer Smith. Essex, who was Leicester's successor in the Queen's favours, was also his successor in the Sweet Wine Farm, and it was the Queen's refusal to renew the Farm at the end of October 1600 which helped to drive the Earl to rebellion three months later. In 1604 the main customs revenues were consolidated into a single Great Farm and let to contractors—a speculation out of which the Earl of Salisbury got a cash gift of £6,000 for patronizing the winning syndicate of merchants. Impositions, which were mostly on luxury imports, were handed out directly to the great courtiers. Peace and the expansion of London as a centre of conspicuous consumption caused a startling increase in these imports and consequently a dramatic rise in profits to the farmers. As a result in the first decade of the century seven peers were enjoying a clear net profit of about £27,500 a year from their role as intermediaries between the Crown and the merchant sub-contractors for the Customs. For all seven this was their most important single source of income.

By these grants the Crown managed both to raise large sums on credit and to satisfy the importunities of its greater clients without directly burdening the Exchequer; the clients managed to receive large annual sums promptly and without arousing too much public indignation; and the merchant financiers managed to get a lucrative stranglehold on the customs service. The system did no great harm to the consumer or taxpayer, except in so far as it provided the Crown with an incentive to burden trade with more and more impositions. But by permitting so much of the profit to pass directly into the hands of court favourites, the Crown weakened its case over its power of levying impositions at will, since it raised serious doubts about the purity of its motives in doing so. Was the King regulating trade in the national interest, or to oblige his friends?

This practice of leasing customs farms was relatively innocuous compared with the complementary habit of granting import or export privileges to favoured courtiers. Parliament by Statute, or the Crown by Proclamation, had placed restrictions on trade in certain commodities for purposes which were directly and explicitly related to the public interest; the Crown then granted to a courtier the right of exemption from these restrictions, a right which the courtier promptly resold to interested merchants. The practice of issuing these exemptions had grown up, on a limited scale, even under the early Tudors and in the 1570's the Queen was tempted to use cloth-export licences as a common method of rewarding an important courtier or official. Three earls, three lords, and three knights between them obtained grants totalling about 320,000 short cloths. Finally in 1601, as compensation for his privateering losses, the Earl of Cumberland not only obtained a licence to export an unlimited quantity of cloths for ten years in return for a rent of £1,000 a year to the Crown, but was also given dispensation from the proviso about dressing every tenth cloth; thus to save the fortunes of the Earl—and to add to her own revenue—Elizabeth abandoned state protection of the native cloth-finishing industry as laid down by Act of Parliament. Nor were the Merchant Adventurers best pleased, since the Earl in his necessity was so grasping that they could not come to terms with him, and it took the arbitration of the Privy Council to impose a settlement. Propping up the house of Clifford was a politically expensive undertaking.

In the early years of James there began a fresh stream of import/ export licences, mostly to importunate Scotsmen. To give but one example, the Earl of Dunbar obtained licences to export 4,000 quarters of wheat and 300 tons of iron ordnance, and secured the monopoly of the import of logwood. Trade in the first was normally forbidden in the interests of the poor, in the second for national security, and in the third to protect the consumer because hitherto the dye was not fast.

It was the royal powers of regulation of internal trade and industry and royal authority to grant monopoly rights which provided some of the lushest pastures for the court aristocracy. The most straightforward and legitimate of these powers was that by which new industrial processes were protected by monopoly patents for a period of years as a means of rewarding the inventor and entrepreneur. In the deliberate efforts in the last half of the sixteenth century to encourage and diversify industrial enterprise these powers were widely used by the Crown, and it was not until the end of the century that abuses began to creep in. By then the Queen's resources were strained to the uttermost by the war with Spain, and she readily acceded to requests for such monopolies as a method of rewarding deserving servants which cost her nothing. Courtiers were not particularly interested in the risks of launching a new technical invention, and preferred to create a lucrative monopoly in some well-established industry, a practice which aroused the bitter resentment of the House of Commons in 1597. Around the ageing Queen there now swarmed the host of

> Courtier leather, courtier pin and soap,
> And courtier vinegar and starch and card,
> And such as shall not court it long, we hope.

At this time monopolies were still mostly modest affairs exploited by the lesser figures about the Court.

Mindful of the turbulent scenes in the Commons in 1597 and 1601, James found it prudent to restrict these monopolies to genuinely new industrial developments. The main difference was that the beneficiaries were now very often peers : industrial monopolies went up in the world in the new reign. Lord Sheffield from the first took a large share in the Yorkshire alum monopoly, if only because the richest seams were to be found on his land. Far more sinister was the monopoly of the manufacture of dyestuffs granted to the Earl of Dunbar in 1605 to complete his stranglehold on the dyeing industry, partly achieved by his monopoly powers of importing logwood. But with three or four exceptions it is doubtful whether these industrial patents brought more than moderate gains to their hopeful patrons. In a few cases the courtier himself took a personal interest in the new process and invested both time and money in its development. In others he acted as a sleeping partner for the provision of capital, but in the majority of cases he was no more than a parasite preying on the talent and resources of others in return for the political influence needed to obtain a monopoly.

More significant as a political irritant and as a source of profit was the abuse by the Crown of its powers of economic regulation and control. Here again the rot set in during the late 1580's and 1590's. Authorized by parliaments inspired by a concern for the national interest, the Tudors had acquired and exercised the widest powers of regulation over economic affairs. Industrial products were searched and stamped to maintain quality standards; prices were controlled to check profiteering, ale-houses were licensed to prevent excessive increase in their numbers, bullion export was carefully regulated to avoid sudden outflows of precious metal; weights and measures were inspected for the prevention of fraud; the printing of books was subject to licensing to prevent the publication of subversive matter. Without an army of paid inspectors many of these controls were obviously useless, and it was not surprising that the Crown should harness the profit motive to the task of enforcement. From the first the paid informer had played a prominent role, but now there developed the practice of giving a monopoly of enforcement to a courtier, who in turn hired his informers as a speculative business venture. Alternatively, if—

as was often the case—the regulations were obsolete or unwork-able, a courtier was given monopoly powers to grant exemptions or to compound with offenders, two powers which in practice tended to be identical in their exercise. Under such grants the Crown ceded to individuals its rights over forfeitures from offenders, a delegation of royal authority against which the judges formally protested in 1604.

A classic case of the obnoxious regulatory grant was that of the alnage of old and new draperies, which in 1604 was given to James's Scottish crony and relative, the Duke of Lennox. This medieval system of controlling quality in cloth-manufacture had long been virtually useless, and its brisk exploitation by Lennox as a kind of private excise on cloth and its extension to the new draperies, which had been begun by Burghley in 1578, caused widespread indignation among the clothiers. There is little evidence that Lennox made much attempt to justify his patent by checking quality of cloth, and he and his factors acted merely as a tax-collecting agency. The Commons of 1621 renewed their protests at the abuses of the system, such as the sale of the seals to the clothier by the bushel, thus making nonsense of any claim to control over quality, and the blackmailing of clothing retailers under threat of persecution by the Duke and his influential friends. By devices such as these the Lennoxes had raised their net profits to £2,400 a year by 1624, and they continued to enjoy this lucra-tive monopoly right up to the Civil War—and again after the Restoration—despite continued protests from manufacturers. Here is another example of the alienation by the Stuarts of an influential section of opinion for the sake of the profits accruing to a favourite aristocratic house.

Customs farms, import and export licences, manufacturing monopolies, and economic regulations and controls are far from exhausting the list of possible royal gifts of fragments of its powers and its resources. Once the principle of farming the revenue was admitted, why should there be any limit to its indefinite extension? Its usefulness was particularly marked in cases of wide but largely disused or neglected royal powers which might profitably be revived. If a great courtier was willing to undertake the task—and to incur the odium—of reasserting the rights, both he as lessee, and the Crown as ultimate owner, would stand to gain. These incentives to individuals to collect for the Crown some of its more difficult dues and arrears were soon accompanied by wholesale subcontracting of branches of the revenue. Even the coinage was put out to farm, the minting of farthing tokens being leased to Lord Harington in 1612 for three years in recompense for the £32,000 he said he had spent in attending the Princess Elizabeth.

From here it was but a short step to even more disreputable methods of preying upon the public. Elizabethan parliaments had enacted strict laws against Catholic recusants and in 1605 James saw an easy way of gratifying his followers by granting the right to enforce these laws and to take the profits. This system lent itself either to extortion, or to total immunity from the laws for the recusant who was granted to a friend. The most active period of these grants was between 1605 and 1611, the commonest form being the gift to a courtier of the fine and forfeiture of eight or ten named recusants. Analogous to these grants of recusants was the ancient custom of giving the wardship of rich minors to influential peers and courtiers, who could then resell them to the mother or relatives or marry them to their own children. The history of this practice, however, follows a different path from that of other grants, since vigorous protests in the Commons and the good sense of the 1st Earl of Salisbury led to a decline in the early seventeenth century.

Failing these many and varied grants at the disposal of the Crown, all that remained to be begged were the powers of the Crown as the fount of honour and as patron of office. The role played by the sale of titles in keeping the court system afloat has already been discussed at length. Between 1603 and 1629 the courtiers were allowed to handle, for a profit, first the granting of knighthoods, then the sale of baronets, and finally the sale of peerages themselves. Between 1603 and 1629 at least £650,000 was raised by this method, over £100,000 of which passed directly into the pockets of existing peers of the realm.

This list gives some idea of the range of gifts at the direct disposal of the Crown. There were, however, possibilities of exercising pressure on others. Bishops were bullied into sharing their wealth with the courtiers, aldermen were cajoled into marrying their rich daughters to royal favourites. And there were other benefits which could be conferred. One, which involved power rather than wealth, was the creation of new borough seats in the

House of Commons. Sir John Neale has proved beyond possibility of doubt that the creation of sixty-two new borough seats by Elizabeth between 1558 and 1586 was the result of pressure from courtiers seeking new forms of patronage. It was some compensation to the nobility for their declining military and social authority to obtain control, if only temporarily, over a handful of borough seats. At the time neither monarch nor patron nor borough corporation could foresee the long-term political consequences of such generosity.

This quest for patronage worked two ways and the great courtier, by reason of his influence in obtaining favours from the Crown, soon found himself besieged by eager clients anxious for his protection. Without any positive encouragement from the Crown, the mere knowledge of this influence was enough to bring clergy, dons, and aldermen scurrying to take cover under the coat-tails of the royal favourites. An easy way of rewarding a courtier or minor official was by bullying an Oxford or Cambridge college into accepting a nominee as scholar, fellow, or head. For the nobility this was no more than compensation for the rights over monastic patronage they had exercised before the Dissolution for their friends and relatives. Jobbing a chaplain into a fellowship or a younger son into a scholarship was a substitute for retiring an old servant with a monastic corrody or stuffing an unwanted daughter away in a nunnery. For the lesser figures about the Court it was a way of looking after the children, a method of exercising influence, and, it must regretfully be admitted, not infrequently the means of making a little money in bribes and gifts from ambitious scholars. For the Crown it was an economical way of fobbing off a suitor by the exercise of powers which at the Reformation it had seized from the Papacy.

These examples could easily be multiplied, but they serve to show the way court patronage was eating into all private spheres of interest. By 1640 there was a very widespread feeling that the influence of the Court had increased, was increasing, and ought to be diminished.

## IV. THE BURDEN OF OFFICE

Hitherto attention has exclusively been focused upon the rich variety of the harvest to be reaped from life at Court. Nothing has so far been said about the hard labour in the fields, about the fate of those whose crops were blighted, or about the inescapable overheads which reduced the profits even of the most successful. For while the scramble for grants is plain enough, it is not so readily apparent that life at Court or in office involved very heavy expenses which could only be met by such grants. It was a point which indignant orators in the House of Commons were apt to overlook when they denounced so fiercely the whole grant system.

It was vital for courtiers to be well dressed in the latest style, at a time when male fashions were at their most unstable and when rich embroidery and lacing were raising the price of clothes to extravagant levels. It was necessary to entertain lavishly, and to have sufficient resources to indulge in that habitual gambling for high stakes which filled so much of the courtier's day. Lastly, there was the rent or upkeep of a house in the west end of London, the purchase and maintenance of a sumptuous coach, the hiring of footmen to provide a suitably impressive retinue. The additional cost of all this in excess of a nobleman's normal expenditure in the country is very difficult to calculate. Even for those without any official position, it can hardly have been less than £1,000 a year in the early seventeenth century. Those with lesser offices might easily spend an additional £2,000 a year one way or another, and the greatest political figures, an Essex, a Salisbury, or a Buckingham, would find themselves spending £5,000 to £10,000 or even more in excess of the norm for a country magnate. If men as favoured as Essex under Elizabeth and Carlisle under James and Charles managed to spend money as fast as or faster than the monarch could hand it out to them, it is not surprising if lesser beneficiaries often ended up in debt.

Medieval monarchs had been peripatetic, moving restlessly from palace to palace, from hunting-lodge to hunting-lodge. By the sixteenth century administrative necessity had long since bound the King to reside for most of the year in the vicinity of London. But their flair for publicity inspired the Tudors, and especially Elizabeth, to tour the country in summer in order to show themselves to their loving subjects—and to sample their hospitality. And so almost every year there set forth a huge caravan led by the Queen, accompanied by her ladies, by some members of the Privy Council, and by noblemen and courtiers, waited on by an army of royal servants and supported by a baggage train of between 400 and 600 carts forcibly impressed from a reluctant peasantry. It was

to accommodate and entertain this nomadic horde that the great
courtiers of Elizabeth and James vied with each other in building
the gigantic 'prodigy' houses—Burghley and Theobalds put up
by Lord Burghley, Holdenby by Sir Christopher Hatton, Hatfield
by the Earl of Salisbury, Audley End by the Earl of Suffolk—the
cost of which alone was enough to drive the owners headlong
into debt.

Once built, these vast palaces then had to be lived in, and also
used to entertain the sovereign. Those anxious to preserve or
increase their favour at Court could not afford to show themselves
niggardly in the country on the occasion of a royal visit. Both
Elizabeth and James expected to be richly feasted and elaborately
amused, and to be sent on their way with expensive parting gifts.
Sir John Thynne gave Elizabeth a jewel costing £140 in 1574,
Lord Keeper Puckering a nosegay of diamonds worth £400 in
1595. The officials of the royal household, the chamber and the
stable, the trumpeters and the guards, all expected their share of
both food and tips, the scale of the latter amounting to as much
as £100 as early as 1561. Elizabeth visited Theobalds no fewer
than thirteen times, and the cost of playing host rose as the royal
appetite for splendour of entertainment grew ever more voracious.
In 1575 a fourteen-day visit to Theobalds only cost Burghley
£309 together with another £32 worth of food sent in by friends,
but in 1591 a ten-day visit cost him £900. A progress cost the
Queen herself about £100 a day in 1560, so that on balance she
was more or less living free.

If we take into account the changing value of money, these late
Elizabethan progresses were among the most expensive ever
staged, and it is hardly surprising that there developed a certain
bashfulness among potential hosts without ambitions at Court.
Elizabeth's notorious inability to make up her mind meant that
every summer the whole country was a prey to agitated speculation as stories spread of an impending visit from Her Gracious
Majesty. Erratic and destructive as a hurricane, summer after
summer Elizabeth wandered about the English countryside bringing ruin in her train, while apprehensive noblemen abandoned
their homes and fled at the mere rumour of her approach. Sir
Thomas Arundell was unwilling to have the name of Wardour
Castle so much as mentioned in a progress time in case the Queen
took it into her head to visit it.

Nor were the Stuarts better received in some quarters. In 1608 King James threatened a descent upon Northamptonshire 'as unwelcom as rain in harvest', and the prudent Lord Spencer promptly fled to Kent. When the blow next fell on Lord Spencer in 1626 with a proposed visit from Henrietta Maria, the old man took to his bed with an ague and the danger was again successfully warded off. It was left to his son, with a higher sense of his social obligations and a laxer grip on the purse-strings, to make handsome amends in 1634 at a cost of £800.

As we have seen, service in time of war was regarded as an obligation which the peerage thought itself morally obliged to fulfil. To get a glimpse of what it cost a leading nobleman to undertake a military expedition, we may glance at the expenses of the Earl of Leicester under Elizabeth. He raised £25,000 by sale and mortgage of some of his land to fit himself out for the Low Countries expedition of 1585, and he borrowed £13,000 from the Queen to pay for an additional troop of horse. When it is argued that he behaved dishonestly in raising his own salary as Lieutenant-General from £6 a day to £10. 13s., this personal investment of nearly £40,000 should not be forgotten. Corrupt he certainly was, but his expenses on military adventures in the last seven years of his life go far to explain, if not to justify, his conduct. If the great court parasites 'lay sucking at the brests of the State', they were also prepared on occasion to give their wet nurse something in return, particularly in time of war.

A nobleman was chosen individually to go abroad as ambassador, and when the summons came it was neither politic nor honourable to refuse. That service upon embassies involved a severe drain on the personal finances of the lord was a convention accepted by both King and peers: it was the other side of the coin of gifts, rewards, and favours. Renaissance diplomacy was conducted on two levels, of which the first was the day-to-day routine, handled by the permanent ambassador in residence; the second was high-level negotiations for a marriage treaty or a military alliance, and the ostentatious display of opulence and splendour on such formal occasions as the christening of a royal child or the conferring of the Order of the Garter. The permanent ambassadors at this time were mostly of lesser rank, men like Sir Edward Stafford or Sir Henry Wotton, who despite their incessant complaints do not seem to have fared too badly. Sir William Cornwallis lobbied for the post as consul in Venice, not, he was careful to point out, with a view to 'service unto Venus' with the famous courtesans of the Rialto, but rather 'in my absence to restore and recover my estate which is shrunk and shaken with so many years service to a prince utterly without reward'. It was the great set-pieces which ran away with the money, and these were reserved for peers. It was not merely that only a man of the highest rank was thought suitable for such occasions, but also that the financial strain was too great to be borne by any but a man of really great wealth. When the summons came, the nobleman had first to equip himself for the journey. He had to have horses, coaches, sumptuous clothes for himself, and rich liveries for his attendants. He had to transport himself and his train across sea and land to the foreign capital. Once abroad, he had to maintain his horde of servants and attendants, to entertain lavishly, and to dispense rich presents to influential officials and politicians about the Court.

Towards these enormous costs the English Crown—as always —made only a grudging contribution. Elizabeth usually, but not invariably, made a modest cash advance of a few hundred pounds for equipment, paid—in due course—an expense claim for travel and postage, and gave a salary for maintenance of between £4 and £6 a day. But this allowance was not adjusted to keep pace with the price revolution—the Earl of Lincoln in 1572 and the Earl of Leicester sixty years later were both given £6 a day for embassies to France—and it was in any case months or even years in arrears. Once the ambassador had presented his credentials, the basic cost of food and housing was expected to be met by the host government, so that in theory the *per diem* allowance should have been sheer gain. In fact the incidental extras ate it all up and there was rarely any money left over. The Earl of Bedford reckoned that two embassies to France and Scotland for Elizabeth had left him at least £3,300 out of pocket. On his departure for home the ambassador might expect a rich present from the prince to whom he had been accredited, and occasionally this was on so gigantic a scale as to convert the embassy from a loss to a profit.

During the reign of Elizabeth the European inflation steadily widened the gap between soaring expenses and an unaltered daily allowance, and in the 1590's things got so bad that for the first time there developed a reluctance on the part of the nobility to continue to serve the Queen upon such terms; the final indignity occurred in 1603 when the ambassador to Scotland, Sir William Bowes, was arrested for debt by a London grocer while he was going about the Queen's business.

The situation was obviously becoming intolerable, but things improved very little in the first years of King James. When in 1604 the Earl of Hertford led an embassy to the Archduke in Brussels, he is said to have spent between £10,000 and £12,000 in excess of his allowance, a figure which his private papers suggest may well be not too far from the truth. Royal service was thus by no means an unmixed blessing. There were a few who gained a vast fortune, some who acquired a modest competence, and many who were enabled to live in a style which would otherwise have been beyond their means. There were many more, however, who gained nothing but debts and disappointment. If life at Court was nearly all kicks under Elizabeth, it was certainly not exclusively ha'pence under James and Charles. In 1661 the Marquis of Argyle warned his son that 'it is possible a man may get an estate at Court, but it is more probable he may lose one; . . . so much is a Court worse than a lottery'.

## V. THE IMPACT OF THE SYSTEM

Just how many of the peerage were in Court at any given time is not at all easy to discover. For what it is worth, it looks as if up to two-thirds of the peerage spent at any rate part of their time at Court in the early and middle years of Elizabeth. Contemporaries believed that numbers were falling off in the late 1590's, and they may well have been right. The accession of the open-handed James saw a flood of peers and squires to Court, and at least three-quarters of the aristocracy were permanent or occasional courtiers between 1603 and 1615. Though the surge into London never ceased, the irresponsible despotism of Buckingham and the moral turpitude of the courtiers prevented any noticeable increase in the number actually in Court between 1616 and 1628. It was not till Charles's personal government, from 1629 to 1640, that the situation was drastically changed. Political and religious opposition combined with enforcement of government regulations about residence in London and the drying up of the flow of favours sharply to reduce the number of Court peers to between a third and a half of the whole body.

In any discussion of office it must be remembered that there were deep-seated structural reasons why only a small, and indeed a diminishing, number of total applicants could hope to be satisfied. Two outstanding peculiarities of England in the sixteenth century were its failure to create a large standing army and its failure to develop a national bureaucracy covering both central and local government. The lack of a permanent army meant that in peacetime there were very few military posts indeed suitable for the nobility. The central organs of government certainly expanded greatly, especially during the 1530's, but several of the new departments disappeared again in the reorganization of the 1550's, and in any case the growth was more in clerks and minor officials than in posts suitable for a magnate. Local government remained firmly in the hands of the unpaid country gentry acting as J.P.s, and the only increase of aristocratic offices under the Tudors was by the creation of the post of Lord Lieutenant of the Shire.

The first task is to discover just how many of the peerage managed to secure for themselves an office which satisfied their desire for employment, prestige, and emoluments. Apart from membership of the Privy Council, under half a dozen of whose aristocratic members held no other office, there were fewer than thirty positions in the late sixteenth century to which peers of the realm could with dignity aspire, and to which they were sometimes appointed. Really great offices carrying serious responsibility were fewer than twenty, a number which hardly altered under James.

Although in England *empleomania* never became anything like the obsession it did in Spain or France, the same pressures were at work, and the gentry were increasingly attracted by the prospect of office. So many families had risen that way in the 1530's and 1540's that the tradition of easy fortunes to be made in office lingered on long after much of the reality had fled. Moreover, the spectacular wealth that still came to the successful few blinded the many to the length of the odds against them. As in the present-day bar, the prestige of the profession and the huge fortunes to be won by a small minority stimulated a rush of aspirants out of all proportion to the rewards that could reasonably be expected. If a guess has to be made—and it can be little more—it would be that the ratio of aspirants to suitable jobs under Elizabeth was about 2 to 1 for the aristocracy, 5 to 1 for the 500 leading county families, and anything up to 30 to 1 for the parochial gentry, Of the 679 gentry of Yorkshire in 1642 only 22 held salaried offices under the Crown in London, Ireland, or at home, and only a further 10 held stewardships of crown lands.

Striking evidence of the explosive demand for office under the Crown in the decades after 1585 is provided by the manuscript lists of offices, office-holders, and fees that found their way into almost every substantial country house in England. Though one or two belong to the middle of the sixteenth century and a handful to the 1570's, they can mostly be dated to between 1585 and 1625. There are at least sixty examples of this period and no doubt there were once hundreds more. This evidence of gentry competition for government office can be supported from other angles. One or two prudent Elizabethan fathers were beginning to provide for younger sons by selling land and using the money to purchase an office. During the reign of Elizabeth this pressure from below was held in check by the social snobbery of the Queen, a prejudice which did much to ensure that at any rate the earls were usually given official employment. But James had few such inhibitions and many favourites and Scottish cronies to reward. In the struggle for office the older peerage—and particularly the barons —were now exposed to the full blast of competition from a masterful and self-confident gentry. There were said to have been 300–400 candidates for the top twenty or so offices in the new household of the little Prince Charles in 1638.

The percentage of eligible peers who held office rose very slightly from the Elizabethan to the Early Stuart period, but this was merely the result of the greater willingness of the Stuarts to elevate to the peerage men who had proved their worth in responsible positions: about 60 per cent. of the post-1603 creations were office-holders. It was also due to the fact that under James the rate of turnover in office was very much faster than under Elizabeth. It is these two factors rather than any real increase in aristocratic office-holding that explains why in 38 years the Early Stuarts employed 84 peers whereas Elizabeth in 45 could only find places for 56. But the true measure of aristocratic office-holding is revealed by the percentage of heirs of peers, as distinct from new creations, who succeeded in obtaining office, and it is here that the important change lies. Whereas 33 per cent. took office under Elizabeth, only 22 per cent. had such luck under the

Early Stuarts. This was the inevitable result of the rapid numerical increase in the peerage, far outstripping the modest increase in the number of jobs. Unless the Crown was willing deliberately to adopt a more aristocratic policy in selecting its officers, the prospects for a born peer inevitably diminished, just at the time when he was increasingly turning to the Court rather than the Country to provide him with a career.

When one looks at the pattern of office-holding it becomes obvious that the experience of individual families differed very widely indeed. Earls had much stronger claims to office than mere barons and were more frequently successful, though there were four successive earls of Bath who held no office at all between 1558 and 1641. Some families seem to have been content with their lot and lived mostly in the country; others had retirement forced upon them by their Catholic beliefs; yet others spent a century vainly seeking office, usually with disastrous financial consequences. One or two families, on the other hand, successfully maintained their grip on royal favour. The Berties and the Herberts held office from generation to generation without a break, and the Comptons and the Howards of Effingham were not far behind. Some, like the Brookes, the Careys, the Cecils lords Burghley, and the Norths, held office continuously under Elizabeth, but failed to retain their influence under the new dynasty. The accession of the Stuarts saw their replacement by new families like the Hamiltons and the Saviles, the Stuarts and the Sydneys, who were all in office for two successive generations.

Attendance at Court and the holding of office are only two of the three factors involved in this problem of the relations between the Crown and the aristocracy. The third is the flow of gifts and favours from the Crown, its amount and its direction. Here again, we cannot rest content with mere impressions and must attempt, however doubtfully, to provide some sort of quantitative measurement (see Appendix II). On balance it is likely that both the incompleteness of the evidence and the method of calculation adopted tend to underestimate the full value of the benefits to individuals. On the other hand, a number of the grants were in compensation for expenditure on state service, the cost of which the Crown would otherwise have been obliged to bear. Moreover, it may be that they exaggerate the true cost to the Crown, since some of the grants were direct, in the form of cash, land, or

annuities, while others were indirect, like monopolies and customs farms, the full profits of which could only theoretically have
been obtained by the Crown itself.

Between 1558 and 1641 the Crown gave away to the peerage
grants and favours to the value of over three-and-a-half million
pounds in Jacobean money. But this huge sum was not distributed
evenly either in time or throughout the peerage as a whole. In the
later years of Elizabeth the scale of giving was only a little over
half what it had been in the earlier (and nearly half of what little
was given poured into the bottomless pockets of a single individual, Robert Earl of Essex). It is hardly surprising, therefore, that
the accession of King James was greeted with rapturous enthusiasm. Six months after the death of Elizabeth, the Earl of Shrewsbury remarked with satisfaction that 'she valued every molehill
that she gave . . . at a mountain; which our Sovereign now does
not'. This was an understatement of the attitude of James, who
scampered south in 1603 to savour what he assumed to be the
inexhaustible wealth that had fallen to him. In his anxiety to please
he was ready to share these riches out among his friends, old and
new, or indeed to hand them out to anyone who cared to ask him
politely. As a result, the rate of giving increased by a factor of
over 13 in the next twenty-five-and-a-half years, when James and
Buckingham succeeded in giving away to the aristocracy alone a
sum equivalent to half the total cost to Elizabeth of the Anglo-
Spanish War from 1585 to 1603.

Such largesse would have been impossible without the making
of peace, a fact that cannot have escaped the notice of the privy
councillors who negotiated the treaty in 1604. It is more than a
coincidence that all the more vociferous members of the anti-
Spanish, war party in the reign of James were either members of
the country gentry group with little expectation of royal favour,
or were fallen courtiers like Ralegh with nothing more to hope for.

But the spending spree did not last. James died in 1625 and the
assassination of Buckingham in 1628 jolted Charles out of his
complacency. The King now determined to rule without Parliament and to launch an administrative new deal. The lavish distribution of favours of the past quarter of a century was a luxury
the Crown could no longer afford, and one which in any case
offended against the spirit of the new order. In consequence the
scale of giving fell away to less than a quarter of its previous rate,

though it was still three times larger than that of the latter years
of Elizabeth. If office and rewards are lumped together, the same
picture of fluctuating distribution emerges.

A further fact to emerge from these calculations is the extreme
inequality of the share-out. If only 117 out of the 342 eligible
peers received some part of the whole, a mere 29 of these 117
obtained 75 per cent., and 9 hogged no less than 45 per cent. Of
these 29 individuals upon whom the sun shone so brightly, 21
received all or most of their grants between 1603 and 1628. Five
of the 21 were members of the Howard family, and 2 of the
Villiers, the first group getting about £400,000 or so, the second
at least £500,000. Of the remaining 21, 5 were Scotsmen, who
obtained about £850,000 during this time, or nearly a third of all
that was going. There is thus some justification for the irritation
of English peers at this invasion of highly favoured carpet-
baggers from the north. Nor does this figure give an adequate
picture of the full measure of favour to the Scots, for a dispropor-
tionately large number of the lesser beneficiaries were also Scotsmen. It was not merely a case of blowing up a handful of favourites
into English dukes and earls, but of rescuing from penury a mob
of 'beggarly blewcaps' who had ridden down hopefully with the
King on their lean horses in 1603.


## VI. THE CONSEQUENCES OF THE SYSTEM

If the sixteenth-century nobility were powerfully attracted by
the Court and were eager competitors for royal office, the Crown
was no less anxious to encourage them in their ambitions. Like
the other monarchs of Europe, the Tudors realized the importance
of an alluring court as a stabilizing political factor. The King
needed a respectable turn-out of nobles to give lustre to his court
and to impress foreigners and gentlemen up from the country
with the splendour and opulence of his way of life. Even Henry VII
had cultivated a luxurious court, and a woman as naturally parsimonious as Queen Elizabeth was careful to maintain a stately and
expensive establishment.

More important, the Court served to distract the nobles from
the dangerous rural pastimes of riot and rebellion, and to occupy
them in time-consuming ceremonial and intrigue, both of which
centred round the Prince and tended to enhance his prestige and

his authority. As the Earl of Northumberland was told in 1566, an absentee landlord could not command the same personal loyalty as a man living on the spot, and in any case potential traitors were more easily watched and their plots more swiftly intercepted if they were at Court than if they were lurking undisturbed in their rural strongholds. So long as the King was powerful enough to make a palace revolution unlikely, he felt safer with his magnates around him.

The first effect of attracting the nobility to court by the lure of office and rewards was to turn them from haughty and independent magnates into a set of shameless mendicants. 'Need obeys no law and forgets blushing', wrote that paragon among Elizabethans, Sir Philip Sydney. Sir John Harington, finding Elizabeth unappreciative of his water-closet, sent King James in Scotland, as a New Year Gift for 1603, a lantern adorned with a crucifixion. Beneath were the words of the good thief on the cross, 'Lord, remember me when thou comest into thy kingdom', an allusion which even James may have found a little hard to stomach. It is very difficult today for us to recapture the hectic atmosphere of the Court with its scurrying intrigues, its hordes of promoters and projectors buttonholing the great with novel schemes for preying on the State and the subject; and at the centre the King, pursued by the wheedling cries of suitors from palace to palace, from chamber to chamber, from bedroom to hunting-field. Exasperated by this ceaseless barrage of importunity James once exclaimed in fury: 'You will never let me alone. I would to God you had first my doublet and then my shirt, and when I were naked I think you would give me leave to be quiet.'

The psychological and financial dependence of the nobility upon the Crown was further strengthened by the fact that many offices and rewards themselves gave rise to fresh entanglements. Under Elizabeth the running up of enormous debts to the Crown became a regular feature of royal service. By this means powerful political personalities were kept sweet, the cost being met by their less influential heirs, who in turn were cowed by fears of demands for immediate repayment and by hopes of favourable treatment. Other grants that could be cut off or renewed at will served a similar purpose of binding the nobility to the Crown. Attracted to the Court by hope of favours, peers were kept docile for fear of losing these elusive benefits, for opposition to the royal will might involve severe economic sanctions. A particularly useful tool for this purpose was the pension list, whose enormous extension under James has already been noted.

If from the point of view of the Crown the Court system was an invaluable weapon in its dealings with the aristocracy, to the latter it was a powerful factor in the advancement or decay of family fortunes. There were those who suspected that the Tudors deliberately set out to clip the wings of the over-mighty subject by absorbing his surplus revenues in expenditure on government service. On the other hand it was equally clear, particularly under Henry VIII and James, that a very large number of families owed their rise to the top at any rate in part to royal office and favour. Though the admixture of other factors in the history of almost every family makes statistical precision impossible, there is one calculation which may perhaps prove illuminating for the early seventeenth century. The gross landed income of the 121 aristocratic families of 1641 was about £630,000—let us say £700,000 to be on the safe side. Capitalized at 20 years' purchase this amounts at most to about £14 million. In the previous 40 years these families had been given by the Crown over £4 million in money of 1640, or in other words about 30 per cent. of their total capital assets at the end of the period. In addition to these grants there should be added the direct profits of office, corruption, and the sale of offices—an unknown and incalculable figure which it would be reasonable to capitalize at not less than another £2 million. From all this one may conclude that office and favour in the previous forty years had enabled between a quarter and third of aristocratic families to live opulently—some even wildly extravagantly—and were responsible for perhaps a quarter of the total capital assets of the group in 1641.

The successful operation of the Court system depended on the maintenance of a delicate and extremely complicated political balance. Since offices suitable to the nobility were restricted in number, the greatest care had to be exercised in the distribution of these few so as to prevent a monopoly of tenure by any one faction. When this occurred, as under Wolsey, Protector Somerset, Sir Robert Cecil, and the Duke of Buckingham, explosive tensions built up among the excluded. The power of promotion and reward was the greatest hold the Crown exercised over the nobility and it was essential that this carrot should continue to dangle before the donkey's nose. Withdraw it altogether and the animal jibbed. As Richard Lloyd of Esclus remarked in 1641, 'it is as neccessary for Princes to have places of preferment to prefer servants of merit as money in their Exchequer'.

The unfortunate consequences of a closing of the opportunity for employment, of allowing a monopoly of political patronage to fall into the hands of a single clique, were most clearly displayed at the turn of the century, for both the Essex Rebellion of 1601 and the Main Plot of 1603 are principally to be explained in terms of thwarted ambition. Elizabeth's tactics on the domestic front had always been to play one group of noblemen off against another: Burghley and Sussex against Leicester and Warwick in her early days; Cecil, Nottingham, and Buckhurst against Essex and his friends in the later. But in 1600 Essex's overweening intransigence destroyed this carefully adjusted political balance, and as a result an important group of courtiers was thrown out into the cold. Similarly, a realignment of the victors after the accession of James pushed out another courtier group of Ralegh, Cobham, and Grey of Wilton, whose hopes of political advancement now seemed permanently blasted. But this is far from being a complete explanation of the revolts and it is hard to avoid the conclusion that financial stress was in all cases an important contributory factor in driving rebels to desperation.

In 1600 the Earl of Essex was a man of 34 who had long enjoyed royal favour, but had suddenly, and it seemed irrevocably, fallen from grace. In the years before the collapse, his personal finances had been slithering towards disaster. Despite the most lavish royal grants of lands and parks, woods, cash, and monopolies, his outgoings had continued to exceed his income. His general style of living, his assiduous cultivation of a huge clientèle to support his political position, and heavy personal expenditure on his military expeditions all combined to run him into debt. By now he was living on the credit of the great London merchants and bankers and particularly on the syndicate which farmed his Sweet Wine monopoly. The end of royal favour and the Queen's refusal to renew the monopoly brought a crisis in his affairs. The refusal meant that he would be obliged to abandon his political position, retire into the country, and sell some of his estate to clear off the debt. He was not faced with financial ruin—there would still be plenty left when the dust had settled—but the old way of life could no longer be maintained. His main psychological incentive was undoubtedly thwarted ambition, but the ceaseless nagging of his creditors, and a realization of the severely reduced circumstances in which he would in future have to drag out his existence were exacerbating factors which drove him to the act of folly that was to cost him his life.

Of his seven aristocratic followers, five—Rutland, Southampton, Sussex, Bedford, and Mounteagle—were angry young men in a hurry, all in their twenties, all chafing at the infuriating grip on office retained by the Cecils. But they too were hard pressed financially, frustration and idleness having led them into courses of extravagant dissipation. The remaining two—Lords Sandys and Cromwell—were embittered men of middle age whose lives had been failures. For years they had hung around the Court or gone soldiering in Ireland in the vain hope of responsible and lucrative office; for years they had struggled with mounting debt, for years they had been selling up the family estates.

The seven aristocratic rebels thus all had one thing in common: they had long been spending at a rate that exceeded their income, and their financial positions were all deteriorating. Some were men of great wealth for whom a period of retrenchment and readjustment was all that was required; others were genuinely poor and were unable to carry on without the aid of some lucrative office under the Crown. It was lust for power and responsibility which had lured these men to Court in the first place, thwarted ambition which had driven them to dissipation, dissipation which had caused the mounting burden of debts, and the necessity to reduce the burden which provided the added incentive to an attempt to seize office by force. It is thus unrealistic to separate power and profit as motives which drove noblemen to seek office under the Crown.

The same picture emerges from an analysis of the Main and Bye Plot conspirators—or intriguers—of 1603. These so-called plots of 1603 are composed of the same basic elements as were observed in the Essex Revolt of 1601: courtiers threatened with loss of power and influence; courtiers and soldiers disappointed at the lack of reward; courtiers infuriated by the monopoly of favour enjoyed by the Cecil–Howard grouping; all, whether rich or poor, with a record of living beyond their incomes and of growing financial difficulties. Faced with the alternative of revolt to seize power or withdrawal into rustic solitude at a seriously reduced standard of living, they chose the former. Such was the magnetism of office and the Court, such the attraction of high living, that the thought of impotent exile on a strict budget was unendurable.

As we have seen, after 1629 the flow of favours was again reduced to a trickle and the numbers at Court were severely restricted. As at the end of Elizabeth's reign, so again in 1640, the King discovered that such a policy dangerously swelled the number of discontented outsiders. After the Civil War was over, the Marquis of Newcastle bluntly told Charles II that his father had had 'no manner of regard of the nobility at all, but some few to monopolize the King and Queen totally to themselves. This did infinitely discontent the nobility and gentry, and was one of the things that brought these woeful times upon us.'

If the political stability of the system was delicately poised, so also was the financial. The sixteenth-century state had to support its bureaucracy and its court and pay for its wars with revenues which were never sufficient for its needs. Without the powerful injection of the wealth of the Church in the middle of the century it could not have survived as long as it did, for the political machine depended on a steady flow of gifts and rewards from the monarch. By their very success in reducing the over-mighty subject the Tudors increased the need for such a flow, for as time went on they were less and less able to call upon a reserve of rich noblemen content to devote a substantial part of their private fortunes to the service of the State. After the magnates had been weakened by the expense of royal service, it became one of the most necessary functions of monarchy so to distribute its favours as to provide rich rewards for its greatest servants, and a reasonable competence for the professional courtiers and for the lesser administrative officers. This burden was no slight one in any case, absorbing as it did in peace-time a very large amount of the finances of the State. But the pressures of inflation, which reduced official fees to what in real terms were derisory levels, and the evasion by the propertied classes of their fiscal obligations, made it an increasingly intractable problem as the sixteenth century wore on.

In the 1580's and 1590's the appalling cost of the Anglo-Spanish War, coupled with a natural parsimony which increased with old age, induced Queen Elizabeth severely to reduce her gifts to all except her favourite, the Earl of Essex—and even he was hard put to it to make ends meet. Her nearest associates gained the impression that the close-fistedness of her later years was due as much to temperamental meanness as to harsh necessity. Thomas Wilson reflected philosophically that 'her years hath now brought with it (the inseparable quality thereof) nearness', and Goodman frankly admitted that 'she . . . grew to be very covetous in her old days'.

This austerity programme had two important and unfortunate consequences, the impoverishment of the Court aristocracy, and the growth of corruption in the public services. With a few exceptions, the greater officers of state found themselves running into debt to maintain the standard of living expected of them, while the position of the unestablished courtiers was even more critical. When we seek the reason for the deteriorating financial position of the peerage at the end of the reign, the unrequited burden of court and office is one of the two most important.

Under these circumstances it is hardly surprising that officials resorted to corruption in an effort to maintain themselves. What started as an attempt to compensate for royal parsimony and static salaries in a time of inflation grew uncontrollably into a permanent and established part of the official scene. This process has been admirably described by Sir John Neale, and needs no further elaboration here. His contention that the 1590's saw a positive deterioration in official morality is supported by the lack of offers of bribes in earlier petitions to the Cecils. It is possible, even likely, that Leicester had been very corrupt, but all the evidence suggests that it was not till the 1590's that venality became widespread. And it is the spread which is important, for if it is admitted that few governments and societies in the history of the world have been free from bribery and extortion, squeeze and protection, wire-pulling and nepotism, it is also true that when carried to extreme lengths these habits have again and again provoked revolts, some successful, some less so, by the exploited classes. The true problem is to define the permissive limit, not to demonstrate the existence of the phenomenon.

Of minor importance were those gifts of 'lamprey pies, salmon, venison red and fallow, and other small tokens' with which Henry Lord Berkeley used to sweeten the course of his lawsuits and petitions, and offers of which bulk so large in the correspondence of Sir Robert Cecil. How they poured in! Smoked salmon, pheasants, hounds, a Barbary falcon, an Irish nag, six cheeses, two firkins of oysters, there was no end to the stream of gifts. Some were too large to be received without demur. When Lord Cromwell gave two horses, one was sent back; there were decencies to be observed. Equally acceptable were those well-established fees which every official exacted from the public for carrying out his duties. If these fees had risen sharply in the last half-century, so had incomes and the cost of living. But what of 'gratuities' paid to courtiers or officials for particular services rendered, whether it be the grant of an office or a patent of monopoly, a pardon for a murderer or a licence to export beer? Professor Aylmer has estimated that by the 1630's these private fees and gratuities came to about £300,000, which is about half of the total ordinary cash income of the Crown.

To this deteriorating situation there was added the temptations and opportunities of war finance, and a distinct weakening of moral integrity on the part of the rising generation of courtiers. It was the impact of merchant capital on a venal court and official world which so gravely accelerated the drift up to and beyond the acceptable threshold of corruption. The lavish bribes of the custom farmers, the careers of men like Lionel Cranfield and Arthur Ingram, prove beyond doubt the degree to which things had deteriorated by the early years of King James.

The greatest casualty of this development was public respect for the highest officers of state. Most of them tried to save their faces by keeping in the background, often adopting the time-honoured device, mentioned by Tacitus, of using their wives as agents. Lord Buckhurst used his daughter Anne Lady Glemham, the Earl of Salisbury his niece the Countess of Derby, and the Earl of Suffolk his wife the Countess. The level to which public morality had sunk when Elizabeth died is perhaps best illustrated by a letter of Sir Robert Cecil to his secretary Michael Hicks, written in February 1604. He is trying to obtain a favour requiring Lord Buckhurst's support. He therefore instructs Hicks to offer Lady Glemham £100 to give to her father, adding the warning not to hand over the cash in advance 'or else she may cozen you'. Finally he adds a postscript: 'For the £100 I will find a ward to pay it.' Here is a letter written by a Secretary of State and Master of the

Court of Wards about a Lord Treasurer. It takes for granted that
the latter's support can be bought, and offers to find the money
for the bribe by a corrupt use of official authority. Such was the
condition to which Elizabeth's parsimony and their own defects
of character had reduced the great officials and court peers.

By 1603 courtiers and officials had got used to these venal ways,
and no improvement occurred now that the largesse of King
James had removed the financial justification for corruption. Unlike Elizabeth, James was unwilling to endure the drudgery of
administrative supervision, and the last check on rampant pecula-
tion consequently collapsed. Royal administration entered its most
squalid phase during the rule of the Duke of Buckingham who
elevated corruption to the status of a system, and it was not until
his death that efforts at a clean-up were begun. But by then it was
too late to restore public confidence, and in any case things had
gone too far for too long for much to be achieved.

If Elizabeth's way of solving the financial problem of the Court
by ruthlessly cutting costs had unforeseen and disastrous consequences, James's alternative was no better. In the first place he
indulged in a massive alienation of royal resources and royal
authority. Between 1603 and 1628 the peerage was given well
over a million pounds' worth of crown lands and rents, which
was perhaps as much as a quarter of all royal estates in 1603. This
erosion of the capital assets of the Crown itself made hope of
financial self-sufficiency more and more unlikely of realization. It
also undermined royal influence on the countryside, since in the
seventeenth century land was still—and was still regarded as—
the basis of prestige and authority as well as a source of income.
But crown lands were not the widow's cruse, and to maintain
his reputation James allowed and encouraged the growth of a
vast ramshackle structure of concealed income and expenditure
administered directly by the courtiers, to whom went all the
profits.

The consequences of these indirect methods of financing the
patronage system of favours and rewards were threefold. By removing the bulk of the operating expenses of the Court from the
official income and expenditure accounts of the Crown, the King
himself, his financial advisers—and subsequent historians—have
all been deceived about its true cost. The total official ordinary
revenue of the Crown in the 1620's amounted to about £500,000

a year; the unrecorded income that passed direct to courtiers and officials by fees from suitors, by grants, by exploitation of their proximity to the throne, by under-assessment for rents or taxes, can hardly have amounted to less than a further £500,000. The burden on the country was not merely far greater than appears at first sight, it was also exacted in the most obnoxious and inequitable way.

Secondly, the peculiarities of the system made radical financial reform extremely difficult, if not impossible. Attempts to raise cash income in one sector merely increased pressure for concealed benefits in another; a transfer of some of the profits of wardship from private to royal hands coincided with a growth of the sale of honours by courtiers; an increase in the customs revenue could only be achieved by compensating the grantees with annuities; a refusal to raise salaries led to the growth of private fees; an attempt to check the rise of these fees merely stimulated corruption; and so on. Viewed in this light, the achievements of financial reformers like Salisbury and Middlesex appear superficial. As they squeezed one part of the balloon, the rubber immediately expanded elsewhere to accommodate the air that was being compressed.

The third consequence of the expansion of the Court system by the Early Stuarts was the sapping of the moral authority of the monarchy. The creeping corruption throughout the administration, the exploitation for personal profit by courtiers of their position as intermediaries between king and subjects, lessened respect for the central organs of government, for the Court, for the nobility, and ultimately for monarchy itself. By the early seventeenth century everyone in government was absorbed in a venal pattern of life as universal as it was discreditable. The financial ethics of the most resolute of reformers, the most devoted of public men, of Salisbury, Cranfield, or Strafford, differed only in degree from those of the parasites they attacked. Not unnaturally such a situation aroused the most violent resentment among those who had to foot the bill, among the country gentry who believed, implausibly, that they themselves would be immune from such temptations were they to come their way. The sense of moral superiority to politicians, which is so normal a feature of public opinion in all times and places, received powerful reinforcement in the early seventeenth century.

It is hardly surprising that the distribution of these favours by the Early Stuarts infuriated the taxpayers and was an important factor in causing Parliament to refuse financial aid. Under Elizabeth government spokesmen could at least ask the Commons to grant taxes with a clear conscience. 'Where', asked Bacon in 1592, 'be the wasteful buildings and the exorbitant and prodigal donatives, the sumptuous dissipations in pleasures and vain ostentations, which we find have exhausted the coffers of so many kings?' Where indeed, if we ignore the grants to Leicester and Essex? But no such defence could be put up for King James. After the Civil War was over and the King dead, Sir Anthony Weldon concluded that 'it may justly be said that King James, like Adam, by bringing the crown into so great a necessity through a profuse prodigality, became the original of his sons fall'.

From one point of view government may be regarded as a device for the redistribution of wealth from the taxpayers to privileged favourites and officials. By the early seventeenth century men were becoming increasingly aware of the polarization of interest between those who ate the King's bread and those who paid for it, a polarization accentuated by the progressive diminution in the share of the tax burden born by the aristocracy and the Court. Not only were peers allowed to run up huge arrears in their payments, but they were progressively under-rated for taxation purposes. The assessed income of approximately the same number of peers, though not all the same families, was about £26,000 a year in 1558 and about £17,500 a year in 1601. If we allow for the fall in the value of money, this represents less than 40 per cent. of the 1558 assessment. It is argued elsewhere that the real income of the peerage was falling during the reign of Elizabeth, but no claim is made for a collapse of quite such catastrophic magnitude. The conclusion is inescapable that the Elizabethan peerage was progressively evading its share of taxation. Moreover, the element of favouritism grew more and more marked, court peers getting off increasingly lightly, whereas country peers like Bath, Vaux, Wharton, Petre, and Robartes were assessed at a far higher rate— though still only at a small fraction of their true income. To quote but one example, in 1624 the Earl of Bath was assessed at £400 and the Earl of Worcester at £200, though the income of the former was probably less than a tenth of that of the latter. Thus even within the peerage class the tax system was grossly inequitable, pressing more hardly on the Country than on the Court, and more hardly on the poor than on the rich.

In their financial relations with the Government the aristocracy would appear to have been almost entirely the beneficiaries, while making very little monetary contribution to the running of the State. In fact, however, this is a false picture, since the contribution of the aristocracy was indirect—in maintaining the pomp of the Court, in giving hospitality on royal progresses, in conducting sumptuous foreign embassies, all at considerable personal cost. But this indirect contribution was not readily appreciated by the taxpayers, and it is easy to see why the House of Commons came to look upon the Court, and in consequence most of the aristocracy, as a purely parasitic order preying on the country at large.

So inept was the Crown that it aroused feelings of exploitation and exclusion among the country gentry without the compensating advantage of satisfying all its clients. Given the extraordinary expansion of royal grants under James, it might have been supposed that political opposition from dissident sections of the aristocracy would have declined. As we have seen, about half of those eligible now either held office or obtained some reward from the Crown, a significantly higher proportion than in the past fifty years. It was at just this time, however, that a small group of men in the House of Lords began vigorously opposing royal policy at all levels, and giving influential backing to the rising tide of criticism in the House of Commons. This must principally be attributed to the growth of real political issues, which inspired men to act without regard for their immediate selfish interests. In part also it was due to the passionate hatred engendered by the rise to absolute power of George Duke of Buckingham, whose upstart pretensions to universal control and whose irresponsible distribution of titles and offices in his own interests generated fierce hostility among the older noble families.

The main reason, however, is that the appearance of widespread generosity is deceptive. It was not merely that office increasingly went to new men, the fraction of sons of peers who obtained office falling from a third to less than a quarter, though this in itself goes far to explain the rising opposition among the Lords. Equally serious was the inequitable and irresponsible manner in which royal favours were distributed. Right from the start friction was generated by the royal policy, for equality of misery creates less discontent than arbitrary distribution of wealth. It was easier for Sir Robert Sydney to put up with Elizabeth's refusal to make him or anyone else a peer, than it was for the older comital families to endure the elevation of George Villiers to a dukedom. Lord Sheffield found it easier to suffer Elizabeth's universal meanness than James's selective generosity, while many an Englishman found it hard to endure with equanimity the sudden rise to affluence of the Scottish courtiers.

The last phase in royal treatment of the problem of the Court opened in 1629 with the death of the Duke of Buckingham and Charles's decision to dispense with Parliament. As it turned out, the sequence of events could not have been more unfortunate for the popularity of monarchy. Elizabeth by her parsimony first endangered the Court system and made corruption an essential ingredient of public service, while at the same time Lord Burghley allowed the propertied classes to fall into the habit of evading their tax responsibilities. James and Buckingham then dissipated royal resources in extravagant gifts and absurdly opulent court festivities. The policy enraged the Commons and provided a legitimate excuse for the refusal to make more parliamentary grants. This refusal in turn obliged the King to auction off his powers for economic regulation, appointment to office, and the creation of new honours, actions which still further exacerbated the political situation. Now there came a period of radical reform, including a sharp reduction of royal largesse, an attack on increases in official fees, heavy taxation of the nobility and upper gentry through wardship and forest fines, and a highly unpopular religious policy. Not only did these measures still further exasperate the country gentry, they also alarmed the administrators, whose fees and perquisites were threatened, and alienated many of the Court nobility.

If in 1640 there was substantial opposition to royal policies in the House of Lords, the basic cause was undoubtedly dislike of Charles's religious and political objectives. Men like Southampton, Clare, and Saye and Sele had been in political opposition since the 1620's. There were some, like Holland and Pembroke, who were devoid of feelings of gratitude towards the Crown upon which they had so long preyed, and others, like Salisbury and Northumberland, who were jealous of the greater rewards that had been showered upon rivals and upstarts. Many had been alienated by their failure to obtain office, a prospect made increasingly unlikely as too many peers chased too few jobs. The exasperation of the disappointed place-hunter was thought by Newcastle to be an important factor in generating aristocratic opposition, and is well reflected in Viscount Chaworth's despairing appeal in 1638: 'Were it to be the King's dog-keeper I would do it and readily too.' Whether successful or not in the quest for office, almost all had been disappointed by the retrenchment of the 1630's, aggrieved by the unaccustomed burden of taxation, and embittered by the contraction of the Court to an exclusive coterie. Men accustomed to a glittering life at Court could ill adapt either to exile in the country or to the sharp reduction in living standards consequent upon the contraction of royal bounty. Charles had few friends in 1641, and one reason was his failure to create strong ties of mutual interest in the maintenance of the *status quo* between King, nobles, and officials. He was not the last autocratic ruler to discover that reform does not pay.

An important by-product of these events and policies was the almost complete alienation of Court from Country, an alienation sharply accentuated by Charles's attempts to drive the gentry and superfluous nobility out of London. By the reign of Charles the concept of harmony within the Commonwealth had broken down, the two words 'Court' and 'Country' having come to mean political, psychological, and moral opposites. As Professor Zagorin has pointed out, 'the term "Country" suggested that the men whom it designated should be regarded as persons of public spirit, unmoved by private interest, untainted by court influence and corruption, representing the highest good of their local communities and the nation in whose interests they, and they only, acted'. This alienation was not confined to politics, for in the 1630's England was experiencing all the tensions created by the development within a single society of two distinct cultures. The one was adopted by the majority of the nobility and a tiny handful of court gentry; the other by the majority of the gentry and a minority of country peers. Dekker was ranged against Massinger; Milton against Davenant; Robert Walker against Van Dyck; Artisan Mannerism against Inigo Jones; suspicion and hatred of Italy as vicious and popish against a passionate admiration for its aesthetic splendours; a belief in the virtues of country living against the sophistication of the London man-about-town; a strong moral antipathy to sexual licence, gambling, stage-plays, hard drinking, duelling, and running into debt, against a natural weakness for all these worldly pleasures and vices; a dark suspicion of ritual and ornament in church worship against a ready acceptance of the beauty of holiness advocated by Laud; and lastly a deeply felt fear and hatred of Papists and Popery against an easy-going toleration for well-connected recusants and a sneaking admiration for Inigo Jones's chapel in Saint James's, got up in full Counter-Reformation fig for the use of Henrietta Maria and her Catholic friends.

It might appear from this analysis that the English Court system collapsed in 1640 because it was too swollen, too expensive—a view which was certainly that of the contemporary Country party. Looked at in a European setting, however, it is clear that the real weakness of the English Court and administration was that it attracted all the odium of the vast tentacular institutions of France and Spain without the compensating advantages of size and strength. Unlike the systems of the Continent, the *ancien régime* in England possessed no standing army to provide employment for the nobility; no paid local officials at all except for feodaries, escheators, and receivers of crown lands; and a central bureaucracy which at the lower levels was not very well paid and was limited in number. The reason for this is political, that the Tudors never managed—and indeed they scarcely tried—to break the hold of the country gentry over local government and over taxation. As a result they could neither expand the administration nor pay for it if they did. At the same time they were trapped by the rigidities of the Common Law, which stopped them from obtaining rights over mineral resources such as were acquired by other nation-states and which went far to protect office-holders from royal interference. Spain waxed rich on a monopoly of silver, the Pope on alum, Sweden on copper, France on salt; all exploited the sale of offices for revenue purposes. But whether for lack of initiative or lack of ability, the English Crown was debarred from these important sources of revenue so successfully tapped by its continental neighbours. It was therefore always short of money and unable to build up a large and loyal vested interest of satisfied place-men. The clumsy and half-hearted efforts of the Early Stuarts to remedy the situation did little either to increase the revenues of the Crown or to swell the numbers of its adherents.

Since the Court and the administration were relatively so

restricted in size, their total cost to the taxpayer, even in the halcyon days of the Duke of Buckingham, was certainly small compared with the burden in France or Spain, even allowing for the huge mass of concealed taxation in fees, bribes, sales of titles, exploitation of monopolies, and so on. In about 1628 it was reckoned that Normandy alone provided Louis XIII with revenues equal to the total ordinary incomes of Charles I. The influential landed classes were certainly being made to pay a little more like their proper share of taxation in the 1630's, but even then the weight of taxation on the rich was still trivial compared with what it was to become at the height of the Civil War a few years later. The resentments aroused were out of all proportion to the hardships suffered, and were directed more against the arbitrary methods of levy and the supposed purposes to which the money was to be put than against the weight of taxation as such.

Finally, the resources available to the Crown were not shared out in an equitable manner. There were therefore large numbers within the system who were dissatisfied with their share of the profits, and were ready to desert their paymaster in 1642. When it came to the push those on the inside were not sufficiently numerous, or sufficiently powerful, or sufficiently conscious of their personal stake to resist assaults from without. By 1640 the Court had contrived to arouse the same resentments as those of the Continent, but had failed to create a vested interest large enough to protect it against the legion of its enemies. Such were the consequences of half a century of ineptitude, by three very different monarchs, in the handling of the patronage system.

# IX

## CREDIT

The moneys employed at interest in this nation are not near the
tenth part disposed to trading people . . . but are for the most
part lent for the supplying of luxury and to support the expence
of persons who, though great owners of lands, yet spend faster
than their lands bring in.

SIR DUDLEY NORTH, *Discourses upon Trade*, 1691, pp. 6–7

No account of the financial situation of the nobility would
be complete without an examination of the uses to which
they put the system of credit. Nor indeed would a history
of the money market and of interest rates make much sense without an analysis of the role of the nobility as borrowers. Sir Dudley
North was speaking with greater knowledge of the money market
than of the problems of landowners, and his explanation of the
latter's dependence upon credit is not entirely fair.

Some borrowing can be explained as a reasonable measure to
adjust fluctuating income to fluctuating expenditure, being used
either as a temporary overdraft or as an anticipation of certain
windfalls in a few years' time; some of it was for purposes of
investment in trade, industry, or fen drainage. When all is said
and done, however, there can be little doubt that most noble
indebtedness, and indeed all the more spectacular examples, were
caused, as Dudley North alleged, by personal extravagance. Some,
like Henry Lord Berkeley, cheerfully went on spending beyond
their income for year after year, decade after decade, content to
see income reduced by land sales and swallowed up in interest
charges. Others, like the 1st Earl of Suffolk, ran up fantastic debts
by excessive building. Some measure of borrowing was dictated
by general factors applicable to all, but it was personal deficiencies
in character and intelligence which time and again turn out to have
been the decisive causes of serious indebtedness.

The only sure way of avoiding the necessity of occasional borrowing was by building up a substantial cash reserve, a policy
fathers were always anxious to press upon their sons, even if they

themselves tended to honour the advice more in the breach than in the observance.

By the middle of the sixteenth century a wide range of choice in the means of borrowing was already available to the nobility. In the first place they could adopt the age-old practice of letting their tradesmen's bills run up until they had exhausted the patience of their suppliers and could get no more goods and services. This has always been a common method of borrowing, but it is regulated by the basic financial resources of the debtor. Those whose need is greatest are least likely to find their tradesmen obliging. None the less the great luxury suppliers of London, the silkmen, mercers, tailors, jewellers, and goldsmiths, were catering for a limited if expanding market and were too greedy to turn away a customer. They adjusted their prices to allow for interest charges, and hoped for the best. As a result some of the greatest noblemen in the kingdom were able to accumulate a really astonishing range of debts to tradesmen. The most striking example of all is that of Thomas Earl of Arundel, who at his death in 1646 had managed to run up shop debts amounting to £16,176. Tradesmen extended credit on this imprudent scale partly because they had little choice. The patronage of a magnate was a prize worth having, and it required iron will and a willingness to cut losses to refuse further credit to a feckless nobleman. Once debts had been run up, it was difficult to know where to stop. The shrewd peer knew this and acted like Middleton's Lord Owemuch, who was 'free of the mercers, and there's none of 'em all dare cross him'.

The leading jewellers and silversmiths also found themselves tempted into the not unprofitable trade of pawnbroking, taking back again as 'gages' or 'pawns' items they had sold to the customer perhaps a few months or years before. All noblemen accumulated substantial quantities of valuables, which in case of need could be turned into ready cash. It is true to say that on the whole the pawning of valuables was a desperate measure, only indulged in by those in the last stages of financial decay. The most tragic case was that of William Lord Vaux, who in 1593 came up to London to do his duty and attend the House of Lords. But, alas, he had pawned his parliament robes to a Londoner, who refused to lend them back for the occasion on payment of interest and stood out obstinately for his principal, which Lord Vaux was quite unable to procure. Well might his lordship describe himself as the 'infortunatest peer of Parliament for poverty that ever was'. Among the less affluent men-about-town such predicaments were common enough, and the trappings of many a gallant passed into the hands of Frippery, the 'filthy-slimy-lousy-nittical broker, pricked out in pawns from the hatband to the shoestring'.

Apart from these minor devices of running up tradesmen's bills and pawning valuables, four principal legal instruments were used by the nobility and gentry for raising money: bills and bonds; recognizances; statutes; and mortgages. All consisted of an acknowledgement of a debt of a certain sum. This was qualified by a clause, which was either written at the bottom or on the back, or set out in a separate instrument called a defeasance. This took the form of an agreement to stay the execution of the penalties of the instrument if certain conditions were fulfilled. The conditions could be the repayment of capital and interest, the former of which after about 1570 normally amounted to half the face value of the instrument.

Bonds, recognizances, and statutes were nominally valid only for very short periods, usually six months. This meant that they were most inconvenient to both creditors and debtors as a means of long-term investment or loan, since they had to be paid off or renewed at such short intervals. On the other hand such was the suspicion of a debtor's trustworthiness that few creditors would allow their money to go out on any other terms. This did not mean that in fact the capital was always called in every six months, and many loans were renewed year after year, as long as the interest continued to be paid. But each renewal required fresh negotiations, fresh writings, and therefore fresh costs and fresh trouble.

There were two special drawbacks to making loans to peers on the security of these instruments. The first was that their social standing made it very difficult to bring them to justice in the local and even in the central courts. The second drawback was that by law a peer of the realm was immune from personal arrest in a civil suit, a privilege which deprived the baulked creditor of his most fearful—if often most futile—weapon. This privilege of freedom from arrest was vigorously defended by the Lords against repeated attempts at encroachment by exasperated creditors in the early seventeenth century. As late as 1646 the Lords were still successfully imprisoning over-zealous creditors for arresting peers, but the end was near. In 1648 a creditor shouted at Lord Cromwell:

'You are a base-conditioned fellow, and I will have my money
or I will tear your cloth from your back.' Within a few months
the House of Lords was abolished and defaulting peers became
as liable to incarceration in the Fleet as other mortals had always
been. In 1651 no less a personage than the Earl of Arundel was
forced into ignominious hiding. So relentless was the pursuit of
bailiffs acting for his creditors that he had to confess that 'I dare
not be seen or suffer it to be known where I am, for . . . I am
waited for both in London and the country to be taken'.

It was all very well for the 2nd Earl of Essex—of all people—
to assert that 'I am in conscience persuaded that the bonds of
noblemen . . . are more safe than those of ordinary merchants, who
go bankrupt every year'. More sensible was Sir Robert Cecil's
frank admission to Alderman Rowe that 'it may be you will be
loth to deal with a baron of the realm without some collateral
securities of meaner quality'. It might indeed! Since the bodies
of peers were immune and suits against them difficult, creditors
often insisted that a nobleman's friends or his leading officers
should join with him in a bond, recognizance, or statute. Owing,
perhaps, to a natural reluctance of friends to get too deeply involved, the commonest sureties used by peers were their own
servants, whose position they then covered by transferring to
them by a trust deed property either in perpetuity for sale, or for
a term of years.

A not altogether unpremeditated by-product of the indefinite
prolongation of the life of the Long Parliament was that it conferred immunity from arrest for debt not only upon M.P.s but
also upon lords' servants, thus making the peers immune from
the most effective form of pressure for repayment. In 1641 the
City protested that M.P.s, peers, and their servants owed it almost
a million pounds, and described this indefinitely extended mora-
torium as a greater grievance than monopolies or ship-money. A
petition to abolish the immunity altogether for lords' and M.P.s'
servants, and to suspend it for M.P.s, was greeted by both Houses,
and particularly by the Lords, with cries of indignation at so subversive an attack upon the fundamental privileges of Parliament.

The weakness of all these instruments had really become intolerable for merchants and in the late thirteenth and early fourteenth
centuries they had devised their own machinery of credit, the
statute merchant and the statute staple, which were swiftly en-

forceable on the body, lands, and goods of the debtor. In 1532
the latter was officially made available to the population at large
in the form of a 'Recognisance in the nature of Statute Staple', and
a central registration office was set up under a Clerk of Recognizances. This allowed the landed classes to draw on the resources
of the London moneyed men by offering the latter guarantees of
swift enforcement. All creditors had to do to recover their money
was to obtain a certificate from the Clerk of Recognizances that the
statute had not been cancelled, and present it and the original
recognizance to the Crown Clerk in Chancery. Without the necessity of any suit at law this would automatically result in the issuing
within ten days of a writ ordering the impounding of the lands
of the debtor. The sheriff would be instructed to place an 'extent'
on the property, which meant that he was to value and seize part
or all the estate of the debtor and pay the rents to the creditor
until capital, interest, costs, and damages were all cleared off. This
cheap, simple, and expeditious procedure was very reassuring to
the creditor, though sometimes painful to the debtor who found
himself temporarily dispossessed of his rents. It was a London
alderman who obliged Francis Curzon to write from 'Kedleston,
my extended poor house'.

Given the swift enforcement of statutes by extents upon land,
the frequent use of sureties, and the fixing of a maximum interest
rate, after 1572 there was at last a credit machinery that was both
flexible and fairly reliable, and one which was extensively used by
the nobility for borrowing substantial sums of money.

The last instrument for raising money was the mortgage of
land, a device which in some ways resembled the extent and in
others the sale of a rent-charge. Debtors were afraid of mortgages
and avoided them when they could. The situation of Lord Mountjoy, who in the 1560's had mortgaged all but £5 a year of his
estates, was not exceptional: it was unique. But those who were
already heavily in debt often found it impossible to raise money
by any other means. Mortgages are therefore not as frequently
met with as bonds, recognizances, and statutes; they tend to be
for fairly large sums; and were mostly used by men who had
already tried other means of borrowing. The reason why they were
so disliked and feared was that in theory, and sometimes in practice, failure to repay the capital on a given day could lead to the
absolute forfeiture of the estate. Estates could rarely be mortgaged

for their full commercial value for fear of prior encumbrances such as earlier mortgages, extents, jointures, or uses for trusts. As a result of this frequent undervaluation, the debtor was faced with the possibility of serious loss if he forfeited his estates through failure to repay the capital on time, a possibility made all the more likely by the fact that nearly all mortgages were nominally for only six months or at most a year. In 1587 the Earl of Leicester claimed that he was about to forfeit, amongst other things, property worth £13,000 for failure to clear mortgages of £4,300. There can be no doubt that foreclosure was regarded as an ever-present threat, a sword of Damocles suspended above the heads of many Elizabethan noblemen.

On the other hand the thread that kept the sword from falling was a good deal stouter than many contemporaries were willing to admit. An important strand was the equitable jurisdiction of Chancery, which was becoming increasingly active in this field and was intervening to protect the debtor whenever he could offer some reasonable excuse for his failure to pay on time. Secondly, in practice creditors were usually willing to pay additional sums to obtain free surrender of title, and indeed this seems to have been normal practice. Thirdly, there was very often a verbal agreement to allow the mortgage to be renewed. City men were not always anxious to saddle themselves with the responsibility of administering scattered landed properties, even if they could be snapped up on very advantageous terms. They often preferred to keep their debtors on the hook and to continue to rake in their steady 10 per cent. interest. And so although there are plenty of examples of forfeited mortgages, there are also plenty more in which the day of redemption was renewed year after year. The Earl of Cumberland mortgaged Brancepath manor in 1588 for six months, lost it by default, recovered it a year later on payment of capital and arrears of interest, remortgaged it two years later, left it in mortgage for six years, and finally sold it outright for a substantially larger figure than that for which it was mortgaged.

This practice of prolongation was supported and encouraged during the first decades of the seventeenth century by the tendency of the Court of Chancery to use its equitable jurisdiction no longer for the protection of the individual with a special grievance but to establish a general principle of granting creditors the equity of redemption of a mortgage. By 1625 the court was assuring the defaulting debtor virtually automatic protection from sudden forfeiture provided that he offered repayment of principal, interest, and costs within a reasonable space of time. Indeed it was going even further, and allowing the debtor to retain possession of the land beyond the date of expiry of the mortgage so long as he continued to pay the interest. Contrary to general belief, however, this did not mean an immediate revolution in the credit structure. Although in theory landowners had at last obtained a reliable instrument of long-term borrowing without endangering their estates, there is in fact no evidence for more than a modest increase in the use of the mortgage for borrowing before the Civil War. Only about half the royalist compounders who borrowed any money used the mortgage, and then only for about half their total debts.

Given the very short-term nature of all credit instruments, with six months to a year as the commonest periods of loan, the problem of repayment bulked large in the minds of both debtors and creditors. The private papers of any large debtor, a Robert Earl of Essex or a Robert Earl of Salisbury, are full of elaborate lists of debts falling due in the next few months, with annotations of prolongation or unsuccessful negotiations to that end, and notes of fresh loans incurred to pay off the old. The system was a gigantic merry-go-round, with the great moneyed men of London in effect paying each other off every six months or so. When in 1593 the Earl of Shrewsbury was trying to borrow £5,000 from Sir Horatio Palavicino to clear off a debt to Thomas Sutton, the former remarked that 'Mr Sutton was his neighbour and it had been his hap to be his paymaster many times'.

It was usually only death which provoked a final settlement. The personal estate of the deceased, freehold property set aside for the purpose, and the goods and chattels were then valued and sold in order to liquidate all or most of the outstanding debts. Despite all the precautions taken, despite the very short term of normal loans, this was the only moment when creditors could feel reasonably sure of recovering their capital. In the life of a noble family it was the moment of truth, when for a brief instant they faced up to the realities of their financial position, balanced their assets against their debts, and estimated how much of gross revenue would have to be allocated to debt liquidation.

'We see that the exorbitance or moderation of interest for money lent depends upon two circumstances: the inconvenience of parting with it for the present, and the hazard of losing it entirely.' Blackstone's succinct analysis of the factors affecting the rate of interest is true enough in itself, but needs amplification. Money will never become very freely or cheaply available in a society which nourishes a strong moral prejudice against the taking of any interest at all—as distinct from objection to the taking of extortionate interest. If usury on any terms, however reasonable, is thought to be a discreditable business, men will tend to shun it and the few who practise it will demand a high return to compensate them for being generally regarded as moral lepers. This feeling was still powerful in the sixteenth century, sufficient indeed to cause legislation on the subject and to deter most of the landed classes from employing their money in this way. Apart from a brief interval between 1545 and 1552 interest on fully secured loans was totally forbidden until 1571. During this period interest naturally continued to be demanded and paid, the rate varying mostly between 12 and 15 per cent. It was the need to accommodate the realities of business life and the desire of the Crown to borrow on the English market that forced Parliament to modify its position in 1571. Public penalties were prescribed for charging interest in excess of 10 per cent., and face was saved by denying legal sanction to the charging of any interest at all. In practice the courts upheld interest rates up to 10 per cent. and borrowers were only too happy to get the money on these terms.

It was clearly in the interest of the landed classes to keep the maximum rate as low as possible, firstly because as debtors they stood to gain, and secondly because it was thought at the time that dear money meant cheap land, and vice versa. It is therefore not surprising to find a draft bill for reduction of the maximum to 5 per cent. in the Parliament of 1607, and another for 8 per cent. in 1614 and 1621, which finally reached the statute book in 1624. The moment was well chosen, soon after a severe trade slump, and the rate in practice fell precisely as the legislators decreed—a remarkable example of successful government interference in the free play of the market. After 1651 the legal maximum was down to 6 per cent. and even men as prodigal as the Earl of Berkshire could borrow three-quarters of the money they needed at a mere 5 per cent., which is between a half and a third of the current rate a hundred years before. This was a revolution with profound and far-reaching economic consequences.

The fiat of the law could not have dictated interest rates without the consent of the moneyed men, and one reason for the success of this legislation was the security already afforded by statutes and mortgages. Coupled with the survival of the nobleman's concept of honour that demanded the ultimate—probably posthumous—repayment of his debts, these afforded the creditor reasonable assurance that his capital was fairly safe, if not easily and swiftly recoverable. Good returns on commercial investments may have been a factor, but the principal reason why the rate was so high was the diversion of capital into purchase of land. So long as the Crown and many old families continued to throw land on to the market in large quantities, so long as landownership carried with it immense and unique social and political prestige, so long would a very great deal of available capital be diverted into this channel.

Before about 1580 the evidence is too scanty to allow any very useful generalizations to be made about the class structure of creditors. Thereafter detailed lists of debts are fairly common, and the picture becomes clear. What first strikes the eye is the very high degree of specialization among a restricted circle of great London merchants, men who first made their money in overseas or retail trading and who then turned to the money-lending business. The most favourably placed for this business were the leading mercers, silkmen, jewellers, and goldsmiths, whose shops were always crowded with the world of fashion. There is little doubt that virtually the whole of this tight little oligarchy was drawn into money-lending between 1580 and 1620. Sixteen goldsmiths and at least forty aldermen are known to have made loans to peers during this period.

The other two groups who were prominent in this business during these forty years—though both were of secondary importance compared with the city magnates—were lawyers and government officials. The fees of the latter were inadequate to support them, and officials concerned with handling revenue were in the habit of holding surplus balances on their accounts and using them for money-lending at interest. Tellers of the Exchequer, Treasurers at War, officials of the Court of Wards, all indulged in this practice. Lord Burghley's secretary, Henry Maynard, first made a fortune from exploiting his position as intermediary between the Lord Treasurer and the buzzing swarm of suitors and clients, and then put it out at interest to let it grow. Then there were the lawyers, whose surplus wealth sometimes sought an outlet in money-lending. Most of them avoided heavy commitments and preferred to put the bulk of their money directly into land as soon as it became available. But one or two plunged heavily.

None of the men and groups hitherto mentioned were specialists in the money-lending field. Money-lending was merely a temporary investment of wealth which had been earned and was still partly employed in foreign trade and retailing in the home market. There were some, however, for whom usury became the main activity and the main source of income. These were the men pilloried by the playwrights, those whom a Jacobean audience would immediately identify as 'Sir Avarice Goldenfleece, second to none for usury and extortion'. One such was Thomas Sutton, the model for Ben Jonson's Volpone, a man who had acquired some capital in fortunate speculation in Newcastle coal-mines, and then moved south to London to set up as a professional money-lender. At one time or another he had on his books the Earls of Salisbury, Sussex, Suffolk, Essex, Huntingdon, and Cumberland, and Lords Compton, Eure, Rich, Mordaunt, Willoughby d'Eresby, and Darcy of Chiche. He also fastened his claws on most of the more obviously decaying of the squirearchy, and when he died he had nearly £45,000 out at interest. There was also Baptist Hicks, the silk merchant and retailer. To the end he continued to vend his wares, but he got increasingly drawn into money-lending, which from being a convenient sideline must eventually have become his major preoccupation. At one time or another he lent to eight earls and six barons, to say nothing of a handful of Scottish lords, and it is scarcely surprising that this prolonged intimacy with the peerage should have ended with the acquisition of a title—by purchase or for similar services rendered to the Crown—and the transformation of the shopkeeper and usurer into Viscount Campden of Chipping Campden.

Precisely the same trajectory was followed a decade later by Alderman Sir Paul Bayning. In 1628 he bought a peerage with a fragment of the fortune first acquired in world-wide commercial activity and then increased by money-lending. When he died a year later, he had more than £136,700 out on loan, to say nothing of a further £12,000 in old and largely irrecoverable debts. As such he was undoubtedly the largest private money-lender (as distinct from crown financier) of the age, a man who in his time had made loans to as many as ten earls, one viscount, and five barons.

Tycoons such as these wielded immense power through their control of the purse-strings, and it is not surprising to find earls addressing letters to 'my very loving friend Mr. Thomas Sutton', or barons poring over their genealogies to find an excuse for saying 'cousin Sutton'. Despite the prejudices of the age, wealth on so heroic a scale could buy at any rate the outward marks of respect.

Bayning was one of the last of his kind. As early as the 1610's shrewd merchants like Cranfield were preferring to use their wealth to speculate in government grants and contracts in general and in customs farms in particular. Others were tying up more capital in joint-stock trading and colonizing ventures, in spite of their disappointing returns. The reduction of the rate of interest to 8 per cent. in 1624 must have increased the attraction of alternative investments, and by the 1630's many of the greatest fortunes of the age were being diverted into other channels than money-lending to the landed classes.

Until the rise of the goldsmith bankers in the 1650's there is reason to think that there is something of a break in the line of really great professional money-lenders working in the private market. This gap—if gap there was—was filled by a striking technical improvement in the money market which mobilized a great mass of hitherto unemployed capital. Small savings of country gentry and city widows were at last made available for loans through the scriveners. The few big landed families with surplus capital had always been able to put out their money, but the Elizabethan with a few hundred pounds to spare must have found it hard to place his savings on reasonably secure terms. By the accession of James the scriveners, who had hitherto acted merely as agents for drawing up legal documents, were beginning to help their clients by putting needy gentlemen and peers in touch with country gentry and city widows with a little capital to invest. There is evidence that some thirty London scriveners, clustered about Ludgate Hill and Cheapside, were procuring money for the peerage in the three decades before the Civil War. Because of the chance survival of his papers the best known is Humphrey Shalcrosse, who before and during the war had between £8,000

and £18,000 out on loan at any one time, only a fraction of it his
own money, and was the agent for ten earls, two sons of earls, one
courtier, six barons, one baroness, six baronets, and thirty-four
knights. By the exercise of this profession he acquired a coat of
arms and sufficient capital to marry off his two daughters with
£2,500 and £3,000 respectively.

Besides making a lot of money, Shalcrosse and his colleagues
also performed a useful service to the community in tapping new
sources of capital for borrowing, and it was probably the example
set by the scriveners which encouraged wealthy squires and
knights to begin putting their money out on loan on their own
account. In the late sixteenth century there had been one or two
nobles who had been willing and able to use their capital in this
way. In the 1590's Bess of Hardwick, Countess of Shrewsbury,
had used her surplus wealth in short-term loans to Derbyshire
gentry. There had also always been a certain amount of lending
between neighbours, a form of mutual self-help within the tight-
knit community of the gentry of the county, but in the sixteenth
century the nobility had had to rely primarily on the London merchants, with some support from royal officials and lawyers.

By 1640 the picture had significantly changed. For one thing
the rapidly rising rents of the previous forty years had created a
great volume of surplus capital in the hands of the more prudent
knights and squires. For another, many had become accustomed
to lending money through the agency of the scriveners, and were
now willing to launch out on their own and save the brokerage
fee. In consequence lists of creditors of the nobility change considerably in character, with country knights and squires and royal
financial officers now taking far more prominent positions.

Contemporaries had no doubt about whether or not it was wise
to borrow to meet sudden emergencies of long-term deficits: they
were against it. With an insistence which seems almost pathological in its repetitious intensity they kept urging one another to
shun the money-lender as they would the devil. Bacon, who was
oppressed with debt all his life, described usury as 'the canker and
ruin of many men's estates, which in process of time breeds public
poverty', and Ralegh used almost the identical words to express
his disapproval. Indeed it is impossible to find a single witness
who thought borrowing was anything but a desperate and dangerous expedient. This universal sense of horror was not mere

lip-service to an outdated medieval tradition. It was deeply and passionately felt by a society in which indebtedness was both an almost unavoidable necessity and a terrible social scourge. The victims talked bitterly of 'usury which biteth to the very bone' and recommended selling land in preference to allowing debts to drag on. The advice was sensible since the acceptable theoretical norm in Elizabethan calculations of the price of land was sixteen to twenty years' purchase, meaning a return of 5 or 6 per cent. on capital, whereas the rate of interest was at least 10 per cent. Even in the middle of the seventeenth century, when conditions were more favourable to borrowers, Lord North was still advising the prompt liquidation of debt 'though it be by a fell of timber, or by selling of that which may seem precious'. It was not until a further drop in the rate of interest, the establishment of absolute confidence in the equity of redemption, and the development of long-term debt mechanisms as a normal part of the system of credit that men began recommending the prolongation of debt in preference to speedy liquidation by sale of land.

In the hundred years between 1550 and 1650 there are records of the debts of about 120 peers, only twelve of which date to before 1585. This imbalance is undoubtedly due in part to the general paucity of records before the latter years of Elizabeth. On the other hand debts by their very nature tend to find their way into the permanent records of the courts of law or the royal ad-ministration, and it is difficult to believe that the flood of evidence after 1585 is purely accidental. There were a number of individuals who, through blind misfortune, calculated policy, or wanton extravagance, succeeded in running up huge debts before 1585. It was misfortune which allowed Lord Grey of Wilton to fall into the hands of the French at Guisnes in 1558, and obliged him to borrow £10,000 to pay his ransom. It may have been calculation which lay behind Lord Treasurer Winchester's failure to settle his accounts with the Crown, thus leaving an accumulated debt to Elizabeth of rather over £34,000. But his debts to individuals of about £12,000 are less easy to explain away, except in terms of over-ambitious building and an inordinately extravagant style of life. But these are exceptions to the rule, and there is little evidence that serious indebtedness was widespread at this time.

After 1585 there was a steady deterioration in the general situa-tion. The cutting off of favours from the Crown coincided with an epidemic of gambling and high living to force a crisis in the affairs of the nobility. The great courtiers adopted the Marquis of Winchester's solution of running up vast debts to the Crown. Others less happily placed were unable to find temporary refuge from the winds of adversity in the royal bosom, and about two-thirds of the peerage seem to have been in growing financial difficulties in the last twenty years of the reign of Elizabeth.

The next thirty years saw a falling off of the frequency of severe and crippling indebtedness, which becomes more the idiosyncrasy of the individual than the hallmark of a class. All the great courtiers continued to pile up vast debts, but their assets were now equally vast and could usually take the strain. The earls of Salisbury survived a debt of £53,000 in 1611, the dukes of Buckingham one of £58,700 in 1628. But the earls of Suffolk never recovered from a debt of £40,000 in 1618, the earls of Dorset one of up to £60,000 in 1624.

For the 1630's the evidence is much more complete, thanks in part to the Royalist Composition Papers, and it looks as if a minority of the peerage, something like a fifth, were in debt to individual creditors (not to Crown or family) to the tune of over two years' income. Truly fantastic private debts had been run up by some of the courtiers—£99,000 by the Earl of Suffolk, £107,000 by the Earl of Strafford, and £121,000 by the Earl of Arundel. Although these gigantic overdrafts were the exception rather than the rule, 57 of the 121 peers are known to have been in debt in 1642, and others may credibly be supposed to have been in the same position. The total indebtedness of the peerage in 1641 to individuals and to the family amounted to about £1½ million, the interest on which, at 8 per cent., comes to £120,000. Since the gross annual income from all sources is estimated at £730,000, interest was absorbing about one sixth, which is approaching the limit which an estate could comfortably support.

The period from 1580 to 1610 in which the nobility first became heavily dependent on credit was the one in which the dangers of borrowing—high interest rates and the potential danger of forfeiting mortgaged estates—were very real. In consequence it was not merely good sense for debtors to sell land to pay off debts; it was forced upon them by the prohibitively heavy costs of borrowing for more than very short periods. The imperfections of the system of credit are therefore a significant factor in the financial

decay of the nobility in the late Elizabethan period. By 1641 incomes had risen very sharply, mortgages were now protected by
the equity of redemption, and the rate of interest had fallen. And
so although the total indebtedness of the peerage had risen absolutely, *per capita*, and as a proportion of gross income, its consequences were now far less serious. Heavy debts were no longer
frightening men into hasty land sales to clear them off. This was
a factor in the stabilization of noble finances in the early seventeenth century inferior only to the creation of life interests, the
rapid rise of rents, the opening up of new sources of income in
urban rents, and the profligate generosity of King James. Moreover, landed income was buoyant in part as a direct result of the
improved facilities for borrowing and the higher rate of indebtedness. One of the commonest and most effective ways of increasing
revenue from land was by raising rents and reducing entry fines
for leases. But this involved a sharp reduction in the capital sums
that could be obtained from the land, and therefore depended on
the availability of credit from the money-lender.

If changes in the rate of interest powerfully affected the fortunes
of the nobility, the demands of the nobility in turn had an important effect on the rate of interest, and therefore indirectly on the
working of the economy as a whole. As we have seen, the main
factor in reducing the rate was undoubtedly a technical improvement of the credit mechanism which enabled gentry and citizens
of modest means to add their savings to the pool of available
credit, savings swollen by a general buoyancy of the economy up
to 1620 which produced a profit surplus to merchants, retailers,
large farmers, landlords, and lawyers. But even at 8 per cent. the
English rate was still nearly double that of primarily mercantile
communities like those of Holland or Genoa, and significantly
higher than that in north-west France.

In the eighteenth century Sir John Dalrymple believed that the
difference between the English and Dutch rates in the sixteenth
century was principally to be explained by differing social backgrounds. Unlike Holland, England not only had a great deal of
land constantly coming on to the market and being eagerly bought
up by merchants seeking to improve their status, but also a wasteful landed nobility constantly seeking large loans and without a
bank to help them out. Dalrymple was right in his diagnosis.
Between 1591 and 1600 seventeen peers drew on the money

market, either by sale of land or by loans from private persons still outstanding in 1600, to the tune of at least £324,000 and probably a good deal more. By no means all the money sunk in land purchase would otherwise have been available for money-lending, but a fairly large part of it certainly would have found its way there sooner or later. By contrast the gross investment throughout the whole of the second half of the sixteenth century in the five major stock enterprises of the age, the Mines Royal and Mineral and Battery Companies for industry, the Russia, North West Passage, and East India Companies for trade, did not exceed £170,000. In 1641 the total investment in all joint-stock companies was probably still less than the money out on loan to the peerage.

If one thinks of the hundreds of knights and squires and lesser gentry who were also borrowing more modest sums on the London market, one can appreciate the tremendous strain imposed by the demands of the landed classes. The amount of available capital which was tied up in loans to and land purchases from the landed classes must have represented a very large part of the whole. The sheer size of their resources and the extreme pressure for conspicuous expenditure to which they were subject made the peerage the largest individual patrons of the market. It is also likely that in aggregate they were a very important as well as the most conspicuous element in the situation. If their consumption was a powerful stimulus to the economy, as it certainly was, the demands they made on the money market were an important cause of the high rate of interest in England. And this in turn put a permanent brake upon the speed of English economic growth.

# X

## CONSPICUOUS EXPENDITURE

Now every one prepares a full table, has good attendance, keeps
horses, wears rich clothes, gives great wages, retains many servants, builds magnificently, furnishes amply, adorns luxuriantly
their bodies, children and houses, by which many costly diversions . . . the paunch of an estate is pinched, and the succulency
sussurated from its amassation.

E. WATERHOUSE, *The Gentleman's Monitor*, 1665, p. 263

AN Englishman of the mid-twentieth century has some difficulty in comprehending how a single individual with a
quarter of a million pounds a year or more—which in
modern money is the sort of income enjoyed by the greater noblemen of the sixteenth and seventeenth centuries—could contrive
to spend it and not infrequently to run up huge debts into the
bargain. The causes of conspicuous display have already been
discussed; it remains to explain where the money went and to
chart the course of the consumptive fever.

As we have seen, the most important factors working for an
abnormally high level of expenditure were the moral obligations
imposed upon a nobleman by society to live in a style commensurate with his dignity; and confusion between the feudal ideal
of generous hospitality and stately living in the country and the
Renaissance ideal of sophisticated patronage and display in the
town. An earl felt obliged to maintain one principal and one or
two subsidiary country seats, a house in London, and a household
staff of between 60 and 100 to run them. He had to keep a generous
table freely open to visitors, and a plentiful supply of horses for
transport and communications.

To understand how it was that so many families, including some
of the richest in the kingdom, contrived at one time or another
to run headlong into debt, it is necessary to illustrate and to
describe in detail the extraordinary temptations to extravagance
that beset the Elizabethan nobleman. It should be emphasized
that the pressure of expenditure on income cannot be ascribed

to the rise in prices, which must have affected the cost of living of the poor far more than that of the rich. The pace-makers in the price rise were foodstuffs and fuel, with wages and industrial goods lagging well behind. But most nobles obtained much of their fuel from their own woods, and a good deal of the food consumed by the household was drawn from the produce of the home farm, rents in kind, or tithes. To this extent, therefore, the basic cost of living of a nobleman, if such a thing can be conceived, must have been a good deal less affected by the price rise than is suggested by the Phelps Brown index of consumption, which was drawn up for a working-class budget. What rose instead was the cost of superfluities like building, life at Court, and marrying off a daughter.

As late as the middle of the sixteenth century most noblemen were still housed very much as they had been in the Middle Ages. In the north and west they mostly huddled behind the massive walls of their castles, enduring with what fortitude they could muster the cold, the dark, the damp, and the draughts. In the lowland zone they were more comfortably lodged in rambling ranges of domestic buildings grouped loosely round courtyards, as at Compton Wynyates. The dissolution of the monasteries had had two important results. Most noblemen picked up at least one monastic site, and as a result found themselves supplied with very large quarries of ready-worked building stone; secondly many of the political grandees acquired town houses along the Strand. A few of the bolder spirits—Sir William Sharington at Lacock, the Earl of Southampton at Titchfield, Lord Sandys at Mottisfont, Lord Rich at Leez—had promptly converted the monastic church to secular use, carving parlours and chambers and bedrooms out of naves, transepts, and chancels without respect for the niceties of ecclesiastical propriety. Many more, like Lord Darcy at St. Osyth and Viscount Montagu at Battle, were content to use the domestic buildings.

Most, however, held back, owing mainly to a natural reluctance to indulge in heavy capital expenditure on property which, if things went badly, might have to be restored to the monks, and partly also to superstitious fear of committing sacrilege by wining, dining, and making love on once holy ground. But reuse of the stone elsewhere was another matter, and country house after country house was built from monastic rubble. The King set an example by demolishing Merton Priory for Nonsuch, and as late as the early seventeenth century, Robert Earl of Salisbury was pulling down part of St. Augustine Abbey, Canterbury, to provide building stone for Hatfield.

By the 1570's and 1580's there had developed overwhelming incentives for new building. Having survived the reign of Mary, holders of monastic property at last felt reasonably secure in their possessions, whatever their private doubts about the long-term prospects of the Anglican settlement. They were therefore now willing to risk their capital on building upon ex-Church land. They had paid off the purchase price of the land and were now free to devote their surplus money to building. Though the new Renaissance style introduced by Protector Somerset and Northumberland and their circle did not catch on, there was clear recognition of an aesthetic obligation to strive for architectural symmetry, while the mannered extravagances of Dutch-inspired architectural embellishments made medieval and early Tudor houses look shabby and down-at-heel. Building materials were plentifully available, what with stone from monastic sites, the rapidly growing output of the brickmaker, and timber from the still extensive woodlands. Men urgently needed more comfortable buildings to live in, with more fireplaces, more private chambers, better plumbing, and better lighting. An architect of genius, Robert Smythson, showed how to take full advantage of new industrial techniques to erect light and airy constructions with huge areas of glass like Hardwick.

In varying degrees these incentives were felt by the landed classes at all levels from the yeoman to the earl. Between 1580 and 1620 England was largely rebuilt in the new materials and in conformity with the new standards of comfort and privacy. All over the lowland zone the yeomen were building the Jacobethan farmhouses so many of which still survive to this day. At a higher level of society the gentry were building as they were never to build again. A survey of four widely spread counties—Derbyshire, Essex, Shropshire, and Somerset—suggests that the amount of country-house building in the fifty years between 1570 and 1620 far exceeded that of any subsequent half-century. At a higher level still, the aristocracy were building great houses in the country and great houses in the City. Some Elizabethans were not content with a single country palace, but demanded two: Hatton had Holdenby and Kirby, Burghley had Burghley House and Theobalds. Most peers were satisfied with one palace and several lesser country seats.

The most striking phenomenon of the period is the gigantic country seat, the so-called 'prodigy house'. The work of the Court aristocracy of the late Elizabethan and Jacobean age, many of these fantastic edifices still lie heavily about the English country-side like the fossilized bones of the giant reptiles of the Carboniferous Age. Their sole justification was to demonstrate status, their sole function to entertain the sovereign on one of the summer progresses. Referring to his own Theobalds and to Sir Christopher Hatton's Holdenby, Lord Burghley spoke of 'her for whom we both meant to exceed our purses', while Hatton described Holdenby as a 'shrine' which 'that holy saint may sit in . . . to whom it is dedicated'. These letters were probably written for effect in the hope that they would be shown to the Queen, but the need to entertain Her Majesty was certainly a key factor, and one that could be openly acknowledged.

The other, unacknowledged, reason for extravagant building was in order to satisfy a lust for power, a thirst for admiration, an ambition to outstrip all rivals, and a wish to create a home suitable for the residence of a nobleman—a particularly urgent incentive to one whose patent was still fresh from the mint. The post-1603 inflation of honours was thus an important cause of this outburst of excessive building which rose to a crescendo between 1580 and 1620 and then began to subside. It was pure ambition to make a show that induced the Countess of Shrewsbury to erect that stately pleasure-dome the New Hall at Hardwick just beside the recently completed Old Hall, an ambition frankly revealed in the huge initials 'E.S.' boldly displayed all round the parapet. It is symptomatic of this desire for display that so many of these new houses were erected on the tops of hills where they would be visible for miles around.

Such extravagance begot envy, and before long an epidemic of over-building broke out as politicians and courtiers struggled to match each other's architectural feats. This competition among the great courtiers was echoed by the struggle of the lesser nobility and ambitious squires, and Sir Henry Slingsby noted how in Yorkshire 'we see an emulation in the structure of our houses'. 'No kingdom in the world spent so much in building as we did in

[King James's] time', reflected Godfrey Goodman. The orgy began to peter out even before the death of James in 1625, and the fifteen years before the Civil War saw relatively few really ambitious building projects. By and large the era of the prodigy house was over: Inigo Jones had chosen his moment badly.

One reason may have been that there were now enough palaces to go round—even the great Duke of Buckingham bought Newhall from the Earl of Sussex and added to it, instead of building from scratch. Another was the decline in the habit of the royal progress, and the growing unpopularity of the Crown. Not only were men less willing to put themselves out for Charles than they had been for Elizabeth; there was now less danger of a royal visitation. Thirdly, men were at last discarding the medieval notion that a nobleman must live for ever in a crowd, surrounded by hosts of servants, retainers, and guests. They therefore no longer needed such enormous houses with ranges of state apartments and guest and servant accommodation. Moreover it is possible that more direct acquaintance with Italy was leading them to revise their ideas about the importance of size. The very modest scale of the Villa Rotunda, the Palazzo Medici, the Gozzoli Chapel, must have come as something of a shock to Englishmen accustomed to the gigantic splendours of Audley End. Finally there was a growing awareness of the appalling cost and the hideous inconvenience. 'It hath been observed as a great unhappiness to our nobility and gentry that generally they are over-housed', lamented the 4th Lord North. Such houses were ruinous to build, expensive to maintain at a proper level, and miserable to live in with a skeleton staff. Only a few families, however, contrived to get rid of these white elephants.

The demand for capital for the initial building was often the signal for the decay of a family. This 'expenseful though bewitching delight', as the 5th Earl of Huntingdon feelingly described it, was a frequent cause of exorbitant debts, and prudent parents were in the habit of quoting Sir Edward Coke's sage advice: 'Put not your finger in the mortar.' These buildings were mostly the work either of private individuals who sold some of their estate to pay for them or else of successful politicians with easy access to the resources of the Crown and a none too scrupulous way with suitors. Wolsey's monument was Hampton Court; the Duke of Somerset spent over £15,000 in three and a half years on

Somerset House and Syon House in 1548–51; the Earl of Salisbury £40,000 at Hatfield alone between 1608 and 1612. Nor was this the end of the expense, since these enormous houses had then to be kept up. Ambitious building, remarked Lord North, causes 'the owner to hoist up more sail then the bottom can bear, which draweth on his ruin'. Long after they had lost all belief in the way of life as an ideal, noblemen continued to hire crowds of under-employed domestic servants and to maintain an open table for visitors, simply in order to justify the existence of echoing halls and sumptuous state apartments, and to keep at bay the melancholia and loneliness of a half-empty mansion.

The determination of many Tudor and one or two Early Stuart noblemen to maintain the open-handed semi-public way of life of the medieval prince was an important cause of their financial difficulties. In 1554 the Venetian ambassador had observed that the English nobility lived mainly in the country 'where they keep up very grand establishments, both with regard to the great abundance of eatables consumed by them as also by reason of their numerous attendants, in which they exceed all other nations'. If the number of servants and guests was often enormous, the size of the meals themselves was gargantuan.

Aristocratic households consumed tremendous quantities of meat, especially beef and mutton, usually in about equal quantities. All the figures we have tally perfectly with an estimate of the Earl of Bath in the middle of the seventeenth century that a household of 80 persons consumed 1 ox and 5 sheep a week. Nor was this all, for the household also ate pork, about 25 to 30 animals a year in a large establishment, veal and lamb, 30 to 40 animals a year, and huge quantities of rabbits and poultry. In the Christmas week of 1588 George Earl of Shrewsbury consumed 3 quarters of wheat, 441 gallons of beer, 12 sheep, 10 capons, 26 hens, 7 pigs, 6 geese, 7 cygnets, 1 turkey, and 118 rabbits. Even if we assume that there were between 100 and 150 persons in the house that week, this still represents a formidable consumption of proteins. Owing to uncertainty about the weight of sixteenth-century animals, the number of guests, and the amount of waste distributed daily to the poor at the gates of the great house, it is impossible to work out any firm figures for the consumption of meat *per capita* in the aristocratic household. It probably did not differ very much from the 8½ lb. per head per week that the 1st Duke of Chandos was allowing to his servants at Cannons in the early eighteenth century. However one reckons and whatever allowances and deductions are made, consumption was greatly in excess of the average among the upper classes of twentieth-century England.

Apart from meat the main items of food were bread, beer, and 'fresh acates', meaning milk, butter, cheese, eggs, game, fresh fish, and fruit. Surviving records suggest that these large households estimated beer consumption at between 5 and 8 pints per person per day—no wonder foreigners were struck by the English capacity for beer-drinking. In addition, between 750 and 1,250 gallons of wine a year were consumed, mostly claret and lesser quantities of white wine and sack. The normal household diet thus consisted basically of huge quantities of meat and bread washed down in oceans of beer and wine. Vegetables were rare in the sixteenth century, and only in the years before the Civil War did imported Mediterranean fruits and the produce of English vegetable gardens begin to lighten this unwholesome fare.

The tradition of providing these generous allowances of foodstuffs for large numbers of persons was inherited from the Middle Ages. A new feature, however, was the Trimalchian rarity of the dishes for special occasions, exotic foods and exotic cooking becoming increasingly important features of fashionable entertainment in London. The judges of Star Chamber were weekly treated to a formal dinner at the public expense, at which they notoriously gormandized. 7 June 1594 fell on a Friday, and was therefore a fish day. But it can hardly be called a fast day, for the ten judges ate ling, green-fish, salmon, pike, gurnard, dory, carp, tench, knobberd, grey-fish, plaice, perch, sole, conger, barbel, flounder, turbot, whiting, lobster, crab, and prawns—to say nothing of eggs, capons, chickens, rabbits, artichokes, peas, strawberries, apples, gooseberries, oranges, lemons, quinces, and barbaries.

Second only to the variety of the ingredients came the exquisite fantasy of the cooking. Massinger spoke of

> Their thirty-pound butter'd eggs, their pies of carp's tongues,
> Their pheasants drench'd with ambergris, the carcases
> Of three fat wethers bruised for gravy to
> Make sauce for a single peacock.

Reality was scarcely less bizarre. In 1618 Sir George Goring celebrated Prince Charles's birthday by bringing to the table 'four huge brawny pigs, piping hot, bitted and harnessed with ropes of sausages, all tied to a monstrous bag-pudding'. Quite apart from such ingenious conceits, there was a general demand for more refined cooking, and chefs with French training were as highly prized 350 years ago as they are today.

The stupendous cost of the great banquet in the early seventeenth century was thus partly due to the rarity of the dishes, partly to the exquisite refinement of the cooking, and partly to sheer exuberance of scale. Even the cautious Burghley found these follies contagious. The £363 he spent on a feast to the French Commissioners in 1581 might perhaps be explained on grounds of public policy. But what are we to make of the £629 spent on three days' junketing at the marriage of his daughter a year later? At this vast party there were consumed, among other things, about 1,000 gallons of wine, 6 veals, 26 deer, 15 pigs, 14 sheep, 16 lambs, 4 kids, 6 hares, 36 swans, 2 storks, 41 turkeys, over 370 poultry, 49 curlews, 135 mallards, 354 teals, 1,049 plovers, 124 knotts, 280 stints, 109 pheasants, 277 partridges, 615 cocks, 485 snipe, 840 larks, 21 gulls, 71 rabbits, 23 pigeons, and 2 sturgeons.

It was in 1617 under the leadership of Lord Hay, later Earl of Carlisle, that culinary extravagance reached its apogee. Hay had picked up ideas in Paris while on an embassy the year before, and he introduced them into London society on his return. The most spectacular of his exploits was a feast to the French Ambassador at Essex House in 1621, organized 'with that sumptuous superfluity that the like hath not been seen nor heard in these parts'. According to John Chamberlain 100 cooks were employed for 8 days concocting 1,600 dishes. There were 12 pheasants in one dish, 24 partridges in another, 144 larks in a third, a couple of swans in a fourth, a couple of pigs in a fifth. There were half a dozen enormous salmon from Russia, 6 feet long. The sweetmeats cost £500, the 6 lb. of ambergris used in the cooking cost another £300. The total bill for the day's work was said to run to £3,300. It was Carlisle who invented that most conspicuous and most wasteful of all devices for conspicuous waste: the antesupper. The guests sat down before a huge and succulent banquet, which was promptly whipped away by the waiters before the guests could touch it, to be replaced by another yet more lavish.

The medical profession was, as usual, very keen on dieting. Thomas Elyot fulminated against the excessive consumption of meat, and Henry Earl of Huntingdon believed that over-eating and over-drinking were killing more people than the wars. One cannot point to any direct casualties of the table—except perhaps the 1st Lord Coleraine who in 1667 was 'choked endeavouring to swallow the rump of a turkey'. But over-eating must have been the main cause of the rumbling, belching, and stomach pains of chronic dyspepsia of which almost every member of the propertied classes seems to have been a victim. It is also difficult to avoid the suspicion that the fact that so very many suffered the agonies of stone in the bladder or kidneys was not in some way connected with their gluttonous habits.

Medical objections to a heavy diet were complemented by the disapproval of the moralists, who regarded an over-loaded table as a scandalous waste of money. The futility of thus stimulating the digestive cycle was proverbial: 'a great housekeeper is sure of nothing for his good cheer save a great turd at his gate' was the elegant aphorism of the yokels of Gloucestershire. But few of the nobility and greater gentry heeded the warning, and more than one of them could be said to have 'sent all his revenues down the privy house'.

Second only to hospitality as a status symbol and as a vehicle for conspicuous consumption were clothes. One cause of unnecessary expense was the bewildering speed with which fashions changed, another the inordinate profusion of embroidery and gold and silver lace. Foreign observers like van Meteren were struck by the fashion-consciousness of the English. Tailors crouched anxiously behind the pillars in old St. Paul's watching for a new cut of doublet or a novel pair of hose displayed upon the gallants exhibiting themselves in the aisles.

The pace was set by the monarchs themselves, even Elizabeth regarding her wardrobe as an exception to her normal rules of parsimony—and being caricatured for her pains as a strutting bird of fantastic plumage. Her attitude to fashion was both imperious and unpredictable, and great were the lamentations in 1594 when she summarily ordered the Court back into short cloaks just when everyone had fitted themselves out in the New Look. As for King James, over a period of five years from 1608 to 1613 he bought a new cloak every month, a new waistcoat every three weeks, a new suit every ten days, a new pair of stockings, boots, and garters every four or five days, and a new pair of gloves every day. King Charles continued to set the same example of dazzling splendour as his parents. Indeed he actually excelled them, by buying no fewer than 513 items of footwear—boots, shoes, galoshes, and slippers—in the course of a single year, 1626-7.

Inspired by this example from on high, the courtiers strove to emulate their sovereign, and so spread the new fashions in ever-widening circles, first in the City and then in the country houses of rural England, where wives began brooding grumpily upon the dowdiness of their wardrobes and started bullying their husbands to take them up to town to see the fashions.

Nor were the men at all behind their wives in this competition in ostentation. It was the Court that led the fashion, and a philandering queen followed by a homosexual king no doubt gave an added incentive to the movement: both Elizabeth and James had an eye for the well-dressed young man. As a result men may even have led the race to deck themselves out in silks and satins, embroidery, and gold and silver lace. This taste for extravagant clothes among the courtiers and men of fashion was a serious drain upon the resources of all but the wealthiest of magnates. In the late 1590's Roger Earl of Rutland was spending £1,000 or more a year on his clothes, and the Duke of Buckingham reckoned to be spending £1,500 a year in 1623 and £3,000 a year in 1627. Lesser mortals could not stand the pace.

Once dressed up in their finery, these peacocks and popinjays had to be transported in fitting style. The reign of Mary had seen the first imported example of the heavy coach with its four big wheels and braced suspension, but it was not till about 1590 that most earls could boast of one of these formidable new status symbols, and it took another quarter of a century to become a common possession of the middling gentry. Sir John Oglander, who only came to live at Nunwell in 1607, records that he owned the second coach in the Isle of Wight. Tricked out with its owner's arms and crest, lavishly adorned with gilding without and silks and satins within, the cost of a town coach was comparable to that of the modern Rolls Royce, though its effective life was very much shorter, and the likelihood of breakdown infinitely greater. Travel was not cheap in the sixteenth and seventeenth centuries.

The other great item of personal expenditure after food, clothes, and transport was that opium of the idle, gambling. This was a vice hated by the Puritans, and feared for its consequences by every prudent parent. To the nobility, however, play within moderation was a suitable pastime for a gentleman, one of whose functions was to live in idleness with elegance and grace. It was as important to know how to play cards or handle the dice as it was to be able to ride a horse or dance a galliard. The two standards of behaviour are enshrined in English history in the popular notions of the typical Cavalier and the typical Roundhead, but the dichotomy was leading to trouble long before it came to civil war.

Bets were offered and taken on dice, 'those true outlanders', on card games, horse-racing, foot-racing, cock-fighting, bull-baiting, hunting, tennis, ninepins, chess, shooting, or bowling. Was it to improve his public image as a man of the world that the austere and preoccupied Lord Burghley had himself painted engaged in a card game for high stakes? Politics were harnessed to the same cause, men offering odds of two to one against Monsieur's coming to England in 1579 and three to one against the Queen's marriage; bets were offered on travel or the birth of children. George Conquest paid Sir Ralph Conquest £10, on a promise to be repaid £30 if and when Thomas Fynett returned from Babylon.

As Sir John Harington pointed out at the time, gambling is a product of the triple vices of idleness, which creates boredom and thus a demand for palliatives; of pride, which makes men play for higher stakes than they can afford in order to give an impression of magnanimity and carefree opulence; and of avarice, which feeds on hopes of making a killing. What is very striking about the period from 1580 to 1640 is not so much the extraordinary range of subjects of betting, as the phenomenal rise in the stakes. On both counts it is arguable that gambling was turning from a pastime into an obsession, from an innocent amusement into a social scourge.

It was at Court that the increased scale of gambling was particularly significant. At all times a court is something of a glorified gambling saloon, if only because courtiers need some distraction with which to while away the prolonged periods of waiting for something to happen. When the monarch himself takes part in the game, it is apt to prove expensive to the other players, particularly when he or she is of an economical and domineering turn of mind. Henry VIII was a fairly habitual gambler, but he very rarely lost as much as £100 in a single session, and was usually content to play bowls or tennis, cards or dice for a few pounds or even

shillings. Queen Elizabeth hated losing, and, according to Ben
Jonson, habitually played with loaded dice. An ambitious courtier
like Lord North found it prudent to allow her to take up to £40
a month off him at cards as an insurance against loss of favour.
But it was not till the accession of King James that gambling
orgies at Court, particularly over Christmas, became a by-word
for prodigality. In 1603 Sir Robert Cecil was reported to have
lost over £800 in a single night; in 1605 he lost £1,000 at dice to
the King (for whom the favourite, the Earl of Montgomery, was
throwing that evening). A few years later such gains and losses
were common form. The Duke of Buckingham won £3,000 on a
foot-race in 1618, Baptist Viscount Campden gambled away his
wife's portion of £2,500 at tennis, Theophilus Lord Howard of
Walden over £1,500 in a day playing bowls at Hackney in 1623.
Stakes on horses rose at the same dizzy pace: the 2nd Earl of
Rutland had cautiously put £1 or £2 on a horse in 1549; the 5th
Earl rarely staked less than £100 on a race in the 1590's.

Gambling on this early seventeenth-century scale was more than
any man could reasonably afford: divines and casuists denounced
it as a moral evil, playwrights and plain observers of the human
scene were convinced, apparently with reason, that it was a major
cause of the frequent decay of families. Many devices were tried
to check the disease, though with conspicuous lack of success.
One of the few recorded instances of a reformed character is that
of the 4th Earl of Southampton, who in 1635 sold all his race-
horses, forswore all deep play—and emerged twenty-five years
later as the spoil-sport Lord Treasurer of the Restoration.

Ostentatious in his lifetime in clothes and hospitality, transport
and housing, in some respects an Elizabethan peer had his finest
hour only after he was dead. So grandiose in scale and portentous
in style were the funeral arrangements of the nobility that the most
contemptible of human beings on earth could hardly fail to be
ushered out of it to universal admiration. Of many could it be said
that nothing became them so much as their going; it was the last
tribute of a deferential society to the dignity of a title.

The first thing to be done on the death of a peer was to summon
a surgeon and an apothecary. These technicians were required to
embalm the dead, for it took time to mount the arrangements for
the funeral and meanwhile the corpse had to be preserved above
ground without giving too much offence to the standers-by. The

trouble taken varied according to the rank of the subject and the estimated time between the death and the funeral. A minor gentleman like Thomas Fermor was disembowelled by a barber for 5s. in 1580; a substantial gentleman like Sir Heneage Proby was properly embalmed for £20 by a doctor-surgeon in 1663. Exceptional care was taken over an earl, the elaboration of whose funeral and the distinction of whose person demanded special treatment. After the bowels had been removed and the body embalmed, it was sealed in wax and placed in a leaden coffin moulded to the shape of the body, seventeenth-century examples of which are visible today in the crypt of the chapel at Farleigh Hungerford, Wiltshire.

The arrangements for the funeral were made by one of the heralds, who immediately posted down as soon as notification of the death of a peer reached the College of Arms. So complicated was the ceremony that it rarely took less than a month to organize. The sort of funeral an earl might expect if he was to be buried in full Elizabethan style was that accorded to Edward Earl of Derby in 1572. The procession marched the two miles from Lathom House to Ormskirk Church: first came 100 poor men fitted out in blacks for the occasion, the choir of 40 in their surplices, followed by an esquire on horseback bearing the late earl's standard. Next came 80 gentlemen of the earl, his 2 secretaries, 2 chaplains, and 50 knights and esquires, the preacher, the Dean of Chester, the three chief officers, and an esquire on horseback carrying the great banner. At this point appeared the splendid spectacle of four heralds, riding horses with black trappings ornamented with escutcheons reaching to the ground, and carrying the late Earl's helmet and sword. The heralds directly preceded the black-draped chariot with the coffin, drawn by four horses and surrounded by ten hooded esquires on horseback. Behind the chariot walked the chief mourner, the new earl, with his two ushers, his two sons, and eight other distinguished mourners headed by Lord Stourton. The tail of this great procession was composed of 500 yeomen and all the servants of the gentlemen taking part in the ceremony.

On arrival at the church, the coffin was removed from the chariot by eight gentlemen and solemnly borne inside. The church itself was in heavy mourning, the pulpit, the communion table, and the arches of the aisles being swathed in black drapes. In the centre stood the hearse upon which the coffin was laid. This was

a gigantic affair 30 feet high, 12 feet long, and 9 feet wide, covered
with black taffeta and velvet, and adorned with numerous heraldic
escutcheons. The funeral service opened with Norroy King of
Arms pronouncing the name and titles of the deceased, followed
by a sermon from the Dean of Chester and the epistle and gospel
read by the vicar. The new earl then offered the heralds a piece of
gold for the deceased, and was himself solemnly offered by the
chief mourners the late earl's arms, sword, target, standard, and
banner. After the other mourners down to the yeomen had made
their offerings to the deceased, the majority of the congregation
again formed up and marched off home, leaving the burial itself
to be conducted by two of the heralds, the twenty-odd attendant
esquires, gentlemen, and yeomen, and the chief officers of the late
earl. These latter broke their staves of office over their heads and
threw them down into the open grave before the earth was
shovelled in. Though the service took place in church, the master
of ceremonies was not the parson but the heralds, and the affair
was characterized more by the rituals of antiquarian feudalism than
by those of Christianity. It was, remarked the Separatist Henry
Barrow, 'as if Duke Hector, or Ajax, or Sir Launcelot were buried'.

These ceremonies were rounded off by great feasts, for which
enormous quantities of food and drink were provided, and which
often took on the aspect of an Irish wake. For the servants of
the dead the funeral heralded the break-up of the old household,
and unless the new master chose to keep them on they would soon
have to set out into the world to seek fresh employment. They
thus had every incentive to get very drunk, and the occasion sometimes degenerated into a saturnalia. At the funeral of Bess of Hardwick in 1607 some of her servants, a prey to conflicting emotions
of relief at the death of the tyrant and anxiety about the future,
indulged themselves very freely and there were orgiastic scenes
below stairs at the Old Hall that day. The funeral was also an
occasion for the distribution of largesse on a gigantic scale. Between 3,000 and 4,000 poor people are said to have been fed from
the left-overs from the funeral feast of Edward Earl of Rutland in
1587. Late that evening or early next morning the guests and the
crowds dispersed, having seen a great Tudor nobleman into his
grave in a style that was suitable for his estate and degree.

The cost of these ostentatious rituals was commensurate with
their size, amounting at their height to not far short of a year's

income. About three-quarters of the cost went on the purchase of black cloth to drape the house, the church, the chariot, and the hearse, and to dress the hundreds of mourners. Although a few items might be hired from an enterprising herald, between 500 and 1,200 yards of black cloth of various qualities had to be purchased for the average great funeral.

After 1580 there was a noticeable reduction in the number of opulent funerals. Though some ancient families like the Talbots and the Manners continued to indulge in the old-style shows, though a few genuinely new men still tried to make their mark by the pomp of their interment, increasing numbers now deliberately tried to economize. The shift in attitude is most fully explained by Robert 2nd Earl of Dorset, who in his will drawn up in 1608 ordered that he should be buried 'without any blacks or great solemnity of funeral but in a Christian manner as other persons are of meaner sort, because the usual solemnities of funerals such as heralds set down for noble men are only good for the heralds and drapers and very prejudicial to the children, servants, and friends of the deceased and to the poor which inhabit thereabout, towards all of which the deceased might otherwise be much more liberal'.

The principal cause of the decline must have been a dawning realization that the cost incurred was out of all proportion to the prestige earned. There took place a profound change in the accepted forms of symbolic justification, a change that was in part stimulated by puritan criticism that such displays of worldly pomp were more pagan than Christian. A further factor that helped to undermine the tradition of the stately funeral was the revolt of a minority against embalming. A handful, especially of women, began to express their new-found sense of individuality by refusing to submit their bodies to gruesome mangling by the embalmer's knife, a refusal which automatically made necessary a swifter and therefore more economical interment. The extreme romantic view was taken by Frances Duchess of Richmond, who ordered in her will 'that I may be speedily buried and not opened, for so my sweet Lord out of his tender love commanded me that I should not be opened. I may be presently put up in bran and in lead before I am fully cold.'

The demand curve of the great figured tomb follows rather a different pattern from that of the lavish funeral, rising to a peak between the middle years of Elizabeth and the death of James. The size of some of these monuments—for example, those of Henry Lord Hunsdon in Westminster Abbey and Edward Earl of Hertford at Salisbury—is breathtaking in its arrogance. The free-standing four-posters were some of the largest and heaviest monuments to private individuals that England had seen since the days of the round barrow. They were made all the more conspicuous, moreover, by the vivid colouring and gilding with which they were liberally adorned, a feature which judicious restoration in recent years is now beginning to bring out once more. Ostentatious in scale and decoration, these tombs were also ostentatious in siting. Sometimes, as at Chenies for the Russells or Great Brington for the Spencers, they occupy an aisle or private chapel. More frequently, however, they crowd out the chancel, as do the Manners's tombs at Bottesford, effectively converting what had for centuries been a place of public worship into the private mausoleum of a single family. Some, like the Earl of Cork in Dublin Cathedral and Sir John Newton at East Harptree, Somerset, had the effrontery to substitute a family monument for the communion table at the east end of the church.

Such magnificence was not cheap, and by the 1580's the normal amount spent on a tomb, in terms of 1480–1500 money, was between £50 and £100, and some were prepared to pay far more. Lord Hunsdon left £1,000 (= £250) for his tomb at Westminster in 1594, and Nicholas Stone was commissioned in 1616 to make one for Lord Harington for £1,020. These high prices persisted as long as the fashion lasted for large monuments with towering superstructure above full-length effigies recumbent or reclining. But the shift of taste in the late 1620's and 1630's to simpler and smaller architectural surrounds and to busts instead of effigies meant a substantial fall in the price, as the notebooks of Nicholas Stone make clear. Expenditure on both funerals and tombs was thus declining well before the Civil War.

All these various forms of excessive expenditure sprang from an attitude of mind which put generosity and display before thrift and economy, and which was encouraged by the growing popularity of attendance, often unrequited attendance, upon a deliberately and conspicuously extravagant court. This generalized ostentation in manner of life and death reached its peak in the late

Elizabethan and Jacobean period, and can be attributed mainly to the fierce competition for social status which in a transitional period of uncertain values tended to find expression in both medieval and renaissance forms, in hospitality and servants in the country, and clothes and gambling at the Court. Superimposed upon this general tendency, however, was a personal recklessness of behaviour whose cause was more psychological than social. This private malaise was particularly common in the 1580's and 1590's as there grew up a whole new generation of high-spirited young aristocrats in open rebellion against the conservative establishment in general and Lord Burghley in particular. Very many, like Oxford, Rutland, Southampton, Bedford, and Essex, had been wards of the old man and were reacting violently against his counsels of worldly prudence. Such a development is hardly surprising. To listen to Polonius for a few moments in a theatre is one thing; to have to put up with him pontificating at every meal-time for years on end is another. No wonder these young men adopted a way of life of absurdly prodigal extravagance; it was the only revenge they could take on a guardian to whom waste and imprudence were deeply horrifying. The knowledge that so many of his charges had both disliked him and gone to the bad must have puzzled and saddened this well-meaning old gentleman.

It would be dangerous to rely too heavily on a few notorious cases in order to make generalizations about a class as a whole. On the other hand, although the aristocratic rake is always with us, he appears to have been peculiarly common at this period. This must have been due partly to the difficulty of finding suitable employment after the collapse of the tradition of service in war, partly to the ease with which it was possible to draw on family capital to finance personal pleasure, and partly to the existence of a widespread social convention which idealized the opulent and open-handed manner of life. Between 1570 and 1630 the social structure creaked and groaned under the stresses of accommodating more and more new families, and of adjusting itself to the decay or disappearance of more and more old landmarks. In an effort to prop it up the ideal of generosity became twisted into a frenzied competition in ostentation which it was beyond the capacity of many a family to support. Thus the outburst of extravagant building, extravagant funerals, and extravagant tombs must surely be connected with the unprecedented mobility of landed society. All three served as symbolic justifications of rank and status. That all three should have declined in the years before the Civil War is to be ascribed not to increasing financial stringency but rather to some relaxation of social pressures and a reassessment of the optimum social returns on invested capital: what was saved on building, funerals, and tombs was now spent on marriage portions to catch the socially desirable husband.

It was not until the early seventeenth century that the English nobility at last began to free themselves from the medieval preoccupation with publicity and open-handedness by which a man's status was judged by the number of his attendants and the scale of his hospitality. The shrinkage in the numbers of servants, the decline of the great funeral, the withdrawal at meal-times from the semi-public great chamber to the private dining-room, the withdrawal on journeys from the equestrian cavalcade to the privacy of the coach or sedan-chair are all symptoms of the same thing: a readjustment of values by which emphasis was laid less on publicity and display and numerical quantity and more on privacy and luxury and aesthetic quality. It is another facet of that movement towards the assertion of the individual which also found expression in the demand for realistic portraiture in pictures and funerary sculpture, the rise of the autobiography as a literary genre, the refusal to be cut about by the embalmer after death, and the demand for a greater share in the choice of a marriage partner. In terms of expenditure this shift in values meant that less money was spent on huge houses, servants, horses, and food, and more on books, pictures, sculpture, furniture, and gardens. In terms of way of life it meant a retreat into greater privacy: the dumb-waiter in the private dining-room is as characteristic of the eighteenth century as is the posse of gentlemen waiters in the great chamber in the sixteenth. In terms of mental attitudes, it meant a demand for a simple family burial and a monument which expressed the personality of the dead and his emotional relationship to his wife and his children. The movement is thus one more sign of that humanizing of family relationships and that growth of respect for the individual which is so striking a feature of the seventeenth-century scene, in life, in literature, and in art.

Disastrous to not a few noble fortunes, and harmful to the prestige of the peerage as a whole, this heavy expenditure by the aristocracy and greater gentry was of critical importance in galvanizing into activity the sluggish Tudor economy. In an age characterized by an under-employed labour force, the use of so much male manpower in the largely unproductive activity of personal service was probably beneficial rather than harmful. But the important factor was not the persistence of medieval extravagance over manpower or food, but the Renaissance demand for luxuries. If one looks at those sectors of the economy which were showing signs of undeniable growth, they are almost all the product of an upper-class demand for new and better standards of comfort and taste. The building of country houses between 1570 and 1620 must have been the largest capital undertaking of the period.

Luxuries like wines and silks headed the field in the growth of imports, generating an adverse trade balance which may have horrified statesmen but which stimulated efforts to increase exports. The phenomenal growth of London was largely due to its unique role as a centre for luxury goods and professional services —doctors and lawyers, actors and bear-wards, drapers and silkmen, scriveners and money-lenders, goldsmiths and jewellers all prospered exceedingly.

Apart from the expansion of agricultural output and coal-mining, both of which were stimulated by rapid demographic growth, such dynamism as this pre-industrial economy showed was largely directed towards satisfying the demands of an upper-class *élite* obsessed with a desire for conspicuous expenditure. Had this specialized demand not existed, had the nobility skimped and saved, it is just possible that growth would have taken place in other, perhaps more generally beneficial, ways; but, given the current social structure and distribution of wealth, it is far more likely that the only result would have been stagnation. English economic growth at this period, its character, its achievements, and its limitations, owe much to the scale and nature of consumer demand from the landed classes, the lesser members of whom tended to follow, mostly at a respectful distance, the lead given them by the aristocracy.

PART THREE

# MINDS AND MANNERS

---

# XI

## MARRIAGE AND THE FAMILY

AMONG the wealthier members of the propertied classes the family was not the small conjugal unit of today, but a large establishment consisting of the husband, the wife, the household officers, the gentlemen and gentlewomen in waiting, the ceaseless throng of guests, and dozens or even hundreds of inferior servants. It was a community in which all members, and particularly the head and his wife, lived in a perpetual crowd; there was much boredom but little solitude in a country house. The composition of this family unit itself did not alter very greatly between 1560 and 1640. In most cases the eldest son and his wife and their children spent at any rate the early years of their married life under the parental roof, before setting up on their own. The peerage nearly always owned a dower house for the widowed grandmother, so that it is only lower down the social scale that the family unit commonly spanned as many as four generations. At no time, however, was much encouragement given to younger sons to remain at home, and daughters were almost invariably married off at an early age. Nor is there much evidence that even in the early sixteenth century the noble household had taken the form of an extended family built up of a host of brothers and sisters, uncles and cousins. Certainly one or two relatives sometimes formed part of the household, as companions of the lord or lady or as administrative officials, but this seems to have been as much the result of personal choice from a wide field of acquaintances as of a sense of family obligation. More commonly relations were employed as stewards and land agents living independently on the scattered family estates. Certainly no relative, not even a brother or sister, could claim membership of the household as of right.

The family was far from being the stable and enduring thing that it is commonly taken to be. Owing to the premature death of husband or wife, over a third of all first marriages lasted less than fifteen years, and in most cases the survivor hastened to remarry and create a fresh family (Fig. 11). The main cause of this rapid

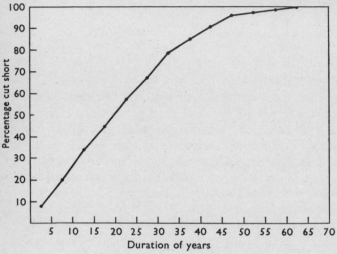

FIG. 11. Duration of First Marriages, 1588–1641

turn-over was the very high death-rate of women during or after childbirth. The chance of the wife's dying in the first fifteen years of marriage was over double that of the husband, being almost 1 in 4 (Fig. 12). It must further be remembered that, in addition to release by death, a number of aristocratic couples were formally or informally separated, so that for one reason or another the early break-up of the family was a very frequent occurrence indeed— probably just as frequent as it is today.

Secondly, children spent very little of their lives under the parental roof. As infants they were usually put out to wet nurses rather than kept at home, and at a relatively early age they were sent off, in the early sixteenth century to take service in another noble household, and a hundred years later to go to school. Only the girls, and perhaps the eldest son in the care of a private tutor, were likely to remain at home until the age of 14. Thirdly, the high infant-mortality rate meant that the long-term prospects of a family's enduring in the male line were very poor. Not more than 60 per cent. of a random sample of families could hope to survive for a hundred years, a situation which had far-reaching consequences in a society which put a premium on male primogeniture.

Since marriages were not based on prior attraction and since children saw so little of their parents, the institution of the family was held together by law, custom, and convenience rather than by ties of sentiment or affection. The Tudor family was an institution for the passing on of life, name, and property, and it was not until the early seventeenth century that it began to be regarded as an instrument of religious and moral improvement.

Outside this conjugal unit there were the looser bonds of kinship and cousinhood, still widely recognized by a society so obsessed with its own genealogy. The family vendettas that flourished in the Elizabethan countryside, and the construction of political alliances around the family connexions of the Howards and the Villiers in the Jacobean Court, would suggest some feeling of loyalty towards the extended family. On the other hand such alliances easily fell apart again and the fissures which were opened up within so many families by the Civil War suggest that it would be unwise to lay too much stress on the role of the clan in seventeenth-century society.

This sixteenth-century aristocratic family was patrilinear, primogenitural, and patriarchal: patrilinear in that it was the male line whose ancestry was traced so diligently by the genealogists and heralds, and in almost all cases via the male line that titles were inherited; primogenitural in that most of the property went to the eldest son, the younger brothers being dispatched into the world with little more than a modest annuity or life interest in a small estate to keep them afloat; and patriarchal in that the husband and father lorded it over his wife and children with the quasi-absolute authority of a despot. None of these features was new, but the first two became more marked in the later Middle Ages and reached their extreme development in the sixteenth century. As Donne pointed out, 'children kneel to ask blessing of parents in England, but where else?' Though he was 63 when he inherited the title in 1666, Sir Dudley North, eldest son of Lord North, 'would never put on his hat or sit down before his father, unless enjoined to it'.

As will be seen, many factors contributed to a slow readjustment of relationships within the family. But one partial change in child-rearing habits must have had consequences which not only Freudians would regard as of considerable importance. In the sixteenth century it was the normal practice in aristocratic and upper-gentry circles to put the new-born baby out to a wet nurse, who would suckle it for up to three years. The reason for the practice is not clear, though some contemporaries ascribed it to the desire of women to preserve the shape of their breasts and thus their sexual attraction for their husbands. As a result it was not uncommon for the child to develop an attachment towards his nurse far deeper than that for his natural mother, whom he saw but rarely. Shakespeare's picture of Juliet's intimate ties with her nurse and her stiff and formal relations with her mother—who could not even remember her exact age—was taken direct from life.

In the early seventeenth century there was a reaction against this practice, ostensibly on nutritional rather than psychological grounds. Sir Hugh Cholmley ascribed his weak and stunted frame as a child to the fact that he had been put out to a nurse who was pregnant, and whose milk was consequently poor. In 1628 the Countess of Lincoln published a book urging mothers to feed their own children, a work which coming from so noble a source must have had considerable effect. In so far as this practice became more common in the seventeenth century, it would tend to strengthen the emotional ties between mother and children and to give her a share in the rearing of her children, from which she had hitherto been almost entirely excluded.

Long before there took place any change in the demographic pattern of high birth-rate and high mortality, children, like wives, were beginning to play a more important role within the family. Before the sixteenth century those who died in infancy were easily forgotten, not even being recorded by the heraldic genealogists. But by the beginning of the seventeenth century the memory of these infants was being carefully preserved on the tombs of their parents. Wrapped up like mummies in their swaddling clothes, their tiny effigies lie close beside those of brothers and sisters. Contemporaries felt that relations between parents and children were altering for the better in the seventeenth century, and Aubrey was reflecting on the recent past when he wrote that 'then . . . sons must not be company for their father . . . [the] child perfectly loathed the sight of his parents as the slave his torture'.

Under these conditions of family life it was perfectly natural, indeed inevitable, that marriage should be arranged by parents, and that scant attention should be paid to the personal wishes of bride or groom. The marriages of this class might determine the social and political landscape of a county, or even the nation, and therefore became matters of high policy. In any case, since it was only in bed that husband and wife would find themselves alone and thrown on their own resources, successful marriage depended less on mutual affinity than on adaptability to the ways of the establishment as a whole. Under these circumstances the choice of marriage partners by parents is likely to be as sound as, or sounder than, that by the children themselves. Obedience to parental orders was therefore held not only to be a moral duty, but also in a child's best interests.

To these social factors in favour of parental control of marriage there was added the suspicion and dislike for passionate love between the sexes which had been shared both by the Ancient World and the medieval church. Dorothy Osborne's brother expressed the general view when he told her that 'all passions have more of trouble than satisfaction in them, and therefore they are happiest that have least of them'.

The most severe parental pressure was inevitably exercised on daughters, who were most dependent and sheltered, who were regarded as members of an inferior sex, and who had little alternative to obedience since celibacy was even less attractive than an unwanted husband. Parents felt themselves morally obliged to marry off their daughters, and daughters were both unwilling and unable to resist. Fathers in their wills were prone to make their bequests conditional upon strict obedience, the 2nd Earl of Southampton ordering both portion and maintenance to be cut off entirely if his daughter disobeyed the executors. Such clauses were common in the sixteenth and continued to appear in the early seventeenth century, though with diminishing frequency and with diminishing effect. Sometimes parents went so far in their wills as to nominate a particular husband for a daughter, and in the early sixteenth century these authoritarian dispositions of children are to be found in all classes and in all areas.

It was a very long time before a woman's right of veto came to be generally accepted, and it was not till the early seventeenth century that most parents, like the 1st Lord Montagu, at last admitted the need not merely for acquiescence but also for 'affection'. Conditions varied from family to family according to the temperament of the father, and daughters continued to be under heavy parental pressure for several centuries, but on the whole contemporary comment suggests that this significant advance in the history of the emancipation of women took place between 1560 and 1640. Concrete proof of this shift of opinion is provided by changes in the nature of testamentary bequests. When a father stipulated that a daughter's marriage portion was dependent on the consent of the mother or guardian, he now often tended to limit this power to the years of the minority. Moreover by the third decade of the seventeenth century many parents in their wills were leaving their daughters' portions free from any strings at all, and payable at a certain age, regardless of whether the girl was married or not. With few exceptions the age varied from 17 to 21, with 18 as the most common—though this did not mean that girls were legally free thereafter, since the Canons of 1603 made marriage of children under 21 dependent on consent of parents or guardians. But fierce dispositions were by now exceptional, and the furthest that most parents were now willing to go was to offer an additional reward for obedience in addition to a free basic portion.

By the 1620's aristocratic marriage settlements were beginning to stipulate in advance the portions payable to future daughters of the union if there were no sons. This was a device much disliked at first by old-fashioned parents, and when in 1628 a treaty was under discussion for the marriage of Anne Cecil to Lord Percy, the 9th Earl of Northumberland refused point-blank to consider such a suggestion. He told the Earl of Salisbury that it was 'a new device rarely used' and drew attention to the dangers of thus freeing children from parental control. 'I will never be an instrument to breed that disobedience', he concluded. But despite Northumberland's attitude the practice spread rapidly and had become almost universal among the aristocracy by the 1640's.

Finally, with the introduction of the 'strict settlement' in the late seventeenth century, the portions of all future children were usually laid down at the time of their parents' marriage. A daughter was at last in a position to defy her parents without depriving herself of her marriage portion. It should be emphasized, however, that this new freedom did not mean that girls were now likely to ignore the old social and economic bases for selection. It was a late-seventeenth-century writer who observed that 'women in this age, like hens, desire only to lay where they see nest-eggs'. Nor was the traditional moral obligation to defer to parental wishes very much less effective. Most girls would for centuries continue to obey their parents, since this was what they had been taught to regard as their Christian duty. All that had been established was the moral claim and the economic power to exercise a veto in the last resort. Mary Astell did not realize what an advance she was registering when she complained in 1700 that: 'A woman indeed can't properly be said to choose, all that is allowed her is to refuse or accept what is offered.'

For eldest sons, freedom of choice was little less restricted than it was for daughters. The desire to prevent marriage from passing out of the family control because of wardship, and the financial importance of the settlement, prompted the father to marry his son and heir during his own lifetime to a woman he had chosen for him. The son was usually at the mercy of the father since he depended on him for an allowance during the latter's lifetime and for the provision of a jointure for his widow, without either of which marriage was virtually impossible.

On the other hand if the father needed the cash portion, it was in his interests to urge his son to marry, and there was consequently some slight freedom of manœuvre. As with daughters, there was a softening of opinion in the early seventeenth century, and in about 1613 Henry Earl of Huntingdon was advising against forced marriages. 'I myself was married when a child and could not have chosen so well myself nor been so happy in any woman I know, but because one proves well it must not beget a conclusion.' By the middle of the century most parents had admitted the right of veto to their eldest sons, though many still hankered after their former absolute powers. When in 1653 Sir Owen Wynn remarked that his son was 'a free man, to be disposed of as God Almighty and his parents think fittest for him', he was doing no more than express the current, muddled, doctrine.

For younger sons the evidence is much scantier, but it is likely that they always enjoyed rather more freedom than their elder brothers since little financial importance attached to their choice. Almost always poorly endowed, they either did not marry at all, or married late and relatively humbly. The doctrine of filial obedience, and the dependence on father or elder brother to provide maintenance and jointure, meant that matters did not go entirely unsupervised. But when provision for younger sons was made in wills, it was rarely tied to marriage by consent of guardians or relatives.

To support this ancient belief in strict parental control and the weighty economic reasons in its favour, there was added a further, institutional, factor. By feudal law the King enjoyed rights over the lands and the disposal in marriage of any of his tenants in chief who inherited his estates while still a minor. This was a common enough occurrence in days of high mortality, more than one in every three peers being under 21 when he inherited his title, and therefore a ward of the Crown. The Tudors revived this authority as a fiscal device, the Court of Wards being set up to sell to individuals the Crown's rights over the minor's person and one-third of his lands. The child could be bought from the Court, either to be married to one of the purchaser's own children or to be auctioned to the mother or to another. The will of the 1st Lord Rich, drawn up in 1567, provides a striking example of the cynical detachment with which such slave-trading was still regarded in the mid-sixteenth century. Among other offspring Lord Rich left an illegitimate son Richard, for whom he now made provision. He instructed his executors to 'provide or buy one woman ward or some other woman having manors, lands, and tenements in possession of the clear yearly value of two hundred pounds by year over all charges at the least, for a marriage to be had and solemnised to the said Richard'. If Richard should refuse to marry the girl the executors were 'to sell the said ward . . . to the uttermost advantage'. The possibility that the ward might refuse Richard was not even thought worth considering.

The notorious abuses of the system were coming under increasing criticism at the end of the sixteenth and the beginning of the seventeenth centuries. Though the distinction should not be pressed too hard, in the sixteenth century the main objection was that the traffic in wards undermined the natural authority of parents and relatives by giving the power of marriage to strangers, and endangered the long-term family fortunes by placing a third of the property at the mercy of rapacious guardians. If natural rights were offended, at this stage they were more the natural rights of parents to authority than of children to freedom of choice. The abuses of wardship became a frequent subject of complaint in the House of Commons, and playwrights and poets soon joined in the assault. In the early seventeenth century, however, emphasis was shifting from criticism of abuses of the system to direct attacks on the system itself. In 1607 George Wilkins devoted a whole play to illustrating the immorality and cruelty of wardship, and by the middle of the century even an arch-conservative like the Marquis of Newcastle was advising Charles II to reform the Court, so that 'wards may not be bought and sold like horses in Smithfield'. The Court of Wards was tolerated as long as the society upon which it preyed had itself little respect for individual freedom of choice, and as long as there was a strong vested interest in its continuance. Only when that freedom began to win a grudging acceptance, and when the Crown reduced the vested interest by monopolizing more of the profits for itself, did its overthrow become inevitable. Blackstone was right when he called the abolition of feudal tenures in 1660 'a greater acquisition to the civil property of this kingdom than even Magna Carta itself'.

Wardship was not the only method by which the Crown could control the choice of marriage partners. Among the propertied classes there was always the danger of royal interference through the unfettered exercise of the prerogative, either to reward a courtier with a rich prize or to favour or obstruct a match on grounds of personal whim. The early Tudors seem to have exercised this authority sparingly, and there are only a handful of recorded cases under Henry VIII. Elizabeth interfered frequently, but hardly ever positively, her main ambition being to prevent the marriage of her courtiers and her aristocratic young Maids of Honour. Her objections were based partly on straightforward feminine jealousy and partly on a desire to preserve the Court as the focus of interest of every English man and woman of note. For those around her it was difficult to know what to do. The Court was the one place in England where young people could escape parental vigilance and had the opportunity to engage their affections as they pleased. But if they asked the Queen's permission to marry they were beaten, like Mary Shelton, or rebuffed, like

Mary Arundell. If they married secretly but were found out, their husbands were imprisoned, like Robert Tyrwhit and Sir Walter Ralegh. If they delayed matters till they were with child and then married hurriedly, both partners were liable to imprisonment, as Elizabeth Vernon and the 3rd Earl of Southampton discovered. If they allowed themselves to be seduced without prospect of marriage they were equally in trouble, like Mary Fitton and William Earl of Pembroke. There was really no way out, except for those who renounced all thought of marriage in deference to the Queen's wishes, like Sir Christopher Hatton and Sir Robert Cecil after his wife's death; or others who were said to have taken the risk of marriage in 1601–2 and kept it secret until the Queen's death. Things were not easy for lovers at the Court of Elizabeth.

With the accession of James, the pattern of royal interference changed dramatically, for royal efforts were now entirely directed towards the encouragement of marriage. Though himself a homosexual, the King was not jealous of the wives of his favourites, and did his best to help them. To smooth the course of true love he provided money and lands for the marriage settlements of Montgomery and Somerset and bullied the bishops into giving the Countess of Essex her divorce. A passionate believer in the union of the two kingdoms, he looked with especial favour upon Anglo-Scottish marriages. Later on in the reign, James was persuaded by Buckingham to use his influence to procure rich wives for his less affluent courtiers. These efforts of James in his declining years prepared the way for the behaviour of Charles, under whom the most frequent and most arbitrary interference occurred. An extreme case occurred soon after the accession, in 1626. Charles had already planned to marry the son and heir of Thomas Earl of Arundel to a daughter of the Earl of Argyle, when the young man suddenly and secretly married a daughter of the Duke of Lennox instead. Charles promptly threw the boy's father into prison on suspicion of complicity. During the 1630's letters of recommendation came thick and fast, but it is a revealing commentary on the growth of opposition to the royal will that on all but one occasion these attempts to influence marriage were without success.

Finally there are a number of cases on record in which leading politicians and officials used their positions to force marriage on clients. The most notorious examples of this form of blackmail were those perpetrated by the Duke of Buckingham, who arrived at Court bringing in his train an almost inexhaustible supply of indigent female relatives. Well might the satirist inquire:

> Hast thou no niece to wed, is there no inn
> Nor bawdy house to afford thee any kin
> To cuckold lords withall?

On the other hand it must be admitted that many peers needed little pressing to take the hand of a relative of the Duke, and a later pamphleteer had some justification for accusing them of 'scrambling for his dirty nieces'.

Despite the ubiquitous authority of parents and guardians and despite occasional pressure from the Crown or politicians, marriage as a result of personal choice was not entirely unknown among the nobility. Two circumstances made this possible. If when his father died the heir was over 21 and still unmarried, he could choose his own wife. Secondly at Court, as nowhere else, he could associate with young women of high birth sufficiently frequently and freely for mutual attachment to develop.

On the basis of surviving evidence it would seem that the doctrine of the absolute right of parents over the disposal of their children was slowly weakening in the late sixteenth and early seventeenth centuries. King James himself declared that 'parents may forbid their children an unfit marriage, but they may not force their consciences to a fit'. When one looks for the causes of this change of attitude, it seems likely that a preponderant part was played by the puritan ethic. Various tendencies were at work to stimulate the growth of individualism, not merely in man's relation to God but also in economics and in politics. But superimposed upon them there was the strong working of moral and religious enthusiasm for a Christian society based on secure family relationships. The puritan divines put forward an idealized view of the relationship of love and marriage, based on traditional Christian morality but adapted to new conditions and expressed in Biblical terms that would fire the imagination of their readers. The most advanced parents like Sir Walter Mildmay or Edward Lord Montagu were men of deep puritan conviction, and an examination of puritan pamphlet and sermon literature shows criticism of the marriage for money and of the double standard— the two basic presuppositions underlying the arranged marriage. Criticism of the manipulation of marriage for material ends had

certainly always existed, but its volume seems to have been increasing in the early seventeenth century. Although most critics
wanted to preserve parental control of marriage, their argument
in fact destroyed the main incentive for such control.

Secondly the old tradition of the double standard of sexual
morality for men and women came under heavy criticism, one of
the features of puritanism being a refusal to accept the normal
tolerant attitude towards adultery by the male. This tightening of
sexual *mores* made forced marriage to an unloved partner insup-
portable to men, and must have been a powerful influence in
encouraging sons to assert themselves. The double standard is
essential to the arranged marriage, and any attack on the one must
lead to an undermining of the other. One of the principal effects
of puritan thinking on marriage was thus entirely unintended, just
as were its effects on capitalism and science.

Contemporary 'Letters of advice to a son' which fathers were
in the habit of composing make it clear that what men sought in
marriage was firstly companionship, an objective to which lip-
service was duly paid by Tudor writers but which only took on
a real importance as marriage began to develop into a union for
spiritual support and consolation under puritan inspiration in the
early seventeenth century. Secondly, marriage was the 'prescribed
satisfaction for irrational heats' as Milton put it; that is to say, it
provided an alternative to fornication, which is sinful, brings
scandal, and—in days before contraception—is likely to lead to
embarrassing and expensive consequences; thirdly, marriage met
the urgent need to produce an heir male to carry on the family
line and property; and fourthly, it offered the hope of financial
and territorial advantage. The first three objectives could, it was
thought, be achieved by any random association of male and
female, and the main motive for selective marriage was the preservation and increase of the patrimony. Essentially, marriage was
not thought of as a personal union for the satisfaction of psychological and physiological needs so much as an institutional device
to ensure the perpetuation of the family and its property.

The greatest attention was therefore paid to the financial benefits
of marriage. The most extreme position was stated in the middle
of the seventeenth century by Francis Osborne, who in a printed
'Advice' which ran to seven editions in two years was prepared to
defend the position that 'as the fertility of the ensuing year is

guessed at the height of the river Nilus, so by the greatness of a wive's portion may much of the future conjugal happiness be calculated'. Relatively few seventeenth-century parents or children were willing to go as far as this. The most famous letter of advice in the early seventeenth century, and one which had great influence on current thought, was that of Lord Burghley to his son Robert. Burghley's counsel was just as cynical but a good deal more subtle and judicious than that of Osborne.

Enquire diligently of her disposition and how her parents have been inclined in their youth. Let her not be poor, how generous soever, for a man can buy nothing in the market with gentility. Nor choose a base and uncomely creature altogether for wealth, for it will cause contempt in others and loathing in thee. Neither make choice of dwarf or fool, for by the one thou shalt beget a race of pigmies, the other will be thy continual disgrace and it will irk thee to hear her talk. For thou shalt find it, to thy great grief, that there is nothing more fulsome than a she-fool.

In the late sixteenth century religious factors began to influence the choice of partners. After about 1570 the great Catholic families began increasingly that practice of religious apartheid that was to cut them off from the main stream of the English landed classes. Though there were still numerous cases of recusant wives of Anglican peers and gentry in the late sixteenth century, they tended to become increasingly rare. Of course this policy was not solely the result of deliberate choice but also of necessity, as Protestants also began to be aware of the disadvantages and dangers of mixed religious marriages. Their concern for 'marrying in the Lord' led Puritans to make similar demands for spiritual harmony in marriage, and in consequence the great Puritan houses of the early seventeenth century also began to draw apart in some measure from the main Anglican body. This was a development which had political consequences in forging a further link to bind together the opponents of the rule of Laud and Charles I.

This religious factor added a new criterion to the old ones of wealth and social status, and so enhanced the importance attached to the personal qualities of both bride and groom. Moreover puritan middle-class ethics stressed the need for love and the importance of a wife as a helpmate, and these ideas percolated through to the more pious of the greater gentry and the peers. The first unvarnished statement of the new approach came from that unbending Puritan, Sir Walter Mildmay, who in 1570 flatly advised his son to 'choose thy wife for virtue only'.

We have seen that wills, correspondence, and contemporary comment strongly suggest that the negative right of veto was more freely conceded during the late sixteenth and early seventeenth centuries and that marriages exclusively or even primarily for money were coming under increasing popular disapproval. But the degree to which parents or children put money before other considerations in making their initial selection or final choice is another matter altogether. So far as the aristocracy is concerned it is possible to give an answer to this question in statistical terms. Among the families elevated before 1603, some 20 per cent. of the marriages between 1540 and 1599 of holders or heirs apparent of titles were with heiresses. Thereafter there is a sudden jump to 34 per cent. for the next sixty years. It is thus evident that around the turn of the century the growing financial embarrassment of the peerage drove them into a far more single-minded pursuit of wealthy marriages than had previously been their custom.

Some families—old and new—devoted themselves wholeheartedly to this objective. The Howards dukes of Norfolk and earls of Arundel married four heiresses between 1555 and 1606; the Howards earls of Suffolk and the Norths married three in a row, and the Russells four. Taking the peerage as a whole, one marriage in every three was with an heiress in the early seventeenth century. When it is considered that these figures exclude marriages with women with huge portions but who were not heiresses, it is evident that wealth was the most important single consideration in very many early-seventeenth-century marriages, and that its supremacy was increasing. Whereas social and political factors had predominated in many earlier marriages, the greater fluidity of landed society led to a growing emphasis upon exclusively financial considerations. When contemporaries grumbled about this development they were not thinking back to an age when parents were more concerned with moral virtue, but to one when the preservation of class distinctions took precedence over the quest for optimum financial benefits. Even so, there is reason to believe that this hypothetical golden age was something of a myth. Aristocratic marriages may have been more mercenary in the seventeenth century than in the fifteenth, but the difference is one of degree rather than of kind.

If these material considerations dominated first marriages, which were usually arranged by parents or guardians, the same was not necessarily true of remarriages, which were normally the result of the free choice of the individuals concerned. It should not be supposed that they were a rarity, for mortality among married women was very high, some 45 per cent. dying before 50, a quarter of these deaths being a direct result of child-bearing (Fig. 12). Some-

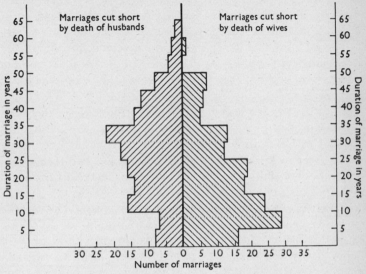

FIG. 12. Termination of First Marriages, 1558–1641

times the desire for more children in order to perpetuate the name and title was the chief reason for a second marriage. This was certainly true of the 1st Duke of Newcastle, of whom his second wife records that 'he having but two sons purposed to marry me, a young woman that might prove fruitful to him and increase his posterity by a masculine offspring'. In very many cases, however, other factors predominated. In a large establishment with servants to be supervised and children to be educated a mistress of the household had a useful function to perform, particularly if the husband was preoccupied with court affairs. Moreover in perhaps the majority of cases this was the first time in which the man was entirely free to make his own choice. If not love-matches, these second marriages were at least the result of personal decisions, the widower seeking a pleasant companion for his middle years as much as a mother for his children or a fortune to swell his coffers. The 1st Lord Guildford ultimately repented of his decision not to remarry, partly on the ground that 'he fancied that, in the night, human heat was friendly'.

There was also a health factor inducing second marriages. Though contemporary medical science was only dimly aware of the stresses set up by sexual frustration, doctors frequently recommended to their patients a regular though moderate ejection of semen, for the same reasons that they prescribed seasonal purges and occasional blood-letting; all three were methods of discharge for 'corrupt humours'. Since the most convenient method of such 'evacuations' was within the marriage bond, this must certainly have been an additional inducement to avoid being wifeless for long.

Quite apart from these more personal considerations, there were sound financial incentives for a second marriage. Sir Charles Guise explained with endearing frankness how 'I . . . was indebted above 2000 . . . so that . . . I found myself in a manner enforced to look after another match'. For the bride was expected to produce a substantial cash portion, which would now go straight into the pocket of the groom instead of that of his father. All he was asked to do in return was to settle a jointure for the life of his widow, a burden which would only affect the estate after his death.

This desire for someone trained in domestic management, mature in sexual experience, and of roughly the same age was one reason why as many as 40 per cent. of the second marriages of peers were with women who were already widows. Nor was there any shortage of supply, for the mortality pattern of peers reveals a high death-rate throughout early middle age. It is easy to see why widows were so eager to marry again. This was a man's world, and a single woman found herself at a severe disadvantage in coping with the normal problems of life. 'Continual troubles, wanting a discreet and helpful friend . . . made me think of marriage', explained the dowager Countess of Sussex in 1646. Moreover these women, now for the first time free to dispose of themselves at their pleasure, were often pathetically anxious to secure that domestic felicity which had hitherto been denied them. Sometimes this contempt for financial considerations turned out well. On her monument in North Cadbury, Somerset, there is a wistful record of the two marriages of Margaret Lady Hastings:

When choice of friends brought her to marriage-bed,
With just renown she passed those her days
And though her youth were tied to age far spent,
Yet without spot she lived and was content.
Her second match she made of her own choice,
Pleasing herself who others pleas'd before.

All too often, alas, such widows married in hope of love only
to find themselves shamelessly exploited. They often suffered
bitter disillusionment, though few had to endure the humiliations
inflicted by Oliver Lord St. John on his second wife, the rich
widow of Sir Edward Griffin. Turning to her in a public gathering
he remarked: ' ". . . your ladyship hath truly paid for your place.
Therefore if any can now make a penny more of you, I would he
had you", wherewith the tears stood in his lady's eyes.'

Part cause and part effect of the pursuit of wealthy marriages
was the development of a nation-wide marriage market centred
on London. In the sixteenth century non-courtier families confined their alliances almost exclusively to the local nobility and
gentry, often within the county. In the north of England even the
peers were limited in their geographical range during the first
two-thirds of the sixteenth century; with only one exception each
the families of Wharton and Ogle married in the north till the end
of the century. The three sisters of the 9th Lord Scrope all married in Yorkshire, and even a magnate as great as the 7th Earl of
Shrewsbury married all his children into the aristocracy of the
north of England. The southern nobility usually allowed themselves a rather greater geographical range. The proximity to
London, the better roads, the less ferocious winters, all made com-
munication easier and reduced parochialism, but even so there is
a strong tendency to regional emphasis at least up to the third
quarter of the sixteenth century.

It was the growth of London as a central matrimonial clearing-
house in the late sixteenth century which finally broke down this
regionalism. Under Elizabeth some thirteen earls or future earls
and five barons found their brides at Court among the Maids of
Honour of the Queen, while for the squirearchy the contacts provided by the increasingly popular London season offered similar
opportunities. At the same time the concentration of knowledge
about settlements in the chambers of a few highly skilled London
conveyancers must also have increased the importance of the

capital as a marriage market. It was in London that the Yorkshire
Wentworths and the Norfolk Pastons sought news of suitable
brides for their children in the early seventeenth century. The old
geographical barriers were breaking down and by this time it is
very difficult to find among the aristocracy examples of regular
local marriages to compare with those of half a century earlier.

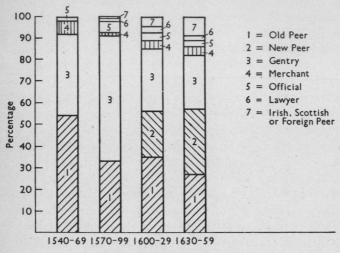

FIG. 13. Social Status of Wives, 1540–1659

If the geographical spread of aristocratic marriage was steadily
widening to the limits of the kingdom, the social range followed
no such regular curve. Of course younger sons throughout married mostly among the gentry, and their situation may be dis-
regarded. Daughters had a choice between peers and gentry, and
the degree to which they succeeded in capturing a nobleman obviously depended on the type of partner the latter was seeking.
Between 1485 and 1569 over half the marriages of titular peers
and their heirs male were within the peerage class, but between
1570 and 1599 the proportion fell to a third (Fig. 13). Inter-
marriage within the peerage had declined sharply, no doubt for
the reasons offered by the Earl of Huntingdon to his son in about
1613 : 'Being allied to most of the nobility, match with one of the
gentry where thou mayest have a great portion, for there is a
satiety in all things, and without means honour will look as naked
as trees that are cropped.' But from 1630 to 1659, when the new

peerage may be said to have been absorbed, the nobility as a whole had reverted to its pre-1570 position of marrying rather more than 50 per cent. within itself. However, since there were now twice as many families, this did not represent quite that strict exclusiveness that had characterized the mid-sixteenth century.

Apart from successful lawyers, who usually came from gentry stock and were rapidly reabsorbed into it at a higher level, the only other extremely wealthy group in England was the London merchants. This vein was already being tapped by the peerage in the fifteenth century, and it continued to be exploited in the early sixteenth with marriages to the widows or daughters of London aldermen of Lords Zouche, Mountjoy, and Marney and the Earl of Kent. Moreover in the later years of Henry VIII there were very close links between the City and high government officials, some of whom had just risen or were about to rise into the peerage. Once established, however, the Elizabethan aristocracy consciously set out to emphasize its new status, and as a result for thirty years after 1561 there was only one case of inter-marriage with the merchant class. The erection of this barrier is as interesting as its weakening in the 1590's. It was built partly on an urge by the newly elevated to cut themselves off from their more humble background, partly on a sharpening of social distinctions, and partly on the temporary removal of the financial necessity for such alliances thanks to the rich booty of monastic estates.

For reasons which are discussed elsewhere, very many peers in the late Elizabethan period found themselves in grave economic difficulties, one result of which was that a few bolder or more desperate spirits began to leap across the barrier that for thirty years had divided peers from merchants. There is no doubt whatever that the initiative came not from aldermen anxious to improve their status but from noblemen determined to grab the rich prizes offered by City widows and daughters, and particularly by City heiresses. The first sign of the new trend came in about 1591 when Lord Stafford wrote to Burghley asking him to use his influence to put pressure on 'a rich citizen for his only daughter and heir to be married unto my son'.

By the end of the sixteenth century it was the gentry—either the impoverished or the ambitious—who had swallowed their pride and were courting the merchants. Several of the new nobility had married into the merchant class before their elevation, and in

doing so they were merely following the tide. By 1618 the example
set by some of the gentry, the decay of old standards of morality
and propriety in the age of the Duke of Buckingham, and the
soaring fortunes and ambitions of the aldermen all conspired to
bring about a spate of matrimonial projects and alliances between
peers and merchants, such as Alderman Sir William Cockayne:
his son bought an Irish viscountcy and his five daughters between
them married three earls, a viscount, and a baronet. After his
death, his widow went one further and married the 1st Earl of
Dover.

That there was something very squalid about these barter agree-
ments of money for title was generally recognized. But at a time
when mercenary marriages were the rule, and when merchants
like Hicks and Bayning and merchants' sons like Craven were
buying their way into the English peerage, the process was inevitable. In the thirteen years from 1618 to 1630 there were nine
alliances or attempted alliances between titular peers or their heirs
male and the daughters or widows of merchants, compared with
six in the seventy years from 1548 to 1617 and three in the thirty
years from 1631 to 1660. The third decade of the century witnessed a degree of mingling between the peerage and the City
without parallel both before and after. The sale of titles died away
after 1630 and for the next forty years the new peerage, like their
predecessors after 1553, cut themselves free from these bourgeois
entanglements.

Since financial considerations played so crucial a part in the
arranged marriage, the legal transactions which preceded and
accompanied the ceremony must be examined with some care.
The terms of the agreement were set out in two documents, the
contract between the fathers of bride and groom, and the settlement of his estate by the father of the groom to trustees for uses.
The two were often combined in a single deed, and the late sixteenth and early seventeenth centuries witnessed an extraordinary
growth in their size and complexity. As a result it is a far cry
from the simple one- or two-page document of the early sixteenth
century to the settlements of the late seventeenth and eighteenth
centuries, the largest of which covers about 300 square feet of
parchment.

The father of the bride had to provide a substantial cash sum,
known as a portion, usually payable in several instalments over

one or two years, the bride's trousseau and jewels, and usually the marriage feast as well. This last was a gargantuan orgy which on occasions spread over several days of eating and drinking.

In return for these straightforward payments the father of the groom had to undertake a far wider set of obligations. The most important was the provision of an annual allowance for support of the bride if and when she became a widow, and the ratio between this jointure, as it was called, and the cash portion was the main issue around which negotiations turned. Calculated as a net income, the jointure usually took the form of physical ownership of land, including living quarters, either a mansion on the jointure estate in the case of peers and great landowners, or some rooms in the family manor house in the case of lesser squires.

Second in importance to the jointure, and particularly significant if the bride's father had his daughter's present comfort at heart, was the allowance made to the groom in his father's lifetime. This also might take the form either of an annuity or of a direct transfer of property and a house, often the same as the jointure. In either case the father of the groom usually undertook to give the pair lodging in his own house for the first few years.

A third obligation written into an increasing number of settlements after about 1620 was that of settling on trustees a fixed annual sum, later known as pin-money, to be at the free disposal of the bride. This was a new development, and is symptomatic of the increasing economic independence of women. To give but one example of these complicated arrangements, when in 1661 the Earl of Salisbury was negotiating to marry his grandson to a daughter of the Earl of Rutland, the latter wrote: 'My lord of Salisbury shall have with my daughter £9000 . . . and for jointure [I] expect £1600 per an., and that land to be for the present maintenance of the young people, that, if it be found inconvenient there being family with parents, they may live by themselves; out of this £1600, £300 I desire for my daughter's personal allowance, made over to trustees for her.'

Fourthly, the father of the groom was expected to make clear the proportion of his estate which he proposed to settle on his eldest son after his death. This settlement of the estate was the crucial factor which governed the stability of the family inheritance, and the technical changes which occurred were of far-reaching consequence. As has been seen, the sixteenth century was a period of exceptional freedom for the head of the family in the disposition of his inherited property. The growing popularity of the life interest first limited this freedom, and then, in the late seventeenth century, the invention and widespread adoption of the 'strict settlement' brought it virtually to a close. Thereafter the father of the bride could rest assured that his daughter's jointure was safe, and that the eldest son of the marriage would inherit the estate intact.

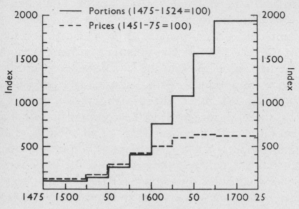

FIG. 14. Marriage Portions and Prices, 1475–1724

The size of a portion offered with a daughter varied according to a number of factors, such as the degree of paternal affection, the number of sisters competing for portions, and the need to compensate for lack of beauty or a discrepancy in social status.

However, sufficient evidence is available for these deviations from the norm to be taken into account, and some judgement made about the average size of portions. Between the second quarter of the sixteenth and the third quarter of the seventeenth century, portions given with daughters of the aristocracy increased approximately ten times. As Fig. 14 shows, the rise kept in step with the general increase of agricultural prices up to about 1600 but thereafter it soared ahead: between 1600 and 1650 prices increased by a third and portions almost trebled. Aristocratic incomes were probably lagging behind the price rise in the late sixteenth century and advancing ahead of it in the early seventeenth, though not to this degree. We must conclude that in the seventeenth century parents were devoting a very much higher proportion of their incomes to marrying off their daughters than were their grand-parents in the sixteenth. By the early seventeenth century few fathers, and then only those with numerous children, were offering less than the equivalent of one year's income as portions for their daughters. As Mary Master remarked in 1663: 'Now, no gentlewoman of what beauty, quality, or qualities soever is thought of, without 3, 5, or 7 thousand pounds. Everybody for a great fortune. Some are plagued, yet it is not warning to the covetous rogues.'

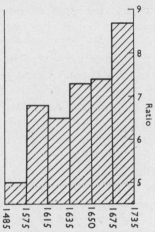

FIG. 15. The Portion/Jointure Ratio, 1485–1734

Statistics of jointure can be drawn up on the same pattern as those for portions, but at present they are based on too small a sample for much reliance to be placed upon them, and they cannot be used as a basis for calculation of average values. However, it seems fairly clear that jointures, at any rate among the aristocracy, now tended to be less than a third of the rental. It is self-evident that the striking rise in portions and the stagnation or decline of jointures in relation to income must involve a major shift in the portion/jointure ratio. Fig. 15 suggests that the average ratio among peers and squires increased by about 75 per cent. between the early sixteenth and late seventeenth century. It is likely, more-over, that owing to the inclusion of unusual cases these statistics slightly underestimate the degree of shift in the ratio. In fact the current norm probably moved from about 5/1 in the mid-sixteenth century to about 10/1 in the early eighteenth century.

By 1640 not only were very much larger portions being offered, but a given portion could buy far less future jointure than it could in 1560. The principal cause of these striking changes is the simple factor of supply and demand: the number of marriageable girls exceeded that of eligible boys. Parents had always felt themselves responsible for disposing of their daughters in one way or another, but the seventeenth century saw a growing contempt for old maids as the Catholic ideal of virginity gave place to the puritan exaltation of matrimony as a holy and honourable state. John Evelyn told his wife that there was 'nothing . . . so ignomineous as an overyeared maid, nor so much despised', and Sir John Lambe brutally advised his daughter to consider the adage 'better louse in pot than no flesh'. Spinsterhood on a modest pension was not respectable, partly because useful or even decorative employment did not exist. Suppression of nunneries by Henry VIII had exacerbated the situation, for they had been used by the aristocracy as 'convenient stowage for their withered daughters', to use Milton's rasping phrase. After 1560 it was only in recusant families that there existed the grim alternative of exile in a nunnery in France or the Spanish Netherlands.

Under conditions of universal marriage for girls, an important factor in upsetting the balance may have been an increased number of children born per marriage, or an increased proportion who survived to a marriageable age, or both. There was certainly a steady increase in population in the late sixteenth and very early seventeenth centuries, which may well have been caused by one or other of these factors. Either would produce a larger number of daughters to be married off and a larger number of younger sons, but only a very small increase in the number of heirs male with whom the daughters could be mated. If this in fact occurred it would in itself go far to explain the increase in the size of portions.

Furthermore daughters of the nobility were faced with growing competition from daughters of the squirearchy in the late sixteenth century, and to a lesser extent from the daughters and widows of City aldermen in the early seventeenth century. The supply of eligible husbands of good social standing failed to keep pace with this rising demand. Daughters of peers had always been ready to marry the heirs male of the greater gentry, so there was no compensatory social break-through to ease the strain, except in so far as there had been an increase in the numbers of these rich gentry. On the other hand the emphasis on patrilinear descent meant that it was still not considered decent to marry your daughter to a mere merchant's son, even though your son and heir might at a pinch marry his sister. This concentration on heirs male is a reason for thinking that the death of many heirs to landed estates in the Civil War, and the subsequent decline—if decline there was—in the proportion of younger sons who married, could have had very little effect on the situation in the seventeenth century. The death of an heir male merely meant his replacement as an eligible husband by his younger brother, and since younger sons were in any case rarely able to compete in this expensive marriage market, any trend towards bachelordom could not have affected the situation. On the other hand the premature deaths of fathers and heirs male in the Civil War must have burdened families with an abnormal number of jointures and therefore raised the premium to be paid for a reasonable jointure in the future.

The time has now come to examine the effects of these various developments upon the two individuals who were the subject of so much careful scheming and plotting. On the wedding day the pair were often still more or less strangers to one another, for it was quite usual for them to have been permitted no more than a few hours in each other's company before the ceremony. Some prospective bridegrooms thought even this formality superfluous. Sir Nicholas Poyntz could hardly bring himself to be civil to a widow he was pursuing. 'Let me not win her love like a fool, nor spend long time like a boy. As God shall help, I am much troubled to think I must speak to any woman one loving word.'

Once fathers came to give their children the right of veto, these brief and formal encounters took on considerable importance, since it was upon them that the agonizing decision of acceptance or refusal had to be based. It was on the basis of a lack of positive antipathy revealed by a little polite conversation that many, perhaps most, noble marriages were concluded. These interviews only took place after the parents had agreed on the contract and settlement, and as soon as the deeds were signed public rejoicing began. The marriage ceremony itself was a public affair, followed by a huge feast for the wedding guests ending not infrequently in the public bedding of the couple, with all the ancient ceremonies of casting off the bride's left stocking and of sewing into the sheets.

And there, naked within the drawn curtains of the great four-poster, the room still echoing with the parting drunken obscenities of the wedding guests, the two strangers were left to make each other's acquaintance. Nor was this always the end of the publicity, for if either bride or groom was a royal favourite King James would cross-question them closely the next morning to extract the last salacious details of the events of the night. In 1617, when Frances Coke was at last forcibly wedded to Sir John Villers, they had to stay in bed the next day until the King came to conduct his habitual *post-coitum* interrogation.

It was not at all unusual for the spousals or verbal engagement, the contract, the marriage, and the consummation to be widely spaced in time. Sometimes parents entered into marriage contracts for their children when they were still very young indeed, the marriages taking place many years later. The reason for the delay was that in law the age of consent was 12 for girls and 14 for boys. If a formal engagement was entered into earlier, it could be broken by either party at the age of consent.

Very few of the nobility and gentry were in fact married the moment it became legally possible (Fig. 16). Only 6 per cent. of the peerage married at 15 or under in the late sixteenth century, and only 5 per cent. in the early seventeenth. Moreover there was a significant trend towards the postponement of marriage to a more reasonable age. In the earlier period 21 per cent. of the peers were married by 17, but in the later only 12 per cent., whereas by 25 the figure was virtually the same, at 78 and 76 per cent. The shift was thus confined to a movement out of the middle teens into the early twenties. This change was due partly to the slow and hesitant introduction of ideas about individual freedom of choice, whose effect has been observed in other spheres, and partly to changing views about the right age for consummation.

Against early consummation there were three arguments whose weight was increasingly recognized as time went on. The first was that very young boys and girls produce stunted children. Secondly men believed, following Plato, Galen, and Avicenna, that the sperm was a vital fluid that governed all growth, and that immoderate discharge in adolescence would therefore impair a man's physical and intellectual development. Thirdly, there was some feeling that parturition by a girl below the age of 16 or so was immediately dangerous and permanently damaging

By the end of the sixteenth century parents thus found themselves in a very awkward situation. To avoid interference from the Court of Wards, to snap up heiresses, to be able to dispose of children at their pleasure, they wanted to marry them off early. To be legally watertight the ceremony had to be consummated, and yet they were assured that early consummation was bad for both parties and likely to produce sickly children. Caught on the

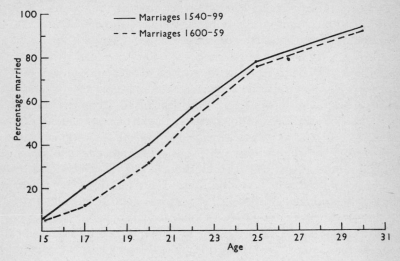

FIG. 16. Age at First Marriage, 1540–1659

horns of this dilemma, they tried three methods of getting themselves off. The first was to put the medical advice first and to delay marriage, the result being, as we have seen, a tendency for the age of marriage for men to move from the late teens to the early twenties. Secondly, the marriage was allowed to take place early but consummation was postponed, sometimes for several years, the girl continuing to live with her parents and the boy proceeding with his education. Failing the postponement of the marriage itself, or marriage and the postponement of consummation, the third and last alternative was marriage accompanied by a unique or even token consummation followed by prolonged separation. In 1610 Francis Willoughby, just down from Oxford, was married to Cassandra, the 11-year-old daughter of Sir Thomas Ridgway. Sir Thomas reported that they were bedded at 4 a.m. after the wedding feast, 'my wife and I relying on his faithful promises to use nothing but fair play till his return out of France etc.'—a journey which lasted nearly four years. Indeed it was a common practice in the early seventeenth century for the marriage to take place a day or two before the young man set out for a year or more of travel on the Continent to finish his education. By this means lengthy cohabitation was effectively postponed and the young man was prevented from getting trapped into an unsuitable marriage abroad. 'Travel when thou art married?' asked Marston. 'Ay, 'tis your young lord's fashion to do so, though he were so lazy being a bachelor that he would never travel so far as the university; yet when he marries her, takes off.'

Once they had reached maturity, there were no longer any external restraints placed on sexual relations between man and wife. There was, however, a good deal of advice given on the subject. Following Aristotle, Thomas Cogan advised moderation always, and total avoidance during the heat of summer, counsel which was certainly followed by Pepys. The recommendation of moderation was fortified by the current view, first advanced by Galen, that gout, which was both very common and much feared among the nobility, was caused in part by excess of venery. John Evelyn, whose prurient pen was constantly returning to the subject, thought that 'too much frequency of embraces dulls the sight, decays the memory, induces gout, palsies, enervates and renders effeminate the whole body, and shortens life'.

Marriage took place very early, the partners were often virtually strangers to each other and were chosen by their parents, the first years of their married life were usually spent in the house of the parents, consummation tended to occur in a blaze of publicity or else some years after the marriage ceremony itself, and was followed more often than not either by total sterility or by an infinitely repetitive cycle of child-bearing. Despite the physical and psychological strains imposed by these arrangements, the majority of marriages survived without open and serious breakdown, and in many cases there developed genuine affection and trust. The number of aristocratic wills in which husbands refer to their wives in friendly terms, leave them bequests, and saddle them with responsibilities makes it clear beyond doubt that very many unions at any rate provided satisfactory working partnerships.

In view of the tremendous religious, social, legal, and economic pressures directed at holding the family unit together, it is none the less remarkable how many marriages publicly and completely broke up. If we disregard entirely the evidence of illegitimate children, in the ninety years between 1570 and 1659 we find forty-nine known cases of notorious marital quarrels, separations *a mensa et thoro*, or annulments among the peerage, which is about 10 per cent. of all marriages. The worst period seems to have been between 1595 and 1620, when something like one-third of the older peers were estranged from or actually separated from their wives.

Why this generation should have been so exceptionally restless is hard to explain. It may be that it was the first reaction by women to the novel doctrine of greater equality between the sexes which was being put about by some puritan pamphleteers. Moreover the legal position of women was improving, and with it their ability to obtain satisfactory terms for a separation—a new situation which may have gone to the heads of some discontented wives. It was between 1580 and 1640 that successive Lord Chancellors gave judgements which substantially altered the law concerning married women's property by creating the doctrine of the Wife's Separate Estate. By the early seventeenth century the economic penalties of a separation for a woman had been substantially diminished.

It is possible that thereafter friction was reduced by the growing reluctance of parents to press children too hard to marry against their inclinations; it may be that the further spread of the puritan conscience damped down these public displays of temper; but it is unlikely to be an illusory product of imperfect evidence, though this may be the explanation of the more modest level recorded in the early Elizabethan period. The great majority of these separations occur in well-established families which had held a title for at least three generations, presumably because only the socially secure felt themselves at liberty to indulge in this unorthodox behaviour. It is also noticeable that trouble very often arose in cases of marriages deliberately designed to capture an heiress or to cement a political alliance, when the compulsion used may be supposed to have been particularly severe: for example the marriages of the Cavendish family were as disastrous personally as they were successful financially.

To what extent were matrimonial discords at this period accompanied by scandal? In England, as in all other European societies, marriage gave the husband monopoly rights over the sexual services of the wife, but conferred on the wife no reciprocal mono-poly over the husband. In the early sixteenth century open main-tenance of a mistress—usually of lower-class origin—was perfectly compatible with a respected social position and a stable marriage. Peers clearly saw nothing shameful in these liaisons, and up to about 1560 they are often to be found leaving bequests to bastard children in their wills.

In practice, if not in theory, the early-sixteenth-century nobility was a polygamous society, and some contrived to live with a succession of women despite the official prohibition on divorce. Presumably in deference to puritan criticism of the double stan-dard, this casual approach to extra-marital relationships dis-appeared after 1560 and between 1610 and 1660 evidence for the maintenance of regular, semi-official mistresses becomes rare. There is no very obvious explanation of this fact, though the following hypothetical model at any rate provides a possible solution. In the Middle Ages and the early sixteenth century, the arranged marriage was often accompanied and made tolerable by the mistress and the illegitimate children. This was a situation accepted by the wife and openly admitted by the husband, and as a result marriages held together as working business arrangements. But impressed by Calvinist criticisms of the double standard, in the late sixteenth century public opinion began to object to the open maintenance of a mistress, which would explain the increas-ing number of breakdowns of marriages, and the reluctance to mention bastards in wills. The arranged marriage was unable to stand the strain of the shutting down of this safety-valve and the scale of separations became so alarming that parents began relaxing the pressure and giving their children some limited right of veto over the choice of marriage partners. As a result the number of open breakdowns of marriage and the number of illegitimate children declined after the first decade of the seventeenth century (though there may well have been an increase in both after the Restoration).

At the same time as there was a tightening up of the sexual *mores* of the nobility and gentry as a whole in the early seventeenth cen-tury, a small minority was moving swiftly in exactly the opposite direction. One of the most striking features of Early Stuart society was the growing cleavage in outlook and behaviour between Court and Country. An aspect of this development which attracted much contemporary attention and criticism was the sexual licence at the Jacobean Court, which may well have rivalled or excelled the more notorious conditions at the Court of Charles II. Although court behaviour under Henry VIII appears to have been fairly lax, in the middle and late sixteenth century peers had taken lower-class mistresses but had jealously guarded the honour of their wives. It was only after about 1590 that there developed general promiscuity among both sexes at Court. Accustomed to the exercise of power, with little training in self-control, and with all the time in the world on their hands, noblemen have probably always been substantially more free in their sexual behaviour than gentry, yeomen, or merchants. When the general atmosphere of the day is tolerant, however, no harm is done to the prestige of the class, and it is only in times like the early seventeenth or the mid-nineteenth centuries that trouble is likely to arise. It was an unfortunate coincidence that the behaviour of a minority—but a spectacular and much publicized minority—of the aristocracy was declining after 1590 as fast as general disapprobation of loose conduct was rising.

The real break-through into promiscuity at Court only occurred under James. The popular reaction was that of Simonds D'Ewes, who spoke of 'the holy state of matrimony perfidiously broken and amongst many made but a May-game . . . and even great personages prostituting their bodies to the intent to satisfy and consume their substance in lascivious appetites of all sorts'. As early as 1603 Lady Anne Clifford said that 'all the ladies about the Court had gotten such ill names that it was grown a scandalous place'. Both the royal favourites were notorious pursuers of women. 'I know those', wrote Lord Thomas Howard in 1611, 'who would not quietly rest, were Carr to leer upon their wives as some do perceive, yea, and like it well too they should be so noticed.' Buckingham was actively encouraged by King James in his amatory exploits and Mrs. Dorothy Gawdy is said to have saved herself from his advances only by climbing out of a window.

More unusual, perhaps, was the dubious reputation enjoyed by so many wives of noblemen about the Court. The playwrights were only voicing a widely held belief when they pointed to the different sexual *mores* of Court and Country. 'That is right court-fashion : men, women, and all woo ; catch that catch may.' 'A close friend or private mistress is court rhetoric ; a wife, mere rustic

solecism.' 'Do your husbands lie with ye?' asked Marston. 'That
were country fashion, i' faith.' The Country was convinced, with
mingled fascination and distaste, that at night the Court was the
regular scene of 'most strange surquedries'.

The greatest damage to the reputation of the Court and the
aristocracy was done by their association in the public mind with
homosexuality, an abnormality which aroused deep horror in the
ever-widening circles of puritanism. With the accession to the
throne of a king who made no attempt to disguise his tastes,
the Court became a haunt of homosexuals. From his behaviour
in public the worst was assumed—probably rightly—of James's
physical relations with his favourites, and the Court itself acquired
an evil reputation. This tendency in royal and aristocratic circles
soon affected female fashions, somewhat to the irritation of King
James, who attacked the wearing of 'broad brim'd hats, pointed
doublets, their hair cut short or shorn, and some of them stillettoes
or poignards'. The playwrights noticed what was happening and
gave it further circulation by their satirical comments. 'We're all
male to the middle', remarked Middleton, 'mankind from the
beaver to th' bum. 'Tis an Amazonian time; you shall have women
shortly tread their husbands.'

Public attention was finally riveted on the sexual behaviour of
the aristocracy by a series of sensational scandals which found
their way into the law courts. The first was the annulment in 1613
of the marriage of the Earl and Countess of Essex in order to leave
her free to marry her lover, the Earl of Somerset, on the grounds
that she was *virgo intacta*—a hypothesis to the falsity of which a
number of men about town could testify. Two years later there
exploded the news that the Earl and Countess of Somerset were
on trial on a charge of murdering Sir Thomas Overbury, a former
friend of the Earl and a dangerous witness to the true facts of the
divorce. At the trial the whole sordid story came out, embellished
with obscene letters of the Countess and highly incriminating
ones by the late Earl of Northampton. Hardly had the public
recovered from the shock of these revelations than a new scandal
broke out in which Lady Roos first accused her husband of impotence, and then charged the Countess of Exeter with 'adultery,
incest, murder, poison, and such like peccadilloes'. In the end
Lady Roos's accusations were exposed as lies, and she herself con-
victed of incest with her brother.

Although the Court of King Charles was a far more respectable place than that of his father, the situation could not be restored overnight, and the puritan gentry, brooding in their country manor-houses upon the evils of the day, continued to be regaled with news of aristocratic scandal, almost all of it associated with the Court group. As a result of this flood of scandalous gossip, sexual licence became ineradicably associated with the aristocracy and with the Court. The consequent erosion of respect for the peerage in conventional minds is well reflected in the diary of Sir Simonds D'Ewes. In 1616 he noted the current anagram upon the name of Frances Howarde (Car finds a whore), but added primly that it was 'somewhat too broad an expression for so nobly extracted a lady'. Ten years later people were not so squeamish.

By virtue of their rank the nobility were obliged to live in a blaze of publicity, in the light of which the impression was given, not without justification, that their sexual habits were laxer than those of other classes. In fact, of course, these scandals only involved a small minority, but they were heavily written up in the correspondence of the professional letter-writers and so gave the appearance of a general collapse of sexual standards. Nor did it help the reputation of either King or peerage that, even when the scandals led to prosecution, the principals usually escaped with little more than loss of office and royal favour. It looked as if the aristocracy had reason to think themselves immune from both the dictates of conventional morality and the penalties of the law. Charles did something in 1630 to restore confidence in royal justice by declining to interfere in the death-sentence imposed by his peers on the Earl of Castlehaven for a series of outrageous sexual offences, but by now the damage had been done. Throughout the whole of this period archidiaconal courts and town magistrates had been treating the sexual peccadilloes of the lower orders with extreme severity, and the discrepancy between the generally enforced moral code and the licence of the Court became an established part of public belief. Impinging upon the puritan conscience, this was a powerful factor in undermining the moral authority of both the peerage and the Court.

It is clear that between the early sixteenth and the late seventeenth century family patterns and marriage customs underwent profound changes. The most striking feature is the emergence of a sense of family responsibility for personal harmony and moral virtue. In the Middle Ages the marriage state had been second best to a life of chastity, and it was the ethical exaltation of marriage by protestant divines that began the transformation. The household shrank in size as the number of superfluous servants was pruned away and as the keeping of open house to all comers gave way to the issue of invitations to personal friends. In conformity with this emphasis on privacy and intimacy, the family withdrew from the hall to the great chamber and the private dining-room; by the end of the seventeenth century corridors were being built to avoid the necessity of tramping through rooms to get from place to place, the promiscuous habit of putting up truckle beds here, there, and everywhere was giving way to the establishment of private bedrooms. The concept of an inward-turned, isolated, conjugal family, already familiar to the *bourgeoisie*, was well on the way to acceptance among the aristocracy.

The most remarkable change inside the family was the shift away from paternal authority, a shift made possible by the extension of the power of the central government. As the state and the law courts came to provide greater protection to wives and children, so the need for subordination to husband and father declined. This greater awareness of personal relations between husband and wife and parents and children marks an important stage in the growth of the child-orientated family and in the growth of the freedom of the individual in Western Europe, an aspect of what Professor Riesman would call the shift from a tradition-directed to an inner-directed society. The aristocracy were not the pacemakers in this social revolution, which was primarily the work of the urban *bourgeoisie* and the puritan divines. What is so striking, however, is the readiness with which they absorbed the new ideas and used them to adapt the structure of the family and the institution of marriage as they had inherited them from the Middle Ages in order not only to fit their obsession with patrilineal and primogenitive inheritance, but also to suit the social, ethical, and religious conditions of the modern world.

# XII

## EDUCATION AND CULTURE

Alas, you will be ungentle gentlemen, if you be no scholars:
you will do your prince but simple service, you will stand your
country but in slender stead, you will bring your selves but to
small preferment, if you be no scholars.
G. PETTIE, *The civile Conversation of S. Guazzo*, 1586, sig. A^v

Between 1540 and 1600 there occurred one of the really
decisive movements in English history by which the propertied classes exploited and expanded the higher educational
resources of the country. By doing so they fitted themselves to
rule in the new conditions of the modern state, and they turned
the intelligentsia from a branch of the clergy into a branch of the
propertied laity. At last it was possible to be an intellectual without having to endure the intolerable hardships of celibacy.

The drive to give a more intellectual training to the children of
the nobility and gentry in the early sixteenth century sprang from
two sources. The ideals of Italian humanism were seeping in, a
century late, through educational reformers like Colet, Vives, and
Erasmus; and there was developing a growing anxiety about the
prospects of the nobility maintaining their grip on the key positions in the political system. Rule by clerics of humble birth like
Wolsey was familiar enough to the Middle Ages; what was new
was the replacement of the clergy in high political and administrative office by talented laymen from the lesser gentry or even below.
As this revolution gathered momentum there developed open
competition for the seats of power between the hereditary nobility
and lower social groups among the laity. This threat to the established order alarmed conservatives everywhere, and stimulated a
demand that the old aristocracy should again fill their rightful
place in the councils of the nation. What had happened was that
the technical requirements for public service had altered. The
demand for military expertise had slackened, and the demand for
intellectual and organizational talents had increased. As the state
bureaucracy grew and as the modern diplomacy took shape, the

highest public offices went to those who had been trained to think clearly, could analyse a situation, draft a minute, know the technicalities of the law, and speak a foreign language. There was a demand for men who could give a sense of perspective to current problems thanks to a familiarity with classical and modern history and with the institutions and economies of the other states of Europe.

These two forces, humanism and the desire to preserve a fixed social hierarchy, interacted one upon the other, the former being a powerful support for the latter. What distinguishes the English humanists of the second quarter of the sixteenth century from their foreign colleagues is the relative poverty of their scholarship. No great corpus of learning, no monumental encyclopaedias came from the English presses. Instead there poured forth a flood of translations for the benefit of gentlemen anxious to absorb the lessons of the classics without going to the trouble of mastering the language. The leading educational figures of the middle of the century were not remote and ineffectual dons but academic politicians and government officials like Sir Thomas Smith and Sir John Cheke, absorbed in the power struggles of court and university. They were the Jowetts of their day, who regarded the production of an educated *élite* to rule the country as a more important objective than the pursuit of scholarly research. And who is to say they were wrong?

These educational reformers were unable to solve the problems posed by the waywardness of the laws of heredity operating in a partly closed society. But at least they could see to it that the number of idle and ignorant aristocrats was reduced to a minimum, and that chances of promotion for the talented 'new man' were consequently restricted. And so there was launched a sustained and in the end remarkably successful attack upon the ignorance of the nobility. Again and again it was hammered home that the justification of the privileges enjoyed by the nobility was service to the commonwealth; that the definition of nobility was not exclusively good birth, but ancestry coupled with virtue; and that virtue consisted not only in devotion to God and the Established Church (whichever it might happen to be at the time), not only in moral rectitude, but also in the mastery of certain technical proficiencies. Among the latter were now counted book-learning, languages, and history as well as the ancient attributes of good manners and proficiency in the military arts, for only by acquiring this new training could the nobility fit themselves to serve the Prince in peace as well as war.

In their zeal for the new learning, the reformers expressed a passionate contempt for the late medieval and early Tudor noble-man. Richard Pace reported a conversation with a gentleman who exploded: 'I swear by God's body, I'd rather that my son should hang than study letters. For it becomes the sons of gentlemen to blow the horn nicely, to hunt skilfully and elegantly, carry and train a hawk. But the study of letters should be left to the sons of rustics.' Thomas Elyot admitted that gentlemen normally despised learning, thinking it a positive disqualification for responsible office, and Edmund Dudley frankly said that he thought that the English nobility were 'the worst brought up for the most part of any realm of christendom'.

What truth is there in this sustained onslaught? There can be no doubt that some late medieval gentry families, like the Pastons, took a bookish education seriously, but then they were an excep-tionally literate family. But the extreme scarcity of surviving correspondence suggests that in general the nobility and gentry did not write, and presumably felt no deprivation because of it. The upper classes conducted most of their affairs by word of mouth, and the records were kept by clerical scribes. As late as the reign of Elizabeth there was one privy councillor, the 1st Earl of Pembroke, who was said to be unable to read or write, and who certainly had the greatest difficulty in scratching his signature on official documents.

By the middle of the sixteenth century, however, peers and gentry were at last convinced, both by the propaganda of the humanists and by the evident success in life of those with educa-tion, that it was time to bestir themselves and get some profes-sional training. There resulted an astonishing explosion of higher education in England, and one that temporarily embraced even women among the aristocracy. The mid-sixteenth century was the first great age of the blue stocking: there were the celebrated More, Cheke, and Cooke ladies, there was Lady Jane Grey, and there was Queen Elizabeth herself. The Howards were for genera-tions outstanding for their insistence on giving their children a sound education, which at this period even extended to their daughters. Katherine, daughter of the luckless Earl of Surrey and wife of Henry Lord Berkeley, kept up with her Latin grammar, was skilful in French, perfect in Italian, a student of natural philosophy and astronomy, familiar with globes and quadrants, and was an admirable player on the lute into the bargain. Whether or not she made a good wife is another matter.

In this first, heroic, phase of the educational revolution, peers and gentry possessed an enthusiasm for pure scholarship that far outran the practical needs of an administrative élite. They rushed headlong into a course of study that stands comparison in its academic austerity with that of any educational system of twentieth-century Europe. Men like Elyot were well aware that their purpose was to train a governing class, but they tended to exaggerate the academic side of the programme. In his enthusiasm Sir Henry Slingsby began to teach his son Latin (by Montaigne's method) at the age of 4. In 1632 Sir John Strode told his son that 'learning to a gentleman is like a diamond set in a gold ring: one doth beautify the other', and Richard Evelyn successfully instilled into the mind of his son John the notion that it is 'better to be unborn than untaught'. Here is learning exalted not merely as a means to virtue and public service, but as an end in itself.

The key figure in the transformation of the education of the aristocracy was Lord Burghley and he may thus claim to have done more in the long run to preserve the class than any other man. As Chancellor of Cambridge and as the most influential old member of St. John's, he was tireless in encouraging sound scholarship. As Master of the Court of Wards, he made himself guardian and educational director of many young fatherless noblemen, while his reputation and influence led other parents to entrust their children to his care. Upon one and all he poured out his passion for learning as the pathway to virtue, godliness, and capacity for high office, and if his efforts were not crowned with the success he felt them to deserve, at least he had created a fashion for a bookish education.

What Burghley meant by learning may be gauged by the programme he had laid down for the studies of Edward Earl of Oxford in 1562. Thirty years before, a progressive-minded parent, Thomas Cromwell, had been satisfied that his son and heir aged about 13 should divide his time between 'the French tongue, writing, playing at weapons, casting of accounts, pastimes of instruments', etc. To be precise, the day began with Mass, fol-

lowed by a reading from Erasmus's *Colloquies*, then an hour or two
at writing and as much again in reading Fabian's *Chronicle*, the rest
of the day being spent in playing on the lute or the virginals. On
his frequent rides his tutor told him stories from Greek and
Roman history. For recreation he hawked, hunted, and practised
with the long bow. The 12-year-old Earl of Oxford in 1562 had
a much more formidable programme to endure:

| A.M. | | | P.M. | | |
|---|---|---|---|---|---|
| 7–7.30 | Dancing | | 1–2 | Cosmography | |
| 7.30–8 | Breakfast | | 2–3 | Latin | |
| 8–9 | French | | 3–4 | French | |
| 9–10 | Latin | | 4–4.30 | Writing | |
| 10–10.30 | Writing and Drawing | | 4.30 | Prayers and Supper | |
| 10.30 | Prayers and Dinner | | | | |

On holidays the boy was to read the epistle of the day in Latin or
English before dinner, and after it the gospel in English or Latin.
The rest of the holiday Burghley allowed to be spent in riding,
shooting, dancing, and other commendable exercises, except for
the times of prayer.

All records of Tudor education indicate that the hours of work
were very arduous, and that, in spite of lofty ideals, much of the
teaching was a dreary linguistic grind consisting of the mechanical
feeding in of facts about the grammar and vocabulary of a dead
language. It is hardly surprising that masters were only able to
maintain discipline and enforce application to the task on hand by
a liberal use of physical punishment, applied equally to noblemen
and others. It was as headmaster of Westminster, the most fashionable school in the country, that Dr. Busby acquired his formidable
reputation as an enthusiastic flogger. The Elizabethan grammar
school was a place where the middle- and upper-class boy acquired
a technical proficiency, namely low-grade Latin, at the hands of
a man succinctly described by Ben Jonson as 'a pure pedantic
schoolmaster sweeping his living from the posteriors of little
children'.

The Tudor educational system was characterized by a total lack
of stratification by age, and by increasingly determined attempts
to ensure stratification by class. Today the greatest attention is
paid to age, and each child tends to move forward automatically
with his own peer-group. No such system prevailed in the sixteenth
and seventeenth centuries, when boys of widely varying ages were

assembled together to pursue the same courses of study. There was no universally accepted age for admission to school or to university, and parents often found it convenient to send two or more brothers forward together.

How far education was socially stratified is a very difficult matter to determine. That such was the desire of many influential people can hardly be in doubt. It lay behind the repeated suggestions for a government-supported academy for the training of young noblemen, and behind the repeated proposals to exclude men not of gentle birth from certain schools, from some university scholarships, and from the Inns of Court. One reason for these proposals was a fear that, if given equal educational opportunities, the sons of the humble would squeeze the sons of gentry out of the limited jobs available, and that in turn sons of mere gentry would squeeze the aristocracy out of the limited number of high political and administrative offices.

By the early seventeenth century two developments can be detected. Firstly, peers and gentry began to congregate in a limited number of fashionable schools, which became more exclusively upper-class in composition. Secondly, the upper classes came in larger numbers to the universities and there cut themselves off from their inferiors by various devices. They lodged and fed separately as gentlemen commoners, were attended by their own servants, and were marked out by distinctive dress when they walked abroad. They could not have had much social contact with the scholars and sizars from professional, mercantile, or clerical backgrounds struggling to obtain a degree and a country parsonage. In any case there was a marked concentration of noblemen and upper gentry in the more fashionable colleges. The fact that in schools and universities there were boys from both gentle and non-gentle backgrounds is no more evidence of genuine social interplay and social cohesion than the attendance today of negroes and whites at integrated American schools, or of sons of peers and sons of paupers at the more exclusive Oxford and Cambridge colleges.

There was a good deal of argument in the sixteenth century about the ideal place of education for a nobleman. In the Middle Ages he had been brought up first at home and then in service attached to a great aristocratic or royal household. Though some noble households continued to provide educational training grounds for young gentlemen and noblemen during the reign of

Elizabeth—that of Edward Earl of Derby was one, of Lord Burghley another—the practice had all but died out by the seventeenth century. The apogee of the private tutor, however, was just beginning, and there can be little doubt that the great majority of peers were educated at home up to the age of 14 or thereabouts, and often beyond. The purely academic duties of a tutor in a serious-minded household were not to be taken lightly. In 1606 the tutor to the 1st Earl of Salisbury's son wrote to complain of his difficulties during a jaunt into Lancashire with his pupil. 'Although we speak Latin both travelling and hunting, yet the sound of it is so harsh amongst a cry of dogs as it comes not with a wonted facility.' It is difficult to know whether to feel sorrier for master or student in this predicament. These tutors usually doubled the role of chaplain and were treated—as tutors and governesses always are—with widely varying degrees of respect and friendship.

Even in the late sixteenth century very many sons of noblemen and leading squires continued to be privately educated without contact with either school or university. A striking feature of the age, however, is the increase in the number of gentry and even nobles who began to patronize places of communal education. This was perhaps the most active period of school expansion in our history. In 10 sample counties, there were not more than 34 schools open to the laity in 1480; by 1660 another 305 had been endowed and a further 105 founded but not endowed. The main beneficiaries were of course the yeomen, artisans, and small shopkeepers who could at last get their children equipped with some of the intellectual tools for social and economic advancement. These schools were not exclusively patronized by the non-gentry classes, however, for from 1560 onwards one finds increasing numbers of sons of squires, knights, and even peers attending first little local schools and then a select number of institutions which became increasingly the preserve of an upper-class clientele. For some time parents, though convinced of the virtues of boarding-school education, were bewildered by the variety of choice. Before proceeding to Balliol John Evelyn got his education first in the three R's by 'one Frier' at the church porch of Wotton, then in Latin and writing by a Frenchman at Lewes, then at Mr. Potts's School in the same town, and finally at the Free School at near-by Southover.

Gradually, however, this wide-ranging, free-wheeling educational process began to give place to a concentration of the aristocracy and leading gentry upon a limited number of fashionable schools in or around London. One of the most successful was that run by Dr. Thomas Farnaby, who is said to have taught upward of 300 noblemen and gentlemen during the reign of Charles I. It is symptomatic of the persistent desire for sound learning that the prime cause of Dr. Farnaby's success was his reputation as a classical scholar and the excellence of the academic teaching at his school. The other two most popular aristocratic schools on the eve of the Civil War were Westminster, where the ferocious but efficient régime of Dr. Busby was just beginning, and Eton. The records of both schools are woefully incomplete, so that no statistical picture of attendance is possible. But we have a glimpse of Eton in the early 1630's showing two sons of the Earl of Peterborough, a son of the Earl of Dover, two sons of the Earl of Cork, four sons of the Earl of Southampton, and two sons of the Earl of Northampton sitting down to dinner at the second table with knights' sons. The picture is a familiar one; Eton has arrived.

The most powerful factor making for social exclusiveness in these schools was already the high cost of board, lodging, and tuition. When the Earl of Cork sent his two sons to Eton, it cost him no less than £914. 3s. 9d. for three years' diet, tutoring, and clothes for themselves and their servants. Though there were the usual complaints that the boys were learning nothing but to drink, swear, and smoke, the idea of the expensive and exclusive boarding school had taken firm hold among the nobility and gentry of England.

In the early sixteenth century very few gentlemen attended the universities, and in 1549 William Thomas described them as the homes of 'mean men's children set to school in hope to live upon hired learning'. After about 1550, however, it became increasingly fashionable for sons of gentry, and even some sons of noblemen, to pass on to the universities, which partly for this reason and partly to supply an educated clergy were just embarking upon one of the three great expansionist phases of their history. The effect of this movement on the political life of the nation is reflected in the change in the number of university men in the House of Commons, which rose from 35 per cent. in 1593 to 57 per cent. in 1640. The two groups most deeply affected by this new trend were the gentry, large and small, and the professional classes, but it is clear that the peerage also felt the pull. From the admittedly incomplete matriculation registers, it looks as if the high point of popularity with the nobility for both universities was in the 1570's (Fig. 17). The great increase in the numbers of the peerage in the early seventeenth century is not reflected in any proportionate rise in the number of future peers attending the universities, although under Charles I the attraction of Oxford was much higher than that of Cambridge.

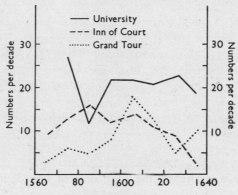

FIG. 17. Education, 1560–1639

These young aristocrats at the universities lived and worked more or less independently, often under their own private tutors, always attended by their own servants. Just what they studied at the universities is still not clear. Though they certainly read some sections of the official course, particularly classical literature, logic, rhetoric, and ethics, they virtually never proceeded to a degree. Some parents were now demanding an education primarily utilitarian in character, concentrated on the study of more recent authors and mainly conducted in English. The early-seventeenth-century universities housed two distinct groups of undergraduates pursuing two overlapping programmes of study: the younger sons of gentry and the professional and mercantile classes taking the official course with a view to acquiring the professional qualification of a degree to fit them for an academic or clerical career; and the eldest sons of squires and noblemen studying certain parts of this official course as well as reading widely in a general way to fit them for public service and to give them the polish needed for conversation in polite society in the age of the virtuoso.

University education never became the *sine qua non* of the cultivated nobleman. Not everyone could find a progressive college tutor willing to experiment with subjects outside the fossilized scholastic curriculum. Many were stuck with a dull conservative pedant, became bored with their studies, and took to dissipation instead. Aristocratic parents soon realized that a good private tutor could look after the purely academic side of the educational process as well as a college fellow. All that the university had to offer was a communal discipline and social intercourse, both of which could be had just as well in other places, at the Inns of Court or the great French academies. 'There are but few noblemen's sons in Oxford', remarked Lady Brilliana Harley in 1638, 'for now for the most part they send their sons into France when they are very young, there to be bred.'

At this period there were in practice not two but three universities in the kingdom. The third was the Inns of Court, whither increasing numbers of young noblemen and gentry resorted in order to study the law and at the same time pick up some of the airs and graces of the near-by Court. In the late sixteenth and early seventeenth centuries more nobles and landed gentlemen acquired a smattering of a legal education than at any time before or possibly since. Indeed although the popularity of both the universities and the Inns of Court rose together, the Inns were at all times more frequented by the gentry than both the older universities put together. It is noticeable that the high peak of aristocratic attendance at the Inns is the 1570's and 1580's, and that thereafter numbers fall off considerably. In this respect the educational trend of the aristocracy differs markedly from that of the squirearchy.

The purpose of giving a nobleman some knowledge of the law was explained by Edward Waterhouse in 1665 : 'To study and be versed in [the laws] concerns noblemen and gentlemen above others, as they have great estates, and great trusts in government; in which ignorance of the laws will not well set them off.' The high proportion of legal books in any contemporary library, the evident familiarity with land tenure and legal procedures displayed by so many noblemen and gentry in their day-to-day affairs, the strongly legalistic terms of reference within which the great political debates of the day were conducted, all suggest that early-seventeenth-century landed society was deeply permeated with the factual equipment and mental attitudes of the Common Law. It is reasonable to suppose that this was acquired primarily during the period of residence at an Inn of Court.

The university or Inn of Court was by no means always the end to the education of a nobleman. Afterwards, or instead, he was packed off abroad for two or three years. It was not till about 1530 that there developed the idea that foreign travel was an important part of training for future life. At this stage Italy was still the great intellectual power-house of Europe, and the view that learning was a desirable attribute of a gentleman inspired visits to the centre of Greek studies. This was a short-lived phase, however, and only marginally affected aristocratic education. Far more important was the rise of the new nation state and the new diplomacy. Since a nobleman's function in life was to enter the administrative or political service of the Prince, he needed foreign languages and a broad knowledge of the institutions and political systems of Europe. Most of the finer accomplishments of a gentleman also could only be acquired abroad. Riding the great horse had to be studied in Paris or Florence, fencing, dancing, and music were best taught in France and Italy. Those few who still adhered to the medieval tradition of preparing themselves for military command had perforce to go abroad to get experience during the long periods of peace in England under Elizabeth and the Early Stuarts. The art of fortification, the techniques of siege warfare, the new tactics and strategy could only be learned in the camps of Europe. In the early seventeenth century men began to travel for a new reason, since it alone could teach them the aesthetic, art-historical, and antiquarian knowledge and understanding which went to make a virtuoso. Five overlapping cultural ideals, those of the man of war, the man of learning, the statesman, the polished cavalier, and the virtuoso all demanded educational training abroad, and thus contrived to stimulate a remarkable growth of foreign travel among the English nobility and gentry.

The admixture of these various objectives is well brought out both in the courses of study actually followed and in the numerous letters of advice that anxious parents gave their sons before they set out upon their perilous travels. In 1571, when his young ward Edward Earl of Rutland was about to set off for France,

Burghley set out the ideal programme for the intelligent young nobleman. Above all he was to continue in the worship and fear of God; he was to become fluent in modern languages; he was to keep a diary in which he was to set down a wide range of information: the fortifications, garrisons, and governors of towns; the administrative and judicial systems; the state of the Court with the characters and ages of the leading courtiers; the state of royal finances; details of the monetary system, the university, and the estates, finances, and administrative arrangements of the nobility. Nor was he to forget to make a note of such Roman antiquities or natural phenomena as he might come across.

What is notable about this programme is the absence of any mention either of the acquisition of courtly accomplishments or an appreciation of contemporary art and architecture. The latter did not become a subject of serious study before the middle years of King James, when men like the Earl of Arundel at last began to look seriously at classical architecture and to make a collection of Renaissance paintings. The former, however, had always been an essential part of foreign travel, and one that became increasingly important in the early seventeenth century. When in about 1610 Sir Henry Slingsby dispatched his son William to the Continent, his tutor was ordered to guard his pupil's religious orthodoxy, keep him to his Latin—Cato, Æsop, and Terence—teach him modern history, and always to converse with him in French or Latin, except in emergencies. In addition the young man was to practise writing, the use of weapons, dancing, and riding, all classified by Sir Henry as 'extraordinary learning'.

It was just these physical accomplishments which were catered for by the great Parisian academies, of which the most famous was that of M. de Pluvenel. The main emphasis of these establishments was on riding the great horse, that extraordinary study of equestrian technique which captivated so many early-seventeenth-century minds. The art of the *manège* had been one of the marks of a gentleman even in Sir Philip Sydney's time, and the horsiness of the landed classes was a thing of long standing. 'If I had not been a piece of a logician before I came to [the Imperial riding master at Vienna] I think he would have persuaded me to have wished my self a horse', remarked Sir Philip, always the intellectual among gentlemen. The value attached to this esoteric art increased in the seventeenth century, and one of the Duke of Newcastle's main claims to distinction was a remarkable knowledge of horses which led to his publication in 1658 of that magnificently illustrated document of human absurdity, *La Méthode et Invention Nouvelle de Dresser les Chevaux*. Clarendon accurately reflected the values of his age when he described the Duke as 'a very fine gentleman, active and full of courage, and most accomplished in those qualities of horsemanship, dancing, and fencing which accompany a good breeding, in which his delight was'.

The Parisian academies were precisely designed to turn out 'fine gentlemen'. At M. de Pluvenel's in 1610 Lord Clifford learned to ride, to fence, to dance, and to play the lute, together with a little mathematics and philosophy. He had to go elsewhere to get his French, Latin, and history.

If the subject-matter of education abroad passed first through a more intellectual and then a more social and aesthetic phase, the geographical range of travel also varied with time. In the early years of the sixteenth century the few who travelled made for Italy. In the middle years of the century the more protestant-minded travellers visited their co-religionaries in Germany. Under Elizabeth, however, France became the main centre of attraction, particularly the Loire valley where the best French was supposed to be spoken. Orléans, Blois, and especially Saumur must have been full of young Englishmen in the lulls between the French civil wars. By the turn of the century the restoration of peace in France, the peace with Spain, and a more tolerant attitude by the Papacy reopened the whole of Europe to the English traveller, and encouraged a flood of young gentlemen and noblemen to develop and then set a pattern that was to last for centuries: a winter or more on the Loire learning languages, fencing, etc.; a summer tour of southern France; a few months in northern Italy, including Florence and Venice; a spell in Paris attending one of the academies.

The value derived from this educational process depended partly on the temperament and abilities of the young man, but even more on the strength of character of the tutor. The latter's task was not an easy one, for his young charge was surrounded by every temptation to dissipation. If the boy went badly off the rails the tutor might be faced with the alternative of becoming either a complacent boozing companion like Ben Jonson, whose charge once trundled him about the streets dead drunk in a cart for the amusement of the by-standers, or a carping and ineffectual nagger like Thomas Windebank with the young Thomas Cecil in 1561.

All too often their charges went to the bad despite their efforts, and concurrently with the spread of the fashion for travel among the nobility there grew up an increasingly vociferous opposition to it. The first element in this hostility was a by-product of that strident jingoism which echoes again and again in later Elizabethan literature. Lord Burghley wanted noblemen first to know their own country, its architecture and antiquities, before rushing off to see the sights abroad, and is said to have refused them passports if they displayed ignorance of English history. It was probably true in 1630—as it is again today—that many young gentlemen were more familiar with the Pont-du-Gard, St. Denis, and the Château at Blois, than they were with Hadrian's Wall, Rievaulx Abbey, or Audley End.

The second and more common charge was that travel merely taught new vices and deplorable foreign fashion. Italy was particularly disliked, as a menace to both body and soul. It was no longer admired as a centre of classical scholarship and was only just beginning to be valued for its wealth of art and architecture. It was reputed to offer facilities for every variety of heterosexual perversion as well as to be the main European stronghold of homosexuality. Francis Osborne warned that: 'Who travels Italy, handsome, young and beardless, may need as much caution and circumspection to protect him from the lust of men as the affections of women.' It was the home of Macchiavelli and so of subversive and cynical political attitudes. And lastly it was a standing threat to the religious constancy of Protestants, who were liable to be dazzled by the aesthetic splendours of the Counter-Reformation Church, overwhelmed by the grandeur of popes, cardinals, and prince-bishops, and quite incapable of refuting the subtle arguments of the Jesuits and other Catholic evangelists. The golden rule for travel was never to be lured into discussion about religion, and the English government tried, somewhat ineffectually, to make things doubly sure by excluding Rome from the places which a tourist was permitted to visit. As a result, some parents and advisers turned their faces resolutely against all travel in general, and travel to Italy in particular. In 1570 Roger Ascham violently denounced 'an English man Italianated' and in 1665 Edward Waterhouse summed up a century of mounting irritation with foreigners and their ways: 'the less youth knows of the levity, liberty, shifts, prophaneness, atheism, subtlety, and lubricity of other nations, the more are they probable to be solid, circumspect, plain, devout, pious, modest.'

This educational pattern was restricted by its high cost to the leading county families and the aristocracy. In the 1580's Sir Robert Dallington reckoned that a gentleman by himself could just manage on £80, but that if he took a servant and learnt to ride the great horse it would cost him £150 a year. When the system really got going in the next decades, costs rose rapidly. In the 1630's the Earl of Cork gave his eldest son £750 a year and two younger ones £500. One cause for the high cost was the fact that a nobleman could not travel light. A mere gentleman could move around with one or two servants, but if a peer was to maintain status he had to have at least ten attendants at his heels. The greatest spendthrift tourist of all was Edward Earl of Oxford, who in fourteen months in 1575–6 was sent no less than £4,561.

To judge from the scanty evidence available, it looks as if there was a trickle of peers and heirs of peers abroad during the 1570's and 1580's, which began to swell after about 1594 as peace returned to France. The quarter of a century between 1594 and 1620 seems to have been the most active period of education by travel by the peerage, and the one when the Grand Tour took shape. Though it was to pick up again in the 1630's, the pace slackened in the 1620's, presumably because of the rumblings of the Thirty Years War, mounting fears of the dangers of conversion to Catholicism resulting from some unfortunate examples like Lord Roos, and the publicity given to the satirists' criticisms of the debauchery and vanity of the returned traveller. Between 1570 and 1639 about 150 peers went to Oxford or Cambridge and about 75 to the Inns of Court. During the same period, about 65 are known to have spent two or three years on an educational tour abroad, and the true number is probably nearer 80 or more (Fig. 17, p. 311).

The new educational pattern of the aristocracy made a revolutionary impact upon English culture. In the Middle Ages authorship had been virtually confined to the ranks of the clergy, who had formed an intellectual and managerial *élite* working for and under the direction of their masters, the King and the nobles. In the late sixteenth century the situation was very different. The secular rulers of the State were now highly educated men capable of evaluating problems and situations in intellectual rather than intuitive terms. The character of their training and their need to understand the issues at stake in the great theological debate encouraged men of property and power to turn to their books for enlightenment. In all our history there have never been such well-educated and scholarly kings and queens as Edward VI, Lady Jane Grey, Elizabeth, and James I, while only Henry III and George IV can rival Charles I for knowledge and appreciation of the arts.

Peers, statesmen, and courtiers were not only personally interested in things of the mind; by force of circumstance they were left to shoulder the burden of scholarly and artistic patronage. In the Middle Ages the greatest patrons of arts and letters had been the King and the higher clergy. It was they who planned and built the great cathedrals, commissioned the sculpture to adorn them, and maintained in their households scholars to write books and artists to execute manuscript illuminations. The feudal aristocracy had played a part in this system by hitching scholars and poets to their entourage, in much the same way as they collected dwarfs and fools. But as late as the days of Wolsey their patronage had been of less importance than that of the bishops, and it was only after 1530 that the roles were reversed. Archbishop Parker was an important collector of manuscripts, Archbishop Laud the builder of the quadrangle at St. John's College, Oxford, which bears his name, but by and large bishops were now a negligible force in English cultural life. Nor was the Crown any longer the great patron of arts and letters. Henry VII had led the country with his chapel and tomb at Westminster, Henry VIII with his spectacular palace of Nonsuch. But until the building of the Banqueting Hall ninety years later, the Crown fell out of the running as a patron of the arts. Henry VIII had been generous in his encouragement of intellectuals, whom he hoped to use to advance his political ambitions, but for all her own mental accomplishments Elizabeth did little or nothing in the way of literary or scholarly patronage.

By the eighteenth century poets, playwrights, scholars, and theologians could stand on their own feet and live off the public at large. The more successful playwrights and acting companies could appeal directly to the public by about 1600, but other authors and artists remained dependent on wealthy patrons until the end of the seventeenth century. The invention of the printing-press and the spread of literacy had produced a spate of authors out of all proportion to the increase in patrons. 'The multitude of writers of our age hath begotten a scarcity of patrons', lamented Thomas Evans in 1615. Men now sought a patron not in order to find shelter and food under his roof but to secure protection from clerical and governmental censorship, and the necessary leverage to thrust them into comfortable jobs in the Church, the universities, and the royal administration. With the ramifying extensions of the clientage system into every sphere of private and public power and office, the role of the patron had become less that of a dispenser of cash or food, and more that of a puller of strings. So far from being a period of decadence in the medieval tradition of literary patronage, this was in fact its Indian summer.

Many noblemen were now men of letters, scholars, and connoisseurs in their own right and therefore only too willing to act the part of Maecenas. From the Earl of Surrey under Henry VIII to the Earl of Oxford under Elizabeth, noblemen had a greater share in the production of English imaginative literature than at any time before or since. The influence of the Sydney family was particularly important. Sir Philip Sydney himself was a major figure in the development of Early Elizabethan literature. His sister, Mary Countess of Pembroke, wrote pastorals, his daughter, Elizabeth Countess of Rutland, and his nephew, William Earl of Pembroke, were also poets, his niece Lady Mary Wroth was the author of *Urania*. The Herberts and Sydneys kept open house to the intelligentsia at Wilton and Penshurst, and were directly responsible for the growth of arcadian romances and pastoral poetry. In a lesser key busy statesmen like Lord Buckhurst wrote tragedies, idle men-about-town like the Earl of Oxford wrote comedies, both of which were highly thought of at the time. Performance as well as patronage were attributes of the Renaissance courtier.

Although literature of the imagination bulks large in the eyes of posterity, in fact it represented only a tiny fraction of the output of the presses. Most published work was theological, historical, political, legal, or scientific in content. Many noblemen were passionately interested in theology. The 4th Earl of Bedford was the author of ten folio volumes of theological reflections. The 8th Lord Mountjoy was an enthusiastic student of divinity, especially of the Fathers and the Schoolmen. Fynes Moryson thought him 'the best divine I ever heard argue, especially for disputing against the Papists', a talent he put to good use in dissuading his mistress, Penelope Lady Rich, from succumbing to the blandishments of the Jesuits.

In the days before bibliophily developed as a collecting mania in its own right, the possession of a substantial library may reasonably be taken as proof of intellectual interests. There is firm evidence that between 1580 and 1640 more than a dozen noblemen were the owners of several hundreds of books, and the true figure must be very much larger. Even more modest collectors took great pride in their libraries, as is proved by the fact that many of them mentioned their books specifically in their wills. Oliver Viscount Grandison bequeathed as an heirloom 'all my books as I have calendared them alphabetically after every letter subscribed with my hand'. The few major libraries of which we have record cover a huge variety of subjects, and give proof of that polymathic breadth of intellectual interests so characteristic of this unspecialized age. One of the most interesting collections is the 1,500-odd items owned by Lord Paget, which in a catalogue of 1617 were classified under headings of theology, law, history, philosophy, medicine and chemistry, mathematics (including architecture), grammar and vocabulary, rhetoric, logic, poetry, war and fortification, letter-writers, and miscellaneous. The last embraced books on such diverse matters as chess and duelling, the use of the silk-worm and the *Satyricon* of Petronius. Of the many small noble collections of books, that in the library of the Earl of Thanet in 1664 may perhaps stand as an example. There were about 100 books in all, including a number of chronicles and histories, a dictionary and a lexicon, fifteen books of Latin and French, five law books, a book of statutes of the realm, Burton's *Anatomy of Melancholy*, and the plays of Beaumont and Fletcher— a useful working library for a fairly cultivated man of affairs.

The direction and scope of aristocratic patronage of living authors was in part inspired by this genuine love of letters and scholarship. It also had less disinterested motives. Some noblemen may have come close to Dr. Johnson's definition of a patron as 'commonly a wretch who supports with insolence and is paid with flattery'. Hardly a book appeared from the press without a dedication to some courtly or aristocratic figure—the *Faerie Queen*

was not only dedicated to the Queen herself, but underwritten by
the inclusion of sonnets to no fewer than sixteen influential persons and 'all the gracious and beautiful ladies in the Court'.
Spenser was taking no chances. Noblemen rarely refused these
public offerings, for by them authors 'not only shield and succour
their cause, but also advance their patrons' name with high renown
throughout all posterity'. Shakespeare reminded his readers that
giving a lift to a great poet could be a more durable investment
than sinking capital in a great tomb:

> Not marble, nor the gilded monuments
> Of princes, shall outlive this powerful rime

Apart from this titillation of the ego, a desire to promote public
causes in which they were concerned was another and equally
important motive behind aristocratic support of authors. Much of
Leicester's wide-ranging patronage was inspired by a desire to
encourage moderate puritanism at home and military aggression
abroad. If he also allowed dedications to be made to him by trans-
lators from the classics, educational reformers, scholars, scientists,
and poets, this all forwarded his ambition to build a network of
supporters throughout the world of intellect. The clientage system
dominated scholarship and letters as well as elections to the House
of Commons; both were aspects of the new structure of politics
and the new role played in it by the Court aristocracy.

Another element in the patronage system was the demand by
the Court for entertainment. Either for reasons of economy or
from an ingrained love of indirection and ostensible delegation of
responsibility, Elizabeth herself was reluctant openly to support
actors and masques. The burden therefore fell on her leading
courtiers. So far as the players were concerned, an influential
patron was essential to keep them from being flogged as vagrants,
and to prevent puritanical town authorities from closing down
their theatres. Financial support was again less important than
political influence. As a result the history of the Elizabethan stage
is the history of the Companies belonging to the Earls of Oxford,
Warwick, Leicester, Worcester, Derby, Shrewsbury, Nottingham,
and others.

Of course willingness to take on a theatrical company was not
motivated exclusively by disinterested love of the stage. The players
were travelling advertisements for the greater glory of their patrons

and it became a question of status to have a company to one's name. On the other hand it would be a mistake to suppose that these noblemen took no interest in their protégés' activities. There is plenty of evidence to prove that many put a good deal of time, energy, and money behind these theatrical ventures. Leicester was prepared to risk the fulmination of his puritan allies for the sake of his Company. Southampton and Oxford were keenly interested in the theatre, and William Earl of Derby's wife encouraged him in this relatively harmless and inexpensive pursuit in order to keep him out of worse mischief.

If the Elizabethan stage owed much to aristocratic patronage, the Jacobean masque owed it everything. It was the enthusiasm of the Jacobean Court ladies, now headed by Queen Anne, which led to the flowering in England of this strange Italian mixture of singing, dancing, music, acting, and painting, laced with allegory. That the ladies managed to find two men of genius in Inigo Jones and Ben Jonson to satisfy their requirements was an accidental bonus of the gods.

The literary, theatrical, and scholarly flowering of the Elizabethan age owed more than mere permission to function to the enlightened patronage of the aristocracy. The delegation of this duty by the Prince to his courtiers and the financial and moral attrition of the clergy left the nobles alone in the field. They beat off attacks from clerical censorship against doctrinal eccentricity; they defied puritan protests against the paganism of poetry and the immorality of the theatre; they jobbed their protégés into royal or clerical or academic offices. Because of the diversity of their interests, almost every branch of scholarship received encouragement from someone; because of the diversity of their views, English literature and the English stage were allowed to develop in comparative freedom, the only—but important—inhibition being against radical criticism of the existing social order: Crown, Court, and peerage could not be touched.

The early seventeenth century witnessed a shift in interest away from purely scholarly towards more aesthetic pursuits, which is reflected in the content of education. It is no accident that the learned King James was succeeded by the artistic King Charles. Appreciation and knowledge of the arts was now one of the hallmarks of a gentleman, and even the practice of the arts ceased to be despised. A gentleman, Epiphanius Evesham, was the best sculptor in Early Stuart England; a knight, Sir Nathaniel Bacon, was one of the best painters; another, Sir Roger Pratt, was shortly to emerge as one of the most progressive of mid-seventeenth-century architects.

Patrons played an unusually large part in architectural design at this period. This was firstly because the jobbing architect-builder could no longer blind his employer with the now valueless science of medieval building craftsmanship. Secondly, most of the ideas for new buildings now came from books in foreign languages in the libraries of the employers, who alone had sufficient linguistic and mathematical education to understand them. As a result the role of the architect sank, that of the patron increased. This dependence for designs upon books is not difficult to document, and there is plenty of evidence to show how Burghley derived his ideas from books and imposed them upon his buildings. So great was his reputation as an architectural expert that his advice was widely sought after by friends like Sir Christopher Hatton and George Earl of Shrewsbury. When we admire and puzzle over the cold symmetry of Longleat or the gilded domes of Burghley House, it is to their owners that we must turn for enlightenment. The plan and the style of these Elizabethan palaces reflect the ambitions, the needs, the personal tastes, and the learning of men like Sir John Thynne and William Lord Burghley more than that of the shadowy, often nameless, architects or surveyors.

The most impressive architectural achievements of this period can best be understood if they are viewed as a means of satisfying the social and psychological needs of the same restricted group of noblemen and courtiers which exercised such influence over literature and the theatre. The distinction between 'Court' and 'Country' is here fundamental. To entertain the Queen, to improve their status, and to satisfy their competitive urges, the great courtiers embarked upon the 'prodigy houses' of the age, which differed from normal country houses in planning, in organization, and in style. Later, in the 1620's and 1630's, with the advent of an architect of genius, Inigo Jones, the Court aristocracy tried to introduce classical architecture to England. In the country Jones began putting a vast Italianate façade on the old house at Wilton of the great courtier, Philip Earl of Pembroke, only to abandon it half-way when the money ran out. It was lack of funds again that prevented Charles from going ahead with the design by Jones for a vast new palace at Westminster to rival the Louvre. Meanwhile the country gentry continued to put up their conventional, comfortable Jacobethan houses as if these revolutionary buildings did not exist. They associated Inigo Jones with the popery, tyranny, and vice which they believed to be the predominant characteristics of the Caroline Court. They would have none of them, and England had to wait for Lord Burlington before it received Palladio.

Though intrinsically a more personal activity than architecture, easel painting at this period was scarcely less dependent on social and political conditions, and was functional rather than aesthetic in purpose. Noblemen and gentlemen wanted above all formal family portraits, which take their place along with genealogical trees and sumptuous tombs as symptoms of the frenzied status-seeking and ancestor-worship of the age. The result was a huge output of facile, glossy, linear portraits which could be hung up about the house, the sixteenth-century equivalent of the 'studio' photographs of today. For the average country gentleman or even nobleman, a handful of pictures of himself and his close relatives was enough. He had no further ambitions.

The great court magnates, however, had other interests. The new diplomacy with its interminable series of high-level negotiations created a demand among politicians for pictures of foreign princes and statesmen, so that a face could be attached to a document or a political upheaval. The huge collection of drawings assembled by Catherine de Medici served just such a purpose, and many English privy councillors owned similar if more modest collections. Leicester collected portraits of the leading Dutch political figures with whom he had to deal during his stay in the Netherlands. Moreover, the growing cult of monarchy which was so important a feature of the new nation-state induced noblemen to equip their houses with portraits of the reigning sovereign and his immediate ancestors. The innumerable pictures of Elizabeth and James which are to be found in almost every great house in the country are the by-products of emergent theories of divine right; while the classical bias and humanistic emphasis on the hero in contemporary education gave rise to a fashion for portraits of worthies, and particularly of Roman emperors; there was also a select market for refined pornography thinly disguised as scenes from classical mythology or occasionally the Bible. Courtiers collected pictures which were almost certainly foreign imports, but which from the lack of attribution must have been cherished more for their subject-matter than their artistic merit. Somerset could take his lubricious wife for a stroll down his bowling alley lined with pictures of Bacchus, Venus and Cupid, Venus and Ceres, Venus and Adonis, and Susanna and the Elders.

The amassing of a substantial collection of pictures was delayed for a long time by the problem of where to hang them. The early sixteenth century saw a major attack on cold and draughts by covering all available wall-surfaces with painted cloths, buckram, and tapestries. So long as the nobility stuck to tapestries as the most expensive and most sumptuous of wall decorations, little room was left for the display of pictures. It was, therefore, quite late in Elizabeth's reign before large collections began to be made, even by the aristocracy. As late as 1600 John, future 1st Lord Petre, had no pictures at all at Ingatestone except in the Long Gallery. There he could show his guests his father Sir William, Henry V and Henry VIII, Cleopatra and Diana, a male and a female Turk, and nine painted shields with posies. Not a very impressive collection, and yet richer than that of the 11th Lord Willoughby d'Eresby at the same date, which consisted of pictures of the owner, his wife, and St. John the Baptist.

The first really large collection of which we have record is that of Robert Earl of Leicester, who died in 1588 owning some 180 pictures. John Lord Lumley possessed about 230 (nearly all portraits) at the same time, and 15 years later Henry Lord Cobham had 77 at Cobham Hall and Blackfriars. The handful of big collections of pictures by noblemen of the Early Stuart period are still very moderate in size compared with some of the great aristocratic collections of the late seventeenth and eighteenth centuries, and there can be little doubt that the vast majority of the pictures in them were low-grade, hack portraits of relatives and notables, dead or alive. If Lord Lumley possessed the odd Dürer, Mor, and Holbein, this was incidental to the subjects. The pleasure to be derived from them was social and utilitarian rather than visual. It was not until the arrival of Van Dyck that the courtiers found an artist who could at last satisfy both their functional desire for glamorous portraiture and their rising standard of aesthetic appreciation.

The early seventeenth century saw the emergence of the new cultural ideal of the virtuoso, a concept which deserves some attention.

A virtuoso is one whose main concern in life is with scientific experiment and the collecting of natural or artificial curiosities, with antiquarian research, with aesthetic appreciation, and with the purchase of antique sculpture and old masters. He is a gentleman of leisure whose ambition is to deepen his appreciation of the arts and build up a famous collection. He is primarily concerned with himself, and no longer seeks to be of service to Prince or Commonweal. One cause of this striking change in aspirations was the shortage of posts in royal service. Since only a diminishing minority could hope to find useful employment, there was a compelling need to find an emotionally satisfying alternative.

Aristocratic dabbling in semi-scientific experiment has a long history behind it, and in the mid-sixteenth century we are told that the 2nd Earl of Cumberland 'was much addicted to the study and practise of alchemy and chemistry and a great distiller of waters and making of other chemical extractions for medicines, and very studious in all manner of learning, so as he had an excellent library both of written hand books and printed books'. In the early seventeenth century the 9th Earl of Northumberland earned his sobriquet 'the wizard earl' from his researches into anatomy and cosmography, alchemy and distillation, but nothing of moment emerged from the first three, and the fourth was designed more to provide choicer and more potent alcoholic spirits for his lordship's table than to advance the cause of pure science. The only noblemen to make a positive contribution were those like the 5th Lord Dudley who encouraged and financed new technological processes in industry.

Along with this uncoordinated and unmethodical experimentation went the collecting of curiosities, natural and artificial phenomena, and mechanical toys. This was a hobby which catered for man's innate love of magic and mystery and stimulated his admiration for the handiwork of God; it also enhanced the prestige of the collector and contriver. But its scientific content was superficial.

The first major natural-history collection to be made in England was that assembled by John Tradescant the elder in the 1620's under the direction of his patron the Duke of Buckingham. Supported by this powerful influence, Tradescant persuaded the great trading companies to supply him with elephant and hippopotamus skulls, strange birds, fishes, and reptiles, and all sorts of snakes, dried fruits, and shining stones. But although carefully catalogued under clear subject headings, not all the contents were of purely scientific interest. There was 'The claw of the bird Rock (who, as authors report, is able to truss an elephant)', half a hazel nut with seventy pieces of household stuff in it, boots to fit a giant and a midget, 'an Italian lock, *custos pudicitiae*', and 'blood that rained on the Isle of Wight, attested by Sir John Oglander' (was *this* the blood with which Sir John penned his much quoted remark about the decline of the mere gentry?). Similarly the dons of St. John's College, Oxford, cherished the skeleton of a woman who had had seventeen husbands, and a gall-stone extracted from Bishop King of London; and John Lord Lumley decorated the screen of his hall with 'six rare heads of beasts', including an elephant, and 'the claw of a griffin, very wonderful'.

The same love of rareties lay behind the bizarre gardens of the day with their artificial rocks, streams, and pools, their mechanical pumps for dousing the visitor with water, their speaking statues, their shell-studded grottoes, and other bizarre contrivances. The formal garden flourished in the sixteenth century and reached its apogee with the fantastic layout contrived in the 1630's by Isaac de Caux for Philip Earl of Pembroke at Wilton, with its hydraulic device for mechanical singing birds, based, presumably, on that at Tivoli.

This quest for rarities, mechanical, natural, or antiquarian, was the very antithesis of the Baconian ideal and effectively diverted upper-class interest away from science proper until the middle of the seventeenth century. So far from conforming to a rational programme of controlled research, it encouraged the mentality of the fair-ground peep-show. The amateurish pursuits of the Early Stuart nobility played little part in the history of English technical and scientific progress.

If the pre-1640 virtuosi failed as scientists, they were remarkably successful in their main ambition to shine as collectors and connoisseurs. The most determined collector of them all was Thomas Earl of Arundel. He conducted excavations in Rome, thus becoming the first Englishman to dig in the city since Henry of Blois in the twelfth century, and set up his finds and his other purchases in the garden at Arundel House. The surviving monument to this important episode in the history of English taste are the Arundel marbles in the Ashmolean Museum at Oxford.

Between 1610 and 1640 the same handful of enthusiastic noblemen first introduced into England large quantities of Italian and, to a lesser extent, Flemish and German art. What they went for was not so much the work of living artists—the sole important exception being Rubens—but the old masters of the sixteenth century. By 1642 Arundel had a collection of some 800 pictures. He had managed to acquire over 40 works by his great love Holbein, as well as the famous book of portrait drawings, 13 Breughels, and 16 Dürers, but otherwise his taste ran mostly to the usual Venice school, with as many as 37 pictures by Titian, and many more by Tintoretto, Veronese, Bassano, Parmigiano, Giorgione, Raphael, and Correggio. In 1621 the Duke of Buckingham entered the field on a massive scale, using his enormous wealth and political influence to build up a private collection second only to that of Arundel. It was from these two that Charles first got his passion for art which led him to spend £18,000 in 1628–30 in buying up the Duke of Mantua's entire collection, and to go on to build up a gallery of astonishing size and splendour.

It is common knowledge that English patrons of the eighteenth century brought back with them large numbers of later Italian paintings. What is not so well known is the amazing quantity and quality of Italian art from what some would regard as the best period which had reached England before the Civil War. Thanks to Charles I, Arundel, Buckingham, Pembroke, and Hamilton, by 1640 London could boast of four or five picture galleries which between them displayed a collection of Italian old masters, particularly of the Venetian school, which was unrivalled in Europe, and which had an important influence on the style of William Dobson. 'C'est nous qui avons les perles des Italiens', boasted Sir Balthazar Gerbier as early as 1624. Most of these collections were dispersed again among the galleries of Europe during the Interregnum, and it was not till the 1690's that the second wave of Italian art began to reach these shores.

It would be idle to pretend that these lovers of art were anything but a tiny minority, or that all who experienced the educational process of the early seventeenth century either enjoyed it or derived much benefit from it. But this is true of every educational system which has ever been devised, and if stupid and boorish wastrels still existed in really high society in the early seventeenth century at least every effort had now been made to reduce their numbers to a minimum. What the cult of the virtuoso accomplished was to offer talented but politically thwarted or indifferent noblemen an alternative outlet for their surplus time, energy, and wealth. If denied an important official position, they could devote themselves to antiquarian research, architectural and pseudo-scientific experiment, and the collection of books, paintings, and *objets d'art*. They were encouraged to patronize poets, writers, intellectuals, scientists, sculptors, artists, and architects, and so preserved their influence on English culture well into the nineteenth century. It familiarized them with Europe and taught them to understand at least one and often two modern languages as well as their own, and so helped to bring English arts and letters into intimate contact with those of the Continent.

This educational revolution passed through two phases, both of fairly short duration. The former laid most stress on the academic, bookish element in education, and on training for future political leadership; the latter tended rather to emphasize the accomplishments of the 'perfect cavalier', coupled with aesthetic and antiquarian appreciation. After a brief phase of scientific enthusiasm in the mid-seventeenth century, the concept of the virtuoso gave way to that of the dilettante, which was the undoing of the Royal Society and has been the curse of the English governing classes ever since. The period from 1560 to 1640 is thus one of exceptionally intensive intellectual and artistic training, squeezed between centuries of ignorance on the one hand and centuries of dilettantism on the other.

Within the landed classes this educational revolution had a double, and opposite effect. *In the short run*, it increased the opportunities of the gentry to compete for office on more equal terms with the nobility. Since so many of the former had fitted themselves for a responsible position in the commonwealth, they began encroaching upon offices which had hitherto been a preserve of either the aristocracy or the higher clergy. The spread among the gentry of education at school, university, and Inn of Court was therefore an important factor in the shift of power away from the peerage in the years before the Civil War.

*In the long run*, the enthusiastic, though belated, adoption of the new educational pattern by the aristocracy was a major cause of their survival as a ruling *élite*. In the 1560's well-qualified observers of the peerage had been full of gloom and foreboding. Laurence Humphrey complained that there was nothing 'at this day more lamentable then the ignorance of magistrates and nobles, head cause of all evils, both in the state and religion', and yet a hundred years later a foreign observer wrote that 'la noblesse d'Angleterre est presque toute savante et fort éclairée', a judgement echoed by a not normally over-sanguine English commentator, Edward Waterhouse. Both the pessimism of the 1560's and the optimism of the 1660's may have been somewhat overdone, but there can be no doubt at all that things had changed. Few revolutions of a revolutionary age were of greater importance.

The educational system as it developed in the seventeenth century tended to divide landed society in two. Since the full-blown educational process—private tutor, boarding school, university, Inn of Court, and the Grand Tour—was so very expensive, it was largely confined to elder sons of the aristocracy and the greater county families. Macaulay undoubtedly exaggerated the sluttish ignorance of the minor rural gentry after the Restoration, but the distinction between the insular fox-hunting squire and the travelled and cultivated nobleman was one that cut deep into seventeenth- and eighteenth-century society. Partly it was based on the differing cultural patterns of town and country, but at its roots lay a difference in training. Many of the benefits of the improved educational opportunities were enjoyed by all layers of the upper and middle classes, as the multiplicity of grammar schools amply proves. But this was mainly a dreary academic grind in the classical languages. Training in French and Italian, political economy, modern history, gentlemanly accomplishments, aesthetic appreciation, all the essential qualifications for social and political advancement at the top, were mostly limited to the rich who could afford to pay for them. The educational system gave the social *élite*—peers and leading gentry—a head-and-shoulders start over their inferiors, including the lesser gentry, in the struggle for political power and lucrative office.

It also gravely accentuated the psychological split between Court and Country, which was so marked a feature of the 1630's. The tastes of the virtuoso for the architecture of Inigo Jones and the art of the Venetian school was exclusively cultivated by a tiny court coterie. To the average country gentleman Italy was a land of popery and vice, and Italian art, with its emphasis on religious imagery, *putti*, and the nudes of classical mythology, bore visual witness to both these perils to the immortal soul: if the sophisticated courtier was entranced, the puritan gentleman was repelled. In the eyes of the bulk of his influential subjects the picture galleries of King Charles and his intimates were evidence of their incorrigible leanings to frivolity and extravagance, popery and pornography.

Lastly the educational revolution, coupled with the inflation of honours, turned out men able and anxious to hold high office in numbers far in excess of the capacity of the society to employ them. This was an important reason for the dissatisfaction of many peers with the government of Charles I in 1640, and their unwillingness to fight for the cause of monarchy in 1642. It also created even more severe frustrations among the aspiring gentry, a far smaller proportion of whom could hope for a post in government, and among the middle-class intellectuals who were being turned out in larger numbers than either the Church or lay society could absorb. 'The core of rebellion', wrote Thomas Hobbes, 'are the universities.' 'For it is a hard matter for men, who do all think highly of their own wits, when they have also acquired the learning of the university, to be persuaded that they want any ability requisite for the government of a commonwealth.' It was for this reason that the Marquis of Newcastle advised Charles II to reduce the numbers in grammar schools and Inns of Court and cut the intake of the universities by 50 per cent. From the point of view of monarchy he was quite right.

# XIII

## RELIGION

THE religious opinions of any individual in the past are rarely easy to discover. Most men were very reticent, or very ambiguous, or genuinely very uncertain, or more or less indifferent, in their public attitude towards the competing churches and doctrines of sixteenth-century England. Since death by torture could be the penalty for plain-speaking, a certain prudence was mere common sense, although in fact an English peer ran little or no risk of being burned to death for his theological opinions. Such penalties were not thought suitable for men of such exalted social status—which was perhaps the main reason why persecution was so ineffective—but a nobleman certainly faced loss of office and influence, erosion of social prestige, and possibly a heavy fine if he too openly defied the authorized religion of the State.

Even when the opinions can be identified, there remains the problem of setting up a satisfactory sociological model which will comprehend the full range of sixteenth-century religious views and actions. For the Catholics the most useful categories are 'recusant', for those who utterly refused to compromise with the national church; 'non-communicant', for those who attended Anglican services but did not take communion; and 'schismatic', for those who took communion while remaining at heart in sympathy with Catholicism. A member of either of the last two groups may be described as a 'Church Catholic', one who 'parts his religion betwixt his conscience and his purse, and comes to Church not to serve God but the King'. For Anglicans by far the most important category was the indifferent, which undoubtedly embraced the vast majority; but there was also a slowly growing body of convinced activists, who after 1625 began to split into Laudian and anti-Laudian groups. For the Puritans the problem is even more difficult since the term embraces a wide spectrum of dissenting opinion and since for long periods most of them were full members of the Anglican Church, although ceaselessly agitating to change its organization and liturgy. Only the separatists, the independent sectaries, were at all clearly defined before the Civil War, though many of the more extreme Presbyterians had found an identity in the 1570's and 1580's.

The view that an established church was an essential support for a hierarchical society and a monarchical government was almost universally held in the sixteenth century, and accounts for the easy acceptance of the slogan *cuius regio, eius religio*. It was thought that a state could not long survive unless its members subscribed to a single church and a single doctrine. Peers were under particular pressure to conform to the Established Church, whatever it might happen to be. By virtue of their rank they were at the apex in the social and political hierarchy and thus had a vested interest in the maintenance of order, discipline, and conformity. So long as their personal interests were looked after, and Henry VIII took great care to deal generously with them when it came to dissolving the monasteries, they had a strong personal incentive for not causing too much trouble.

A man like Edward Earl of Derby was brought up a Catholic, swallowed the monastic estates when the opportunity offered, raised no open protest against the Edwardian innovations in religion, was a loyal supporter of Mary and the Catholic reaction, and an equally loyal servant of Elizabeth and fairly diligent as a magistrate in enforcing Anglican worship after 1559. His real views about the problem of salvation are obscure, to say the least: his policy was one of support for established authority and the maintenance of social and political order. Indeed religion to some was little more than a Marxist opium of the people devised to protect property and sanctify the social order. It was the Marquis of Newcastle who reminded the exiled Charles II of the political benefits of religion: 'were there no Heaven and no Hell you shall see the disadvantage for your government.' As for the Anglican Church, he described it to His Majesty as 'an ecclesiastical government pretending to no power over the king at all, nor no power under the king neither, but from him and by him; teaching active obedience to all lawful commands of lawful authority, and passive obedience even to those commands that are not lawful, so the authority commanding them be not unlawful'.

Only a minority, though a vitally important one, seem to have chosen their religion as the unique vehicle for the salvation of their souls. One test of the strength of a man's religious views is the attention he paid in his will to the future of his spirit. The majority dismissed the subject in a sentence and passed on to the more urgent business of disposing of their body and their real and personal estate. It is very significant that of the 30 peers who between 1558 and 1641 showed signs in their wills of strong religious feelings, no fewer than 7 were recusants or schismatics, and 12 were Puritans or Puritan sympathizers. Under Elizabeth extreme Protestant sentiments were strengthened by a crude nationalism stimulated first by Mary's disastrous foreign policy and later by the threat of Spanish invasion. For Leicester in particular, religious beliefs found political expression in the demand for a war of aggression at sea and military intervention in Europe, though even with him there seems no reason to doubt his sincerity.

At work at this level of society there was no obvious economic incentive to tempt men for or against a religious faith other than that established by law. The desire to hang on to ex-monastic estates can easily be exaggerated as a factor favouring Protestantism. Almost all peers and leading squires owned church property, but some of the greatest predators under Henry VIII like the 1st Lord Rich or Sir William Petre remained staunch Catholics, and the acceptance by the Pope of the *fait accompli* under Mary had quieted the worst fears of dispossession.

The main incentive to Anglicanism was loyalty to the established order and ambition to earn office and favour at Court. On the other flank of Anglicanism the Puritans found that their beliefs not only hindered their political advancement, but also ran directly counter to their financial interests. Their desire for an educated and zealous clergy was difficult to reconcile with the system of lay impropriations. These formed useful additions to the income of peers and squires, but reduced many clerical stipends to pitiful levels and were a direct incentive to pluralism and non-residence, the two evils which Puritans never tired of denouncing.

Puritan landlords thus found their material and their spiritual interests pulling in different ways, a fact which severely limited the possibilities of effective reform. So far as the peerage is concerned, the relationship between economic interests and religious beliefs is far more complex and far less close than is usually assumed nowadays. But more important for our purposes than hypothetical speculations about the causes of religious opinions, which are usually impossible to disentangle anyway, are the effects of these opinions both on the peers themselves and on the society in which they lived.

Given the preponderant authority of the aristocracy in the countryside in the early years of Elizabeth, the success of the Anglican settlement depended very largely on their active co-operation or passive acquiescence. By their influence in local affairs they could see to it that the local justices exposed or protected dissident clergy, suppressed or encouraged radical preaching and pamphleteering, punished or ignored defiance of the laws concerning church-going and religious conformity among the laity. The situation in the first decade of the reign was ominous in the extreme. In the north there was a solid phalanx of openly Catholic peers. On the other hand the convinced Protestants, mostly with Puritan leanings, were concentrated in the south and midlands. There was thus a fairly clear geographical split which if things had taken an ugly turn could have provided secure bases for two sides in a civil war. In this respect in 1568 the England of Elizabeth was not unlike the France of Catherine de Medici.

Though others had a vital role to play—Puritan ministers and Catholic missioners, city artisans and pious country gentlewomen —if the peers and leading squires had distributed their support otherwise between 1558 and 1588, the religious configuration of seventeenth-century England would undoubtedly have looked very different. It was the casual indifference of the majority which allowed Anglicanism to get itself accepted as an established institution; it was the triumph of political loyalty over religious opinions which kept the majority of the Catholic sympathizers from giving encouragement to assassination plots or schemes of rebellion. But it was resistance to government orders by a handful of magnates on either side which allowed Catholicism and Puritanism to dig in and take root within this tepidly conformist society.

The dependence of the Catholic revival upon the nobility for shelter, encouragement, protection, and financial backing is writ large in the records of the Elizabethan missioners and Early Stuart bishops. In every county it was the peers and leading squires who took the initiative in breaking with the Anglican Church. The utter dependence of the Jesuit mission of the 1580's upon these upper gentry and aristocratic hosts is admirably demonstrated by Father John Gerard's frank and vivid account of his activities.

He first settled at Grimston in Norfolk, the house of Edward Yelverton. 'I stayed openly six or eight months in the house of that gentleman. . . . During that time he introduced me to the house and circle of nearly every gentleman in Norfolk, and before the end of the eight months I had received many people into the Church, including one of my host's brothers, his two sisters, and later his brother-in-law.' From Grimston Father Gerard moved to Lawshall in Suffolk, the house of Henry Drury, where he was kept safe for two years from persecution, provided with funds, and given opportunities for proselytizing the neighbouring gentry at hunting parties and other social occasions. A generation later the first two Catholic bishops who worked in post-Reformation England were similarly dependent on a restricted group of rich patrons. When the Jesuits set up a novitiate in London in 1625, it was in a house hired for the purpose from the Earl of Shrewsbury.

Archbishop Mathew has observed that it was 'a defect of the Tridentine organization that the missioners in southern England should have concentrated so much attention on the noble patron and have taken such satisfaction in the conversion of the *generosi*'. This is a questionable judgement, for it was only in these great houses that the priests were safe from denunciation and arrest. When the dowager Lady Vaux was planning to rent Kirby Hall for use as a Catholic centre, Father Gerard remarked with approval that 'it was large and well-built, and stood remote from other dwellings, surrounded by fine orchards and gardens—people could come and go without anyone noticing them.' Priests could live quietly in some remote corner of the house without attracting the attention of the servants, and could set up a chapel in an empty room for the hearing of mass, while the sheer size of the house guaranteed some warning of the arrival of a search-party and offered plenty of scope for secret hiding-places. They could not easily be observed in their comings and goings, and by taking part in the active social life of the gentry and nobility they could proselytize unobserved. Furthermore they knew quite well that, if they could convert a sufficient number of the nobility and leading gentry, all the rest would be given unto them. Their concentration on the nobility was not mere snobbery : it was plain common sense. Indeed, in so far as Catholicism remained a threat to the Anglican settlement, it was not because of a widespread latent sympathy with Catholic ritual and superstition among the people at large, but because a significant proportion of noblemen and leading squires had been reconciled to Rome by the Elizabethan missioners.

The fact that its strength lay in large households headed by men of an assured social status explains why English Catholicism could not be suppressed; it also explains why it so rapidly relapsed into passivity. After a brief activist phase in the late Elizabethan period most of the upper-class laity broke with the Jesuit missioners and retreated into self-imposed isolation. The tacit understanding they reached with the Crown, if not with their Puritan neighbours, was that so long as they remained inactive they would be left in relative peace to cultivate their gardens and worship as they chose.

For all intents and purposes seventeenth-century Catholicism was a quietist sect of aristocratic and upper-gentry families. They maintained priests for their personal use, but would not let them minister to the poor outside the park gates for fear of trouble. Their leaders were peers—in 1605 Viscount Montagu was described as the 'great captain and firm pillar of the papists'. They intermarried, their children were educated at home by private Catholic tutors; in the reign of Charles I they even attended Catholic private schools, provided as usual by the great lay patrons. Many sons of recusants subsequently moved on to Catholic universities abroad, also in defiance of severe legal penalties. They were dissident in religion but politically extremely loyal, indeed they cultivated a reverence for the Stuart monarchy that many Anglicans found excessive. Though they only exercised real influence at Court and in the Council at rare intervals in the early seventeenth century, they were at all times a presence to be felt around the monarch. With the arrival of Henrietta Maria at the English Court their activity was given an assured focus, and there were a number of spectacular conversions of court ladies. Even when power was exclusively in the hands of their most bitter enemies, their reserves of wealth and local influence were sufficient to protect the most important of them from serious persecution. Men like the successive Earls of Worcester at Raglan Castle enjoyed *de facto* immunity from the laws about religious conformity.

Recusants were not all from old-established families, nor were they in humble or declining economic circumstances. On the contrary about half the Catholic peers of 1641 were new creations, the cream of the risen gentry, and most of the rest were above the average in wealth and showed no signs of recent decay. The only Catholic peers who had been going downhill for some time and were now in relatively humble circumstances were the Stourtons, the Touchets, and the Vaux. Catholic recusancy was thus a product of three factors : the conservatism of some early Elizabethan gentry families who sent their children abroad to be trained as mission priests; the courage and devotion of these missioners in the late Elizabethan period; and the physical protection and financial support of some noblemen and leading squires which gave English Catholicism its peculiarly upper-class character and ensured its survival in the face of a rising tide of anti-papist sentiment in the country at large.

The geographical pattern of seventeenth-century Catholicism, which was a rural not an urban movement, was consequently determined in large measure by the attitude of a handful of leading families in each county. What in the early years of Elizabeth had been a widely diffused scatter of passive conservatives had by the end of the reign become a series of isolated little pockets of dedicated recusants, each one centred around and dependent upon a great house. Thus in Yorkshire in 1590 3 per cent. of the parishes contained 48 per cent. of the recorded Catholic recusants.

In its early stages Elizabethan Puritanism was a confederation of ministers and laity, semi-sectarian but still within the fold of the Church. It pressed in Parliament and the Privy Council for reform of liturgy and ceremony, and for a cleaning up of administrative abuses and corruption, it was active locally in preaching and practising the new ethic of godliness. It differed from Catholicism in that the initiative came from the laity, which demanded, and finally obtained, a clerical wing which served to spread the word throughout the populace at large. It was therefore even more powerfully influenced by a few great magnates, but much less exclusive in its social composition. It is to the activities of a handful of peers, notably the Earls of Bedford, Huntingdon, Leicester, and Warwick and the irrepressible Duchess of Suffolk, that early Elizabethan Puritanism owes its remarkable success.

For the first thirty years of Elizabeth's reign there was always an influential group of Puritan peers and knights in the Privy Council, where they successfully fought off the most dangerous attacks on Puritan preachers. They supported plans for moderate reform in 1575; and when the crisis came in 1584–5 they did all in their power to mitigate the ferocity of Archbishop Whitgift's anti-Puritan drive. Lord Burghley—who was no fanatic—was driven to compare Whitgift to his face with a Catholic inquisitor. So long as the Privy Council contained this powerful group of Puritan peers, the more moderate preachers had little to fear from the bishops. When Archbishop Sandys tried to suspend William Whittingham from the deanery of Durham, he was successfully obstructed by the Earl of Huntingdon. Even when Puritans were arrested, strings were usually pulled to have them released within a few weeks, and when danger threatened they were given shelter as chaplains in private country houses. The well-known pressure for moderate Puritan reform in Elizabethan parliaments was conducted in the House of Commons, but it would be naïve to assume that the great Puritan lords were not pulling strings in the background. The Commons were bold because they knew that an influential section of the Privy Council and the Lords was on their side, so long as they moderated the tone and content of their demands.

It was to these peers and squires that the Puritan clergy looked for maintenance and preferment. Since the laity controlled so many advowsons and rectories, it was not difficult for a Puritan minister to find himself a living. If his views were too radical to meet acceptance with a bishop, he could be appointed a lecturer in a town or a chaplain in a private house. The Dudley brothers and some local gentry established a consortium to finance itinerant preachers in Warwickshire; Lord Rich kept Robert Wright as his chaplain at Rochford, where he catechized all and sundry in the great hall and held services in the chapel, although he had never been consecrated by a bishop and never used the Book of Common Prayer. Puritan peers were also invaluable in getting printed material past the censor. It was difficult to suppress a book or pamphlet which had been dedicated, with the patron's approval, to a privy councillor or powerful magnate, and thanks to some half-dozen men like the Earls of Leicester, Bedford, Huntingdon, and Warwick, and Lord Rich, the English press was for many years wide open to Puritan propaganda.

Perhaps the most important of all the achievements of the Puritan nobility was their success in harnessing large sections of the educational system to the cause. Between 1565 and 1575 Cambridge produced no fewer than 228 Puritan ministers and schoolmasters, to say nothing of the hundreds of young gentlemen who went out into the world with a firm belief in the need for a Puritan reformation of the Anglican Church. Control of the universities was achieved partly by the active exercise of his power as Chancellor at Oxford by the Earl of Leicester and the passive tolerance of the moderate Puritans by Lord Burghley at Cambridge; partly by the deliberate creation of fellowships for Puritans, like the four founded by the Earl of Huntingdon at Emmanuel; partly by the provision of scholarships for devoutly Puritan children; and partly by successful lobbying at Court for the appointment of puritanically minded heads of houses.

The importance of patronage in the movement can be demonstrated by looking first at the career of the organizer of the abortive Elizabethan Presbyterian movement, and then at the activities of a few of the more prominent Puritan peers. By 1565 John Field had been taken under the wing of the Earl of Warwick, who was probably responsible for getting him ordained at the uncanonical age of 21. When he was silenced and imprisoned in 1572, Leicester and Warwick were behind his removal from Newgate to the comfortable and lax confinement of an alderman's house, and his release within a few months. Despite Bishop Aylmer's anxiety to deport him to the north, he managed to stay on in London under his patrons' protection. He dedicated books to the Earls of Leicester, Warwick, Huntingdon, and Bedford, and in 1579 Leicester persuaded the University of Oxford to give him a licence to preach again. What worried Bishop Aylmer most was that Field 'had entered into great houses and taught . . . God knows what'. When he was imprisoned and sentenced again in 1581, Leicester once more got him released and restored his licence to preach.

Leicester has been described as 'the keystone of the whole edifice of Elizabethan Puritanism'. As the leader of the moderate Puritan group in the Privy Council, he could block moves to persecute his protégés, and could get them out of prison; he could see that their books passed the censor, and as Chancellor of the University he could find them jobs at Oxford. In 1564 he is said to have stopped the Privy Council from authorizing Parker's Advertisements. He was the patron not only of Field and Cart-wright, but also of scholars and educators like Laurence Humphrey, the Puritan President of Magdalen College at Oxford, and William Fulke, the Puritan Master of Pembroke Hall at Cambridge. His death was the signal for the great assault upon the Presbyterians and moderate Puritans which Hatton, Whitgift, and Bancroft had been itching to launch for years, and Thomas Digges was not distorting the shift of official opinion when he wrote that 'when the Earl of Leicester lived, it went for currant that all the Papists were traitors in action, of affection. He was no sooner dead but . . . Puritans were trounced and traduced as troublers of the state.'

Another key figure in the growth of moderate Elizabethan Puritanism was Henry, 3rd Earl of Huntingdon, brother-in-law of the Dudleys. His own household was a Protestant seminary in miniature, with prayers, fastings, and catechizings. He filled such advowsons as he controlled with men of the left, his chaplains were nearly all nonconformists of one type or another. He put in Puritan ministers at Leicester and Loughborough and set up Anthony Gilby as lecturer at Ashby de la Zouch, which consequently became the headquarters of radical reform within the county and beyond. On his initiative, the Leicester Corporation ordered that one member of every household in the town should attend sermons on Wednesdays and Fridays, so as to encourage 'those that love the gospel'. Having thus ensured the local clergy a captive audience, he installed a theological library in the parish church to raise their intellectual tone, while to improve that of the parishioners he founded a strongly Protestant grammar school at Ashby and reorganized that at Leicester. He endowed both with scholarships at the universities and created four fellowships at Emmanuel.

Huntingdon also used to the full his powers as President of the Council of the North and a leading member of the High Commission in the North to plant sound Protestants, very often moderate Puritans, as preachers in the market towns of the north; he protected a nest of Puritans up in Durham from the onslaughts of the archbishop. It is almost certainly through Huntingdon's influence that John Udall was appointed minister at Newcastle in 1590, only to be condemned to death two years later for his share in the Marprelate Controversy. As a result of his personal labours, Protestantism, even moderate Puritanism, was greatly encouraged

in the north, and Leicestershire took on a radical religious tone
which it was to retain for at least a century. One may suspect,
though it has yet to be proved, that it was at any rate partly thanks
to similar influence exercised by the earls of Bedford that alone
among the west-country shires Devon became a centre of militant
Protestantism.

Two generations later the same pattern repeated itself, with
ministers silenced and hounded by Laud being protected and
maintained by the great Puritan lords. George Hughes, ejected
from his lecturership in London, found refuge at Warwick Castle
as chaplain to Lord Brooke, the 'great patron and Maecenas to the
pious and religious ministry'.

An extremely important factor in the religious life of Elizabethan England was the influence of women. Then as always
religious enthusiasm was confined to a smallish number of men,
and a much larger phalanx of women, who, as Hooker observed,
'are propense and inclinable to holiness'. Given the idle and
frustrated lives these women lived in the man's world of a great
country house, it is hardly surprising that they should have turned
in desperation to the comforts of religion. It was to the women in
the big houses that John Gerard appealed in the 1580's, and it was
through them that he approached their husbands. It was women
who were particularly susceptible to the new wave of Catholic
propaganda in the 1630's. Similarly, it was to the wives of his
gentry supporters that the Puritan Wilcox mostly wrote at the time
of his troubles in the 1570's. It was Frances Countess of Sussex
who refounded Sidney Sussex as a seminary for the reformed
religion.

Given the influence exerted by these magnates and the piety of
their wives, it is hardly surprising that the Government should
have taken energetic steps to tear the children of prominent
Catholic families from their mothers' charge. The ancient power
of wardship, first revived by the early Tudors for purposes of
finance, now took on a new function as an instrument in making
the country safe for Anglicanism. Lord Burghley was far more
successful in his self-appointed task of giving aristocratic heirs a
taste for Protestantism than he was in inducing them to buckle
down to their books. In family after Catholic family the process
can be seen at work. The 1st Lord Wharton died an open Roman
Catholic in 1568; his son had been a supporter of Queen Mary,

and King Philip of Spain had stood godfather to his grandson in 1555. But on the death of the 2nd Lord Wharton in 1572 the heir was entrusted to the care of Lord Burghley and the Earl of Sussex. He was thus effectively shifted into the Protestant camp, and one of his sons became 'a professed enemy of popery and prophaneness'.

The story of the Wriothesleys, earls of Southampton, is very similar. The 2nd Earl was brought up by his mother during Mary's reign as a devout Catholic and in 1565 was married into another openly Catholic family, the Brownes, viscounts Montagu. When he died in 1581 his son and heir, who was only 8 years old, was removed from his mother's charge and put into Burghley's house to be brought up with his other aristocratic wards. When he arrived, the child was already so well indoctrinated that at first he refused to attend Anglican service. But he was carefully re-educated, and although his religious orthodoxy remained uncertain before about 1605, he was at worst indifferent and in the end became an open supporter of Anglicanism.

This and other similar stories demonstrate both the key role of Lord Burghley in weaning the great families from Catholicism, and the overriding importance of education. 'As we are bred, so we live, and so we die for the most part', observed the Marquis of Newcastle. At this period a very considerable amount of any curriculum was devoted to theology, and his teachers did much to determine the colour of a man's religious views. The ease with which a nobleman could obtain a private education at home from chaplains and tutors of his father's choosing made it exceedingly difficult for the Government to break the religious affiliations of a family once they had been established.

On the other hand the spread of the habit of a public education at school and at the university encouraged acquiescence and acceptance of the established religion, though it would have been far more effective if only the dons had been more orthodox in their opinions. The success of Leicester and Burghley in their capacities as chancellors in purging the two universities of Catholic dons was probably one of the most crucial victories in a prolonged struggle for the allegiance of the political nation. The encouragement given by Leicester at Oxford to Puritans like Laurence Humphrey, President of Magdalen, and the caution and restraint exercised by Burghley at Cambridge in his dealings with the

Puritans there, allowed both universities to become partly infected with Puritan doctrines, and thus to become important centres of Puritan propaganda among the young. Since they were catering for a larger and larger proportion of both the future clergy and the future gentry and nobility of the country, religious radicalism in the universities, to which men were exposed at their most impressionable age, was to have far-reaching consequences. It was this infiltration of the universities which turned Puritanism from the sectional eccentricity of a few great households in the countryside and groups of artisans and small traders in the towns into a nation-wide movement affecting all classes of society. The Marquis of Newcastle was right to advise the future Charles II to take care to establish a tight monopoly of university offices by docile and conformist Anglicans.

It is difficult to escape the conclusion that the formation and preservation of a substantial minority of religious dissidents on either flank of the Established Church depended in very large measure on the patronage of a few dozen dedicated magnates and leading squires. Had it not been for this powerful protection, it is more than likely that official persecution would have succeeded, as elsewhere in Europe, in creating a monolithic state church. Had this happened, the effects on English history would have been incalculable. Freedom of thought and expression, the creation of a plural society held together by a willingness to live and let live, depended on the failure of the Established Church to crush or absorb dissenting opinion in the hundred years between 1540 and 1640.

No division of the peerage into clear-cut religious categories is possible during the first twenty years of Elizabeth's reign. No one, except possibly the Queen herself, can seriously have regarded the botched-up political compromise of 1559 as a final solution which was designed to last for centuries, and although the great majority outwardly subscribed to the Anglican settlement, many were striving to change it in one direction or another. By about 1580, however, the divisions were becoming clearer. The Puritans had been goaded by inept persecution and obstinate refusal to remedy crying abuses into launching more far-reaching attacks upon the Anglican liturgy and organization; many Church Catholics had been encouraged by the Papal Bull of 1570 and vigorous missionary activity into taking up a more uncompromising religious stand. In 1580 there were 66 English peers: 20 of these were Catholic recusants, about 10 were of strongly Puritan sympathies, about a dozen were supporters of the Anglican settlement, and the remaining 24 were relatively indifferent to religious issues and anxious only to back the winner. What is noticeable is the high proportion of Catholics and the small number of convinced Anglicans (some of whom undoubtedly had sneaking Puritan leanings). Even Lord Burghley was sympathetic towards the Puritan objectives of a purge of administrative abuses and a simplified liturgy, although he loyally set his face against change in deference to the wishes of the Queen.

Sixty-two years later, on the eve of the Civil War, the peerage was almost as far as ever from unanimity in religious opinions. Little attention had been paid to religious affiliation in the creation of the new Jacobean peerage, and as a result a number of convinced recusants and zealous Puritans had contrived to slip by. In 1641 something like a fifth of the 121 peers were Roman Catholics, and at least another fifth were in varying degrees Puritan in sympathy. Allowing for the indifferent, substantially less than a half were seriously committed to the Established Church.

These religious divisions among the aristocracy had far-reaching political consequences. In the first place, they split the peers into three distinct clans, Catholic, Anglican, and Puritan, whose members chose both their wives and their friends from within the clan. Some of the most characteristic features of the Puritan ethic, austerity in sex and drink, frugality in clothes and expenditure, and respect for hard work, were responsible for exacerbating relations between Court and Country and thus dividing the peerage against itself on politically significant lines. This explains the increasingly obsessive, indeed at times pathological, character of the Country's attitude towards the immorality, idleness, and extravagance of the Court. Partly because of their different religious affiliations, the peers of 1641 lacked a sense of solidarity and were unable to present a united front in the face of social and political challenge from below.

Secondly, it was Puritanism which led so many peers to side with Parliament when war actually broke out. The hostility of the majority of the peers to Charles I in 1640 can be ascribed in large measure to the failure of the King to multiply jobs to keep pace with the increase of titles, and to the restriction of the patronage

system to a shrinking court coterie. But other factors must be
adduced to explain the apathy of the many and the hostility of the
few when war broke out two years later. It is possible, as did
Clarendon at the time, to find reasons of personal pique towards
Charles and Henrietta Maria, fear of suffering the fate of Strafford,
and hopes of personal financial advantage which led each individual to forsake the traditional loyalty of nobles to the Crown. But
the fact remains that the key figures in the parliamentary opposition in 1642 had all given evidence of Puritan sympathies long
before the crisis. Even the *frondeurs* like Pembroke, Leicester, and
Holland, life-long courtiers who ratted on their old master, may
have been influenced in some measure by this factor. Several of
the neutrals and tepid nominal adherents of the King were torn
between political loyalty to the Crown on the one hand and on the
other a desire for religious reform and a suspicion and hatred
of the swarms of Catholics who were rallying so enthusiastically
round the King. In many cases the result was a paralysis of will.

Finally, religion was a powerful solvent of respect for the
peerage. Because so many peers were Catholics, suspicion was
thrown upon the class as a whole. Publicly on the floor of the
House of Commons, and privately in their diaries, country gentlemen kept anxiously totting up the number of Catholic peers, and
particularly those who held office. Each time the list got longer,
they were pushed one step nearer the conclusion that it would be
both foolish and ungodly to put one's trust in noblemen. Fear and
hatred of the religious beliefs of a minority came to outweigh
respect for the order as a whole, and when the Grand Remon-
strance of 1641 complained of obstruction by 'a party of bishops
and popish lords in the House of Peers', it was sounding the first
trumpet for an assault which was to end in the abolition of the
House itself.

More fundamental, though more difficult to demonstrate, was
the effect of Calvinist theology on men's attitude to the traditional
hierarchy of rank, and to its apex the peerage. The doctrine of the
elect erected a second, independent, hierarchy of spiritual grace
alongside that of temporal authority and dignity. If it was agreed
that the two coincided, all well and good. But what if they did
not? Calvinism gave others than John Knox the courage to attack
the mighty in their seats, and the puritanically minded aristocrat
found himself obliged to listen with what patience he could

muster to outspoken rebukes from his social interiors. The trouble
was that the Puritan scale of values was difficult to harmonize with
the traditional way of life of a great nobleman. During the reign
of Edward VI the family chaplain, James Haddon, was perpetually nagging at the devoutly Protestant Duchess of Suffolk
for her incorrigible love of petty gambling and fine clothes. A
similar rebuke greeted the 2nd Lord Spencer some eighty years
later, when he was organizing an annual race-meeting near
Northampton. In 1632 he and some local gentlemen clubbed
together to raise £200, which they gave to the Corporation. In
return the latter promised to provide a silver gilt cup for the
winner of a horse-race to be run annually at Harlestone on the
Thursday of Easter week. As soon as he heard about it, the Rev.
Richard Samwell wrote to Lord Spencer urging him to abandon
the project, concluding with the frank words: 'I cannot forbear
to tell your Lordship that I hear some that . . . say this is one of the
worst things that ever they knew you give way to.' Even more
striking than this bold rebuke was the way Lord Spencer took it.
Samwell must have been gratified and flattered to receive a long
and courteous reply. Spencer pointed out that he was treating the
clergyman on terms of absolute equality, but reminded him gently
that 'the greatness of noblemen, notwithstanding the pride of any
man's heart, must be remembered. Honour to whom honour belongeth, and it is to be valued above a piece of paper.' After producing a variety of arguments, Spencer played his trump: 'my
counsellors in matters of divinity are clergymen, and they will say
that these sports are not natural in sin.' Both parties thus recognized that questions of divine law and the will of God transcended
the normal respect due to a titular superior. One may well ask at
what other period of history, except perhaps in high Victorian
times, could there have taken place such an exchange of letters
between a peer and a parson about the personal recreational habits
of the former.

The classic statement of the Puritan attitude to aristocracy in the
1630's comes from New England, in the form of replies made to
Lords Saye and Sele and Brooke when they were contemplating
emigration to Massachusetts. The noblemen were anxious to be
assured that their family claims to dignity and power would be
respected in the new environment. The official reply was polite
but firm:

Hereditary honours both nature and scripture doth acknowledge (Eccles. xix. 17), but hereditary authority and power standeth only by the civil laws of some commonwealths. . . .

Where God blesseth any branch of any noble or generous family with a spirit and gifts fit for government, it would be a taking God's name in vain to put such a talent under a bushel, and a sin against the honour of magistracy to neglect such in our public elections. But if God should not delight to furnish some of their posterity with gifts fit for magistracy, we should expose them rather to reproach and prejudice, and the commonwealth with them, than exalt them to honour, if we should call them forth, when God doth not, to public authority.

These exchanges are revealing evidence of the effect of the Puritan conscience in sapping respect for rank and title at all levels of the social hierarchy.

# XIV

## CONCLUSION
## THE CRISIS OF CONFIDENCE

### I. DEFERENCE

'THE essence of social class is the way a man is treated by his fellows (and, reciprocally, the way he treats them), not the qualities or the possessions which cause that treatment.' If we examine the position of the peerage in the light of this classic definition we can see the maintenance of a fairly stout barrier between peers and gentry in the reign of Elizabeth, and the striking, if temporary, erosion of that barrier under the Early Stuarts.

During the reign of Elizabeth the gentry certainly regarded the peerage with some apprehension. Sir William Holles flatly refused to marry his daughter to an earl. 'Sake of God', he said, 'I do not like to stand with my cap in my hand to my son in law. I will see her married to an honest gentleman with whom I may have friendship and conversation.' Up to the late sixteenth century noblemen still lived in semi-regal state, surrounded by swarms of attendants who formed a minor court around them. They never moved without their train, and as they passed through a village bells were rung in their honour and the local gentry turned out to greet them. When they dined they were served by the sons of gentlemen. When their letters were read out in public assemblies, men took off their hats as a mark of respect.

Many commentators struck a note of obsequious deference that appears both ridiculous and nauseating to the twentieth century, but was no more than a natural reflection of the social order and the social ethos of the day. 'Nobility is a precious gift, which so glittereth in the eyes of all men that there is no one corporal thing in this world, whereof we make a greater account', wrote Thomas Twyne in a fit of enthusiasm. 'Men naturally favour nobility', observed the more prosaic Camden. All three monarchs took the same line and Elizabeth did her best to find jobs for her nobility, and to protect them from insult. James was of the opinion that 'virtue followeth oftest noble blood', even if he did little to exploit his biological discovery.

By the early seventeenth century this attitude of respectful subservience was breaking down, despite increasing efforts of the Government to keep it alive. Sir Edward Walker thought that the rapid increase in the number of the nobility after 1615 'introduced a parity in conversation; which considering English dispositions proved of ill consequences, familiarity . . . begetting contempt'. As early as 1578 it was remarked that lords were far more respected in remote areas like Lancashire, Cheshire, and Shropshire, where they were rare birds, than in the Home Counties, where they were a familiar sight. For years the nobility had been the butt of the playwrights and it was not long before this criticism was reflected in real life. Asked if he realized that the Earl of Huntingdon was a gentleman, Sir Henry Shirley retorted curtly, 'I know not that; but if my hawk had flown into any lord's parlour, I would have followed my hawk'. During the 1620's and 1630's significant little incidents kept occurring. A gentleman jostled and swore at the Earl of Carlisle in a narrow passage; two draymen deliberately rammed and overturned the Earl of Exeter's coach; a beggar assaulted the Earl of Westmorland with a truncheon. Meanwhile, tenants ceased to treat noblemen with their wonted deference, the gentry ceased to turn out to welcome them, the yeomanry ceased to vote as they were bid. By the time the Civil War broke out the stock of the aristocracy was lower than it had ever been before, or was to be again for centuries.

The manifold causes of this slump in prestige have already been spelt out at length. They include the decline in the wealth of the peers relative to that of the gentry; the shrinkage of their territorial possessions, in both absolute and relative terms; the decay of their military power in men, arms, castles, and will to resist; the granting of titles of honour for cash not merit, in too great numbers, and to too unworthy persons; the change in their attitude towards the tenantry from suppliers of manpower to suppliers of rent; the undermining of their electoral influence due to the rise of deeply felt political and religious issues; the increasing preference for extravagant living in the city instead of hospitable living in the countryside; the spread throughout the propertied classes of a bookish education, acquired at school and university, and the demand by the State for an administrative *élite* of proved

CONCLUSION: THE CRISIS OF CONFIDENCE      351

competence, irrespective of the claims of rank; the pervasive influence of the rise of individualism, the Calvinist belief in a spiritual hierarchy of the Elect, and the Puritan exaltation of the private conscience, which affected attitudes towards hierarchy and obedience in secular society; and finally the growing psychological breach between Court and Country in attitudes, real or supposed, towards constitutional theory, methods and scale of taxation, forms of worship, aesthetic tastes, financial probity, and sexual morality.

Many of the same forces were at work to bring about a general weakening of the hierarchical framework of upper-class society in the early seventeenth century. Respect for the episcopacy had been reduced by a century of robbery, neglect, and Calvinism; respect for the clergy had been undermined by attacks on their moral and educational shortcomings, and by wider reading of the New Testament; respect for the King had been reduced by his association with a sexually depraved court, a pro-Spanish foreign policy, and a popish queen; respect for the baronetage had been sapped by the admission of men who were not even regarded as gentlemen, respect for the knighthood by the indiscriminate mass creations of James and Buckingham. The early seventeenth century thus saw a hardening of status divisions according to the law, accompanied by a decline of respect for superiors in church, state, society, and family. It is hardly surprising that the sharp decline in the prestige of peers eventually gave birth to a new constitutional theory. The M.P.s had convinced themselves that the House of Commons was by its very nature an infinitely more important body than the House of Lords. John Pym described the latter as merely 'a Third Estate, by inheritance and birth-right', compared with 'the whole body of the Commons of the Kingdom'. Although these ideas were undoubtedly stimulated by the policy clashes on vital issues between Lords and Commons, they struck an immediately responsive chord among the public, and it was this popular reaction which forced the Lords into reluctant retreat in 1641–2. This was the atmosphere which prepared the way for, and does much to explain, the popularity of the Leveller ideas in the late 1640's. William Overton argued historically that William the Conqueror and his successors 'made dukes, earls, barons, and lords of their fellow robbers, rogues, and thieves'. His conclusion, 'away with the pretended power of the Lords', was acceptable in circles far removed from that of his fellow Levellers.

In face of the mounting criticism of their privileges, the growing contempt for their persons, and the erosion of the territorial foundations of their authority, the nobility were foolish enough to attempt to mount a counter-attack, the most visible feature of which was an overweening arrogance revealing their basic insecurity. Aubrey found them 'damnably proud and arrogant, and the French would say that "*My lord d'Angleterre comme un mastif-dog*" '. Immediately after the Restoration the same comments are made. 'La haute noblesse . . . d'ordinaire est insupportablement fière et orgueilleuse en Angleterre. Il semble qu'un mylord s'estime d'une autre espèce qu'un autre gentilhomme, si impérieusement il traite avec lui', noted a French visitor. Peers showed a hypersensitive reaction to slights, real or imagined. When the Mayor of Chester failed to turn out to greet him as he passed through the town in 1635, Thomas Earl of Arundel completely lost his temper. When his worship finally appeared, the Earl snatched away the mayoral staff, shouting 'I will teach you to know your self and attend Peers of the Realm'. This hysterical outburst was symptomatic of an uneasy feeling that things were not what they had been. Another symptom of the same phenomenon was the frenetic interest in heraldry, the diligent commissioning of family histories.

Everyone in the early seventeenth century was busy calling in the past to redress the balance of the present. The common lawyers were grubbing about in medieval parchments to support their pretensions against the prerogative courts and Chancery; the opposition members of the House of Commons were scouring the Parliament Rolls for ammunition against the Crown; on the other side the Laudian clergy were harking nostalgically back to the powers and wealth of the pre-Reformation Church; the Crown was brushing up its medieval rights over the Forest, distraint of knighthood, and scutage. Similarly the peers were only too happy to be reminded of the days when they were the hereditary advisers of the Crown and the judges of ministerial delinquency under the moribund procedure of impeachment; they employed Selden and Hakewill to search out the privileges of the House of Lords, which they then defended with diligent punctilio. In doing so they felt —or were induced by Coke and the antiquarians to feel—that they were the lineal descendants of the barons on the field of Runnymede or the baronial allies of Simon de Montfort. Their greatest moment seemed to come in 1641 when Charles in despair summoned to York a Great Council of noblemen to advise him what to do. For Charles himself was an active supporter of this attempted aristocratic revival, and royalist and courtier peers were as anxious to encourage it as were the members of the opposition. The whole framework of personal government in the 1630's depended on a reassertion of privilege in Church and State. Hence the ferocity with which critics of bishops and challengers of peers were alike punished; hence the abrupt cessation of the sale of titles in 1629, so as to restore respectability to the social order; hence the increase in the proportion of lay peers in the Privy Council from two-thirds to over three-quarters; hence the proposals for a massive increase of the privileges of the titled which were under consideration in 1639–40.

As usually happens, this attempted aristocratic revival merely accelerated the downfall of the old order. The opposition peers failed to realize that both in impeachment cases and in the struggle of 1640–1 they were merely being used by the lawyers and gentry as a battering-ram and a shield. The royalist peers failed to realize that on the Privy Council and in the country they were merely being used by the King as a useful cover for his autocratic pretensions. Their growing arrogance made them new enemies without overawing the old. In England, unlike France or Brandenburg, a firm alliance of mutual self-interest between a highly privileged nobility and an authoritarian Crown was not given time to mature. If it came to the crunch, the English nobles would be ground to pieces between the millstones of King and Commons.

## II. THE END

Divided and uncertain in their allegiance, some peers joined the parliamentarian forces, many more the royalists, and more still were neutrals or turncoats. After the débâcle Sir Edward Walker wrote: 'I am confident that if the nobility had been unanimous to have defended the just rights of the King, the honour and interest of their own body, and the good of the people, it had never been in the power of the Commons to have begun their rebellion.' Walker, as usual, is going too far, but it is certainly arguable that if the leaders of the Commons had not been able to enlist the support of a number of prominent peers, and to rely on the neutrality of an even larger group, they might have hesitated to take up arms against the King. For the first crucial months the parliamentary peers were essential to the cause, not for their talents or their power, but for the air of social respectability they conferred on what would otherwise have appeared as naked rebellion against the combined authority of monarchy, court, aristocracy, and episcopacy. Thereafter their usefulness declined sharply, and they were treated accordingly. Even the peers who joined the winning side gained nothing from the war but destruction of property and contempt of person, while the sufferings of the royalists are notorious.

Soldiers of every persuasion showed themselves so eager to loot the opulent houses of the great that the Earl of Berkshire was driven to the conclusion that both the royalist and the parliamentarian troops had resolved to make their fortunes out of noble estates. During the siege of Oxford peers were two a penny in the overcrowded town, and hungry sentries on watch cried down to the besiegers: 'Roundhead, fling me up half a mutton and I will fling thee down a Lord.' Nor were things any better in London, where a miserable rump huddled, neglected and despised, in an empty House of Lords. In 1645 Lord Willoughby remarked bitterly, 'I thought it a crime to be a nobleman'; by the winter of 1648 there were only a handful of peers left to 'sit and tell tales by the fireside in their House in hope of more Lords to drive away the time'. A few months later the House of Lords was abolished, and with it the privileges which had hitherto helped to distinguish peers from gentry. This act was not a mere by-product of the dynamics of war; it was the culmination of a crisis of confidence which had been maturing for well over half a century.

## APPENDIX I

### Estimates of Total Manorial Holdings, 1558–1641

| Date | Type of family | Number of families | Manors held (to nearest 10) | Average number of manors per family | Number of families holding | |
|---|---|---|---|---|---|---|
| | | | | | 40 manors or more | 10 manors or less |
| 31 December 1558 | Extant on December 1559+Kent | 63 | 3,390 | 54 | 39 | 2 |
| 31 December 1602 | Extant on 31 December 1602+Essex and Southampton | 57 | 2,220 | 39 | c. 19–21 | 5 |
| 31 December 1641 | Pre-1602 creations still extant in 1641 | 48 | 1,640 | 34 | 14 | 9 |
| | Post-1602 creations still extant in 1641 | 73 | 1,440 | 20 | 9 | 29 |
| | Total families extant in 1641 | 121 | 3,080 | 25 | 23 | 38 |

# APPENDIX II

## Rewards, 1558–1641

| | | | UNITS | |
| Periods | Dates | Duration in years | Total units | Average p/a |
| --- | --- | --- | --- | --- |
| I | 1558–76 | 19 1/12 | 268 | 13·8 |
| II | 1577–1603 | 25 1/2 | 203 | 7·8 |
| III | 1603–28 | 25 1/2 | 2,741 | 105·4 |
| IV | 1629–41 | 13 | 329 | 25·2 |
| | 1558–1641 | 83 1/12 | 3,541 | 42·7 |

To illustrate the variations in the rate of giving at different periods, the eighty-three years from 17 November 1558 to 31 December 1641 have been divided into four periods. The breaks have been chosen so as to bring out the changes in the scale of giving which resulted from the mounting pressure on Elizabethan finances from the threat and actuality of war after 1577; from the accession of the open-handed James in 1603; and from the death of Buckingham and the inauguration of the new political programme in 1628. By a happy coincidence these divisions provide two central periods of twenty-five and a half years each, which makes direct comparison from Elizabethan parsimony to Jacobean generosity all the easier to draw.

All known grants recorded in warrant books, patent rolls, and other records have been listed, and private and public archives have been combed for evidence as to their value. All grants, whether of annuities, land, or monopolies have then been converted into capital sums, and calculated in units with a value of £1,000 each in period III from 1603 to 1628. To allow for the depreciation in the value of money, all grants have been adjusted approximately in accordance with the Phelps Brown price index. That is to say, the unit has been altered to £600, £800, and £1,200 in periods I, II, and IV respectively. This is a very crude method of correction, but a more elaborate calculation by a moving annual price index would itself introduce new elements of guesswork, and would only serve to create a misleading impression of statistical precision. Grants of land in fee simple have been capitalized at 30 years' purchase of old Crown rents before 1603 and at 40 years' thereafter, and grants in fee-farm at 10 years' purchase before and 20 years' after. Annuities and the profits of patents for life or 21 years have been conservatively valued at 7 years' purchase, though when they in fact ended before 7 years this has been taken into account. Leases of crown lands, exchanges of lands, grants of wardship, and sales of baronetcies and knighthoods have been omitted since it has proved impossible to put a value on them; in any case they are unlikely to have been of really great importance. Restorations of property to the heirs of attainted peers have been included only when there was a real danger that the estate might pass into other hands owing to lapse of time since the attainder. Thus the restorations of land to the Earls of Warwick and Arundel and to Lord Paget have been included, but not those to the Earls of Southampton, Essex, and Strafford, and to Lord Audley. This is admittedly an arbitrary decision, but on balance it seems a reasonable one.

It is important to emphasize once again that these figures can of their very nature be only the very roughest of approximations, for their compilation involves a wide range of both factual uncertainty and subjective judgement. There are a large number of grants, particularly of lands and of monopolies, whose value can only be very roughly guessed at. The evidence is not complete, and some grants have undoubtedly gone unrecorded. Capital values have been calculated by the use of deliberately conservative multipliers.

# INDEX

This index does not pretend to be comprehensive nor to do much more than help the reader to identify the noblemen referred to in the text. For this reason it is mainly confined to peers, and more particularly to those whose surname differs from their title, and those titles of whom several holders are mentioned. Holders of titles are listed chronologically in the title entry, the number in brackets referring to the order of succession. Where several persons have the same name and Christian name, they have been classified in ascending order of rank (e.g. earls before dukes) and alphabetically according to title within each order (e.g. Earl of Arundel, Earl of Suffolk).

Arundel, Earl of, *see* Howard, Thomas (14), Henry Frederick (15).
Arundell, Sir Thomas, 209.

Bacon, Francis, 27, 33, 43, 51–52, 57–58, 88, 120, 178, 227.
Bath, Earl of, *see* Bourchier, Edward.
Bayning, Sir Paul, 1st Viscount Bayning, 44, 56, 170, 242.
Bedford, Earl of, *see* Russell, Francis (2), Edward (3), Francis, 2nd Lord Russell of Thornhaugh (4).
Bergavenny, Lord, *see* Nevill, George.
Berkeley, Lord, *see* Berkeley, Maurice (13), Henry (17).
Berkeley, Henry, 17th Lord Berkeley, 104, 144, 152.
Berkeley, Maurice, 13th Lord Berkeley, 184.
Bertie, Catherine, Duchess of Suffolk, m. 1. Charles Brandon, Duke of Suffolk, 338.
Bertie, Peregrine, 11th Lord Willoughby d'Eresby, 49, 325.
Bertie, Robert, 1st Earl of Lindsey, 171.
Blount, James, 6th Lord Mountjoy, 161, 163, 181, 237.
Bourchier, Edward, 4th Earl of Bath, 227.
Boyle, Richard, 1st Earl of Cork, 54, 264, 310, 317.
Bridgwater, Earl of, *see* Egerton, John.
Brooke, Lord, *see* Greville, Fulke (1), Robert (2).

Browne, Anthony Maria, 2nd Viscount Montagu, 337.
Brudenell, Sir Thomas, 1st Lord Brudenell, 55, 158.
Buckhurst, Lord, *see* Sackville, Thomas.
Buckingham, Duke of, *see* Stafford, Edward; Villiers, George.
Burghley, Lord, *see* Cecil, William.

Cambridge, Earl of, *see* Hamilton, James.
Carey, Henry, 1st Lord Hunsdon, 121, 264.
Carey, John, 3rd Lord Hunsdon, 198.
Carlisle, Earl of, *see* Hay, James.
Carr, Frances, Countess of Somerset, m. 1. and divorced Robert Devereux, 3rd Earl of Essex, 2. the following, 278, 300 1, 325.
Carr, Robert, 1st Earl of Somerset, 278, 299, 325.
Cavendish, Sir William, 1st Lord Cavendish, 1st Earl of Devonshire, 50, 92, 158, 166.
Cavendish, William, Marquis, 1st Duke of Newcastle, 56, 58–59, 283, 314–15, 333, 343–4.
Cecil, Sir Robert, 1st Earl of Salisbury, 17, 43–44, 50, 127, 172, 202, 206, 209, 220, 224, 236, 239, 246, 251, 254, 260, 278, 281.
Cecil, Sir William, 1st Lord Burghley, 16–17, 48, 112, 122, 127, 175–6, 178, 181, 187, 191, 196, 205, 209, 220, 252, 256, 259, 265, 281, 287, 306, 309, 310, 316, 323, 339–40, 342–3, 345.

Cecil, William, 2nd Earl of Salisbury, 118, 137, 148, 151, 154, 158, 198, 229, 274, 289.

Charles I, King, 7, 18, 43, 46–47, 164, 173, 216, 258, 278, 301, 322–3, 328.

Clifford, George, 3rd Earl of Cumberland, 75, 122, 156, 158, 174–5, 182, 202, 238.

Coke, Sir Edward, 16, 179.

Commons, House of, 6–8, 12, 19, 25, 54, 58–59, 127–8, 203, 205, 207–8, 277, 310, 339, 346, 351–3.

Conway, Sir Edward, 1st Viscount Conway, 198.

Cork, Earl of, see Boyle, Richard.

Cotton, Sir Robert, 43.

Cranfield, Lionel, 1st Earl of Middlesex, 27, 41, 53, 58, 89, 224, 226.

Cumberland, Earl of, see Clifford, George.

Derby, Earl of, see Stanley, Edward.

Devereux, Robert, 2nd Earl of Essex, 40–41, 127, 168, 199, 201, 216, 220–1, 223, 236, 239, 265.

Devereux, Robert, 3rd Earl of Essex, 300.

Devereux, Walter, 1st Earl of Essex, 17.

Dorset, Earl of, see Sackville, Thomas, Lord Buckhurst (1), Robert (2), Richard (3).

Dudley, Ambrose, Earl of Warwick, 176–8, 220, 321, 338–40.

Dudley, Robert, Earl of Leicester, 107, 127, 167, 174–6, 178, 181, 201, 210, 220, 223, 238, 321, 325, 334, 338–41, 343.

Dunbar, Earl of, see Hume, George.

Egerton, John, 1st Earl of Bridgwater, 151, 158.

Egerton, Sir Thomas, 50.

Elizabeth, Queen, 9, 39–40, 48–49, 100–1, 112–13, 115, 122, 176, 194, 197, 225, 252, 257–8, 260, 277, 305, 318.

Essex, Countess of, see Carr, Frances.

Essex, Earl of, see Devereux, Walter (1), Robert (2 and 3).

Fiennes, Edward, 1st Earl of Lincoln, 211.

Fiennes, Henry, 2nd Earl of Lincoln, 104, 109, 156.

Fiennes, Theophilus, 4th Earl of Lincoln, 178, 181.

Fiennes, William, 2nd Lord Saye and Sele, 178, 181, 229, 347.

Fuller, Thomas, 52, 90, 174, 185.

Greville, Sir Fulke, 1st Lord Brooke, 10, 101, 169, 342.

Greville, Robert, 2nd Lord Brooke, 178, 347.

Grey, Frances, Duchess of Suffolk, w. of Henry Grey, Duke of Suffolk, 347.

Hamilton, James, 2nd Marquis of Hamilton, 1st Earl of Cambridge, 177, 198, 328.

Hardwick, Bess of, see Talbot, Elizabeth.

Harington, Sir John, 187–8, 193, 218, 259.

Hastings, Henry, 3rd Earl of Huntingdon, 86, 126, 144, 156, 199, 275, 338–41.

Hastings, Henry, 5th Earl of Huntingdon, 118, 286.

Hatton, Sir Christopher, 113, 176, 181, 199, 209, 251–2, 278, 323.

Hay, James, 1st Earl of Carlisle, 53, 163, 256, 350.

Henry VII, King, 48, 99, 318.

Henry VIII, King, 48, 250, 259, 318.

Herbert, Edward, 1st Lord Herbert of Cherbury, 18, 164, 188.

Herbert, Henry, 2nd Earl of Pembroke, 101, 127.

Herbert, Mary, Countess of Pembroke, 3rd w. of above, 319.

Herbert, Philip, Earl of Montgomery, 4th Earl of Pembroke, 154, 198, 229, 260, 278, 323, 327–8, 346.

Herbert, William, 1st Earl of Pembroke, 175.

Herbert, William, 3rd Earl of Pembroke, 278, 319.

Hertford, Earl of, see Seymour, Edward.

Holderness, Earl of, see Ramsay, John.

Holland, Earl of, see Rich, Henry.

Holles, Sir John, Lord Houghton, 1st Earl of Clare, 52–54, 229.

Houghton, Lord, see Holles, John.

Howard of Effingham, Lord, see Howard, Charles.

Howard of Walden, Lord, courtesy title of Howard, Theophilus (*q.v.*) during his father's lifetime.

Howard, Charles, 2nd Lord Howard of Effingham, 1st Earl of Nottingham, 49, 198, 220, 321.

Howard, Henry, Earl of Northampton, 43–44, 196, 198, 300.

Howard, Henry Frederick, 15th Earl of Arundel, 236.

Howard, Theophilus, 2nd Earl of Suffolk, 246, 260.

Howard, Thomas, 14th Earl of Arundel, 17, 58, 177, 196, 234, 246, 314, 327–8, 352.

Howard, Thomas, 1st Earl of Suffolk, 196, 209, 224, 246.

Howard, Thomas, 4th Duke of Norfolk, 122, 141, 196.

Hume, George, 1st Earl of Dunbar, 203–4.

Hunsdon, Lord, *see* Carey, Henry (1), John (3).

Huntingdon, Earl of, *see* Hastings, Henry (3 *and* 5).

Ingram, Sir Arthur, 41, 224.

James I, King, 7, 41–46, 49, 51, 54, 60–61, 120, 188, 194, 197–8, 218, 225, 257–8, 260, 279, 294, 322.

Laud, William, Archbishop, 7, 9, 318.

Leake, Sir Francis, 53–54.

Leicester, Earl of, *see* Dudley, Robert; Sydney, Robert (1 *and* 2).

Lennox, Duchess of, *see* Stuart, Frances.

Lennox, Duke of, *see* Stuart, Ludovic.

Lincoln, Earl of, *see* Fiennes, Edward (1), Henry (2), Theophilus (4).

Lindsey, Earl of, *see* Bertie, Robert.

Lords, House of, 6, 29–30, 57–58, 346, 351–2, 354.

Lumley, John, 6th Lord Lumley, 122, 165, 325, 327.

Manners, Edward, 3rd Earl of Rutland, 262, 313.

Manners, Elizabeth, Countess of Rutland, w. of Roger, Earl of Rutland, 319.

Manners, Henry, 2nd Earl of Rutland, 260.

Manners, John, 8th Earl of Rutland, 289.

Manners, Roger, 5th Earl of Rutland, 105, 221, 258, 260, 265.

Middlesex, Earl of, *see* Cranfield, Lionel.

Mildmay, Sir Walter, 279, 282.

Montagu, Viscount, *see* Browne, Anthony Maria.

Montagu, Edward, 1st Lord Montagu of Boughton, 157, 179, 274, 279.

Montgomery, Earl of, *see* Herbert, Philip.

Mountjoy, Lord, *see* Blount, James.

Nevill, George, 3rd Lord Bergavenny, 99–100.

Newcastle, Marquis, Duke of, *see* Cavendish, William.

Norfolk, Duke of, *see* Howard, Thomas.

North, Sir Dudley, 233.

North, Sir Dudley, 4th Lord North, 102, 143, 245, 254, 271.

North, Roger, 2nd Lord, 176, 260.

Northampton, Earl of, *see* Howard, Henry.

Northumberland, Earl of, *see* Percy, Henry (9), Algernon (10).

Nottingham, Earl of, *see* Howard, Charles.

Oxford, Earl of, *see* Vere, Edward.

Paget, William, 1st Lord Paget, 169.

Paget, William, 4th Lord Paget, 170, 320.

Paulet, William, 1st Marquis of Winchester, 245–6.

Pembroke, Countess of, *see* Herbert, Mary.

Pembroke, Earl of, *see* Herbert, William (1), Henry (2), Philip, Earl of Montgomery (4).

Percy, Algernon, 10th Earl of Northumberland, 501.

Percy, Henry, 9th Earl of Northumberland, 156, 158, 218, 274, 326.

Ralegh, Sir Walter, 105, 107, 120, 133, 143, 220, 278.

Ramsay, John, 1st Earl of Holderness, 177.

Ratcliffe, Robert, 5th Earl of Sussex, 221.

Ratcliffe, Thomas, 3rd Earl of Sussex, 176, 220, 343.

Rich, Henry, 1st Earl of Holland, 178, 229, 346.

Rich, Robert, 2nd Earl of Warwick, 178, 181, 186.

Rich, Robert, 3rd Lord Rich, 339.

Richmond, Duchess of, see Stuart, Frances.

Richmond, Duke of, see Stuart, James.

Roper, Sir John, 53.

Russell, Edward, 3rd Earl of Bedford, 221, 265.

Russell, Francis, 2nd Earl of Bedford, 122, 156, 211, 338–40.

Russell, Francis, 2nd Lord Russell of Thornhaugh, 4th Earl of Bedford, 170–1, 173, 182, 319.

Rutland, Earl of, see Manners, Henry (2), Edward (3), Roger (5), John (8).

Sackville, Richard, 3rd Earl of Dorset, 246.

Sackville, Robert, 2nd Earl of Dorset, 263.

Sackville, Thomas, Lord Buckhurst, 1st Earl of Dorset, 115, 220, 224, 319.

Salisbury, Earl of, see Cecil, Robert (1), William (2).

Saye and Sele, Viscount, see Fiennes, William.

Selden, John, 58.

Seymour, Edward, 9th Earl of Hertford, 86, 212, 264.

Seymour, Edward, Duke of Somerset, 253.

Sheffield, Edmund, 3rd Lord Sheffield, 104, 204, 229.

Shrewsbury, Countess of, see Talbot, Elizabeth.

Shrewsbury, Earl of, see Talbot, George (9), Gilbert (10).

Smith, Sir Thomas, 26–27, 39.

Smyth, John, 3, 17, 137, 152, 189.

Somerset, Countess of, see Carr, Frances.

Somerset, Duke of, see Seymour, Edward.

Somerset, Earl of, see Carr, Robert.

Somerset, Edward, 4th Earl of Worcester, 227.

Somerset, William, 3rd Earl of Worcester, 321.

Southampton, Earl of, see Wriothesley, Henry (2 and 3), Thomas (4).

Spencer, Robert, 1st Lord Spencer, 58, 157–8, 161, 184, 210.

Spencer, William, 2nd Lord Spencer, 209, 347.

Stafford, Edward, Duke of Buckingham, 97, 105.

Stanley, Edward, 12th Earl of Derby, 261, 309, 321, 322, 333.

Strafford, Earl of, see Wentworth, Thomas.

Stuart, Arabella, 50.

Stuart, Frances, Duchess of Lennox and Richmond, m. 3. Ludovic Stuart, 198, 263.

Stuart, James, 2nd Duke of Richmond, 198.

Stuart, Ludovic, 2nd Duke of Lennox, 1st Duke of Richmond, 177, 205.

Suffolk, Duchess of, see Grey, Frances; Bertie, Catherine.

Suffolk, Earl of, see Howard, Thomas (1), Theophilus (2).

Sussex, Earl of, see Ratcliffe, Thomas (3), Robert (5).

Sydney, Sir Philip, 108, 218, 314, 319.

Sydney, Sir Robert, 1st Earl of Leicester, 125, 185, 211, 229.

Sydney, Robert, 2nd Earl of Leicester, 346.

Talbot, Elizabeth, Countess of Shrewsbury, 'Bess of Hardwick', m. 2. William Cavendish, 4. George, 9th Earl of Shrewsbury, 91–92, 166, 187, 244, 252, 262.

Talbot, George, 9th Earl of Shrewsbury, 91–92, 165–6, 168–9, 174, 178, 254, 321, 323.

Talbot, Gilbert, 10th Earl of Shrewsbury, 101, 104, 115, 150.

Vere, Edward, 17th Earl of Oxford, 102, 112, 194, 265, 306–7, 317, 319, 321–2.

Villiers, George, 1st Duke of Buckingham, 7, 44, 46–47, 51–55, 58, 177, 198, 228, 246, 258, 260, 278, 299, 326, 328.

Walker, Sir Edward, 47, 56, 58, 350, 353.

Warwick, Earl of, see Dudley, Ambrose; Rich, Robert, 3rd Lord Rich (1), Robert (2).

Wentworth, Thomas, Earl of Strafford, 7, 226, 246.

Willoughby d'Eresby, Lord, *see* Bertie, Peregrine.

Willoughby, Francis, 5th Lord Willoughby of Parham, 354.

Wilson, Thomas, 28, 223.

Winchester, Marquis of, *see* Paulet, William.

Worcester, Earl of, *see* Somerset, William (3), Edward (4).

Wriothesley, Henry, 2nd Earl of Southampton, 273, 343.

Wriothesley, Henry, 3rd Earl of Southampton, 145–6, 170, 178, 181, 221, 265, 278, 322, 343.

Wriothesley, Thomas, 4th Earl of Southampton, 229, 260.